# HIGH LONESOME

T0345249

# HIGH LONESOME

On the Poetry of Charles Wright

Edited by Adam Giannelli

**Oberlin College Press**
Oberlin, Ohio

Cover photograph: Daniel Kelly
Cover design: Steve Farkas

Oberlin College Press, 50 N. Professor Street, Oberlin, OH 44074
www.oberlin.edu/ocpress

**Library of Congress Cataloging-in-Publication Data**

High lonesome : on the poetry of Charles Wright / edited by Adam Giannelli.
  p. cm.
Includes bibliographical references.
ISBN 0-932440-29-0 (pbk. : alk. paper)
  1. Wright, Charles, 1935- —Criticism and interpretation. I. Giannelli,
Adam.
  PS3573.R52Z65  2006    811'.54—dc22               2006006508

*In Memory of Tom Andrews*

*(1961-2001)*

# Contents

Introduction     xi

**Part One: Reviews**

*Country Music*

  Charles Wright's *Country Music* (1991)     3
    DAVID ST. JOHN

*The Southern Cross*

  *from* "*One for the Rose* and *The Southern Cross*" (1982)     10
    DAVID WALKER

*The Other Side of the River*

  *from* "Lives in a Rearview Mirror" (1984)     15
    DAVID KALSTONE

  *from* "The Trace of a Story Line" (1986)     17
    MARK JARMAN

*Zone Journals*

  *from* "The Pragmatic Imagination and
  the Secret of Poetry" (1988)     25
    MARK JARMAN

  Travels in Time (1988)     29
    HELEN VENDLER

  *Zone Journals* (1991)     36
    SHEROD SANTOS

*The World of the Ten Thousand Things*

  *from* "An Elegist's New England,
  a Buddhist's Dante" (1991)     40
    RICHARD TILLINGHAST

  The Blood Bees of Paradise (1991)     42
    DAVID YOUNG

  Improvisations on Charles Wright's
  *The World of the Ten Thousand Things* (1992)     52
    TOM ANDREWS

Charles Wright's Hymn (1991)                              61
   CHRISTOPHER BUCKLEY

*Chickamauga*

The Nothing That Is (1995)                               68
   HELEN VENDLER

*from* "On Restraint" (1996)                             76
   DAVID BAKER

*from* "Earned Weight" (1995)                            79
   JAMES LONGENBACH

*Black Zodiac*

Guided by Dark Stars (1997)                              83
   CAROL MUSKE-DUKES

*from* "Looking for Landscapes" (1998)                   87
   DAVID YOUNG

*Appalachia*

*Appalachia* (1999)                                      94
   JAMES LONGENBACH

Between Heaven and Earth (1999)                          98
   ADAM KIRSCH

Ars Longa (1999)                                        101
   J. D. MCCLATCHY

*Negative Blue*

An Enchanted, Diminished World (2000)                   111
   RON SMITH

**Part Two: Essays**

The Transcendent "I" (1979)                             115
   HELEN VENDLER

Tracing Charles Wright (1982)                           126
   CALVIN BEDIENT

Under the Sign of the Cross (1989)                      142
   J. D. MCCLATCHY

"Things That Lock Our Wrists to the Past":
Self-Portraiture and Autobiography in
Charles Wright's Poetry (1989)    154
   JAMES MCCORKLE

Gospel Music: Charles Wright and
the High Lonesome (1992)    186
   MICHAEL CHITWOOD

Charles Wright and Presences in Absence (1994)    192
   JULIAN GITZEN

The Capabilities of Charles Wright (1992)    203
   STEPHEN CUSHMAN

Metaphysics of the Image in
Charles Wright and Paul Cézanne (1994)    221
   BRUCE BOND

Resurrecting the Baroque (1997)    230
   PETER STITT

The Doubting Penitent: Charles Wright's
Epiphanies of Abandonment (1998)    255
   LEE UPTON

Poetic Standard Time: The Zones
of Charles Wright (1998)    285
   CHRISTOPHER R. MILLER

Charles Wright, Giorgio Morandi, and
the Metaphysics of the Line (2002)    304
   BONNIE COSTELLO

Charles Wright's *Via Mystica* (2004)    325
   HENRY HART

Charles Wright and "The Metaphysics
of the Quotidian" (2005)    345
   WILLARD SPIEGELMAN

Bibliography    374

Contributors    382

Acknowledgments    386

# Introduction

"Has any other American poet been writing as beautifully and daringly over the past twenty-five years as Charles Wright?" wrote Philip Levine when awarding Wright the Lenore Marshall Prize in 1996. "Possibly. But I cannot imagine who it would be."[1] Levine's comment attests to Wright's status as one of the most important figures in contemporary American poetry. His vibrant voice—a blend of incantatory music, reverberating imagery, and visionary reach—has influenced other poets and elicited a thoughtful array of literary criticism.

Wright has claimed, "All my poems seem to be an ongoing argument with myself about the unlikelihood of salvation" (*HL* 37).[2] This search for transcendence, an examination of the natural world within the confines of language, has haunted his poems for over thirty years. The singularity of Wright's vision has led him to probe deeper, to embed his inquiries within more intricate structures, to rise to new strains of eloquence. Over the span of his career, he has compressed language in tightfisted lyrics, documented the earth's plentitude and mystery in long verse journals, and distilled his vision in serene poems of understatement and abstraction. His work fuses a wide range of influences, from Ezra Pound's modernist fragments and Giorgio Morandi's ghostly bottles to the country tunes of the Carter family. The titles of his poems show this diversity: "Thinking of Georg Trakl," "Homage to Paul Cézanne," "Portrait of the Artist with Hart Crane," "To Giacomo Leopardi in the Sky," "Waiting for Tu Fu," "St. Augustine and the Arctic Bear." One is even called "Elizabeth Bishop and Miles Davis Fake the Break." The landscapes his poems inhabit are equally varied: the rivers and foothills of Tennessee, Italy's olive trees and stone streets, the California coastline, Montana's high country, and his own backyard in Charlottesville, Virginia. Such a distinctly flavored and ambitious body of work offers many points of entry, and it is no surprise that the critical response to Wright's work has been large and diverse. This book hopes to gather the most significant of these responses, tracing the unfolding reactions to Wright's poetry and clarifying his achievement.

*High Lonesome* is a continuation and revision of *The Point Where All Things Meet: Essays on Charles Wright* published by Oberlin College Press ten years

---

1. Philip Levine, "Citation: Philip Levine," *American Poet*, Winter 1996/97, 25.

2. Wright has published two books of essays and interviews: *Halflife: Improvisations and Interviews 1977–87* (Ann Arbor: University of Michigan Press, 1988) and *Quarter Notes: Improvisations and Interviews* (Ann Arbor: University of Michigan Press, 1995). References to these books, abbreviated as *HL* and *QN*, are cited parenthetically in the text.

ago. That volume, edited by the late Tom Andrews, was the first book of crit-
icism dedicated entirely to Wright's work and made the first significant step
in appraising his poetry. Many of its essays have been reprinted here, and I
am grateful to Tom Andrews, whose careful judgment provides the founda-
tion for this book. I have tried my best to sustain his vision. Since the pub-
lication of *The Point Where All Things Meet*, however, Wright has published six
more books of poetry and received numerous awards, including the Pulitzer
Prize and the National Book Critics Circle Award. He has also continued to
elicit criticism of a high caliber. Not only has his recent work attracted at-
tention, but these past few years have allowed critics time to reflect on his
earlier achievements and the trajectory of his work as a whole. I have tried
to incorporate these new insights while retaining the vital criticism of ear-
lier commentaries.

These last years also mark the completion of Wright's trilogy of trilogies,
"The Appalachian Book of the Dead," a project of Dantean proportions that
encompasses thirty years, the bulk of his life's work. Over the course of his
career, Wright has compiled three separate but sequential volumes of selected
poetry: *Country Music* (1982), *The World of the Ten Thousand Things* (1990), and
*Negative Blue* (2000). All three books follow the same search for the divine
among the world's mysteries, yet they mark distinct changes in Wright's style.
A glance at the books' covers is instructive. Each has a work of art that
Wright admires, and their diversity hints at the scope of his project. The
cover of *Country Music*, a book characterized by compression and compact
imagery, has a black-and-white line drawing of a landscape by Morandi. *The
World of the Ten Thousand Things*, in contrast, is graced by Cézanne's *Bend in
the Road*, a vibrant and layered landscape, which is indicative of the elaborate
structures developed in that collection. Finally, the cover of *Negative Blue* has
a painting by Giovanni di Paolo that portrays Adam and Eve being expelled
from heaven. Although it depicts the mountainous earth, it is the only one
of the three that is not a landscape. It presents a vision of Paradise, akin to
Dante's cosmology. The earth is surrounded by concentric circles, the plan-
ets and constellations embedded within them. Beyond them, God glows in
celestial light and Eden is dense with flora. In the other two, the landscape
hints at the unknown—through sparseness in Morandi and lushness in
Cézanne—but here the natural world is incorporated within a larger frame-
work. The beyond is made visible. This seems appropriate for Wright's third
and final installment, his own "small-time paradiso" (*NB* 173), where the
speaker raids the heavens with his gaze.[3] Commenting in the second edition

---

3. Quotations from Wright's books of poetry are cited in the text with the following
abbreviations: *CM—Country Music: Selected Early Poems*, 2nd ed. (Middletown, CT:
Wesleyan University Press, 1991); *WTTT—The World of the Ten Thousand Things: Poems
1980–1990* (New York: Farrar, Straus & Giroux, 1990); *NB—Negative Blue: Selected Later
Poems* (New York: Farrar, Straus & Giroux, 2000).

of *Country Music* on the body of his work, Wright muses, "It has also been suggested—again by Jorge Luis Borges—that everything a man writes, in the end, traces the outlines of his own face. I find it has been that way with me" (*CM* xxiii). Wright has always turned inward towards his own losses and obsessions. It could be said that these three books sketch the same face, the same life, only—as the covers indicate—with different colors, shadows, and textures. But since Wright is a poet and not a painter, one might also say that the structures, even the rhythms, change, while it is always the same song.

Wright was born on August 25, 1935, in Pickwick Dam, Tennessee. His father, a civil engineer, worked on damsites for the Tennessee Valley Authority, bringing electricity to regions in the rural South. Wright had a nomadic childhood, living in parts of Tennessee, Mississippi, and North Carolina, as the family moved from one damsite to another, finally settling in Kingsport. His mother, born and raised in the Mississippi Delta, wrote short stories and encouraged Wright to read William Faulkner. As a teenager, he spent four summers and one year at Sky Valley, a school of eight students "under the evangelical thumb of the daughter of the Episcopal Bishop of South Carolina" (*QN* 5). His final two years of high school, he attended an Episcopal boarding school, Christ School, nicknamed "Jesus Tech" by the students. Although he soon abandoned organized religion, Wright's poems maintain a spiritual impulse and Christian overtones. He explains this debt to his past in an interview: "We take the vocabulary we are given—in my case, Christian—and use it to our own ends. We try to develop and expand what we are given" (*QN* 120). He graduated from Davidson College in 1957 with a degree in history, but called his college career "four years of amnesia, as much my fault as theirs" (*HL* 60).

After college, he served in the US Army Intelligence Service for four years, three of which were spent in Verona, Italy. His time abroad provided Wright with the intellectual development that he did not attain through college. Reflecting on his army career, he wrote, "I cared for nothing it had to offer and yearned for everything around it that it stood staunchly against—art, literature, foreigners, past history, and small cars."[4] He spent his off hours immersed in poetry, painting, and Italian culture. Urged by a friend, he read Pound's "Blandula, Tenulla, Vagula" by the ruins of Catullus's country villa on Lake Garda, the location memorialized in the poem. He was drawn to its music and saw in Pound's poem—arranged through lyrical association rather than narrative—a form that he might emulate and use to express himself: "My life was changed forever. No kidding. I was at that time twenty-three or twenty-four. You can't get more romantic than that, can you, unless you're Gauguin?" (*HL* 60).

After the army, Wright entered the University of Iowa's Writers' Workshop in 1961. His admission into the program was allegedly "a fluke"

---

4. Charles Wright, entry in *Contemporary Authors Autobiography Series*, vol. 7, ed. Mark Zadrozny (Detroit: Gale Research Inc., 1988), 295.

(*HL* 170). He applied late in the summer; the university admitted him for study, but none of the professors at the workshop had read his manuscript. Wright, who had little formal training in poetry, proved a diligent student, learning quickly from his teachers and fellow students: "Immediately I knew I was in over my head, so I kept my mouth shut for two years and my ears and eyes open."[5] Donald Justice, as a teacher and mentor, was influential in Wright's development and taught Wright about prosody and literary history: "I was the blackboard and he was the chalk. I like to think that some of what he first wrote on there still remains" (*HL* 174). Mark Strand also influenced Wright, encouraging him to experiment with prose poems and translate Italian poetry. Wright graduated in 1963 and then returned to Italy for two years as a Fulbright scholar. He studied Dante and Eugenio Montale at the University of Rome and translated Montale's book *La bufera e altro* (The Storm and Other Poems, 1956). Montale, like Pound, was one of Wright's major early influences. The metaphysical overtones in Montale's poems appealed to Wright, and the careful act of translation improved his understanding of poetic craft. Montale taught him "how to move a line, how to move an image from one stage to the next. How to create imaginary bridges between images and stanzas and then to cross them, making them real, image to image, block to block" (*HL* 63–4). Wright eventually published his translation in 1978 with Oberlin College Press and was awarded the PEN Translation Prize.

He returned to the University of Iowa in 1965 to earn a Ph.D. but abandoned the program after a year when offered a teaching position at the University of California, Irvine. He was offered "a half-time, visiting, nine-month lectureship" but ended up staying for seventeen years, settling in Laguna Beach.[6] During his third year at Irvine, he returned to Italy again as a Fulbright lecturer at the University of Padua and lived in Venice. In the spring of 1969 he married the photographer Holly McIntire. The couple has one son, Luke. Through family Wright and his wife inherited a small ranch in the mountains of Montana, where they spend their summers. Like the landscapes of the American South and Italy, it is a source of inspiration and sustenance in Wright's work. In 1983 he left California and accepted a position at the University of Virginia, returning to his Southern roots after twenty-five years. He still lives and teaches in Charlottesville.

*Country Music*, awarded the National Book Award in 1983, gathers eighty-eight poems from Wright's first four books. In compiling the collection, he decided not to include any new poems, unusual for a selected works, and chose only five prose poems from his first book, *The Grave of the Right Hand* (1970), dismissing it as an "apprentice volume" (*QN* 103). Instead, the collection preserves what Wright feels comprises a trilogy that represents the past, present, and future: *Hard Freight* (1973), *Bloodlines* (1975), and *China Trace*

---

5. Ibid., 297.
6. Ibid., 299.

(1977). As the title *Country Music* suggests, the volume evokes the unbridled landscapes of Tennessee and North Carolina, the yearning for salvation that dominated Wright's Episcopalian upbringing, and the cadences of gospel music and prayer. In an interview, Wright acknowledged, "All my poems are prayers and songs. Hymns" (*HL* 130). *Country Music* begins in earnest with Wright's second book, *Hard Freight*, a collection of disparate lyrics. The book's strongest poems explore Wright's childhood, probing the past, not through conventional narrative, but through place. In "Dog Creek Mainline," which he calls "one of my first decent poems," Wright commemorates the lush wilderness near Hiwassee Dam, North Carolina, one of the damsites where his family lived.[7] Through spondaic lines and compact metaphors Wright captures the dense landscape in language: "Spindrift and windfall; woodrot; / Odor of muscadine, the blue creep / Of kingsnake and copperhead" (*CM* 36). This compression of sound and image is characteristic of his early work.

His next book, *Bloodlines*, continues to elegize the past and grapple with its ghosts. It is divided symmetrically by two twenty-poem sequences, "Tattoos" and "Skins." One of Wright's favorite poems, Montale's "Mottetti" (Motets), a group of twenty love poems, inspired him to experiment with the sequence form. The poems in "Tattoos" each capture a specific incident in the poet's life, a moment that marked his consciousness, "a psychic tattoo" (*HL* 67). Memories range from a bout of blood poisoning as a child to seeing a sideshow stripper at a county fair to encountering Piero della Francesca's *The Resurrrection* in Italy. Taken together, the poems comprise a dense and elusive autobiography. The second sequence, "Skins," composed in sonnet-like blocks of fourteen lines, is more conceptual than its companion and presents a series of elliptical meditations. By adopting an abstract subject matter in "Skins," Wright turns away from memory to the present moment and prepares to encounter the future in his next book, *China Trace*.

When writing *China Trace*, Wright limited himself to poems of twelve lines or less, and this condensed approach produced works of stunning lyric concision. There is even a one-line poem ("Bygones") and a two-line poem ("Death"). Although it consists of fifty short poems, *China Trace* can also be considered one book-length sequence, its individual parts interwoven by a submerged narrative. Wright explains the concept in an interview: "I think of the book as a long poem with fifty chapters...fifty little doors you open, click shut, and then go on to the next" (*HL* 97).[8] Taken as a whole, the book follows one man's journey from childhood to a partial ascension into heaven. It is a deeply spiritual volume, which David St. John calls "a pilgrim's book...the soul's search for salvation, a man's yearning for the *other*" (*CM* xvii).[9] The

---

7. Ibid., 289.

8. The revised version of *China Trace* that appears in *Country Music* includes only forty-six poems.

9. St. John's essay appears in *High Lonesome*.

central figure—often referred to as "I," sometimes as "you," and finally as "he"—desires to unite with the everlasting and, in reaching towards the unknown, hints at the future. The speaker's spiritual yearning is evident in "Clear Night": "I want to be bruised by God. / I want to be strung up in a strong light and singled out" (*CM* 152).

Despite their metaphysical themes, the poems in *China Trace* are rooted in everyday life and the natural world. Place names, months, seasons, and phases of the moon bind and awe the speaker. Influenced by Pound's translations of Chinese poetry in *Cathay* (1915), Wright grounds his meditations in the landscape around him, a method borrowed from the poets of the T'ang dynasty. According to Wright, the poems in *China Trace* "are *like* Chinese poems in the sense that they give you an idea of one man's relationship to the endlessness, the ongoingness, the everlastingness of what's around him, and his relationship to it as he stands in the natural world" (*HL* 77). Ultimately, *China Trace's* preoccupation with this world inhibits its pilgrim from attaining a Christian transcendence into the next. In the final poem, "Him," the protagonist rises into the night sky and transforms into stars: "Look for him high in the flat back of the northern Pacific sky, / Released in his suit of lights, / lifted and laid clear" (*CM* 156). Wright, using the vocabulary of Dantean cosmology, acknowledges the limitations of this transcendence: "He ends up a constellation in the heaven of the fixed stars—not enough belief to be able to get beyond what he can see, into the empyrean" (*QN* 103). In Dante, the empyrean is the highest heaven, outside of time and space—a leap Wright's earthbound pilgrim fails to make. A yearning for transcendence and its contradictory impulse, the love of worldly things, contend throughout *China Trace* and continue their wrenching sway in Wright's subsequent work.

*The World of the Ten Thousand Things*, Wright's second volume of selected poems, collects a decade of achievement: *The Southern Cross* (1981), *The Other Side of the River* (1984), *Zone Journals* (1988), and a brief coda, *Xionia* (1990). The themes of *Country Music*—landscape, memory, mortality, salvation—continue in *The World of the Ten Thousand Things*, but Wright's work undergoes a stylistic shift. A longer, more relaxed line allows more everyday details into the poems. The book's title derives from the *Tao Te Ching* by the Chinese philosopher Lao Tzu, who used the phrase to express the diversity of the universe: "Tao produced the One. / The One produced the two. / The two produced the three. / And the three produced the ten thousand things."[10] These poems are rich in texture, strewn with anecdotes and particulars. A wider range of diction and shades of humor also develop in Wright's voice, creating poems that are candid and human. In an interview, Wright explains his move away from the crystalline concision of *Country Music*: "I…tried to compress my line and my poems into a handful of matter, to squeeze everything down to its essences as much as I could….After

---

10. Lao Tzu, *Tao Te Ching*, in *A Source Book in Chinese Philosophy*, comp. and trans. Wing-tsit Chan (Princeton: Princeton University Press, 1963), 160.

that, I wanted to open my hand and let the line and poems expand as far as they could toward prose, without *becoming* prose."[11] Wright's "The Southern Cross," the title poem to his fifth book, exemplifies his switch to more fluid forms. In twenty-five sections of various lengths, the poem unravels Wright's own past, drifting from scene to scene, image to image, the way memory drifts: Venice's lapping canals, the English Cemetery in Rome where Keats and Shelley are buried, the dark hills of Kingsport. Instead of a continuous narrative line, filaments of narrative flash one after another. Wright describes this process to an interviewer: "Anyone's autobiography…is made up of a string of luminous moments, numinous moments. It's a necklace we spend our lives assembling. That's what 'The Southern Cross' is about, saying some of those beads" (*QN* 107). By presenting his life in snippets, as a collage of surfaces and sensations, Wright forces what's mentioned to grow in poignancy against the silences. The incidents feel drawn from a larger, anonymous whole. His autobiography becomes half his own, half everybody else's.

Wright continues splicing together narratives in *The Other Side of the River*, and as the stories unfold, whether they're about sucking gin from a watermelon or a near-death experience in a helicopter, people begin to populate his landscapes. Human presences—names like Rose Dials, George Vaughn, Doagie Duncan, and Miss Sweeney—are counted among the ten thousand things. Wright adopts even looser structures in *Zone Journals*, his next book, where the poems pose as journal entries. The diary form, which finds its material in daily events and the passage of the seasons, allows him to linger among the details. The book's centerpiece, the forty-page "Journal of the Year of the Ox," chronicles the entire year of 1985 and uncovers a diverse array of material: American history, personal reflections, winter landscapes, a stretch of summer months in Northern Italy, a detailed description of Renaissance frescos in Ferrara, pilgrimages to the places where Emily Dickinson, Edgar Allen Poe, and Petrarch once lived. Wright, however, is not content to merely record the surfaces but to envision what they once were or what they might become. He pays homage to the sacred ground of the Cherokees, nearly forgotten on the way to the golf course. Later, Dante wanders his garden in a gown and speaks. The seemingly ordinary is transfused with ghosts and murmurs of the divine, merging the visible and the invisible, what Wright calls "the metaphysics of the quotidian" (*HL* 22). The everyday world is imbued with a celestial glow, while, at the same time, Wright's visionary concerns become heartbreakingly tangible.

Throughout *The World of the Ten Thousand Things*, Wright's loose structures are accompanied by long lines that often drop down a step and continue across the page:

---

11. Charles Wright, "An Interview with Charles Wright," by Louis Bourgeois, *Carolina Quarterly* 56, no. 2/3 (2004): 32.

> As the morning begins to take hold
> > and the palm trees gleam.
> > > (*WTTT* 48)

> And the dark lets all its weight down
> > to within a half inch of the ground.
> > > (*WTTT* 116)

> The grass knows, stunned in its lockjaw bed,
> > but it won't tell.
> > > (*WTTT* 154)

The dropped line or "low rider" (*HL* 52) derives from Pound, but Wright has made it his signature. Unlike Pound's dropped line, which sometimes appears more like an indented second line, Wright's staggers directly downward and across in one fluid motion, so it can be conceived of as one line, not two. It creates dissonance in the flow of the long end-stopped line and unites William Carlos Williams's frenetic energy with Walt Whitman's expansiveness. The dropped line also alters the physical shape of Wright's poems. The text, jagged and creviced, spans both the length and width of the page, creating what Wright dubs "an American sprawl of a poem" (*QN* 116). As Bonnie Costello notes, "The Father of American sprawl is Whitman," and this connection seems fitting for the ambulatory speaker in *The World of the Ten Thousand Things*, who rummages the landscape for sights and sounds.[12] Wright even makes the comparison himself: "Places and things that caught my eye, Walt, / In Italy. On foot, Great Cataloguer, some twenty-odd years ago" (*WTTT* 19). Wright's speaker crumbles a handful of dirt in Clark County, Virginia, the home of his ancestors. He walks through Kensington Gardens in London, admiring the dogs and "the limbs of a leafless chestnut tree" (*WTTT* 129). He visits Poe's old room in Charlottesville, knocks twice on the doorjamb, and moves on.

The third volume of Wright's selected works, *Negative Blue* (2000), contains *Chickamauga* (1995), *Black Zodiac* (1997), *Appalachia* (1998), and *North American Bear* (1999). Refining his style once again, Wright synthesizes his previous techniques. He returns to the short lyric poem, the form taut with intensity throughout *Country Music*, abandoning the larger structures of *The World of the Ten Thousand Things*, but the long, loping line remains, as does the skeleton of the verse journal. The titles no longer label the poems as journals, but Wright's musings are still guided by the changing seasons. The poems flow one into the next, winding through the year as they intermingle physical description, philosophical inquiries, and quotes from other authors. Taken as a whole, the book can be viewed as one long sequence. Instead of the terse titles of *China Trace*, which propped up the poems the way you might hang a picture frame on a nail, the titles in *Negative Blue* tend

---

12. Bonnie Costello, "Charles Wright, Giorgio Morandi, and the Metaphysics of the Line," *Mosaic* 35, no. 1 (2002): 165. This essay appears in *High Lonesome*.

to be longer, often anecdotal and humorous: "Thinking of David Summers at the Beginning of Winter," "Looking West from Laguna Beach at Night," "After Rereading Robert Graves, I Go Outside to Get My Head Together." Tied to incident and seasonal change, the titles reinforce the journal form, and their casual, playful tone softens the divisions between poems.

In "Sprung Narratives," Wright traverses the past, accumulating narrative shards in a method like that of "The Southern Cross." But more often, the speaker in *Negative Blue* is content with the present moment, to sit in his backyard east of the Blue Ridge Mountains and ponder what is before him. These are meditative poems, the physical and mental landscapes intimately merged. In shortening his poems, Wright sloughs off the details of the ten thousand things and condenses his insights through abstraction and aphorism:

How strange to have a name, any name, on this poor earth.　　(*NB* 45)

One life is all we're entitled to, but it's enough.　　(*NB* 51)

Death is into the water, life is the coming out.　　(*NB* 78)

Love is more talked about than surrendered to.　　(*NB* 131)

A line of poetry's a line of blood.　　(*NB* 139)

Like late Williams, Wright, as he ages, relies more on the declarative statement and less on the imagistic one: "Why not just sit out in the open and talk about it. It won't talk back, as I've discovered, so camouflage and wily evasions no longer seem *as* necessary, though sometimes they still feel prudent."[13] His ruminations frequently incorporate quotes from other authors, introducing them with phrases such as, "Blake reminds us" (*NB* 40), "according to Cioran" (*NB* 120), "Borges wondered" (*NB* 170), "Simone Weil says" (*NB* 172). Wright has always paid homage to his influences, but this technique of assimilating other voices into his own is more characteristic of his later work. Instead of visiting the houses of Dickinson and Petrarch, as he does in "The Journal of the Year of the Ox," Wright now holds dialogues with his predecessors' disembodied voices. He seems less concerned with tracing the rhythms of the earth. Instead, the mind itself sways in contemplation. His speaker is less ambulatory, more static. Wright's description of Emily Dickinson could easily be applied to his later poems: "She sat in her room and the galaxy unrolled beneath her feet. She sat in her room and the garden and orchard outside her window took on the ghostly garments of infinity....Inside the tube of the climbing rose, the River of Heaven flowed. Under the oak's throat, the broken ladder of Paradise waited for reassembly" (*QN* 39–40).

---

13. Charles Wright, "Interview," by Willard Spiegelman, *Literary Imagination* 2, no. 1 (2000): 116.

If *Country Music* explored Wright's roots and *The World of the Ten Thousand Things* depicted the diversity of the earth, *Negative Blue* looks upward at the sky. The title *Negative Blue* focuses our attention on the sky's immensity and how it conjures the unknown. Heaven, however, is never glimpsed. Instead, the blue expanse sets our lives in relief, in negative, making what emerges fragile and cherished. Nectarine-colored sunsets, drifting clouds, and constellations pass overhead in these poems, somber and brilliant. *Country Music's* divisions of the past, present, and future, are mirrored in *Chickamauga, Black Zodiac,* and *Appalachia*. Like its companion volume *China Trace, Appalachia* is a sequence of short lyrics that conclude with an upward ascent, entertaining the possibility of transcendence. The closing pages of *Negative Blue* are abundant with celestial imagery. The speaker, with "one eye cocked toward heaven" (*NB* 147), continuously ponders the constellations and what might lie beyond them, the night sky recast through metaphor as "a code card punched with holes" (*NB* 156) or "a sequined dress from the forties" (*NB* 182). The poems have titles such as "Star Turn," "Star Turn II," and "Sky Diving," and the concluding sequence of seven poems, *North American Bear,* is named after the costellation Ursa Major. "What a sidereal jones we have!" Wright self-deprecatingly declares (*NB* 201). Despite this assault on the heavenly spheres, *Negative Blue,* like *China Trace,* ends in the heaven of the fixed stars, Wright's pilgrim unable to transcend the visible world: "We live our lives like stars, unconstelled stars, just next to / Great form and great structure, / ungathered, uncalled upon" (*NB* 193). In the title poem "North American Bear" he solemnly declares, "There is a final solitude I haven't arrived at yet" (*NB* 198). Wright's trilogies end here, on a note of disappointment and wonder. It is an elliptical conclusion filled with the yearning, transience, and rediscovery that churn throughout his work. His speaker is still waiting to be gathered, still apart from the celestial lights. And because of such distances, still in awe of them: "Who is to say some angel has not / breathed in my ear?" (*NB* 197).

Since *Negative Blue,* Wright has published two more books: *A Short History of the Shadow* (2002) and *Buffalo Yoga* (2004). The books are stylistically and thematically similar to his other work, and these resemblances have brought the integrity of the trilogies into question. In 2005 the AWP Conference in Vancouver presented a panel on Wright's work, and one of its panelists, Elizabeth Dodd, preferred to look beyond the divisions of the trilogies. Dodd, focusing on the verse journal as a unifying structure, claimed, "The ultimate structural discoveries first achieved in *Zone Journals* resist his placement of that book in the second of his trilogies, *The World of the Ten Thousand Things;* that is to say, I find that the poems are most revealing when considered *not* as a part of a distinct trilogy, but as part of a larger effort of 'seeing' that will comprise all his subsequent work."[14] J. D. McClatchy in his essay "Ars Longa" is also unconvinced. He points out that "the symmetry is slightly askew," since Wright's trilogies collect poems from twelve books, not

14. Elizabeth Dodd, "'Looking Around': A Fidelity of Attention in Charles Wright's Transcendent Journals" (unpublished essay).

as one might suspect, nine. Then he adds, "It may be that when Charles Wright has published three more collections, they will be sheaved together and talk will start of The Tetralogy."[15] Given the inexhaustible nature of Wright's search, such assessments are warranted, but I hope the overview I have provided also shows that the trilogies coalesce in an overall design. According to the numbers alone, McClatchy is correct about the symmetry. *The Grave of the Right Hand*, however, only contributes five prose poems and *Xionia* and *North American Bear* are both chapbooks. Each volume of selected poems is primarily based on three books, and each is characterized by new developments in style.

Wright's work has always wavered between contradictory impulses. An otherworldly ascension is weighed down by the shrill and fragrant earth. A nostalgia for the past reveals memory's tainted shards. A yearning for expression abuts the limits of language. Willard Spiegelman writes, "There is no American poet who combines so neatly the rival tendencies to summarize, epitomize, or conclude…and to speculate, wonder, and question." Henry Hart adds that Wright "fragments Dante's architectonic design, scattering shards of infernos, purgatories, and paradises throughout his sequence."[16] It is no surprise that all of these oppositions are not resolved in the final pages of *Negative Blue*. Such a transcendence would impose a narrative conclusion onto a lyric sequence and ultimately betray Wright's project. For Wright, Paradise is not found in that last step beyond the stars, but in "walking to and fro on the earth" (*CM* 101), the image of the pilgrim occurring frequently in this work. It seems fitting that the trilogies culminate with his most prolonged thrust heavenward. His two most recent books plummet back down to the earth, to its griefs and cycles. They provide a falling action to the climax of *Appalachia* and *North American Bear*. Wright, like Dante, maps the span of human experience, but does so piecemeal, in revelations and concessions, in Pound's "gists and piths."[17] If paradise is to be found on earth, such an elaborate weave is necessary, the luminous embedded among the quotidian. Wright's trilogies, in all their intricate grandeur, attest to this vision: "What we have, and all we will have, is here in the earthly paradise. How to wring music from it, how to squeeze the light out of it, is, as it has always been, the only true question" (*QN* 120).

Given the welter of attention Wright's poetry has received, this book could easily have been twice as long. I have done my best to produce a collection

---

15. J. D. McClatchy, "Ars Longa," review of *Appalachia*, *Poetry* 175, no. 1 (1999): 79, 88. This essay appears in *High Lonesome*.

16. Willard Spiegelmen, "Charles Wright and 'The Metaphysics of the Quotidian,'" in *How Poets See the World: The Art of Description in Contemporary Poetry* (New York: Oxford University Press, 2005), 103. Henry Hart, "Charles Wright's *Via Mystica*," *Georgia Review* 58, no. 2 (2004): 410. Both of these essays appear in *High Lonesome*.

17. Ezra Pound, *The ABC of Reading* (New York: New Directions, 1960), 92.

that is thorough but readable. For the sake of concision, not all the essays from *The Point Where All Things Meet* have been reprinted. On occasion, they have been replaced with recent work by the same author, who has extended his or her original ideas. Peter Stitt's "Resurrecting the Baroque," which appears here, incorporates insights from his reviews in *The Point Where All Things Meet*. Likewise, I have opted against including Bonnie Costello's "The Soil and Man's Intelligence: Three Contemporary Landscape Poets," an essay from *The Point Where All Things Meet* that discusses landscape poetry, comparing Wright with Gary Snyder and A. R. Ammons. I have, however, included her more recent piece "Charles Wright, Giorgio Morandi, and the Metaphysics of the Line," which focuses exclusively on Wright, investigating the Italian painter's influence on his poetry.[18] *High Lonesome* concludes with a selected bibliography that lists Wright's publications as well as many secondary sources. Readers interested in additional responses to Wright's poetry are encouraged to consult it.

In revising the book, I have divided it into two parts. The first collects book reviews. They trace the chronology of Wright's books and are arranged accordingly. Thus, David St. John's preface to the second edition of *Country Music*, although it appeared nine years after the book's original publication, is organized according to *Country Music*'s position in the chronology. The second part of *High Lonesome* is comprised of essays that span several books, provide overviews, or investigate Wright's work from specific angles. For example, Michael Chitwood's "Gospel Music: Charles Wright and the High Lonesome" explores Wright's connection to country music, while Stephen Cushman's "The Capabilities of Charles Wright" examines formal issues in Wright's poetry and his commitment to free verse. These are arranged by publication date in a loose chronological order. I hope this organization allows the reader to follow the response to Wright's work volume by volume, while also providing more sustained glances at his achievement. It should be noted that these divisions, though useful, are far from rigid. Reviews of Wright's selected volumes—*Country Music, The World of the Ten Thousand Things,* and *Negative Blue*—encapsulate decade-long spans in his career and provide significant overviews. Also, J. D. McClatchy's "Ars Longa," a review of *Appalachia*, extends beyond that one book to examine its place at the conclusion of Wright's trilogies.

Readers familiar with Wright's work will note some omissions in the chronology of the reviews. There are no reviews of his first four books: *The Grave of the Right Hand, Bloodlines, Hard Freight,* and *China Trace*. Individual reviews of these books were omitted from *The Point Where All Things Meet*, and I have chosen not to amend Tom Andrews's decision. Early responses to

---

18. Costello, who frequently comments on Wright's work, has written a third essay: "Charles Wright's *Via Negativa*: Language, Landscape, and the Idea of God," *Contemporary Literature* 42, no. 2 (2001): 325–46. Although not included in *High Lonesome*, it merits attention.

Wright's work tend to be short, his books mentioned glancingly in omnibus reviews. Nevertheless, these early books are given extensive treatment in *High Lonesome*. David St. John's preface to *Country Music* provides an ample overview of Wright's early poems. Several of the essays in the second half of the book also examine this period, notably Helen Vendler's "The Transcendent 'I'" and the essays by Calvin Bedient, James McCorkle, and Peter Stitt. Wright's two most recent books, *A Short History of the Shadow* and *Buffalo Yoga*, comprise another omission and are scarcely mentioned in this collection. The publication of *Negative Blue*, the concluding volume in the trilogies and the culmination of Wright's thirty-year project, seems like an appropriate point to pause and assess his achievement. The final phase of Wright's development is still unfolding and, aside from several book reviews, has not yet received the same scrutiny as his trilogies. His work continues to grow, and as it does, it is sure to engender more criticism and influence new generations of poets. I welcome those discussions and hope *High Lonesome* will help future readers enter and explore Wright's exquisite music. If *The Point Where All Things Meet* was the first step in assessing Wright's accomplishments, this book wishes to be the second of the many that follow.

David Young kindly offered me the opportunity to assemble this collection. I would like to extend my gratitude to him and David Walker for their guidance and patience. I also thank Charles Wright, for his suggestions and generosity; the University of Virginia Libraries, whose resources were instrumental in compiling the book and bibliography; Linda Slocum, for her diligent work at the office of Oberlin College Press; and the contributors and publishers who generously made available these essays. Lastly, I thank my parents for their love and support, which have been bountiful.

# Part One

# Reviews

DAVID ST. JOHN

# Charles Wright's *Country Music* (1991)

I t has been ten years since the first edition of Charles Wright's *Country Music: Selected Early Poems*, which gathers work from his first four collections of poetry: *The Grave of the Right Hand*, *Hard Freight*, *Bloodlines*, and *China Trace*. In that time, Wright has dazzled his readers with four more quite extraordinary new volumes: *The Southern Cross*, *The Other Side of the River*, *Zone Journals*, and *Xionia*, which have now been collected into one volume entitled *The World of the Ten Thousand Things*. For the many readers who have been longtime admirers of his poetry, it has been gratifying to note that the critical reception to Charles Wright's work has also kept pace with the widening of his audience, an audience which has been increasingly drawn to his poetry by its great power and beauty, its incisive spirituality and meditative elegance.

Certainly, the fact that Helen Vendler, David Kalstone, Peter Stitt, Calvin Bedient and others have championed his poetry in their thoughtful and perceptive reviews has helped this audience at large to recognize that Charles Wright is without question one of our preeminent American poets. His many prizes, including the 1983 National Book Award for *Country Music*, the Academy of American Poets' Edgar Allan Poe Award, and the Brandeis Creative Arts Citation for Poetry, have also shown the high regard in which he's held by his peers. Yet it strikes me that Charles Wright's poetry is highly unusual in that it stands not only in the context of its own time (and such temporal accolades), but that its lucid illuminations are also intended to reflect far into—while casting light upon—those dark recesses of our futures. For his readers, Charles Wright's poetry often serves as a kind of prayer book, a kind of poetic hymnal or speculative field guide we might carry with us on our own metaphysical journeys.

Over the past twenty years Charles Wright has written an impressive and demanding body of work that can stand in its accomplishments as the equal of *any* poet's in the latter part of the twentieth century. This has been not only an artistic achievement of notable dimension but a spiritual one as well. Quite simply, Charles Wright has emerged as the most visionary American poet since Hart Crane; he is that most rare of poets—one who is stylistically (and tirelessly) inventive, yet who speaks to and from a tradition that harkens back to Dante. With the mirror of his collection *The World of the Ten Thousand Things* so recently before us, it seems to me a proper occasion to look back at the rich and complex harmonies of Charles Wright's selected early poetry, *Country Music*.

★

Throughout his career, Charles Wright has been a highly adept literary ar-
chitect; he is not only a formal master, he is also an endlessly imaginative
sculptor of larger unifying structures for his work. *China Trace*, Wright's
fourth full collection, completed the triptych of books begun with *Hard
Freight* (his second volume) and which he'd continued through his much
praised third book, *Bloodlines.* In *Country Music*, Wright has selected only
five brief prose poems from his first book, *The Grave of the Right Hand*, as
a kind of prologue to this triptych of his subsequent books.

It has always seemed natural to me (after the finely crafted, visually
acute and precise poems of his debut volume) that Wright should feel the
need to gather his past, in some sense to write—and rewrite—not only
that past, but also the self (the poetic self and voice) which he was bring-
ing to maturity in his newer and more ambitious poems. Clearly, in terms
of both style and subject matter, this new direction was signaled by the
poem "Dog Creek Mainline" from the book *Hard Freight*. Knotty, rhyth-
mically muscular, alliterative, yet still highly imagistic and visual, Wright's
poetry took on a beautiful rasping quality; his work began more deliber-
ately to reflect the abstract concerns embodied in his retrieval of the past,
all the while exhibiting the enjambed music that seemed to arise so mag-
ically from his lines. Wright also began revealing in these new poems
from *Hard Freight* and *Bloodlines* his self-conscious choice to use both
overt and covert autobiographical subject matter. These now familiar im-
pulses in Wright's poetry began to grow, it seems, along with his convic-
tion that the "unknown," or the spiritual and metaphysical, could best be
encountered or mediated through the "known." For Wright this meant a
reclamation of his past, an attempt at the recuperation of his childhood,
was necessary before he could begin to look toward the yearnings and
desirings of the "*beyond*" we find so delicately considered in the volume
*China Trace*, the final panel of Wright's triptych.

In *Hard Freight* (and to some extent in the poems of *Bloodlines*) familial
memories and episodes of Wright's youth in Tennessee and North Carolina
mix quite easily—"naturally" we might say—with the rich landscapes of
their settings. Yet, in *Bloodlines*, Wright begins the rigorous process of not
only attempting to orient himself to his past, now as a mature speaker, but
of orienting himself in relation to his own *present* and *presence* as well.
*Bloodlines* is a fiercely elegiac book, detailing the losses of people, places, and
times that have passed out of the poet's life. In addition to the powerful ele-
gies for his parents, Wright provides a double axis of personal reckoning to
*Bloodlines*; the intimate losses of the book revolve around two masterful po-
etic sequences, "Tattoos" and "Skins" (each consists of twenty numbered
sections and each sequence serves to echo the concerns of the other).

"Tattoos" illustrates a list of psychologically potent events which have,
each in some distinct way, "marked" Wright. "Skins" is a highly abstract
inquiry into the materials of existence, from the most elemental to the

most ethereal. The philosophical and metaphysical issues of "Skins" combine in a complex verbal music. And even though he questions his own ordering of the present, Wright nevertheless attempts to lay to rest his reclamation of the past while looking toward the certain—if ill-defined—terrain of his future, a terrain which takes as its horizon Wright's own death. Although, in *China Trace*, Wright will ask what may exist beyond that horizon (albeit in his own yearnings and imaginings), it is in *Bloodlines*, at the end of the final section of "Skins," that the meditations found in *China Trace* really begin:

> And what does it come to, Pilgrim,
> This walking to and fro on the earth, knowing
> That nothing changes, or everything;
> And only, to tell it, these sad marks,
> Phrases half-parsed, ellipses and scratches across the dirt?
> It comes to a point. It comes and it goes.

So, it is with these "sad marks" that Wright begins his attempt to tell not only what it comes to, but where—and why—his pilgrimage must continue.

*China Trace* remains one of the most remarkable books of American poetry of recent years. Though made up of individual pieces, *China Trace* functions also as a single book-length poem, beginning with the speaker's childhood and concluding with his assumption into the sky, into what Wright has called "a man-made heaven." *China Trace* is a personal history pushed toward its future; its speaker reaches toward his own death and the desired salvation it may or may not bring. In the course of these poems, Wright often clearly does *not* believe, yet he feels called upon to continue the search that his spiritual yearnings have prompted. The book is filled with portents of what's to come, as in the poems "Next" ("I want to lie down, I am so tired, and let / The crab grass seep through my heart, / Side by side with the inchworm and the fallen psalm . . .") and "January" ("In some other life / I'll stand where I'm standing now, and will look down, and will see / My own face, and not know what I'm looking at"). Much as in the poem "Skins," it is the elemental regeneration of a life—its death into decay, the body passing through its cycle of water, earth, fire, and air—which seems as much as one might ask of salvation. Here in "Self-Portrait in 2035" is Charles Wright imagining himself at 100 years old:

> The root becomes him, the road ruts
> That are sift and grain in the powderlight
> Recast him, sink bone in him,
> Blanket and creep up, fine, fine:
>
> Worm-waste and pillow tick; hair
> Prickly and dust-dangled, his arms and black shoes

> Unlinked and laceless, his face false
> In the wood-rot, and past pause . . .

> Darkness, erase these lines, forget these words.
> Spider recite his one sin.

The poems in *China Trace* are often offered as small cosmologies, many posited by Wright as approximations of both what is and what's to come. Even if, as he says in the poem "Morandi" (for the great Italian painter), it is "the void / These objects sentry for, and rise from," it is clear that the poems of *China Trace* are firmly rooted in the objects of everyday life, in the earth itself (as well as in natural landscape), and in the domestic experience reflected in the journal-like quality of many of the poems. It is no accident these poems are often fixed not only by place names, but by specific times of day or night, phases of the moon, dates, and personal references as well. In his diary of passage, the quotidian and the natural must balance what otherwise could simply seem the illusions all dreamers must perform. Thus, it remains vital to Wright that he must continuously mark and notate his search with the facts of his existence. Otherwise, without these resolutely concrete notes in the log, what future resonance could such a spiritual search have?

*China Trace* is a pilgrim's book, the same "Pilgrim" who is addressed at the conclusion of "Skins." It carries a strong and dramatic narrative—the soul's search for salvation, a man's yearning for the *other*. *China Trace* also shows Charles Wright to be one of the most formally inventive poets writing. The weblike structures of his poems reverberate with his characteristic verbal music, and their individual images seem to radiate through *Country Music* as a whole. *China Trace* grows slowly into a guidebook of spiritual passage, with nods to fellow travelers along the way. Sometimes, we feel that the speaker of these poems has suffered his own silence, in seclusion, for a long while. Sometimes, we listen as the poems take on the tone of a wanderer who has walked off from the tribe, the city, in order to turn and speak for it, at last. In "Depression Before the Solstice" Wright sees:

> The watchers and holy ones set out, divining
> The seal, eclipses
> Taped to their sleeves with black felt,
> Their footprints filling with sparks
> In the bitter loam behind them, ahead of them stobbed with sand,
> And walk hard, and regret nothing.

Many have remarked upon the hermetic tone of *China Trace*, attributing it in part to the influence of Eugenio Montale, the superb Italian poet whom Wright has translated so well. Yet the impulse to touch mystery has always been present in Wright's work. In the illuminating *instants* of *China Trace* we are in the presence—as in all of the finest religious works—of the mystery of the *one*, the individual, confronted by the expanse of the greater and more fluent *other*. Here is the poem "Stone Canyon Nocturne":

> Ancient of Days, old friend, no one believes you'll come back.
> No one believes in his own life anymore.
>
> The moon, like a dead heart, cold and unstartable, hangs by a thread
> At the earth's edge,
> Unfaithful at last, splotching the ferns and the pink shrubs.
>
> In the other world, children undo the knots in their tally strings.
> They sing songs, and their fingers blear.
>
> And here, where the swan hums in his socket, where bloodroot
> And belladonna insist on our comforting,
> Where the fox in the canyon wall empties our hands, ecstatic for more,
>
> Like a bead of clear oil the Healer revolves through the night wind,
> Part eye, part tear, unwilling to recognize us.

Once again, Wright tries to explore the nature of our proper relationship to what "lies beyond," since fear and acquiescence are both regarded as inadequate. For Wright, this simple search always leads back to language; for that reason his poetry has, over the years, developed a more heightened and extremely graphic sense of what characterizes verbal enactment. As a result, Wright has often been called "painterly" in his use of wordplay and in his execution of dazzling verbal chromatics. It is as if many of Wright's poems keep seeking some ideogrammatic form, and as such exist almost as some other language—something between the language we know and the glyphs of an obscure, yet resilient poetic cult. There is, in Charles Wright's poetry, much of the tone of Yeats' occult clarity and Rilke's sonorous passion. It's no accident that the natural elements often appear in the act of "writing" themselves across the face of the earth or the sky. It is this singularly physical signature of passage, both man's and the world's, which so intrigues Wright, perhaps because so much of his poetry reflects his struggle against the impossibility of inscription.

Certainly one can trace Pound behind some of Wright's ambitions, just as one can find echoes of Hart Crane's revisionistsymbolist impulses, or the devotional grandeur of Gerard Manley Hopkins. Yet I'm convinced that, in the forging of this new line and new language for himself, Charles Wright has responded to a tremendously personal, *internal* pressure—a pressure to discover the proper word construct, the right syllable mobile, the most pleasing sound ladder—in his search for an appropriate aesthetic to reflect and convey his anxious, metaphysical explorations.

There is some risk, certainly, when so demanding a notion of language is coupled with so abstract a subject matter. But Charles Wright is an impeccable stylist, and his poems remain rooted in real experience even while seeking some greater, perhaps more universal, equation.

*Country Music* as a whole "traces" Charles Wright's grand passions: his desire to reclaim and redeem a personal past, to make a reckoning with his present, and to conjure the terms by which we might face the future. If we wonder where the road of these poems can possibly end, it is the end we knew would be reached from the very beginning. If we wonder what will become of the "Pilgrim" who has disguised himself so often as "I," "You," and "He," then we are answered in the final poem of *China Trace*, with its devotional pun on hymn, "Him":

> His sorrow hangs like a heart in the star-flowered boundary tree.
> It mirrors the endless wind.
>
> He feeds on the lunar differences and flies up at the dawn.
>
> When he lies down, the waters will lie down with him,
> And all that walks and all that stands still, and sleep through the thunder.
>
> It's for him that the willow bleeds.
>
> Look for him high in the flat black of the northern Pacific sky,
> Released in his suit of lights,
>                     lifted and laid clear.

★

In *Country Music* we see the same explosive imagery, the same dismantled and concentric (or parallel) narratives, the same resolutely spiritual concerns that have become so familiar to us in Wright's more recent poetry. The idea of using a fluid "journal" construct, which becomes the central formal aspect of *The World of the Ten Thousand Things*, can be discovered in the poems of *China Trace*. The charged verbal rhythms and the crystalline music that have become hallmarks of Wright's poetry both have their poetic workbooks contained in *Country Music*. And it is here, especially in those poems of overt autobiographical reckoning, that we come to recognize the importance of Charles Wright as an American poet, most specifically as a Southern poet. The "country" in *Country Music* is meant to signal a fierce regionalism in Wright, as well as to honor the "lyric, the human theme" of country music itself, an art whose story line, Wright says, seldom varies: "change your life or else heaven won't be your home." Yet the title also announces the importance of understanding how elements of landscape in Charles Wright's poems have been first remembered and recovered, then precisely reinvented and constructed as poetic entities (and melodies). In his prose book, *Halflife*, Wright says of his poems from *Zone Journals* something that is applicable to all of his work, that his poems "are about language and landscape, and how they coexist in each other, and speak for, and to, each other." In his poetry, Wright looks to the landscapes that have nourished him, contained him, and inspired him, and tries to give them worthy poetic voices.

We need also to keep in mind the interwoven quality of Wright's spiritual aspirations with the poetic materials of his poems. In Charles Wright's poetry, reticence is a kind of faith and style is an articulation of virtue. As Wright says elsewhere in *Halflife*, "True vision is great style." Wright's poems are not only truly devotional, they are each secular prayers begging to break into a realm far beyond their own seclusion or privacy.

It is perhaps Charles Wright's greatest accomplishment that, while his poems remain very much of the world, they are nevertheless resolutely spiritual in character. It is this, even more than his technical virtuosity, formal prowess, and astounding imaginative range which makes him unique among his contemporaries. Charles Wright's poetic maps are drawn with humor and tenderness, great clarity and imagistic precision; yet it is his reverberating metaphors and complex verbal overlays that continue to dazzle his readers. Like his master, Cézanne, Wright insists that the very nature of perception itself change within us, that we might see more clearly the world which is without. This remarkable volume, *Country Music*, is an essential key to understanding the delicate poetic cosmology that resonates in Charles Wright's poetry. Lastly, let me remind the reader that one of the many rewards of these poems is that they seem so often to arise, in their consummate grace and power, in voices we slowly come to recognize as the simple echoes and lost harmonies of our own.

DAVID WALKER

# from "*One for the Rose* and *The Southern Cross*" (1982)

Charles Wright is at least as much a romantic as [Philip] Levine—his subject is always finally some version of his experience or vision—but even at their most self-conscious, his recent poems are never self-indulgent or self-aggrandizing. After repeated readings, I'm still not sure how he manages it. A description of this book might make it sound attitudinizing or breathy, a sort of Shelleyan effusion. In fact *The Southern Cross* is a controlled, resilient, and absolutely accurate performance, one of the best books I've read since—well, since his *China Trace* (1977) and *Bloodlines* (1975).

Wright's epigraph is a passage from the *Purgatorio* in which Virgil warns a shade not to embrace him because (in Singleton's translation) "you are a shade and a shade you see," to which the shade replies, "Now you may comprehend the measure of the love that burns in me for you, when I forget our emptiness and treat shades as solid things." It's appropriate in a number of ways. The book's mode is deeply elegiac; the poet corresponds with the shades of Cézanne, Pound, Li Po, Hart Crane, and Dante himself, as well as all those earlier avatars of himself that insist on rising from the dead. The theme of a love powerful enough to subsume emptiness is also central here; Wright's world is tragic, but also often heartbreakingly beautiful. Finally, while in the *Purgatorio* everything outside the poet is insubstantial, a series of shades not to be mistaken for "solid things," in *The Southern Cross* the world is manifestly, ecstatically tangible. That's one of the ways Wright escapes self-enclosure, I think, by recreating the world so vividly and acutely that there's no question that his subject is merely himself. Within individual poems, and from poem to poem, the relation of the ghostly to the tangible is explored by interweaving them; the visionary and the domestic alternate and occasionally merge, as in this passage about the dead from the long opening poem, "Homage to Paul Cézanne":

> Sometimes they lie like leaves in their little arks, and curl up at the
>     edges.
> Sometimes they come inside, wearing our shoes, and walk
> From mirror to mirror.
> Or lie in our beds with their gloves off
> And touch our bodies. Or talk
> In a corner. Or wait like envelopes on a desk.

They reach up from the ice plant.
They shuttle their messengers through the oat grass.
Their answers rise like rust on the stalks and the spidery leaves.

We rub them off our hands.

The opening passage of the title poem could stand as a touchstone for all of *The Southern Cross*:

Things that divine us we never touch:

The black sounds of the night music,
The Southern Cross, like a kite at the end of its string,

And now this sunrise, and empty sleeve of a day,
The rain just starting to fall, and then not fall,

No trace of a story line.

With few exceptions, these poems are released from a "story line," from the pressure of narrative or any overt dramatic scenario; they're structured instead as reactions to and meditations on the apparently random sequence of memory and event. We see *glimpses* of the past, of remembered landscapes and situations, but they rarely come into full focus—in other words, the poems remain almost purely lyrical. Yet even in those poems where Wright speaks most directly of his own experience ("Virginia Reel," "Bar Giamaica, 1959-60," "Gate City Breakdown"), there's no posturing or self-inflation, but a sense of utter integrity. And in the book's second section, the five poems each called "Self-Portrait" are all different and all curiously transparent; here's the fifth:

SELF-PORTRAIT

In Murray, Kentucky I lay once
On my side, the ghost-weight of a past life in my arms,
A life not mine. I know she was there,
Asking for nothing, heavy as bad luck, still waiting to rise.
I know now and I lift her.

Evening becomes us.
I see myself in a tight dissolve, and answer to no one.
Self-traitor, I smuggle in
The spider love, undoer and rearranger of all things.
Angel of Mercy, strip me down.

This world is a little place,
Just red in the sky before the sun rises.
Hold hands, hold hands
That when the birds start, none of us is missing.
Hold hands, hold hands.

In painting, the self-portrait is not usually a romantic or expressionist genre; rather, the painter turns the ready subject of the self into an object, a kind of still life to be formally contemplated. Wright seems to use the notion of self-portraiture for its rhetorical possibilities: it provides a network or web into which he can collect a variety of impressions and fragments that are linked by their relation to the self at the center.

This poem begins with a mysteriously located memory of an encounter with a ghostly presence; once that spirit was heavy and earth-bound, but now through the speaker's imagination he can help her to rise. The first line of the second stanza is a kind of pun: evening both is appropriate to us and constitutes us. The speaker then explicitly sees himself from an aesthetic distance, as in a film ("a tight dissolve"), and apparently as a result proclaims his independence ("answer to no one"). Immediately he contradicts this claim through a variation on Donne's "Twickenham Garden": "But oh, self-traitor, I do bring / The spider love, which transubstantiates all, / And can convert manna to gall." Significantly, Wright's "spider love" is less a poisoner than a rearranger, and the poem seems constantly to be rearranging experience—a self-portrait composed of found materials, a Joseph Cornell box radiating possibilities. It closes with a prayer for simplicity and then—in a voice stripped down to that of a child—a chant for comfort and protection. The focus opens widely at the end, reaching out to include the reader in imaginative communion, but its structure has been inclusive from the start. Reading, we focus not on the feelings and personal experience that may have given rise to the poem, but rather on the mood and idea that evolve from this collection of details and gestures. It's a portrait that creates a self more than it expresses one.

As "Self-Portrait" suggests, Wright's language in *The Southern Cross* tends to be more relaxed, not quite as hieratic as in *China Trace*. He can pull out the stops when he chooses:

> And the viridescent shirtwaists of light the trees wear.
> And the sutra-circles of cattle egrets wheeling out past the rain showers.
> And the spiked marimbas of dawn rattling their amulets . . .

But often there seems to be a recognition that a more chastened rhetoric is appropriate for the sort of communion with the past and the dead that is undertaken here:

> We filigree and we baste.
> But what do the dead care for the fringe of words,
> Safe in their suits of milk?
> What do they care for the honk and flash of a new style?

How risky it is to structure a passage simply as a list of things forgotten and things remembered, and how beautifully it works:

I can't remember the colors I said I'd never forget
On Via Giulia at sundown,
The ochres and glazes and bright hennas of each house,
Or a single day from November of 1964.
I can't remember the way the stairs smelled
                              or the hallway smelled
At Piazza del Biscione.
                    Or just how the light fell
Through the east-facing window over the wicker chairs there.

I do remember the way the boar hung
                              in the butcher shop at Christmas
Two streets from the Trevi fountain, a crown of holly and mistletoe
Jauntily over his left ear.
I do remember the flower paintings
Nodding throughout the May afternoons
                              on the dining room walls
At Zajac's place.
                    And the reliquary mornings,
And Easter, and both Days of the Dead . . .

That seems utterly matter-of-fact, but it recreates place, mood, and cul-
ture with wonderful economy. And then Wright merges past into pres-
ent, upping the verbal and emotional ante:

At noon in the English Cemetery no one's around.
Keats is off to the left, in an open view.
Shelley and Someone's son are straight up ahead.

With their marble breath and their marble names,
                              the sun in a quick squint through the trees,
They lie at the edge of everywhere,
                    Rome like a stone cloud at the back of their eyes.

                    ———

Time is the villain in most tales,
                    and here, too,
Lowering its stiff body into the water.
Its landscape is the resurrection of the word,
No end of it,
          the petals of wreckage in everything.

Out of context, the last line might seem overblown or melodramatic; by
quoting the whole passage I've tried to show how it's prepared for, how
in allowing himself the slow and almost prosaic rhythms of the list
Wright earns the heightened vision and diction of the ending. This sort
of progression leads to extraordinarily complex tonalities: I find the fol-
lowing both celebratory and melancholy, for instance:

August licks at the pine trees.
Sun haze, and little fugues from the creek.
Fern-sleep beneath the green skirt of the marsh.

I always imagine a mouth
Starting to open its blue lips
Inside me, an arm
                    curving sorrowfully over an open window
At evening, and toads leaping out of the wet grass.

Again the silence of flowers.
Again the faint notes of piano music back in the woods.
How easily summer fills the room.

Does such a passage grow out of acute observation of the natural world, or out of transcendent vision? The uncanny answer, I think, is that the voice somehow seems to become an extension of the eye—or vice versa—and that nature and spirit appear to merge in a way that feels almost *objectively* true. I don't pretend to understand how this works, but it's breathtaking to witness. *The Southern Cross* is the work of a master writing at the height of his powers, and signals a number of directions that I'd guess some of the best poetry of the eighties will follow.

DAVID KALSTONE

## *from* "Lives in a Rearview Mirror" (1984)

Over the years, Charles Wright has been assembling an arresting verse autobiography out of radiant fragments. There is no pretense of narrative sequence or explanation in his extraordinary poems. Yet behind them one feels an unslakable appetite to know, if not to tell, his story—"There is an otherness inside us / We never touch." Or again:

> It's not age,
> nor time with its gold eyelid and blink,
> Nor dissolution in all its mimicry
> That lifts us and sorts us out.
> It's discontinuity
> and all its spangled coming between
> That sends us apart and keeps us there in a dread.
> It's what's in the rear-view mirror,
> smaller and out of sight.

Memory is only its own traces glimpsed in landscapes and passing scenes. A deep love of place has come to stand for what is fugitive or unknowable about this poet's life. Impression and repression are the twin reflexes his writings explore. The poems are troubled by, and often grateful for, the way the sharp and pleasurable sensations we call description unseat narrative and the compulsive stories of our lives.

In six previous books, Mr. Wright has revisited the same charged landscapes, especially the Tennessee of his childhood and northern Italy (Verona and Venice), where he did military service some 20 years ago. The implied link between those two worlds, the obsessive shuttling between them, was mysterious in the earlier volumes. But it has become increasingly clear that each is for Mr. Wright a theater of the extreme; they throw into sharp relief both ecstasy ("What gifts there are are all here, in this world") and what death holds in ambush. He is in a helicopter, the engine suddenly gone dead, the machine sliding "sideways down the air / As quietly as a snowflake," or in a skid that almost takes his car over the edge of a mountain, wheels spinning in space. Or as a child at summer camp, he is sleepwalking one night toward a precipice, stopped only by coming up against a large black bear. The danger in each case is absorbed in memory by a pleasurable slowing down of narrative, the attention diverted to physical detail. So, recalling himself as the sleepwalking child:

> . . . my left hand, and then my right hand,
> Stopped me as they were stopped
> By the breathing side of a bear . . .

There is an erotic edge to that last detail and to the savored balances of the lines preceding it. He remembers the half-moon and the cloud cover, the way the child threaded his path through the rhododendrons, as much as his escape. The boy doesn't simply waken but becomes "truly awake in the throbbing world."

That recollection has the ring of a fable, one central to Mr. Wright's poems. Both he and his characters are ghostly presences in his work; he generally sees himself alone or among figures from the past, as in fading photographs. It is their insubstantiality—and his sense of his own—that makes Mr. Wright cling so vividly to sensations, like one of those yearning characters in Dante doomed only to remember the physical world:

> We stare at the backs of our own heads continually
> Walking in cadence into the past,
> Great-grandfathers before their suicides,
>                                     Venice in sunshine, Venice in rain,
> Someone standing in front of the sea
>                             watching the waves come in . . .

Those lines come from "Looking at Pictures," a poem that finds him trying "to enter the tired bodies assembled" in postcards and photos of prized works of art displayed on a bulletin board, with dazed admiration for their miniature preservations of the world. We can begin to understand why some of Mr. Wright's best poems are tributes to writers and painters—the earlier "Homage to Paul Cézanne," his finest work, about the impasto of death in representations of the living, and, from the present collection, the visionary poem "To Giacomo Leopardi in the Sky."

*The Other Side of the River* is not as consistently good as its immediate predecessor, *The Southern Cross*, but in such poems as "Italian Days," "Arkansas Traveller" and "To Giacomo Leopardi in the Sky," it can still represent Mr. Wright at his impressive best. In both collections he has replaced the haiku-like stanzas he once used with a long, loping line that, in split-level fashion, sometimes divides typographically into two and has the effect of a meditative intake of breath. His poems now have a retrospective authority, as if he were judging his visionary gift as well as expressing it. He is one of our best middle-generation poets, writing at the peak of his form.

MARK JARMAN

# *from* "The Trace of a Story Line" (1986)

One of the most intriguing parables of the Synoptic Gospels is the parable of the sower; Mark 4:3-9 might be said to be the simplest and most direct version of this story.

> Listen! A sower went out to sow and as he sowed, some seed fell along the path, and the birds came and devoured it. Other seed fell on rocky ground where it had not much soil, and immediately it sprang up, since it had no depth of soil; and when the sun rose it was scorched, and since it had no root it withered away. Other seed fell among thorns and the thorns grew up and choked it, and it yielded no grain. And other seeds fell into good soil and brought forth grain, growing up and increasing and yielding thirtyfold and sixtyfold and a hundredfold.

Completing his parable Jesus admonishes his listeners, "He who has ears to hear, let him hear." Pressed to explain the parable, he makes it clear that what the sower sows is the word, God's Word. His listeners are likened to kinds of soil. According to *The Interpreter's Bible*, the parable is, like all of Jesus's parables, "an earthly story with a heavenly meaning." But it is also another kind of story, one that exists apart from the meaning that Jesus gave it. It is an everyday fact, or was an everyday fact in a world where seeds were sown before the ground was plowed. In this regard it is straight out of the Palestine Farmer's Almanac. Another interesting exegesis in *The Interpreter's Bible*, however, is that Jesus is speaking autobiographically. The sower's experience has also been his experience as a preacher.

What I want to examine in Charles Wright's and Philip Levine's latest books of poetry is how the story to which a meaning might be attached is presented as meaningful in itself, how the earthly story has been created without a heavenly meaning, although there is often in both poets a yearning for some meaning other than the natural fact of experience. In Philip Levine and particularly in his twelfth volume of poetry we have a poet whose natural impulse is toward the significant anecdote, even the extended narrative. Charles Wright in his sixth book is a poet fully aware of what he has often suppressed in previous work—the narrative line— and is now going so far as to call one poem "Two Stories." One important similarity between these two poets is a belief in the redemptive power of nature. For Levine it is that world poised in Romantic opposition to the city where so much of his poetry is also set. For Wright, nature is all that is not human, the country that is better than the people, to paraphrase the quote from Hemingway that serves as epigraph to

Wright's *Country Music: Selected Early Poems.* Often in the past Wright's poems have hurried away from the human milieu, but in *The Other Side of the River* they are at times crowded with people. Levine's poems have always been full of names, some attached to people and some anonymous in their chaste separation from an imaginable body, and *Sweet Will* is no exception. In both books, when name and place come together, story occurs. Why this happens is one question I would like to answer. The other is what is the nature of meaning when the metaphorical form of a story is negated? Levine and Wright are also poets who return again and again to the denial, to insistence on the absence of anyone who might understand or care or remember, even to the insistence that they themselves do not always comprehend what they have written, either now or any longer. They invoke nothingness and its synonyms so often in their poetry that absence takes on an actual presence, like the holy spirit in a tongue of flame. To help me answer this question I will draw on the critic Harriet Davidson's essay "Eliot, Narrative, and the Time of the World," which was published in the Autumn 1985 issue of *The New England Review and Bread Loaf Quarterly.* In that essay she argues that narrative is actually a metonymic structure that expresses the finitude of human life and therefore makes possible a multitude of meanings and at the same time only one.

*The Other Side of the River* is divided into four parts. The first part is set primarily in the South with references to Italy, Montana, and Southern California, Wright's home when he was writing these poems. The poems are made up of blocks of long lines, including the staggered line that Wright perfected in the long title poem of *The Southern Cross.* In fact, "Lost Bodies," the first poem of the new book, begins with the image of a Southern cross, a concrete one outside his childhood home of Kingsport, Tennessee, carved with the words "GET RIGHT WITH GOD / JESUS IS COMING SOON." Time and place thus established, Wright relates the first of this volume's many stories.

> The cross was opposite Fleenor's Cabins below the hill
> On US 11W.
> Harold Shipley told me, when I was 12,
>            he'd seen a woman undressed
>
> In the back seat of a Buick, between two men,
>            her cunt shaved clean,
> In front of the motel office.
> They gave him a dollar, he said, to stick his finger up there.

Nothing else in this book is as blunt and brutal, though much is as mysterious. Furthermore, it is only this story that Wright himself admits makes any response, any attempt to make meaning, nearly impossible.

What can you say to that?
>                    everything Jesus promised,

(My five senses waiting apart in their grey hoods,
Touching their beads,
>                    licking the ashes that stained their lips)
And someone to tell it to.

Part of this message, as you can see, is an image of the poet's demurral and of his renunciation and petition. Still, the story has been told, and the reader is that someone he has found to tell it to.

"What do you say to that?" is the response elicited by many of the short but fully rounded tales Wright embeds in these poems. In his essay on Wright's recent poetry, Wyatt Prunty suggests that Wright in practicing the tall tale of the Southern variety has returned to his origins. That seems an accurate interpretation of Wright's temperament. The fixed location from which the mental traveler, or as Wright calls him "the Pilgrim," actually sets out in these poems is Southern California. He travels to the South, which is the past of childhood and adolescence; to Italy, which is the past of young adulthood; and to Montana, a parallel place, a wilderness retreat, in the present. In all of these travels the personal account cast as a story occurs, but not always as the tall tale that one boy might tell another to stand his hair on end.

At the heart of the second poem in the volume, "Lost Souls," is a theme Wright has treated elsewhere, the deaths of his mother and father.

The last time I saw George Vaughan,
He was standing in front of my father's casket at the laying out,
One of the kindest men I've ever known.

When I was 16, he taught me the way to use a jackhammer,
>                    putting the hand grip
Into my stomach and clinching down,
Riding it out till the jarring became a straight line.

He taught me the way a shovel breathes,
And how the red clay gives away nothing.
He took my hand when my hand needed taking.

And I didn't even remember his name.

What do you say to that? The small failure of tact this records is magnified by the occasion and by the double death in forgetting the name of a father figure at the father's funeral. To consider this story in this way may help explain its emotional impact, but there is also an irrefutable factualness to it that is repeated at the end of the poem.

A little curtain of flesh, Blake said,
For his own reasons . . .
And I had mine to draw it last night on the Wasatch Range
And pull it back as the sun rose
                                over the north fork
And blue weave of the Cumberlands.
It was June again, and 1964 again,
                                and I still wasn't there
As they laid her down and my father turned away,
I still imagine, precisely, into the cave of cold air
He lived in for eight more years, the cars
Below my window in Rome honking maniacally
                                *O still small voice of calm . . .*

Whatever reasons he has to imagine himself drawing the night over the vast geographical middle of the American continent, still Wright has admitted us to their origin through the deft relation of a time, a place, and an event whose disunity he will never be able to bring together and atone for.

The book's third poem is a tour de force called "Lonesome Pine Special" in which Wright surveys the nation's landscape by means of a Whitmanesque cataloguing of roads and highways: US 25E, US 23, Idaho 75, US 52, County 508, US 176, US 2, US 23, Montana 508, and one called Solo Joe after a legendary Montana prospector. Among the lives and landscapes he imagines and describes this story occurs in the eighth section of the poem.

Once, in 1955 on an icy road in Sam's Gap, North Carolina,
Going north into Tennessee on US 23,
I spun out on a slick patch
And the car turned once-and-a-half around,
Stopping at last with one front wheel on a rock
                                and the other on air,
Hundreds of feet of air down the mountainside
I backed away from, mortal again
After having left myself
                                and returned, having watched myself
Wrench the wheel toward the spin, as I'm doing now,
Stop and shift to reverse, as I'm doing now,
                                and back out on the road
As I entered my arms and fingers again
Calmly, as though I had never left them,
Shift to low, and never question the grace
That had put me there and alive, as I'm doing now . . .

There are two other stories Wright tells in which grace, questionable or unquestionable, appears to be involved. One of them is in the next poem, "Two Stories," and tells of how as a boy sleepwalking one night on a camp-out he was impeded from falling off a cliff when the live body of a bear stopped him, woke him, and he was able to make his way safely back to camp. The other story comes in part II of *The Other Side of the River,* in the poem "Italian Days," and recounts a near accident in a helicopter whose engine cuts out "Thousands of feet above the Brenner highway" and Wright, then in U.S. Army Intelligence, nearly became "a squib / in the *Stars and Stripes.*"

Wright himself would be the first to say that these are the events of anyone's life, that any one of us could relate similar anecdotes of times when, but for the grace of God, our lives would have ended before we had fully lived them and perhaps understood them. The sleepwalker in "Two Stories" claims that after he made it back to his tent and to sleep he "never told anyone / Till years later when I thought I knew what it meant, / which now I've forgot." Lest we too easily link this story, as I have done, with the other testimonies of grace, it is necessary to examine the second of "Two Stories." Admitting that this story is questionable, Wright tells of a friend "Who'd killed a six-foot diamondback about seven o'clock in the morning" and chopped its head off. That evening when he reaches in a sack to show a friend the dead snake the headless stump strikes his wrist hard enough to bruise it "for a week." What do you say to that? Here is what Wright says.

> It's not age,
> > nor time with its gold eyelid and blink,
> Nor dissolution in all its mimicry
> That lifts us and sorts us out.
> It's discontinuity
> > and all its spangled coming between
> That sends us apart and keeps us there in a dread.
> It's what's in the rear-view mirror,
> > > smaller and out of sight.

Without a head the serpent cannot bite its tail and roll into proverb or into a Yeatsian cosmology where "all the barrel-hoops are knit." Discontinuity is a serious and elusive thing to demonstrate through the necessary continuity of narrative. But it is the inexplicable, the other side of the river, that Wright always aims to present us in his poetry. That thing we call grace is, finally, an utter mystery.

> I'm 15 again, and back on Mt. Anne in North Carolina
> Repairing the fire tower,
> Nobody else around but the horse I packed in with,
> > > and five days to finish the job.
> Those nights were the longest nights I ever remember,
> The lake and pavilion 3,000 feet below
> > > as though modeled in tinfoil,
> And even more distant than that,
> The last fire out, the after-reflection of Lake Llewellyn
> Aluminum glare in the sponged dark,

Lightning bugs everywhere,
                    the plump stars
Dangling and falling near on their black strings.

These nights are like that,
The silvery alphabet of the sea
                         increasingly difficult to transcribe,
And larger each year, everything farther away, and less clear,
Than I want it to be,
                    not enough time to do the job,
And faint thunks in the earth,
As though somewhere nearby a horse was nervously pawing the ground.
                                    ("The Other Side of the River")

Although he has said with a tongue-in-cheek humor he rarely shows, "There is so little to say, and so much time to say it in," here Wright brings the urgency of that fifteen-year-old working high and alone into the present. There is not enough time to do the job. Again and again throughout *The Other Side of the River*, the story is used to underscore this fact, the fact of finitude, either of the past, which memory represents poorly, or of the future, which will terminate for sure. The time that deludes us by seeming so vast is the present, and the little we have to say also faces us with our limitation, the small space of our lives, the shrinkage of our urgent stories.

Wright's negations, as I have said, proliferate in his poetry as much as Levine's do. Because the fundamental form of his poems is not narrative—so much so that when he employs narrative one detects a significant difference in the matter of his poetry—there is also a more emphatic sense to Wright's treatment of nothingness; it truly is imperiling and against it there may be little that can be done.

To return to the poem "Two Stories" I want to look again at Wright's own response to his tall tale about sleepwalking. He had never told anyone about it "Till years later when I thought I knew what it meant, / which now I've forgot." What is missing? Apparently there was a time and a place and presumably at least one other person listening when Wright related this story and its meaning. So he says. But now he tells it and claims he has forgotten that meaning. Imagine Jesus turning on the disciples and saying to them, "Figure it out for yourself" or "I can't remember why I told that one." But my facetiousness is merely to suggest that a readily applicable meaning is not what Wright seeks. He wishes to express whatever it is that negates meaning. In this case, it is forgetfulness. Wright embodies his negations in other ways, too—along with forgetfulness there are darkness, emptiness and nothingness. Where Levine negates in order to strip the story of sentimentality and to isolate it in its pure factualness, Wright does so usually to understand negation itself. Again, in "Two Stories" he disqualifies age, time, and dissolution until he hits on what he believes is the nature of negation: "It's discontinuity."

Wright's use of narration enables him to characterize experience in the past, the present, and the future always in relation to what is missed. Thus in "Italian Days" where he remembers his youth in the Southern European Task Force,

> On alternate Sundays we'd drive to Soave and Asolo,
> Padova and the Euganean Hills,
> Always looking for the event,
>                    not knowing that we were it.

This not knowing, of course, is the anxiety and glory of youth, for, Wright goes on,

> At the end of the last word,
> When night comes walking across the lake on its hands,
> And nothing appears in the mirror,
>                    or has turned to water
> Where nothing walks or lies down,
> What will your question be,
> Whistling the dogs of mold in, giving them meat?
> And what will it profit you?
>
> No thought of that back then . . .

No, of course not, for had there been, there would have been no youth, none of the experience that rises again and again from the darkness of memory.

One reason Wright gives us for ransacking his past, much as Augustine did his memory to find where God's grace had entered it, comes at the end of the first poem of part IV, "Arkansas Traveller" (readers of Wright should hear the echo of "Delta Traveller" in *Bloodlines*). He recalls his great-grandfather's emigration from Austria, his service in the Confederate army, then settling in Little Rock where Wright himself would spend his childhood summers with his grandparents. The poem concludes,

> Knot by knot I untie myself from the past
> And let it rise away from me like a balloon.
> What a small thing it becomes.
> What a bright tweak at the vanishing point, blue on blue.

I will risk claiming there is a pun in "Knot by knot" on "not by not." Thus Wright's use of memory is to purge himself of memory, to release himself from the past, to negate it. But that is a task, thankfully, he will never finish.

The book's last poem could be read as a satire of people without a history. Called "California Dreaming" it echoes the sentiments of more than one popular song.

> We are not born yet, and everything's crystal under our feet.
> We are not brethren, we are not underlings.
> We are another nation,
> > living by voices that you will never hear,
> Caught in the net of splendor
> > of time-to-come on the earth.
> We shine in our distant chambers, we are golden.

These figures may be "apotheosizic" but they are also part of what makes Wright ask himself "what in the hell I'm doing out here." Whatever Wright has to do is not yet done, not accomplished by *The Other Side of the River*, and this sense of the incomplete, the unfinished, is what is represented by the Aristotelian middle of all stories. The book's penultimate poem, "Looking at Pictures" describes Wright in his study looking at "photographs / And reproductions of all I've thought most beautiful . . ."

> . . . Rothko has a black-on-red
> Painting . . . I'd sink through flat on my back
> Endlessly down into nothingness . . .
>
> But not now. Not now when the hound of the Pope's men
> Is leaping, not now
> > when the banner of St. George
> Dragontails out of the sky. Not now
> When our fathers stand in their riding boots, arms crossed,
> Trying to tell us something we can't quite hear,
> > our ears jugged like Kafka's.
> The devil eats us, I know, but our arms don't touch his neck.

The tension in the poetry of Charles Wright is just this recognition of what he calls the "emptiness" that is "the beginning of all things" and its opposite, another negation, that seduces us without our will or compliance, to which our response throughout our lives is "Not now." This tension is also the factor that raises Wright's poetry, in my estimation, to greatness.

MARK JARMAN

# *from* "The Pragmatic Imagination and the Secret of Poetry" (1988)

> As if nothingness contained a métier . . .
> —Wallace Stevens

K ant believed that though a metaphysics of the immanent or empirical world was possible a transcendent metaphysics was not. Charles Wright subscribes to this belief but writes about the empirical world, the immanent, as if a transcendent metaphysics *were* possible. It is because of the tension between possibility and impossibility that he is able to make the statements he makes. The title of his new book, *Zone Journals*, plays on this tension. The "zone" is unidentified, although image after image, poem after poem locates it in this world. The "journal" is the form that these poems take, a form implicit as well in his two preceding collections, *The Other Side of the River* and *The Southern Cross*; it is the way in which this poet, with his profound distrust of narrative, still follows the ancient chronological pattern. Although time is fixed and place shifts, only in this zone can time be marked, in a journal, as passing.

*Zone Journals* includes ten poems divided unequally into three parts. The sixth poem, "Journal of the Year of the Ox," which comprises all of part two, is forty-eight pages long and its movement, like the movement of the entire book, is toward a greater understanding and the challenges this will require. The challenge to Wright is that his is a metaphysics of absence—what is most important to him is what is *not* in the picture. His journal entries appear preceded by a dash and many of his lines move in a staggered two-step across the page: a portion of a line, then a descent to the rest of the line, allowing a fullness to enter without running up against the margin (as C. K. Williams's lines do, spilling over time and again, a mark of his style as much as Wright's is of his):

> —Exclusion's the secret: what's missing is what appears
> Most visible to the eye:
>                                        the more luminous anything is,
> The more it subtracts what's around it,
> Peeling away the burned skin of the world
>                                        making the unseen seen . . .

Thus in the first poem, "Yard Journal," he shows us his method for the entire book: to make the metaphysical statement, "what's missing is what appears / Most visible to the eye," and by elaboration of imagery, coming before and after, offer the world as proof:

> That rhododendron and dogwood tree, that spruce,
> An architecture of absence,
>                         a landscape whose words
> Are imprints, dissolving images after the eyelids close:
> I take them away to keep them there—
>                         the hedgehorn, for instance, that stalk . . .

What Wright acknowledges is the idealism of most metaphysics that have come before, and against this he opposes his own vision, with a wistfulness at times that is part of the paradoxical nature of so many of his statements. "A Journal of English Days," set in London, fall 1983, shows Wright confronting the spiritual tradition from which his poetry derives:

> How sweet to think that Nature is solvency,
>                         that something empirically true
> Lies just under the dead leaves
> That will make us anchorites in the dark
> Chambers of some celestial perpetuity—
>                         nice to think that,
> Given the bleak alternative,
> Though it hasn't proved so before,
>                         and won't now
> No matter what things we scrape aside—
>                         God is an abstract noun.

The final metaphor, "God is an abstract noun," expresses Charles Wright's metaphysical view, par excellence. It also expresses the pragmatic view, wherein "God" works only as a word—a powerful word, but existing apart from any concrete manifestation. Dante would not have agreed, we know that; nor would have Milton. It is important to understand that a metaphysics is possible without a transcendent or religious view of reality. The paradox of Charles Wright is that his is a religious poetry without a religion, but not without a metaphysics.

As Wright's metaphysics is based on absence, so it must acknowledge the limitation of presence or immanence. As he says at the end of "March Journal," "—Form is finite, an undestroyable hush over all things." The conclusion of the following poem, "A Journal of True Confessions," arrives at much the same point by describing "The last warm wind of summer" shining "in the dogwood trees" and "flamingoing berries and cupped leaves" as a "Veneer, like a hard wax, of nothing on everything." Even words are included in his austere metaphysics, for they are part of the things of the world in which that metaphysics does its work. In "Night Journal" (like the seventeenth-century metaphysical poets, Wright is fond of oxymoron, contradiction, paradox) he says, "—Words, like all things, are caught in their finitude."

In the central poem, "Journal of the Year of the Ox" Wright covers the year of his fiftieth birthday, 1985, from January to December. The use of the Asian name for this year is one indication of Wright's empathy with

Eastern theories and systems. Another might be the combination of Christian and Zen views of the fundamental nature of reality that makes him speak of the immanent in terms of the transcendent. The poem begins with a trope Wright has used before, the persona of the pilgrim, a poor one this time, setting forth to remember. Wright begins, "Each year I remember less." Taking stock of memory has been Wright's theme in a number of his recent major poems—for example in "The Southern Cross," from the book of that name, and in "Lost Bodies" and "Lost Souls" from *The Other Side of the River*. It is a form of confession, of seeking absolution, but it may also be a mode of purgation, of setting oneself free or clearing the decks for action. Although "Journal of the Year of the Ox" includes memories of Wright's years in Italy (touchstone of his greatest creative and spiritual force), running through it is an account of and meditation on Long Island of the Holston River in eastern Tennessee where he grew up, "sacred refuge ground / Of the Cherokee Nation."

"Journal of the Year of the Ox" is about sacred places—those like the Island that are barely memorialized while being desecrated constantly, and others, like the homes of Emily Dickinson, Edgar Allan Poe, and Petrarch, that are kept in relatively decent repair for visitors. He also recalls the beginning of his metaphysics and how he argued, when living in Italy, with "Hobart and Schneeman," two characters who have appeared in his poems before, "that what's outside / The picture is more important than what's in." He admits "They didn't agree . . ."; it sometimes appears that Wright has devoted his poetry to showing that this assertion is true. To this poem he brings "The Cherokee's mystic Nation," "ended for all time," "*with streams of blood every way*"—a powerful and successful expression of the metaphysics of absence. In this case, a people remembered on an obscure plaque as "Wolf Clan, Blue Clan, Deer Clan, Paint Clan, Wild Potato Clan, Long Hair Clan, Bird Clan" is the paradigm of that important absence. These, the remaining clans of the Cherokee nation in eastern Tennessee, are now owners of Long Island of the Holston. Their presence, a set of words on "a rectangular block of marble," points to what's gone.

Ending on Christmas day, the poem closes almost on a note of dissatisfaction, asking, "What is a life of contemplation worth in this world?" But in the penultimate journal entry, speaking of using his son's telescope to watch Halley's comet, Wright anticipates his question with this answer:

> An ordered and measured affection is virtuous
> In its clean cause
> > however it comes close in this life.
> Nothing else moves toward us out of the stars,
> > > nothing else shines.

This is a discovery for Wright. His strength as a poet is to make his refrains sound like fresh recognitions; he is always "making it new." But this does seem to be a new thing, a faith that an abstraction—"affection"—can be mirrored in the cosmos, that it can be "empirically true." *Zone Journals* ends with four poems—"Light Journal," "Journal of One Significant Landscape," "Chinese Journal," and a second called "Night Journal"—about light, a light that demonstrates a fundamental way of being—"to shine but not to dazzle."

Wright's transformation of the natural world into imagery is a search for transcendence in the face of mere immanence. Thus his final, austere but courageous, tautological resolution: the earth is itself; it refers only to itself—although whatever is absent from it (Wright must take this on faith, like all who create a metaphysics) defines it, is better somehow, and worth our search. Wright's diminished metaphysics is as close as we can come to the integrated cosmology of Dante, resting on Aquinas's *Summa*, or to Milton, buttressed by the Reformation. "Night Journal," the book's last poem, says it again, in answer to the question "What's-Out-There":

> I'd say what it says: nothing, with all its verities
> Gone to the ground and hiding . . .

Wright's metaphysics is truly inclusive, as paradoxical as that may sound. Inclusion—the proliferation of detail and image—is what he and C. K. Williams and Philip Levine have in common. Wright's use of the pilgrim as persona is to suggest his forays into the world, in order to discover ways to say freshly what he knows:

> I long for clear water, the silence
> Of risk and deep splendor,
>                                 the quietness inside the solitude.
> I want its drop on my lip, its cold undertaking.

The words "risk" and "undertaking" work against "quietness" and "solitude," indicating Wright's activity, which is to fill the picture in to make what's left out of it manifest.

HELEN VENDLER

# Travels in Time (1988)

> Lashed to the syllable and noun,
> >                          the strict Armaggedon of the verb,
> I lolled for seventeen years
> Above this bay with its antimacassars of foam
> On the rocks, the white, triangular tears
> >                          sailboats poke through the sea's spun sheet,
> Houses like wads of paper dropped in the moss-clumps of the trees,
> Fog in its dress whites at ease along the horizon,
> Trying to get the description right.
> >                          If nothing else,
> It showed me that what you see
> >                          both is and is not there,
> The unseen bulking in from the edges of all things,
> Changing the frame with its nothingness.
>
> >                          ("A Journal of True Confessions")

R estless and observant senses provide the words for the unseen in Charles Wright, as they did for the religious poets Henry Vaughan and Thomas Traherne, both (given that their subject was the unseen) unnervingly visual writers. All ways of formulating the paradox of the unseen felt in the seen falsify the experience of that paradox, in which the reports of the senses are accompanied by some aura (not felt by most of us, perhaps) of what is not there but makes its presence felt—eternity, death, transcendence, extension, rhythm: the unseen can go by many names. Visual reports in poetry rarely go unattended by such an aura; but the creation of the aura in words puts a bizarre stress on the writer. Fog along the horizon could be described by any number of analogies; here, the aura lies in the complex personification, "Fog in its dress whites at ease," but the relaxed formality of that comparison does not exhaust the aura, since the disturbing note of a sheet of water "torn" by sails participates in it, as does the reassuring and slightly absurd metaphor of foam antimacassars on the rocks, and the disorderliness of the littering houses. If the aura of this landscape is the aura of a long habitation ("seventeen years"), then a sense of arbitrary military posting, relaxation in a parlor, seamless experience punctuated by painful rips, and a fate careless of its scatterings of habitation all combine in the "seen unseen" of the bay. Valéry draws a similar harbor with an aura of its own in "Le Cimetière Marin," but he takes care to give a logical air to his images, and would not combine antimacassars and dress whites in the same stanza. The freedom to follow the aura without respect to thematic consistency of imagery is a mark of modernist verse (Eliot's ragged claws cohabiting with bats with baby faces and so on). But this free-dom is also peculiarly and necessarily the mark of poets whose concerns turn inward to the screen of contemplation, away from the sociopolitical world and the world of narrative. For such poets neither narrative (which confers a clue through the labyrinth of consciousness) nor sociopolitical reality (which confers contemporary "urgency") is an available option. They turn inward, and skyward: "There is no sickness of spirit like home-sickness / When what you are sick for has never been seen or heard" ("A Journal of English Days").

The title of Wright's recent book, *Zone Journals*, suggests time modi-fied by space. The time is the region around his fiftieth year; the zones traversed in the volume include California, Virginia, England, and Italy. There are other notable modern journal volumes of the fiftieth year: Lowell's *Notebook*, Ammons's *Snow Poems*, Merrill's *Divine Comedies*. These books, far more quotidian (in the best sense) than Wright's bring into sharp relief the very different nature of Wright's journals—brood-ing, lyrical, painterly, contemplative. No marches on the Pentagon here, no historical emperors and tyrants, as in Lowell; none of the sanguine dailiness or scientific curiosity of Ammons; none of the domestic com-edy of Merrill (Wright mentions his wife and son only glancingly in his verse). Wright's poetry reproduces the circling and deepening concentra-tion that aims at either obliteration or transcendence, blankness or mys-ticism. But Wright stops short of either polarity because he remains bound to the materiality and the temporal rhythm of language, whereas both Eastern nothingness and Western transcendence, at their utmost point, renounce as meaningless both materiality and time.

The very nature of poetry—a temporal art forever reformulated—sug-gests that no object or scene of present contemplation can last any longer than the moment of attention (a Keatsian point dwelt on by contempo-rary poets other than Wright, such as Ashbery in "Self-Portrait"). Seeking recourse against the evanescence of contemplation, Wright turns to the abiding memory of his predecessors in contemplation, who compose an aesthetic pantheon including Li Po, Dante, Petrarch, Leonardo, and Sidney; Keats, Poe, and Dickinson; Picasso, Rothko, and Pound. The ex-emplary quality of the life of the artist, and the question of the function and survival of art, preoccupy Wright in these journals.

At some moments, nothing seems more alive to Wright (as to anyone responsive to the headiness of aesthetically formulated language) than the voice of the great formulators, no matter how long dead. Dante appears here and speaks live words to the poet (as he had appeared to Eliot in the Quartets, as Joyce appears and speaks to Heaney in *Station Island*). "The voice that cannot be stilled by death or the passage of time": this is one definition, the most assuaging one for the poet, of poetry. There are lesser definitions, though still powerful. "The presence that haunts the place it dwelt" might be the definition that for Wright fits Dickinson and Poe, whose houses in Amherst and Baltimore the poet is seen visiting, hearing no voices but finding a place where "the spirits come and my skin sings" ("Journal of the Year of the Ox," 23 May; henceforth quotations from this long poem will be identified by date alone). But presences themselves fade: Petrarch's full life ("the tapestries and winter fires, / The long walks and solitude") comes down after a half-millenium to "the one name and a rhyme scheme" (3 August). What are artists, in fact, but dust? "Fulke Greville lies in his stone boat in the church of St. Mary . . . / Hermetically sealed in stone" ("A Journal of English Days"). As if to emphasize equally both the importance of the artist's birth and his eventual remoteness in time, Wright keeps note of birthdays in his English journal:

"October 17th, Sir Philip dead / 397 years today."
"Cézanne . . . died there today / 77 years ago."
"Sunday, October 30th, Pound's birthday 98 years ago."

And he includes a "Short Riff for John Keats on his 188th Birthday." Our ahistoric "eternal voices" are thereby placed firmly in lost time, where Wright also places, as a past but unobliterable piece of American history, the defeated Cherokees of Virginia, who in 1806 ceded their sacred burial lands to the invaders. Wright knows that as the earlier inhabitants of his territory are, so will he be.

At the same time, history itself preserves not only the shame of massacres and exploitation but also the exemplary lives of saints and artists who confirm the poets' faith in the extension of imaginative possibility, not only in themselves but in us. Cézanne "made us see differently, where the hooks fit, and the eyes go," says Wright's English journal; and the "Journal of True Confessions" carries even further the example of what being imaginative means, by way of a story about Leonardo told by Vasari. Presented with an unusual lizard, Leonardo, dissatisfied even with the uncommon, proceeded to embellish it:

[He] made wings for it out of the skins
Of other lizards,
        and filled the wings with mercury
Which caused them to wave and quiver
Whenever the lizard moved.
           He made eyes, a beard and two horns
In the same way, tamed it, and kept it in a large box
To terrify his friends.
          His games were the pure games of children,
Asking for nothing but artifice, beauty and fear.

Leonardo's coalescing of the biologically real lizard ("The real is only the base. But it is the base," said Stevens), the scientifically invented mercury-wings, the anthropomorphic beard, and the mythological horns becomes a parable of aesthetic energy, delight, and imaginative intimidation.

Artifice, beauty, and fear, all in the elaborate game of metered language, are the materials of Wright's art as well. Leonardo's humor and wit (the lizard, once unmasked as artifice, must have amused) are not present in Wright, whose liturgical solemnity is corrected only by the ironies of death and futility. But at least these powerful ironies are always present: the ultimate evanescence of everything, the round of the seasons making and breaking natural forms, the inevitable self-replaceability of language.

It is in his evocations of the seasons that Wright displays both the gorgeousness of his descriptive equipment and his gift for the pathetic fallacy. At the same time, these recurrent seasonal tableaux, by their ostentatious substitutiveness, call their own reliability into question. If on one day the clouds are "cloud banks enfrescoed," on another they are "Mannerist clouds," on another "cloud-tufts that print a black alphabet / along the hillsides." An infinite number of adjectival substitutions, one feels, are possible for the clouds; and although in another poet visual accuracy would be uppermost, in Wright the symbolic arbitrariness of the mind's play is at least as visible in such passages as any putative appearance of the clouds. For all Wright's debt to Hopkins and Pound and Stevens, he is less hard-edged in description than any of them, more dreamy. His beautiful landscapes are a symbolic means, rather than a visually specific end.

The landscapes consequently abound in the pathetic fallacy, which aims in Wright not at its classical unobtrusiveness but rather at an overt and unashamed pathos:

> The rain lying like loose bandages over the ground;
>
> ("English Journal")

> The rain, in its white disguise,
> has nothing to say to the wind
> That carries it, whose shoulders
> It slips from giving no signal, aimlessly, one drop
> At a time, no word
> Or gesture to what has carried it all this way for nothing.
>
> ("Journal of the Year of the Ox")

These passages may be arbitrary when considered as visual descriptions of rain, but no longer seem purely contingent when considered emotionally as resonances of a suffusing inner life.

The realm of meditation which Wright has made his own has been often described in the vocabularies of theological, philosophical, and psychological speculation. Nonetheless, it does not feel, as we inhabit it, like a place called "mortal sin," or "proprioception," or "the superego." It feels by turns soft, or hard, or brilliant, or drifting, or pallid, or violent. In his discipleship to the Italian futurist poet Dino Campana, whose *Orphic Songs* he has translated, Wright learned a sensuous, rich, and seductive vocabulary for inner sensation. Here, for comparison, are some images from

Campana, in Wright's translation: "The moon . . . rose up in a new red dress of coppery smoke . . . in solitary and smoky vapor over the barbaric clefts and slices." "The telluric melody of the Falterona [mountain range]. Telluric waves. The last asterisk of the Falterona's song gets lost in the clouds." "A long veranda . . . has scribbled a many-colored comment with its arches." Like Wright, Campana was a pilgrim homesick for the eternal ("O pilgrim, O pilgrims who go out searching so seriously"), but his violence of color and utterance have been modulated in Wright into something which, while still sensual and ecstatic at once, is more mournful and less hallucinatory.

Journal-poems are for Wright a departure from his earlier crystalline short lyrics and exquisitely finished sequences aiming for inevitability of effect. A journal-poem allows for the chanciness of travel, and the form serves Wright especially well in the long poem "Journal of the Year of the Ox," the centerpiece of *Zone Journals*. The year 1985, covered by the journal, is crowned by some summer months spent in Italy (where Wright did his military service and studied as a Fulbright scholar). The glowing set piece in the center of the sequence describes the opulent Renaissance frescoes in the Schifanoia Palace of the dukes of Este in Ferrara. These frescoes are important to Wright because they so ideally represent the world as he conceives it—an ampler, more beautiful, and more ordered cosmos than that perceived by the senses alone (though including the testimony of the senses, and expressible only in sensuous forms).

The frescoes, covering the upper portion of the large palace hall, are divided into three levels: the highest level displays the triumphs of gods invoked as patrons of Ferrara (Ceres, Apollo, Venus, and so on); the middle level displays the signs of the zodiac and their graceful attendant wardens or "deans" (so called because each figure is responsible for ten days of the month); and the lowest level displays various civic and social activities of the duke of Este. All three levels are of a striking beauty, but in each case the beauty is of a decorum to match the subject: the gods move in a radiant anagogical atmosphere of light, glory, and throngs of divine attributes; the zodiacal signs and their deans, by contrast, exist in a fixed and allegorical emblematic simplicity of outline against a solid-colored background; while the duke acts in a busy social sphere of Italian civic and geographical detail. Here is Wright responding to the art that so perfectly complies with his sense of life, allowing as it does not only for ideational panoplies and seasonal symbols but also for the realities of courtiers, horses, peasants, and grapevines:

> Through scenes of everyday life,
> Through the dark allegory of the soul
>
>                     into the white light of eternity,
> The goddess burns in her golden car
> From month to month, season to season
>
>                 high on the walls

At the south edge of Ferrara: . . .
Reality, symbol and ideal
                    tripartite and everlasting
Under the bricked, Emilian sun.
. . . . .
Borso d'Este, Duke of Ferrara and Modena, on a spring day
On horseback off to the hunt:
                         a dog noses a duck up from a pond,
Peasants are pruning the vines back, and grafting new ones.
. . . . .
Such a narrow, meaningful strip
                       of arrows and snakes.
Circles and purple robes, griffins and questing pilgrims:
At the tip of the lion's tail, a courtier rips
A haunch of venison with his teeth;
At the lion's head,
               someone sits in a brushed, celestial tree.
. . . . .
Up there, in the third realm,
                      light as though under water
Washes and folds and breaks in small waves
Over each month like sunrise:
                     triumph after triumph
Of pure Abstraction and pure Word, a paradise of white cloth
And white reflections of cloth cross-currented over the cars
With golden wheels and gold leads,
                      all Concept and finery:
Love with her long hair and swans in trace,
Cybele among the Corybants,
Apollo, Medusa's blood and Attis in expiation:
All caught in the tide of light,
               all burned in the same air.

                                                   (25 July)

A hymn of such passion and distinction justifies both itself and the fresco it celebrates. The lavish iconography of the Renaissance, with its fertile mixture of classical, neo-Platonic, alchemical, astrological, and Christian elements, was after all a human invention:

Is this the progression of our lives
                    or merely a comment on them?

Wright's question suggests that the extent to which such a fresco represents our lives, or is an analogy to them, is an earnest of what the fully rich life of consciousness can be, how it can place the "real" (the duke's daily round) in the light of cosmic orderly change (the zodiac) and suffuse it with the light of human motives idealized (Love, Wisdom, Art, Commerce). Here, it is not a political superstructure that gives significance to personal and civic activity; it is rather the superstructure of the sensuous, the affective, and the intellectual that gives meaning to the political.

Summer in Italy releases in Wright a flood of responsive exaltation. At home, in the winter, he is more likely to feel the downward pull of mortality; this is made gentle, in the following quotation, by the song-like mode that Wright allows his meditations to assume from time to time:

> One, one and by one we all sift to a difference
> And cry out if one of our branches snaps
> > or our bark is cut.
> The winter sunlight scours us,
> The winter wind is our comfort and consolation.
> We settle into our ruin
>
> One, one and by one as we slip from clear rags into feathery skin
> Or juice-in-the-ground, pooled
> And biding its time
> > backwashed under the slick peach tree.
> One, one and by one thrust up by the creek bank,
> Huddled in spongy colonies,
> > longing to be listened to.
>
> *Here I am, here I am,* we all say,
> > *I'm back,*
> Rustle and wave, chatter and spring
> Up to the air, the sweet air.
> Hardened around the woodpecker's hole, under his down,
> We all slip into the landscape, one, one and by one.

Folk song and the blues hover here, as elsewhere, behind Wright's poetry, and distinguish him from his most potent mentor, Pound. He is the only one of the tribe of Pound not to feel Pound's aversion to syntax, and Wright's poetry, in its play of syntactic subordination and dominance, reclaims an elaborate intellectuality for the Poundian image. In spite of their intellectuality, the poems remain finally sensuous objects in a pilgrim shrine. "Our lines," says Wright in "A Journal of True Confessions," "seem such sad notes for the most part, / Pinned like reliquaries and stop-gaps / to the cloth effigy of some saint." Wright's Christian upbringing remains imaginatively present to him, secreting a nacreous nostalgia for the vocabulary that, had it only suited his century, would have best suited his sense of things. Without the ability to assert, at least in any conventional dogma, the intuitions of faith, he is left with the biological conservation of matter as the only resurrection he can count on, "juice-in-the-ground, pooled / And biding its time." In his zones of dislocation—between the Christian and the biological, between Europe and America, and between the allegorical and the visible—Wright finds a scene of writing unique to himself and to his historical moment, and phrases it over and over in his musical and grieving half-lines, themselves the very rhythm of contemplative musing.

# Zone Journals (1991)

C harles Wright is a poet of projects and paradoxes, large, ambitious, ongoing projects paradoxically enfleshed in an art that moves— "line after line after latched, untraceable line" ("A Journal of English Days")—less by will than by intuition. Like some huge Gothic stained glass window, his books coalesce into elaborately patterned fragments of perception whose splendor depends on the brilliance of the verbally projected light with which he suffuses their pages. Light, in fact, may be the single most instructive element to enter his poems, the only element that crosses with ease between this world and the next (his twinned perennial subjects), the element from which *Zone Journals* derives its abiding principle of composition: "the more luminous anything is, / The more it subtracts what's around it . . . / making the unseen seen" ("Yard Journal").

Wright seems bent on testing the verse and converse of that axiom: is it also true that the more one subtracts the more luminous the thing becomes? Somewhere within those precepts resides the imagist's and the visionary's paradigm, although (again paradoxically) Wright's shrewdly subtractive style never proves more expansive than in *Zone Journals*. In the course of its packed ninety-eight pages, stories get told; kin of the spirit and kin of the flesh appear, speak, leave their names; dates are recorded religiously ("October 17, Sir Philip [Sidney] dead / 397 years today"); and ideas spool out *almost* to the point of assertion. As he described his method in a recent interview in *The Paris Review*, the ten "journals" that make up this collection inhabit "as loose a form as I can work with and still work in lines" (making them somewhat the orchestral counterpart of *China Trace*, which, ten years earlier, in another interview, he declared "was as tight as I could get it"). "One of the purposes of the journals," he goes on to say, "was to work with a line that was pushed as hard as I could push it toward prose. . . . At the same time, of course, they *are* poems, with all a poem's avoidances and exclusions. Still the word 'journal' is operative, and allows more quotidiana in." If the word "journal" is operative because it best describes the feel of the poems, then the word "exclusion" ("Exclusion's the secret," one poem confides) is operative as the best description of how they work. With sudden cross-cuts into discourse, narrative, quick-image presentation, dreamscape, flashback, interior monologue, the journals set up relations which, mutually stirred, resolve in time, and only in time, into a sustained investigation of his favorite themes: "the difference between the spirit and flesh" ("A Journal of English Days"), "the inarticulation of desire" ("Light Journal"), "the presence / Of what is missing" ("Chinese Journal"), and, everpresently, the feel of how it feels to be "Lashed to the syllable and noun, / the strict Armageddon of the verb" ("A Journal of True Confessions").

*Zone Journals*, Wright's seventh book of poems, brings to a close the second phase of his career. His first four books, republished in 1982 as *Country Music*, mark the first phase; the next three, concluding with *Zone Journals*, mark the second, to be collected this year under the title *The World of the 10,000 Things* (with an addendum called *Xionia*, made up of 15 additional journal poems). Looking back over those books we might now acknowledge that Wright lays claim to a particular set of obsessions, that he has been writing about them from the beginning, and, I suspect, he will keep writing about them until the end. If any one thing could sum them up, this might do:

> —Ficino tells us the Absolute
> Wakens the drowsy, lights the obscure,
> 
> > revives the dead,
> Gives form to the formless and finishes the incomplete.
> What better good can be spoken of?
> 
> > (from "A Journal of the Year of the Ox")

To awaken, illuminate, revive, give form, and finally complete—it would be difficult to find other activities of equal importance in Wright's poems. It would also be difficult to find another contemporary American poet as willing to trace those energies back to the notion of an Absolute (though it's important to note that—instead of "What better good can be *done*"—Wright says "What better good can be *spoken of*," thereby suspending the question of faith). That he has managed to build a career around those calculated uncertainties—in a day and age when such things arouse more skepticism than interest—attests to the solitariness of his enterprise, to the sheer verbal power of the poems. Our era and Wright's cosmology would stifle a less determined poet, but even when reality proves most unyielding, most resistant to his vexed metaphysical probings—as in the following section from the masterful long poem, "A Journal of the Year of the Ox"—resistance itself is anatomized and drawn up into the soulful meanderings of Wright's desperately articulate inner life:

> These monochromatic early days of October
> Throb like a headache just back of the eyes,
> 
> > a music
> Of dull, identical syllables
> Almost all vowels,
> 
> > ooohing and aaahing
> As though they would break out in speech and tell us something.
> 
> But nothing's to be revealed,
> It seems:

> each day the shadows blur and enlarge, the rain comes
> and comes back,
> A dripping of consonants,
> As though it too wanted to tell us something, something
> Unlike the shadows and their stray signs,
>
> Unlike the syllable the days make
> Behind the eyes, cross-current and cross-grained, and unlike
> The sibilance of oak tree and ash.

Given the somewhat anachronistic nature of Wright's concerns—not to mention his lavish iconographic imagination, the architectural planning that goes into his work, and, more particularly, his residual faith in the efficacy of certain personal, recurrent signs—he reminds me of the one modernist poet with whom, so far as I know, he has never been linked, W. B. Yeats. Certainly Wright has more in common with the modernists than with any generation to follow. Much has already been said about Pound's influence—so much so that the label seems to have stuck long past the point Wright outgrew it—and something still remains to be said about Eliot's; i.e., Wright's particular brand of classicism, with its carefully mediated forays on the tradition, derives more from Eliot's connoisseurism than from Pound's vortex. But with Eliot and Pound, each new phase in their work brought an almost violent act of self-revision; with Yeats one has the impression of an evolving core of ideas and personality around which the poem tirelessly struggles to adapt itself. Like Yeats more than the other two, Wright labors to construct a kind of gestalt, a literary equivalent for the total, ongoing life of a man. And though little of Yeats's music finds its way into Wright's line, many of his predilections do. The following, for example, from Yeats's *Ideas of Good and Evil,* not only applies to Wright's kaleidoscopic style, but anticipates one of the central metaphysical issues that haunts *Zone Journals,* the summoning of presences from the "other world":

> All sounds, all colours, all forms . . . call down among us certain disembodied powers, whose footsteps over our hearts we call emotions; . . . and the more perfect [the work of art] is, and the more various and numerous the elements that have flowed into its perfection, the more powerful will be the emotion, the power, the god it calls among us.

The "disembodied powers" Wright calls down among us—powers no less various than St. Catherine, Jefferson, Li Po, Dante, the Cherokee Nation, Buddha, Dickinson, Leonardo, Poe, just to name a few—those powers become, as he says in "A Journal of the Year of the Ox'" his "constituency":

> those who would die back
> To splendor and rise again
> From hurt and unwillingness,
> their own ash on their tongues,

> Are those I would be among,
> The called, the bruised by God, by their old ways forsaken
> And startled on . . .

And their footsteps over these pages account in large part for the slowly developing object of Wright's lifelong quest: this is not spiritual archaeology so much as portraiture by collage, and the portrait, we see, is of the light-filled face of God.

That this stage in Wright's "project" has drawn to a close may permit some speculative comments. Perhaps because of the perilous terrain these poems cross—Banquo's ghost would feel right at home—one grows all that more aware of the conscious elegance of their lines, their keen refinements, their kind of *sangfroid* that, unfaltering, says: This poet never loses his cool. And yet, when one turns back to those many saints, visionary poets, mad seers and mystics who people Wright's poems, one can't help recall that their ventures into "the other world" cost nothing less than apostasy and terror. It wasn't just symmetry, but a fearful symmetry that Blake discovered, a blood-dimmed tide that Yeats foresaw. That Wright has achieved such a profound level of virtuosity is as ominous as it is admirable, for perhaps virtuosity now becomes the obstacle he must overcome. In a bittersweet section from "A Journal of the Year of the Ox," the poet is relaxing outside his home, "The quattrocento landscape / turning to air beneath [his] feet," children in the distance playing "a game [he'd] never played," his son and friend moving "through the upper yard like candles / Among the fruit trees." In the sustained evanescence of that wistful hour the poet begins to sense "That anything I could feel, / anything I could put my hand on"

> Would burst into brilliance at my touch.
> But I sat still, and I touched nothing,
> > afraid that something might change
> And change me beyond knowing,
> That everything I had hoped for, all I had ever wanted,
> Might actually happen.
> > So I sat still and touched nothing.

Who is to say, but perhaps in the next phase of Wright's career he must risk that touch, that change beyond knowing, must risk becoming one of his own constituency, "by their old ways forsaken / And startled on." And so—in the spirit of someone slipping a defunct St. Christopher into the hand of a friend setting off on a trip—I'll close with Wright's own premonitory comments from the previously mentioned interview:

> The problem with all of us as we get older is that we begin writing as though we were somebody. One should always write as if one were nobody. . . . We should always write out of our ignorance and desire and ambition, never out of some sense of false well-being, some tinge of success. There is no success in poetry, there is only the next inch, the next hand-hold out of the pit.

# *from* "An Elegist's New England, a Buddhist's Dante" (1991)

The subtle cadences of his verse, his famously "good ear," have won Charles Wright a select place among contemporary poets. *The World of the Ten Thousand Things* gathers work from *The Southern Cross* (1981) to *Xionia* (1990). Since the early 80s, Mr. Wright has increasingly abandoned short lyrics for journal poems that weave diverse thematic threads into a single autobiographical fabric—more than 200 pages, written over a ten-year period, that can be read as a single poetic sequence worthy of comparison with such extended works as *The Bridge* by Hart Crane, *The Far Field* by Theodore Roethke, and *Dream Songs* by John Berryman. Freed from the stringencies of unity and closure demanded by the sort of poem most readers are used to, Mr. Wright is at liberty to spin out extended meditations that pick up, work with, lay aside, and return again to landscapes, historical events, and ideas.

The culture of Italy, where Mr. Wright was stationed in the Army and where he has returned over the years, runs like a bright thread through his meditations. Like Ezra Pound, he aspires toward Dante as a poetic master. The spirit of the Tuscan poet, in a form reminiscent of Giotto's painting of him—"Laurel corona encircling his red transparent headcap," his "voice like a slow rip through silk cloth / In disapproval"—makes an appearance in "A Journal of the Year of the Ox," the 40-page centerpiece of *Zone Journals* (1988).

One is occasionally reminded of Pound's *Cantos* in these pages. Mr. Wright meanders through cultures—Chinese (as the book's title suggests), Italian, American (the poet explores his Virginia roots and describes the betrayal and destruction of the Cherokee nation in east Tennessee, his native state). But Mr. Wright's intelligence is supple, humane, and inclusive; not for him Pound's crackpot economic and racial theories, his narrowness and crankiness.

*The World of the Ten Thousand Things* records with journal-like intimacy a spiritual quest—an investigation of the relation between the visible and the invisible worlds. Viewing "the fire-knots of late roses / Still pumping their petals of flame / up from the English loam," Mr. Wright exclaims: "And I suddenly recognize / The difference between the spirit and flesh / is finite, and slowly transgressable." These meditations often cross the border separating the living from the dead (family members as well as poetic precursors, including Poe and Petrarch in addition to Dante and Pound). The dead appear with great immediacy. Perhaps paradoxically, however, Mr. Wright takes a philosophical position closely akin to

Buddhism—ontological emptiness is the dimension in which all else is grounded: "this is the dirt their lives were made of, the dirt the world is, / Immeasurable emptiness of all things."

But this is, as it were, a positive emptiness, not an excuse for despair or a refusal to engage the world. The poetry grounds itself firmly in actuality, the "ten thousand things" that constitute the world in its totality—what we cannot see in addition to what we can see:

> I stand on the porch of Wickliffe Church,
> My kinfolk out back in the bee-stitched vines and weeds,
> The night coming on, my flat shirt drawing the light in,
> Bright bud on the branch of nothing's tree.

The dialectic between a philosophy that negates phenomena and a sensory keenness for what Richard Wilbur has called "the world's hunks and colors" energizes Charles Wright's poetry, which is often presented as a dialogue between the poet and ideas taken from his reading: "*Objects do not exist, / by convention sweet, by convention bitter. /* Still, you could have fooled me." This down-to-earth voice makes itself heard from time to time in these meditations, and that's a good thing, because Mr. Wright's bad angel tempts him at times toward abstraction—"Form tends toward its own dissolution"—and sometimes toward a level of rhetoric that does not convince: "Inside the self is another self like a black hole / Constantly dying."

Yet Mr. Wright's gifts for verbal music, his ability to evoke sensory experience and a boldness of metaphorical reference get the juices flowing whenever the language starts to seem a bit desiccated:

> salmon-smoke in the west
> Back-vaulting the bats
> who plunged and swooped like wrong angels
> Hooking their slipped souls in the twilight.

This poet is able to soar with Dante:

> —A bumblebee the size of my thumb
> rises like Geryon
> From the hard Dantescan gloom . . .
> Shoulders I've wanted to sit on, a ride I've wanted to take.

And he can still remain down-home enough to greet the denizens of the Inferno in high-five American style—"Bico, my man, are you here?" He continues to reveal himself as a poet of great purity and originality.

DAVID YOUNG

# The Blood Bees of Paradise (1991)

C harles Wright's new book [*The World of the Ten Thousand Things*] brings together three previous collections and a group of new poems. It covers a ten year span, from 1980 to 1990. Here's how it opens:

> At night, in the fish-light of the moon, the dead wear our white shirts
> To stay warm, and litter the fields.
> We pick them up in the mornings, dewy pieces of paper and scraps of
>   cloth.
> Like us, they refract themselves. Like us,
> They keep on saying the same thing, trying to get it right.
> Like us, the water unsettles their names.
>
> ("Homage to Paul Cézanne")

We're in the presence of jumpy, highly original poetic language. A line may have three internal rhymes. Its length may vary from eight syllables to nineteen. The verbal music is intense: consonants crackling, vowels echoing, rhythms reaching toward the incantatory. But what strikes us most, disorienting us a little, is what we call the content. Here is a series of six or seven assertions, none of which could be thought of as literally true. We aren't dealing, as in some poets, with a literal level of narrative and reportage that then mixes in figurative language to move the level of discourse toward the poetic; instead, as in much of Wallace Stevens, we're confronted with the figurative, the indirect and playful, immediately. The moon's light is a fish-light, the dead wear our shirts, they litter our fields, and we pick up scraps of cloth and pieces of paper that are evidence of their activity, their trying to stay warm. The dew on the scraps gives a "realistic" base to the passage from night to day, but everything else feels metaphoric, metamorphic, hallucinatory, surreal.

This opening set of assertions has to be translated into some kind of account of how we imagine, respond to and care about the dead, why we traditionally dress them in white (the stereotypic sheets here become, surprisingly, shirts), how it might be said that they wear our clothes or litter our fields. The imagination is dilated, the terms on which language communicates are redefined, and we are in a disturbing, exhilarating world. With the figurative base established, we can entertain abstractions. The claim of likeness, familiar signal for the figurative, here moves not toward the image but toward conceptual statements: like us, the dead refract themselves; like us, they keep on saying the same thing. And these assertions of likeness tease us because they ascribe likeness to a community that includes the speaker and the reader, those who are alive. They begin to erase the barrier between living and dead. A more normal mode of discourse would have posited the dead as objects, imagined by us as subjects. Wright's move is to start with the dead as subjects who are different from ourselves and then gradually subtract the differences. Language itself becomes key when both groups are seen as using it repetitively in the interest of precision, "trying to get it right," an attempt that seems never to succeed.

The assertion that closes the stanza returns to the figurative for the third "Like us," and we imagine, variously, gravestones eroded by rain (especially Keats's, with its famous epitaph, "Here lies one whose name was writ on water"), identities dissolved or carried away in floods, selves recognizing their instability by acknowledging kinship with an unstable element. Is this the same water that made the moonlight seem fishy, that dewed the scraps of cloth and paper? We're less apt to try to get literal sense from gnomic statements; we take them as atmospheric, part of the larger pattern of deliberate "misuse" of language to drive toward a visionary sense of being. If we tried to reduce the eight sixteen-line sections of "Homage to Paul Cézanne" to propositional status, that activity might clarify the poem's structure somewhat—the dead are all around us, the dead are more and more with us as we get older, the dead have a rhythm that allies them to the sea, the dead are like the blue a painter like Cézanne puts everywhere in his paintings, etc.—but it would not begin to approximate the poem. The propositions, if we can call them that, are merely there as triggers, opening moves, ways of tuning up the music and the gorgeous, painterly succession of meditative stanzas. Often, they open the sections, as if to get the necessary relation to ordinary language use out of the way so that the enterprise of turning language into music, incantation, re-presentation, color and shape and texture for their own sakes, can get quickly underway. The poem teaches us how to read it (or not read it, if by "read" we mean normal interpretive reading, translating the knowledge and information out for separate use) as we go, and learning how to take in the poem is the first step in learning how to take in the book, this book of ten thousand things.

Those are some observations on the first six lines of a page that has ten more such lines and a book that has 230 such pages. It seems safe to admit that Charles Wright is going to acquire his readers gradually. The intense pleasures and exploding insights that proceed from such concentrated and original poetry can come only from a willingness to submit, to put aside preconceptions about language and experience, from an enjoyment of play and risk and wild invention. Safer to read a poet who is more predictable (as William Logan, reviewing *Zone Journals*, tried to exorcise Wright's originality by invoking what he felt to be the excessive influence of Pound and then betrayed his own limitations by expressing preference for a much less interesting poet because he admired her "hexameters") or better still, a novel, or a mystery story, or, even safer, a television program. Who can blame us for our cowardly ways? We live in an information explosion, a bewildering world, and we would like to think that language is a stable element in that world, not a medium that unsettles our names like water and reflects our obsessions, secret and open, with mortality.

For readers who wish to forge an acquaintance with this book, let me set forth some guidelines and suggestions based on my own acquaintance, as an editor and a friend and an avid reader, with the poems to be found in it. I have already argued that one must put aside preconceptions about language to engage Wright's work successfully. I have touched on some of the symmetries and harmonies to be found in the structure of poems like "Homage to Paul Cézanne." Let me turn next to the question of the self, and especially to our modern and postmodern understanding of the self, for I believe that Wright's explorations of the problems and mysteries of identity and selfhood are central to everything he does. He might well subscribe to Wittgenstein's notion that "The subject does not belong to the world but it is a limit of the world" (*Tractatus*, 5.632), for he is fascinated with the way we can and cannot connect ourselves to the world of appearances and the fortunes of language, elements that sustain us even as they can be said to seduce, subvert, and betray us.

One way to get at this dwelling on the self is to attempt a description of Wright's poetic persona. No doubt this persona is a selective version of the poet himself, but its deliberately designed personality and scrupulously managed obsessions are what we must concern ourselves with here. Wright's persona provides a consistent element in the enormous variety of forms, observations, memories, stories, assertions, and divagations that fill this volume.

This persona is deeply and helplessly in love with the world of appearances, all the weather and seasons, the trees, leaves, flowers, animals, birds, cloudforms, skyscapes, the comings and goings of light, the textures and forms and colors and sounds that fill our senses if we let them. He has certain favorite things—Italy's culture and landscape, the seasons of spring and fall, fruit trees, light on water—but you can put him anywhere and he will find himself constructing a lovesong to the natural world:

<blockquote>

—Up from the basement flat at 43A,
                        up past the Greek college,
Across Walton to Ovington Gardens
Then over to Brompton Road
And across,
         left to the Oratory and right
Up under the chestnut trees to Ennismore Mews,
Up past the gardens and Prince's Gate
Across the main road and Rotten Row,
                  bicycle track
And long grass down to the Serpentine,
Ducks on the water, geese on the water, the paired swans
</blockquote>

Imperious and the gulls
          neat on the slick edges,
Then backtrack and a right turn
To the west, across the road and into Kensington Gardens
And out to the chestnut and beech grove
As the dogs go by
          and the Punks noodle along
In their chrome stud belts and Technicolor hair.

("A Journal of English Days")

This is a London walk from Chelsea to Hyde Park and Kensington Gardens. The observing self may be sustained here by chestnut trees and swans, but it takes in architecture and punks and dogs as well. One wants to accompany Wright's persona first and foremost, I suppose, because of this capacity to notice and enjoy and articulate the crowded phenomena that the world makes available to the senses.

But this lover of the world of appearances is also deeply distrustful of them. He knows they are ephemeral and illusory. They turn back his inquiries, especially his metaphysical ones (does the world bespeak a creator? Is it divine or secular, order or chaos?), and they drive him into a melancholy awareness of the limits of his knowledge and the brevity of his life. In the poem cited above he "meets" another poet, Fulke Greville, who is of course dead, "in his stone boat in the church of St. Mary," and he marks the death-days of other poets, Sidney and Keats, and of his hero Cézanne. Everywhere he turns he finds the presence of mystery and death, "Charon, in slow motion, poling his empty boat." Hints of a god fill his world too, but they are frustrating, tantalizing, always associated with loss and melancholy, "the Norman churchyard, / Grey flake and flame in a hushed mound on Delia Johnson. / *God Knows His Own.*" Late in this poem he muses, "How sweet to think that Nature is solvency," that there is something behind it "That will make us anchorites in the dark / Chambers of celestial perpetuity— / nice to think that, / Given the bleak alternative, / Though it hasn't proved so before, / and won't now / No matter what things we scrape aside— / God is an abstract noun."

But that is only one of the endings; the other is a moment of mystical oneness in a museum courtyard connecting with a Buddha, the oneness an experience of nothingness as well, the self a hand that unclenches and spreads open "finger by finger inside the Buddha's eye. . . ." The eye is a holy thing, of course, because it is the means by which the self most often delights in the world of appearances. *I* is *eye*, one of our most reverberant puns, as in so much of Shakespeare, and vision is both seeing and epiphany, as in mystical poets like Cavalcanti. But where other mystics finally find God, Wright more often finds just himself or his sense of his own limits or his rueful acknowledgment that he is somehow terribly separate from the world he loves. The tension keeps the poems moving forward, stanza to stanza, perception to perception, hint to hint. It is the texture of life itself.

If the persona cannot help both loving and distrusting his world of appearances, finding in it both his pains and his pleasures, his strengths and his weaknesses, his intimations both of total fulfillment and total denial and collapse, he has a similar relation to words: a helpless love and need for them, an endless fascination with them, an irrevocable dependency on them and at the same time a profound sense of how they actually separate him from experience and fail him when he tries to realize himself through them.

This note is struck in the Cézanne poem that I quoted at the outset of this essay. The dead find that their names, verbal identities, are unsettled by water. Even such crucial and irrevocable words as names, names of the dead, prove unstable in this world of change and process. As the poem moves forward, we learn that the dead "point to their favorite words / Growing around them, revealed as themselves for the first time," and that "what they repeat to themselves, / Is the song that our fathers sing." As the sea "explains itself, backing and filling / What space it can't avoid," the dead "Over and over, through clenched teeth," tell "Their story, the story each knows by heart: / *Remember me, speak my name.*" The dead are of course finally us, and our projections of memory and desire, so their obsessive storytelling and singing, their pitiful dependence on speech, is our own. There's something circular and meaningless in our constant conversing with them, they with us, something that may go nowhere but serves a little to relieve our sense of loss and separation: "Our words are words for the clay, uttered in undertones, / Our gestures salve for the wind." Talking to clay or trying to heal the wind is ridiculous, but it is the story of our lives and of our dependence upon words.

The "Journal of English Days" I have also been citing here is less explicit about the love affair with words and the sense of their inadequacy, but it manifests the same preoccupations in its concern with other word-users, with getting things right, knowing the right names for things, and when, near the end, "God is an abstract noun," His disappearance into arid language is precisely the result of the way appearance dissolves and language is unable to effectively take its place.

We could say that Wright's dual sense that the two things he loves most, world and word, betray him by betraying each other is a tragic vision, and that would be partly correct. It would not, however, be the whole story. For the poems also tell us that if the two things that mean the most are notoriously unstable, it is probably their very instability that makes them so meaningful. And their similarity includes the possibility that they can mirror and interpret each other. It links them, unstable and ephemeral and beautiful, and then it links them to life itself, to the poet's and reader's mortality. Thus the melancholy news language and appearance convey, the news that the self must expire, is the very same information the self needs to make its identity complete, to allow it to connect with the world and with words and to know them after all. There's a kind of triple paradox at work here. Three forms of instability—self, world and language—are involved in an intricate dance that choreographs uncertainty and change into a kind of celebration. We must call Wright's world tragicomic because we must include the wry playfulness, the melancholy pleasure, that comes from aligning all the things that enchant and then fail us, including our very own selves.

It is a trick of language and of experience and of self, for instance, to say that the hand unclenches finger by finger inside the Buddha's eye. We should understand that that's a trick, a bit of nifty rhetoric, because this poet keeps nothing up his sleeve. That it's artificial and manipulative does not destroy its value. Here too we come across what looks very much like Wright's allegiance to Stevens, never really articulated to my knowledge (though the "Journal of One Significant Landscape" in *Zone Journals* echoes Stevens's early "Six Significant Landscapes"). The connection may be accidental or deliberate, or both: the poet as clown-phenomenologist, the sleight-of-hand man who makes us believe in meaning even after he has shown us that it may be meaningless.

Now we've come to the heart of this persona (and others in our time, though I won't name names), to the poet's reason for featuring this version of the self so relentlessly and variously. There's a reluctant but necessary narcissism involved in Charles Wright's poetry. To show what he wants to show us about how the natural world mirrors our love, our moroseness, our mortality, he must portray a poet, a language user, discovering how he can play his language lovingly against the world, watching the patterns that emerge and acknowledging the inevitable solipsism of the enterprise. Self-portraiture of a kind is necessary to the equation of tricky world, tricky language and trickster poet, a pilgrim, a traveler, as Wordsworth has it in a line Wright cites here (p. 29), between life and death.

What then are the adventures and parameters of this collection? Where do they take the persona in his pilgrimage, where follow him? They cover the late middle years, age 45 to 55, when memory begins to play a much more active role in the life of the self and when the completed creations that lie behind the speaker/singer/storyteller exert their own subtle pressures, making him wonder if he is simply repeating himself and how he may move on to what Hart Crane called "new thresholds, new anatomies." Wright's answer has been, especially in the second half of the decade, to design larger and apparently looser structures for his persona to inhabit, journal-poems that walk the boundaries between poetry and prose, trivial and profound, random and designed, contingent and self-contained. The risks he has taken in this process will challenge and frustrate even some of his better readers. He will seem to have abandoned the laconic, visionary style that was his hallmark, especially in *China Trace*, and to be indulging himself with a garrulousness and expansiveness that threaten to become swollen, overblown, self-important. Wright has already faced such reactions to the crucial collection, *Zone Journals*, and no doubt he has wondered himself from time to time whether he was up to something he could bring off.

For my own part, I think the journal poems deepen the meaning of the persona-world-word triangle I have outlined. They make the facing of appearances and the ambivalent affair with language a daily matter, a mundane concern, not simply associated with times of ecstasy and inspiration but with getting up and going through the day and going to bed. They bring the whole poetic enterprise closer to the texture of life, a gesture of inclusiveness that may recall Whitman as well as those Stevens poems that deliberately focus on repetition and trivia, that build up and break down, section by section, before our eyes, enacting their meanings by cyclic engagements with skepticism and belief (e.g., "Auroras of Autumn," "An Ordinary Evening in New Haven").

If we think about the journal form for a moment, we realize how flexible a concept it is. The diarist or journal-keeper is only committed to some kind of timely recording of data. It may or may not be regular, but it will be fresh, born of the moment and a certain spontaneity, free of the need to be perfected and included in anything other than the steady stream of experience based on living in time. The data may be as "trival" as the weather, what one ate, the minute events of an uneventful life, or as "profound" as thoughts on life and death, the recording of philosophical or theological musings. I use quotes for these contrasting adjectives because I think that in the journals from the past that we tend to value— Pepys, Gilbert White, Boswell—what is technically trivial is precisely what emerges to us as profound: the capturing of the "dailiness of life" (Jarrell's phrase in "Well Water"), the glimpsing among the details of the quotidian a meaning, or meanings, as if in a powerful metaphor, or in a drama that marries absurdity to loss, as in Chekhov, a way of rendering experience that is ultimately more valuable than that of systems, generalizations, ideologies.

This, I think, is what Wright is after, and in my opinion he captures it. The section I quoted earlier, from the poem about England, is indeed made up of some trivial details: what one passes walking the route that the persona walks to get from Chelsea to Hyde Park and round back to Kensington Gardens. We don't object to this kind of detail in a novel, but we want to feel that poems get beyond it, that they shed the detritus of the mundane and soar up into visionary regions that are their special domain. But we need to admit that poetry has a domestic and mundane side, even in its visionary practitioners (think of Herbert, Wordsworth, Dickinson), and we need to recognize that Wright and his persona never lose their hunger for the absolute, their drive to find answers to the largest questions. "A Journal of the Year of the Ox," the longest (40 pages) of the journal poems, behaves like this in an excerpt I have deliberately chosen at random, an "entry" dated "9 April 1985" (p. 158):

—Such a hustle of blue skies from the west,
the pre-Columbian clouds
Brooding and looking straight down,

The white plumes of the crab-apple tree
Plunging and streaming in their invisible headgear.

April plugs in the rosebud
               and its Tiffany limbs.
This earth is a plenitude, but it all twists into the dark,
The not no image can cut
Or color replenish.
              Not red, not yellow, not blue.

None of the visionary concerns, none of the tension I cited earlier, is missing here. The difference is mainly that instead of being titled and collected as a poem on its own, this is included in a larger structure that is governed by what happens, what is thought about and read and felt, over the course of a year. My Wittgenstein motto, "The subject does not belong to the world but it is a limit of the world," still pertains. The mundane—sky, clouds, blooming crab-apples, budding roses—is cross-roughed by history (pre-Columbian) and by artistic tradition (Tiffany), and the vocabularies of technology (headgear, plugs in) are invited to participate as well. The drive to find adequate generalizations for experience is both fulfilled—the earth as a plenitude that twists into darkness—and frustrated: a pun, slippage in language, is used to admit that imagery can't get at nothingness, can't cut its knot, can't "cut it," as we say colloquially. And I would argue that the mature style is as sure and reassuring as anything Wright managed earlier, in his more predictably shaped and more obviously controlled poems.

We will need time to digest these journal poems, obviously, but I predict that they will become, because they are so ambitious and risky, among this poet's most admired efforts. He remains one of our most exciting current practitioners of the art of poetry, distinctive and powerful, a voice that continues to surpass itself.

I've said nothing negative here, I realize, nothing to qualify my praise for *The World of the Ten Thousand Things*. The task of discriminating relative success and failure seems to me less interesting at the moment than the effort to understand what the poet is up to. I can find lines that I think don't come off (e.g., "What tongue is toothless enough to speak their piece?" in the Cézanne poem), and passages where I think Wright's deliberately overwrought and expressionistic rendering of natural events shades into mannerism and self-parody. But even the weaknesses, in truly original poetry, have a certain endearing tendency to become strengths, to jump on the bandwagon. I admire the courage and risk-taking that this book stands for, the questing spirit it evinces. It is wry, voluminous, high-spirited, and often gorgeously overwrought.

Let me close by quoting part of an out-of-the-way favorite of mine called "Cryopexy," from *The Other Side of the River*. The notes tell us that cryopexy is the name of "an operation to repair, by freezing with liquid Freon gas, a tear on the eye's retina." In other words, we can surmise that

the poem draws on the poet's experiencing such an operation and the re-
covery period it entails, and seizing on it, journal-like, journalist-like (the
journal poems may finally just admit and claim that journalists is what all
poets really are), to choreograph those obsessions and frustrations that
arise from his persona's pursuit of the sirens of appearance and language.
Eye is I, again, here, in a poem that celebrates vision, in all senses of that
word, strangely and with enormous originality:

> Looming and phosphorescent in the dark,
> Words, always words.
>                     What language does light speak?
> Vowels hang down from the pepper tree
>                               in their green and their gold.

> ———

> The star charts and galactic blood trails behind the eye
> Where the lights are, and the links and chains are,
>                                 cut wall through ascending wall,
> Indigo corridors, the intolerable shine
>                           transgressing heaven's borders . . .

> ———

> What are the colors of true splendor,
>                           yellow and white,
> Carnation and ivory, petal and bone?
> Everything comes from fire.

> ———

> Glare and glare-white,
>                     light like a plate of isinglass
> Under the lid,
>                   currents of fox-fire between the layers,
> And black dots like the blood bees of Paradise . . .

> ———

> Radiance comes through the eye
>                       and lodges like cut glass in the mind,
> Never vice-versa,
> Somatic and self-contained.

> ———

> Like soiled stars from the night-blooming jasmine vine
> Espaliered against the sky,
>                     char flakes rise from their blank deeps

Through peach light and apricot
Into the endlessness behind the eye.

———

Blood clots, like numb houseflies, hang
In the alabaster and tracery,
                icy detritus
Rocked in the swish and tug
                of the eye's twice-turned and moonless tides.
Behind them, tourmaline thread-ladders
Web up through the nothingness,
                the diamond and infinite glare . . .

———

I'd love to quote the whole poem—this is a little over half of it—but I've surely made my point. Wright always wrestles with the angel of the mundane, making it admit its heavenly origins. In the process, he gives his readers joy, shock, delight. Inside the healing eye, here, we have the sense of the world, or at least a playing with it, at it, around it. The eye can't normally see itself, another paradox that Wittgenstein remarks on. Here, seeing its own shortcomings and precariousness, it sees nothing and in that nothing, everything, up to the blood bees of Paradise. If there were a heaven for poets, and Charles Wright had nothing but a scrap of his work to show, say these few stanzas, whoever is keeping the gate there, George Herbert or Guido Cavalcanti, would surely wave him in.

TOM ANDREWS

# Improvisations on Charles Wright's
## *The World of the Ten Thousand Things* (1992)

> . . . good work joins earth to heaven.
> —Lu Chi

Thinking about what I wanted to say in this essay brought home to me the truth of something Robert Hass observed in *Twentieth Century Pleasures*: "You can analyze the music of poetry but it's difficult to conduct an argument about its value, especially when it's gotten into the blood. It becomes autobiography there."[1] This is especially true of my encounter with Charles Wright's *The World of the Ten Thousand Things: Poems 1980-1990*, which collects his three previous books, *The Southern Cross*, *The Other Side of the River*, and *Zone Journals*, as well as the chapbook *Xionia*. I think it's only fair, therefore, to begin with a brief account of how I came to hear its music, of how that music has "gotten into the blood."

In 1981 I was a sophomore at Hope College, a small Christian school where I had gone for preparation to become a minister. One year earlier I had entered the school, and the religion department, with full evangelical certainty regarding my choice of vocation. By the next year, however, I had serious doubts about that choice, and I discovered a need for writers who had something to say about the conditions of anxiety and doubt and fear. I remember returning again and again to four books: Paul Tillich's *The Courage to Be*, Owen Barfield's *Saving the Appearances*, Woody Allen's *Without Feathers*, and Charles Wright's newly published *The Southern Cross*. (I did not necessarily read them in that order.)

Somehow the poems in *The Southern Cross* embodied much of what I valued in the other three books: the moral seriousness of Tillich, the visionary reach and language of Barfield, and the perfect timing of Woody Allen. One poem, "October," became for me a kind of hymn:

> The leaves fall from my fingers.
> Cornflowers scatter across the field like stars,
>                                        like smoke stars,
> By the train tracks, the leaves in a drift

---

1. Robert Hass, "Lowell's Graveyard," *Twentieth Century Pleasures* (New York: Ecco, 1984), 3.

Under the slow clouds
                        and the nine steps to heaven,
The light falling in great sheets through the trees,
Sheets almost tangible.

The transfiguration will start like this, I think,
                                            breathless,
Quick blade through the trees,
Something with red colors falling away from my hands,

The air beginning to go cold . . .
                        And when it does
I'll rise from this tired body, a blood-knot of light,
Ready to take the darkness in.

—Or for the wind to come
And carry me, bone by bone, through the sky,
Its wafer a burn on my tongue,
                        its wine deep forgetfulness.

I was astonished, and grateful. Wright incorporated Christian imagery—
e.g., the transfiguration and the resurrection of the body, the sacramental
host and wine—in such a way as to deepen my participation in the mys-
teries of the faith while at the same time articulating my uncertainties.
There was also the startling beauty and ambition of Wright's poems, their
amplitude of desire, their reach for "Things that divine us," as he put it
in "The Southern Cross," no matter that "we never touch [them]." I
knew then that this poet would be important to me for the rest of my
life, and I set about reading everything by him I could find.

I mention all this not because I think my story is unique. Rather, I think
it mirrors the circumstances of many readers who turn to Charles
Wright's poems. Once, when I had a chance to tell him how much the
poem "October" had meant to me, Wright mentioned a letter he had re-
ceived from an ex-nun. She wrote (from what I could gather through
Wright's characteristic modesty) to say that his poems offered rare conso-
lation, especially when she mourned leaving the order, and that she even
kept a copy of "October" in her wallet. My guess is that Wright has over
the years received many such letters referring to many of his poems, a guess
perhaps confirmed by these lines from "A Journal of the Year of the Ox,"
from *Zone Journals*:

The disillusioned and twice-lapsed, the fallen away,
Become my constituency:
                        those who would die back
To splendor and rise again
From hurt and unwillingness,
                        their own ash on their tongues,

Are those I would be among,
The called, the bruised by God, by their old ways forsaken
And startled on, the shorn and weakened.

Unlike Wallace Stevens, for whom seeing "the gods dispelled in mid-air and dissolve like clouds is one of the great human experiences,"[2] Wright's poems speak to, and from, the contradictory longings of "The disillusioned and twice-lapsed, the fallen away" who "would die back / To splendor." Of course Wright's circle of readers is larger than I'm suggesting here; his constituency is made up of more than would-be ministers and ex-nuns. But there's no doubt that his work has a special attraction for the God-haunted among us, those who have experienced the "homesickness" Wright describes in "A Journal of English Days":

> There is no sickness of spirit like homesickness
> When what you are sick for
>                         has never been seen or heard
> In this world, or even remembered
>                         except as a smear of bleached light
> Opening, closing beyond any alphabet's
> Recall to witness and isolate . . .

★

Recently a friend remarked that what he admired most about *Four Quartets* was that Eliot was able to write a convincing religious poem in a secular age. Charles Wright's poems offer similar satisfactions, in an age even more "secular" than Eliot's. I fumigate the word "secular" with quotation marks because I believe a central impulse of *The World of the Ten Thousand Things* is to show how the secular (or the quotidian, the seen world) and the religious (or the noumenal, the unseen) persistently overlap. Wright, I think, would agree with Novalis: "The seat of the soul is where the inner world and the outer world meet. Where they overlap, it is in every point of the overlap."[3] Moreover, for Wright this overlapping occurs whenever we truly concentrate on the natural world:

> From somewhere we never see comes everything that we do see.
> What is important devolves
>                         from the immanence of infinitude

---

2. Wallace Stevens, "Two or Three Ideas," *Opus Posthumous* (New York: Knopf, 1957), 206.

3. Novalis, "Aphorisms" (trans. Charles E. Passage), quoted in Robert Bly, *News of the Universe: Poems of Twofold Consciousness* (San Francisco: Sierra Club Books, 1980), 48.

In whatever our hands touch—
The other world is here, just under our fingertips.

("December Journal")

To know "What is important," Wright implies, to recognize that "The other world is here, just under our fingertips," we must first give our attention, and our affection, to the dense particulars of *this* world. Wright does so with stunning precision and imaginative energy. His poems catalog the ten thousand things with the reverence of a T'ang dynasty poet:

There is, in the orchards of Sommacampagna,
A sleet-like and tenuous iridescence that falls
Through the peach trees whenever it rains.
                    The blossoms parachute to the ground
So heavy and so distinct,
And the light above Riva spokes out from under the clouds
Like Blake,
          the wires for the grapevines beading their little rainbows,
The cars planing by on the highway,
                shooshing their golden plumes . . .

What gifts there are are all here, in this world.

("Italian Days")

The gifts the natural world offers to Wright include the knowledge that "what you see / both is and is not there, / The unseen bulking in from the edges of all things" ("A Journal of True Confessions"). All things, for Wright, are rife with the absolute. Concentrating on them, seeing them as they truly are, dissolves such distinctions as those between the secular and the religious. This insight was articulated memorably by William Blake. Blake, whose marvelous engravings and whose inspiring life as an artist Wright compares in "Italian Days" to "the light above Riva" as it "spokes out from under the clouds" (where the pun of "spokes" suggests both visionary speech and the optical effect of sunbeams radiating through clouds), wrote in *The Marriage of Heaven and Hell* that "If the doors of perception were cleansed every thing would appear to man as it is, infinite."[4] As Wright himself emphasized in his *Paris Review* interview, "The textures of the world *are* an outline of the infinite."[5]

The verse journals Charles Wright began working with in *Zone Journals* are particularly well suited to his vision of the world's textures and hidden mysteries. A journal suggests an inclusiveness of the mundane

---

4. *The Poetry and Prose of William Blake*, ed. David V. Erdman (Garden City, NY: Doubleday, 1965), 39.

5. Charles Wright, "The Art of Poetry XLI," *Paris Review* 113 (Winter 1989): 220.

generally beyond the scope of the lyric poem. It also suggests an author's willingness to record daily events and concerns, and to be candid about the way those events and concerns fall within or conflict with larger pre-occupations. David St. John, referring to Wright's earlier book *China Trace*, described very well the motivation for such a project. Despite the "resolutely spiritual" search Wright's poems arise from, St. John re-marked, the poems are

> firmly rooted in [the] objects of daily life, in the earth, the domestic ex-perience. . . . It is no accident the poems are often fixed not only by place names, but by specific times of day or night, phases of the moon, dates, and personal references. . . . [I]t remains vital to Wright that he continuously mark or notate his search with the facts of his existence, otherwise what point would such a search have?[6]

The journal-poems in *The World of the Ten Thousand Things* make explicit what St. John found implicit in *China Trace*. Again we are talking about the "metaphysics of the commonplace, the metaphysics of the quotidian," as Wright says in "Halflife: A Commonplace Notebook."[7] The journal-poems allow Wright to freely engage the complexity of the world's presence as it appears to him, to shift from precise description to reminiscence to meditation to epiphany and back again at something like the mind's actual breakneck speed:

> —Ashes know what burns,
> clouds savvy which way the wind blows . . .
> Full moon like a bed of coals
> As autumn revs up and cuts off
> Remembering winter nights like a doused light bulb
> Leaning against my skin,
> object melting into the image
> Under the quickly descending stars:
> Once the impasse is solved, St. Augustine says, between matter and spirit,
> Evil is merely the absence of good:
> Which makes sense, if you understand what it truly means,
> Full moon the color of sand now,
> and still unretractable . . .

These lines are from "A Journal of the Year of the Ox," the centerpiece of *Zone Journals*. Because it is the longest and most ambitious poem in

---

6. David St. John, "The Poetry of Charles Wright," *Wright: A Profile* (Iowa City: Grilled Flowers Press, 1979), 56.

7. Charles Wright, "Halflife: A Commonplace Notebook," in *Halflife: Improvisations and Interviews, 1977-87* (Ann Arbor: Univ. of Michigan Press, 1988), 22.

*The World of the Ten Thousand Things*—11 pages covering 1985, the poet's fiftieth year—it offers the clearest single view of Wright's remarkable accomplishment in the book. In the last entry of the poem, dated 25 December 1985, Wright asks,

> What is a life of contemplation worth in this world?
> How far can you go if you concentrate,
>
> > how far down?

Throughout the poem, Wright's powers of concentration and incantatory utterance, his passion "to 'know,' to be among the 'knowers' of this world" (as he has described Montale's aspiration[8]), answer his own questions in the strongest affirmative terms. They are not fashionable questions for a poet to raise nowadays, and part of Wright's achievement in the poem is his ability to compel our assent to their validity. Still, though Wright occasionally explores an extended line of questioning, the poem remains "heroically concrete" (in St. John's phrase), mixing, as always, mundane and visionary urgencies:

> How shall we hold on, when everything bright falls away?
> How shall we know what calls us
> > when what's past remains what's past
> And unredeemed, the crystal
> And wavering coefficient of what's ahead?
>
> Thursday, purgatorial Thursday,
> The Blue Ridge etched in smoke
> > through the leaded panes of the oak trees,
> There, then not there,
> A lone squirrel running the power line,
> > neck bowed like a tiny buffalo . . .

★

In September of 1985, nine and a half months into "A Journal of the Year of the Ox," Wright was interviewed by the *Iowa Journal of Literary Studies*, where he described his struggle for an "overall organization" to the poem:

> Part of my spatial theory of free verse is that structure resembles a giant spider web. It's endlessly expandable, but within a framework. The secret is to find the framework. To have found the framework for this journal has proven difficult. The year, obviously, is one reference point. That's the skin structure of the poem. But you also have to make interior structuring

---

8. Wright, "Improvisations on Montale," *Halflife*, 43.

devices so you know yourself you haven't just been vamping for a whole year—that there are three or four points the whole thing hangs on, that it does make a strange circular movement.[9]

It is fascinating to hear Wright comment on the process of this poem—a poem on which he has a great deal at stake—not from the relative safety of hindsight but while still in the midst of finding a viable framework for it, a framework faithful to the poem's undercurrents or "interior structuring devices" as well as to its "skin structure." (The statement also points to the restless formal and structural investigation that runs throughout *The World of the Ten Thousand Things.* Earlier I said that Wright began working with verse journals in *Zone Journals.* It's more accurate, I think, to say that the journal-poems are the natural extension of Wright's previous experiments with journal-like layering and juxtaposition, begun in *The Southern Cross* and culminating in "A Journal of the Year of the Ox.")

Wright's comments remind me of a remark Miles Davis once made when he was asked why he played over or against his band. "It's always," Davis replied, "a counter-melody to a melody, a melody within a melody. You can just go on and on."[10] In Miles Davis's terms, Wright in "A Journal of the Year of the Ox" has the poem's "skin structure," the references to the progression of the year, work as a counter-melody to the "interior structuring devices." Those structuring devices are strategically-positioned meditations on sacred places, particularly the Long Island of the Holston River in east Tennessee, sacred meeting ground of the Cherokee Nation, and northern Italy, where Wright began writing poems while stationed in the Army. The Long Island of the Holston is mentioned in January, April, September, and December. The long meditation on Italy occurs in the summer entries, the exact center of the poem. The hub of "A Journal of the Year of the Ox," therefore, invokes Wright's artistic birth, the birth of his way of seeing and hearing the world, while the entries devoted to the banishment of the Cherokee from sacred ground make up the poem's seasonal spokes, as it were. Thus the structure itself echoes and informs Wright's preoccupation throughout the poem with the value of a life devoted to finding the sacred in a profane world. The necessary dailiness of that search—embodied so well by a journal format—finds resonance in the poem's architectural design.

When I say that Charles Wright's poems offer religious satisfactions, I do not mean the satisfactions of one orthodoxy or another. At the heart of their satisfaction, I believe, is Wright's refusal to assume any certainty

---

9. Wright, "With Carol Ellis," *Halflife*, 155–56.

10. Interview on videocassette, *Miles in Paris* (Burbank, CA: Warner Reprise Video, 1990).

about his spiritual quest. His poems remain on that threshold where psychic stabilities and instabilities meet, where one's identity is perpetually on the verge of dissolving into a mystical transcendence even as that transcendence is feared by the finite self. In "Composition in Grey and Pink," for example, Wright "dream[s] of an incandescent space / where nothing distinct exists, / And where nothing ends. . . ." By the end of the poem, however, Wright qualifies this vision by acknowledging a human desire to pull back from the absolute, to remain "distinct," "Untied from God":

> I want to complete my flesh
>
> and sit in a quiet corner
> Untied from God, where the dead don't sing in their sleep.

Such qualifications of the transcendent impulse lend his work a trustworthy authority. Wright does not discount his mystical moments. Nor does he set up a soapbox after experiencing them. He presents them as they come to him: baffling, exhilarating, temporary. "Something infinite behind everything appears, / and then disappears," Wright says in "The Other Side of the River." As David Young has written of Wright's work,

> . . . where other mystics finally find God, Wright more often finds just himself or his sense of his own limits or his rueful acknowledgment that he is somehow terribly separate from the world he loves. The tension keeps the poems moving forward, stanza to stanza, perception to perception, hint to hint. It is the texture of life itself.[11]

To find "the texture of life itself" so accurately recreated and so passionately celebrated is, I find, a decidedly religious satisfaction. And it is fitting, I think, to recognize Wright as "a religious poet of a unique sort" a phrase he once used to describe the Italian poet Eugenio Montale. When asked to clarify that assertion in an interview, Wright characterized Montale's work in terms that serve as a portrait of his own:

> It seems to me . . . that La bufera [The Storm, Montale's third book of poems] throughout admits God as a possibility, though how he is taken is often unsure. As though there were flashes of lightning in the nothingness that surrounds and penetrates much of his work. Metaphysical overtones of faith seem to settle in on the wind and then to be swept away again. . . . In his world of time as the steady destroyer, of existence as entropy, the steady process of decay, like the darkness, surrounds us from the inside out. Any relief from that, in him, becomes an intercession, a kind of grace beyond our ability to explain or understand. The mysteries beat just under the surface of everything. He hears that beating, he sees the flashes of light.[12]

---

11. David Young, "The Blood Bees of Paradise," *FIELD* 44 (Spring 1991): 82.
12. Wright, "With Antonella Francini," *Halflife*, 119-120.

★

"Nothing can be omitted, experience drunk and experience sober, experience sleeping and experience waking, experience drowsy and experience wide-awake, experience self-conscious and experience self-forgetful, experience intellectual and experience physical, experience religious and experience skeptical, experience anxious and experience care-free, experience anticipatory and experience retrospective, experience happy and experience grieving, experience dominated by emotion and experience under self-restraint, experience in the light and experience in the dark, experience normal and experience abnormal."

Thus Alfred North Whitehead, describing in *Adventures of Ideas* the conditions necessary for a metaphysics to be considered "empirical."[13] An "empirical metaphysics" is precisely, I think, what Charles Wright has constructed in *The World of the Ten Thousand Things*, and he has done so through the spirit of generosity and inclusiveness Whitehead calls for. The ten thousand things come together in this book, in the kind of glorious embrace Wright evokes in this entry from "A Journal of the Year of the Ox":

> —In the first inch of afternoon, under the peach trees,
> The constellations of sunlight
> Sifting along their courses among the posed limbs,
> It's hard to imagine the north wind
>                                          wishing us ill,
> Revealing nothing at all and wishing us ill,
> In God's third face.
>                          The world is an ampersand,
> And I lie in sweet clover,
>                          bees like golden earrings
> Dangling and locked fast to its white heads,
> Watching the clouds move and the constellations of light move
> Through the trees, as they both will
> When the wind weathers them on their way,
> When the wind weathers them to that point
>                                          where all things meet.

---

13. Quoted in Frank Burch Brown, *Transfiguration: Poetic Metaphor and the Languages of Religious Belief* (Chapel Hill: Univ. of North Carolina Press, 1983), 134.

# Charles Wright's Hymn (1991)

In his *New York Times Book Review* (2/24/91) of Wright's *World of the Ten Thousand Things*, Richard Tillinghast opened his essay with two observations with which I wholeheartedly agree. First and most obviously, he pointed out how Wright's subtle cadences and "famously good ear" have won Wright a select place among contemporary poets. Indeed, for the specific reasons that Tillinghast mentions as well as many others, Wright has proven to be a poet of brilliant and original style. Tillinghast goes on to point out that *The World of the Ten Thousand Things* (Wright's collected work over the last ten years including *The Southern Cross*, *The Other Side of the River*, *Zone Journals*, and most recently *Xionia*) really reads as a single poetic sequence worthy of comparison to the extended works of some of our greatest poets; he mentions Roethke, Berryman, and Hart Crane. This point is the most salient, for it is Wright's abiding vision, his metaphysical argument with the physical, his varied dialog with nature and with time about transcendence—its saving grace, its desirability, its implausibility—that finally makes Wright's poems some of the most important and resonant we have.

The title of his book comes, of course, from oriental philosophy, probably from Lao Tsu's *Tao Te Ching* which warns of the material, the illusions of the "world of ten thousand things." One of Lao Tsu's most telling lines, especially as the work of Wright is concerned, is "Heaven and earth are ruthless." The achievement of Wright's work then is that it so often places us at the crossroads, at that point where there is all the beauty and deflection of the world that may in fact point to transcendence and a metaphysical continuum, but that, given our collective mortal experience, may not finally deliver us. Both the material and spiritual are difficult, and we find ourselves caught between two beauties, two desires.

In the August issue of *Poetry*, J. D. McClatchy, also reviewing *The World of Ten Thousand Things*, speaks to this focus in Wright's poetry: "Wright's poems have a double purpose: to describe those things not of which this world is made but by which it is seen, and then to use them to return to his beginnings." Those beginnings are not only memories from childhood and other autobiographical experiences, they are aesthetic and mystical/ spiritual. McClatchy enunciates the real concern of Wright's work, its progression over the years from these beginnings to a true metaphysical landscape charted from the early tightly imagistic poems, to the longer lines and drop lines of *The Southern Cross* and *The Other Side of the River*, to the looser, inspired speculations of *Zone Journals* and *Xionia*. McClatchy, speaking of this progression, says "these journal-poems are not preoccupied with the self, but with otherness within the self." He continues to point out that Wright's true concern, far and above his concerns with style and craft, had been to write a "spiritual autobiography."

Both Tillinghast and McClatchy see then the progression of Wright's work over the years and especially over the last ten year period and offer insightful, just and salient appreciations of the work. All one could really wish is that a little more space had been devoted to *Xionia*, the newest portion of this work, the poems that serve wonderfully as the coda to this vision.

The fine print edition from Windhover Press consists of 250 signed copies printed by hand from Joanna types on either Johannot or Iyo papers, case bound, quarter cloth, paper over boards. K. K. Merker and Windhover Press have long been known for fine letter press editions of poetry by some of our best poets, and this volume continues that tradition. The page size is ample, but not overwhelming; it allows the necessary space for these poems to "breathe," to baste and whirl as Wright himself might say. Even with Wright's longer journal lines, even with drop lines, the poem is never cramped against a margin or gutter. Merker is known as a printer who thinks of the text first, a printer who wants nothing in the printing to detract from the poem. The quarter bound cloth spine is a deep cranberry color, and this is complemented by a mauve-to-grey paper over boards; it reminds one almost of a hymnal. As book art, this volume is a masterful production, and as a collection of poems, *Xionia* stands wonderfully on its own as well.

*Xionia* is a coda to all poems—their styles and themes—in *The World of Ten Thousand Things. The Southern Cross* and *The Other Side of the River* begin the journey with more narrative and autobiographical attachments—aesthetic concerns of strategies beyond narrative; occasions from childhood, from travel; stories of relatives, of place, and always the spiritual condition and questioning, the examination of the inner landscape as well as the outer. The "spiritual autobiography," as McClatchy names it, begins anchored in the earth, in *event* in these books. However with *Zone Journals*, especially the long virtuoso poem "A Journal of the Year of the Ox," Wright begins to play out the string of his style and his themes, to let them roll symphonically, introducing variations and recapitulations—all in a more condensed imagistic method than in the previous works. The journal poems are vastly more inclusive than anything Wright has previously written, more atmospheric, more textural; they name much, risk much, and include it all in a large vision always testing the possibility of salvation. And so when we come to *Xionia*, it's much as if we have been listening to a symphony—beginning with a theme, following many variations, and now finding ourselves at the resolution, the recapitulation of a big and complete work!

The poems in *Xionia* are the most direct in enunciating themes, in saying it in image and diction without equivocation. Having given all the examples—the narrative vignettes, the autobiographical situations, the long speculative and inclusive litanies, Wright has now earned his way to these more direct statements. These poems are on the whole more condensed in form than anything previous yet they still shine with brilliance and originality of imagery that allows all the specifics and all the thematic connotations to soar; at the same time, he manages to keep it all in focus, in perspective and tied clearly to his metaphysical vision and ideas.

"Bicoastal Journal" is probably the poem in *Xionia* that best gives us Wright's theme over the years, and the one that best exemplifies Wright's directness in these poems. In addressing the struggle between the physical and metaphysical he will not only give us lush imagery which will lead to a larger and speculative resolution at closure, he will now directly include diction and imagery from the metaphysical side. Always, he will balance this with the concrete elements of the environment at hand in the poem, but now more than ever the gloves are off. In this poem he is reading Richard of St. Victor; he is talking directly of the soul and "disincarnate figures."

> Noon light on the jacaranda fans
> Colorless sheen,
>     and distant figures disincarnate
> Every so often among the trunks . . .
>
> The contemplative soul goes out and comes back with marvelous
>   quickness—
> Or bends itself, as it were,
>       into a circle, Richard of St. Victor says.
> Or gathers itself, as it were,
> In one place and is fixed there motionless
> Like birds in the sky, now to the right, now to the left . . .
>
> There are six kinds of contemplation,
>       St. Victor adds:
> Imagination, and according to imagination only;
> Imagination, according to reason; reason
> According to imagination;
>      reason according to reason;
> Above, but not beyond reason;
>      above reason, beyond reason.

Here, Wright sets forth the long battle between love for the world and our love for the luminous edges of the world which might be metaphysical and continuous, and which, paradoxically, might only direct us back to the earth, with our longing and our loss, our bobbing and weaving of transcendence. Here is the conclusion of the poem:

> I'd rather be elsewise, like water
>     hugging the undergrowth,

Uncovering rocks and small windfall
Under the laurel and maple wood.
                                    I'd rather be loose fire
Licking the edges of all things but the absolute
Whose murmur retoggles me.
I'd rather be memory, touching the undersides
Of all I ever touched once in the natural world.

"December Journal"—one of the longer poems in the book—is also as direct in its subject and themes. There is an austerity in the texture of meditations as a result of experience.

God is not offered to the senses,
                                    St. Augustine tells us,
The artificer is not his work, but is his art:
Nothing is good if it can be better.
But all these oak trees look fine to me,
                                    this Virginia cedar
Is true to its own order
And ghosts a unity beyond its single number . . .

I keep coming back to the visible.
                                    I keep coming back
To what it leads me into,
The hymn in the hymnal,
The object, sequence and consequence.

There is a thinking through of the small additions and subtractions in a life that beg the question of transcendence.

Trash cans weigh up with water beside the curb,
Leaves flatten themselves against the ground
                                    and take cover.

How are we capable of so much love
                                    for things that must fall away?
How can we utter our mild retractions and still keep
Our wasting affection for this world?

St. Augustine returns in the poem and reminds us about the soul. And this is a poem of meditation about the nature of "soul," and so an austere poem, one with more concept than the usual lushly imagistic Wright poem. The marvel is that even in speaking of such concepts of love and soul, Wright makes a closure that is nonetheless heartbreaking for its poignant enunciation of our collective condition.

The tongue cannot live up to the heart:
Raise the eyes of your affection to its affection

And let its equivalents
                    ripen in your body.
Love what you don't understand yet, and bring it to you.


From somewhere we never see comes everything that we do see.
What is important devolves
                    from the immanence of infinitude
In whatever our hands touch—
The other world is here, just under our fingertips.


"A Journal of Southern Rivers" opens about as thematically and directly as a poem can, and ties in a little autobiography to anchor its theme before moving on to investigate the evidence of the supporting imagery, those images that witness the relevance and irrelevance of time.

What lasts is what you start with.
*What hast thou, O my soul, with Paradise,* for instance,
Is where I began, in March 1959—
                    my question has never changed.


True to the journal format, Wright moves to Montana, considers the philosophy of Heidegger which moves him to say, "In awe and astonishment we regain ourselves in this world. // There is no other." The battle is on, a pull between this world only and that spiritual "river" that seems to nevertheless wind its way through all the poet's experience. And yet this poem does not resolve in a sure move toward some spiritual epiphany. One thing that keeps Wright's debate about salvation alive is the weight of each side of the argument and in this poem, it is the weight of mortality that seems to finally tip the scales.

How easily one thing comes and another passes away.
How soon we become the acolytes
Of nothing and nothing's altar
                    redeems us and makes us whole
Now for the first time,
And what we are is what we are not,
                    ecstatic and unknown.
What lasts is what you start with.

                    ———


Whose shadows are dancing upside down in the southern rivers?
Fifty-two years have passed
                    like the turning of a palm . . .


And yet the tone here, the rhetoric, diction and texture, do not allow the reader to come away believing the earth is all there is; and paradoxically, the insistence on the swift movement of time and mortality may focus back on "what you start with" which for Wright is the question of his soul and of Paradise.

There are other ideas here also. "Language Journal," to my reading, is a wonderfully subtle poem against the tenets of language poetry and deconstruction. It is a poem of affirmation that says all poetry is "language poetry"—a craft showing a love of and appreciation for language, its sounds and nuances—and at the same time not "language poetry" in the political poetry-faction sense, for, as Wright consistently asserts, the images, the lines, the poem and the world do have meaning for him. Again, as in all of the poems in *Xionia*, Wright has passages that are very direct and to the point.

> To be of use, not to be used by,
> the language sighs,
> The landscape sighs, the wide mouth
> Of March sighs at the ear of evening,
> Whose eye has that look of eternity in its gaze.
> To be of use,
> look of eternity in its gaze,
> Not to be used by . . .
> This English is not the King's English,
> it doesn't dissemble.
> If anything means nothing, nothing means anything,
> Full moon in the sky
> Like a golden period.
> It doesn't dissemble.

Wright turns around the debate about meaning with a quick image; immediately the moon takes on a meaning and remains, refuses to be meaningless. And by the end of the poem, Wright comes very close to using the rhetoric of Language Poetry, uses it to expose *its* lack of meaning.

> I step through the alphabet
> The tree limbs shadow across the grass,
> a dark language
> Of strokes and ideograms
> That spells out a different story than we are used to,
> A story with no beginning and no end,
> a little one.
> I leave it and cross the street.
> I think it's a happy story,
> and not about us.

I read "happy" here as mildly pejorative, not serious, thin, fatuous. And since it is not serious and "not about us" it is overlooking—certainly for Wright—the important questions about our lives.

Overall, these poems have a humble and ecstatic voice and vision, yet one with a moral weight. They pull all of the threads of over ten years' writing together. It is a resounding coda, a final passage that brings this

long sequence and question to a mature, and I would say spiritual, con-
clusion. Wright's short meditation which ends the book, "Last Journal,"
is composed of only direct statement—he has found his way to this place
patiently, and he knows his theme well, his hymn, and is singing better
than most anyone we have.

> Out of our mouths we are sentenced,
>                       we who put our trust in visible things.
>
> Soon enough we will forget the world.
>                       And soon enough the world will forget us.
>
> The breath of our lives, passing from this one to that one
> Is what the wind says, its single word
>                       being the earth's delight.
>
> Lust of the tongue, lust of the eye,
>                       out of our own mouths we are sentenced . . .

# The Nothing That Is (1995)

The title poem of Charles Wright's new book doesn't mention the Civil War battle of Chickamauga or the soldiers who died in it, and in this it is typical of Wright's practice. The poem climbs to a vantage point where the anonymity of history has blanked out the details. What is left is the distillate: that something happened at this place, that its legacy of uneasiness inhabits the collective psyche (Wright was born in Tennessee), that it will not let us go and demands a response. A confessional poet might write about his own family's legacy from the war. A socially minded poet might recount the havoc of battle. A moral poet might debate what Melville called "the conflict of convictions." A landscape poet might describe the vacant battlefield as it is now. Wright is none of these, does none of these things.

What can a lyric poetry be that sidelines the confessional, the social, the moral, the panoramic? It can be—and in Wright's case, it is—eschatological. Eschatology sees the world under the sign of the last things: Death, Judgment, Heaven, Hell. Wright redefines these in his own way: Annihilation, History, Light, Disappearance. If we face annihilation as persons, and we do; if history judges us and disposes of us, and it does; if mass is clarified into energy, and it is; if every object vanishes, and it will—then what kind of language can we use of life that will be true of these processes and true of us?

Wright's earliest manifesto of the lyric that he wanted to write was phrased in negation, in 1971:

### The New Poem

It will not resemble the sea.
It will not have dirt on its thick hands.
It will not be part of the weather.

It will not reveal its name.
It will not have dreams you can count on.
It will not be photogenic.

It will not attend our sorrow.
It will not console our children.
It will not be able to help us.

How was Wright to find a set of positives to accompany these negatives? The three stanzas of "The New Poem" refuse mimesis of the external world (sea, dirt, weather); mimesis of the psychological world (name, dreams, face); and mimesis of the religious world (attendance, consolation, help). No objects, then; and no self; and no God. Has there ever been a more stringent set of requirements for poetry?

If the object of art is not mimesis and not self-identification and not consolation, many of the tones that we associate with poetry must also be forgone. The strict discipline that Wright imposes on himself is visible in all he writes. If an item from the world is mentioned, it must always be remembered that it has been selected and is not simply "there." The word used to mention it, once it has been settled on, has its own history, its own weight and color. If the self is mentioned, it must always be remembered that what has been invoked is merely one aspect of the self, one that fits the purposes of this particular poem and is constructed by the instruments available to this poem—its images, its location, its syntax. If sorrows or needs or desires appear, nobody grander than ourselves can be there to attend to them, help us with them or console our afflictions.

Thus, when we come to the poem "Chickamauga," none of the "warmer" tones of lyric are permitted to attend on the scene. No Civil War color and drama, no embattled Southern polemics, no grief even. There are five stanzas, arranged in Chinese-box fashion. In the middle is the peregrine face of the poet, to whom Chickamauga is a place of haunting significance. Readers cannot know the poet's human face; it lies under the mask of the poem. The masked face is bracketed, fore and aft, by history—first, by history in its cold indifference (discarding all of us "like spoiled fruit"); and second, by history as the trawling force that will haul us up, like fish, into its clarifying light and air where we cannot but suffocate. But this apparently omnipotent history, too, is bracketed fore and aft: by landscape, which banally outlives the history of the battle, and by language, the other enduring, transhistorical force.

Wright's structure—face enclosed by poem, face and poem enclosed by history, history enclosed by landscape and language—is in itself a powerful truth-telling geometry of destiny:

## Chickamauga

Dove-twirl in the tall grass.
                        End-of-summer glaze next door
On the gloves and split ends of the conked magnolia tree.
Work sounds: truck back-up-beep, wood tin-hammer, cicada, fire horn.

———

History handles our past like spoiled fruit.
Mid-morning, late-century light
                             calicoed under the peach trees.
Fingers us here. Fingers us here and here.

———

The poem is a code with no message:
The point of the mask is not the mask but the face underneath,
Absolute, incommunicado,
               unhoused and peregrine.

———————

The gill net of history will pluck us soon enough
From the cold waters of self-contentment we drift in
One by one
               into its suffocating light and air.

———————

Structure becomes an element of belief, syntax
And grammar a catechist,
Their words what the beads say,
                    words thumbed to our discontent.

Such a poem will not be your choice if you are set on lyric that main-
tains the illusion of a direct mimetic personal speech by "suppressing" its
status as composed and measured language. It will also not be your choice
if you prefer "language poetry," which dispenses with structure, syntax and
grammar as authoritarian hegemonic structures that limit what can be said
within them.

Wright offers the interesting example of a poet who wants to ac-
knowledge in each of his poems that a poem is a coded piece of lan-
guage and yet wants also to express, by that very code, the certainty that
a piece of language exhibiting structure, grammar and syntax is not
"found art," but has been arranged by a questing human consciousness
forever incommunicado beneath its achieved mask. He is not alone in
his double desire. The foregrounding of the artifactual status of the lyric
is common coin these days. What makes Wright unusual is his ascetic
practice, his insistence on holding the rest of the poem to account under
this double truth of incommunicado humanity and admitted inhuman-
ness: nothing in the poem is allowed to ignore the strict metaphysics of
its conception.

The "warm" tones of polemic, confession, startle and fear—all those
"immediacies" of direct expression—are forbidden him by his distanced
and meditated stance. His poems, looked at from one perspective, lie
about us like the life-masks they are: immobile, "placed," shaped,
blanched. And yet, from another perspective, his poems are alive, as they
struggle toward the transfiguration of still-life that they will, at their end,
achieve. There are two signs of livingness in Wright, one proper to indi-
vidual poems, the other proper to his total oeuvre: there is temporality, as
the present-tense of any given poem slowly modulates into its dead fu-
ture, and there is the change that takes place in the "objective" world, as
different poems call into being varying perceptions, often stimulated by
seasonal change.

After writing for a long time about the landscape of California, Wright moved several years ago to Virginia, and Charlottesville replaced Laguna Beach as the source of his images. Wright's usual "rule" of composition is that one or more images drawn from the landscape must set the musical tone of the poem. In "Lines After Rereading T. S. Eliot," the tone is set by Wright's own "wasteland between the brown / Apricot leaf and the hedge":

> The orchard is fading out.
> All nine of the fruit trees
> Diminish and dull back in the late Sunday sunlight.
> The dead script of vines
> scrawls unintelligibly
> Over the arbor vitae.

As the season changes, we see the same orchard transformed, no longer a "wasteland," in "Still Life with Spring and Time to Burn," which begins:

> Warm day, early March. The buds preen, busting their shirtwaists
> All over the plum trees. Blue moan of the mourning dove.
> It's that time again,
> time of relief, time of sorrow
> The earth is afflicted by.
> We feel it ourselves, a bright uncertainty of what's to come
>
> Swelling our own skins with sweet renewal, a kind of disease
> That holds our affections dear
> and asks us to love it.
> And so we do, supposing
> That time and affection is all we need answer to.

For some, Wright says, time and affection may be the sole standards. But like Hopkins, who, after crying out "Nothing is so beautiful as Spring," had to answer to his own awareness of the eschatological ("Have, get, before it cloy, / Before it cloud, Christ, Lord, and sour with sinning"), Wright cannot rest in the sensuous moment. He "spoils" every such moment with his Eliot-like vision of "the skull beneath the skin." I pick up the spring poem where I cut it off:

> And so we do, supposing
> That time and affection is all we need answer to.
> But we guess wrong:
>
> Time will append us like suit coats left out overnight
> On a deck chair, loose change dead weight in the right pocket,
> Silk handkerchief limp with dew,
> sleeves in a slow dance with the wind.

And love will kill us—
Love, and the winds from under the earth
                            that grind us to grain-out.

"But we guess wrong." The guess that hazards everything on time and af-
fection omits too much for Wright, whose mind is saturated with death and
the chilling Midas-petrifaction of words. His "But we guess wrong" is a
close cousin of Milton's remark on pagan mythographers: "So they relate,
erring." Milton could not lightly employ Greek mythology, because he con-
sidered it an imaginative fiction that belied the Christian truth to which he
was obliged to adhere. Wright, bound no less straitly by the truths of death
and arranged language, sees the immediate sensuous life (when offered in
language) as no less a mythological fiction than the gods on Parnassus.

During his thirty-year span of writing, Wright has investigated many
ways of folding death into life, absence into presence, deconstruction into
construction. He has tried abstract titles; poems with notes attached so
that details could be left out; titles specifying the occasion that the fol-
lowing poem could be general; white space; desiccation of means; re-
moteness of stance; atemporality of narration. He has invoked a cluster of
authenticating poets, artists and musicians for his aesthetic practice:
Dante, Hopkins, Dickinson, Hart Crane, Pound, Eliot, Tu Fu, Trakl,
Montale; Piero della Francesca, Cézanne, Morandi; and here in
*Chickamauga* there appear, among others, Elizabeth Bishop, Lao Tzu,
Wang Wei, Paul Celan, Miles Davis and Mondrian. More than most
poets, Wright has owned up to being a site traversed by the languages,
images and tones of others, from Christian mystics to composers of
country music. The religious yearning that used to find a home in doc-
trine is now, in that sense, homeless; but in Wright it persists in an urgent
form, demanding to be housed somewhere, anywhere—in image, in
landscape, in allusion, in geometry, in structure.

Piero's monumental figures with their glance fixed on something beyond
the canvas; Cézanne's patches of color on white canvas; Morandi's ghostly
bottles; Mondrian's repetitive figuration: all are symbols, to Wright, of the
austerity of construction that satisfies his sense of rightness. These painters
reprove the voluptuousness of the flesh, the heedlessness of the passing mo-
ment, the domesticities of contentment. The Chinese poets stand, in Wright,
for the observer lost in the observation, for Buddhist emptiness, and for the
stringencies of classic form. And the religious poets authenticate, for Wright,
what used to be called the analogical level of experience—that which is not
literal, nor figurative, nor emblematic, but which escapes direct representa-
tion by fact, or image, or emblem, and which drives poets to hints, intima-
tions and expressions of the ineffable. Country music and jazz are symbols
of indigenous rhythms known to Wright since his youth.

This, more or less, is the map of Wright's poetics. Since his readers do
not share all of Wright's talismanic obsessions, it has been his task to take
us under the tent of his poems and make us care, not so much for his

fetishes as for the harmonies that they create when they are assembled to-gether. "This is a lip of snow and a lip of blood," says a 1981 poem called "Childhood's Body": those who want lips of blood will be put off by the chill of snow, those who want lips of snow will be put off by the stain of blood. Readers of modern poetry are well aware of the voice of the body ("Dance, and Provençal song, and sunburnt mirth") and the voice of the mind ("Nothing that is not there and the nothing that is"), but it is rarer to find the voice of the soul, especially the soul in its still-embodied state, conscious of its lip of snow meeting the body's lip of blood.

None of these voices is interesting to poetry, of course, unless the heart is present, too. It is in the junction of feeling heart and embodied soul that Wright locates his poetry. "This is too *hard*," protests the un-willing reader: "let me subside into blood or snow, one or the other." The Wright poem creates an anxiety that is very difficult to live within, since its constantly ticking clock adds certain loss to each daily gain:

> The subject of all poems is the clock,
> I think, those tiny, untouchable hands that fold across our chests
> Each night and unfold each morning, finger by finger,
> Under the new weight of the sun.
> One day more is one day less.

What, then, are the rewards for subjecting oneself to the severity of Wright's pages, for living on his dissolving interface of feeling, between life and death? For a start, the brilliance of his images. His images, changing with the seasons, set the musical tone for each poem, and they are conceived in a manner that never ceases to astonish. One can never guess what word will come next on the page in a poem by Wright. Here is Venice, brilliant at night, dwindled at dawn, from *Chickamauga's* "Venexia I":

> Too much at first, too lavish—full moon
> Jackhammering light-splints along the canal, gondola beaks
> Blading the half-dark;
> Moon-spar; backwash backlit with moon-spark . . .
>
> Next morning, all's otherwise
> With a slow, chill rainfall like ragweed
>                             electric against the launch lights,
> Then grim-grained, then grey.
> This is the water-watch landscape, the auto-da-fé.

In this sequence of images, sexual and visual energy shrivels, as a torture of exhausted observation succeeds the Hopkinsian intoxication. That is one reason to live in the poem with Wright: that emotional accuracy and verbal plenitude. Another is the floating tide of his musical line, which lifts the reader along its irregular cadence, as in "Easter 1989":

Instinct will end us.
The force that measles the peach tree
                              will divest and undo us.

The power that kicks on
                    the cells in the lilac bush
Will tumble us down and down.
Under the quince tree, purple cross points, and that's all right

For the time being,
                    the willow across the back fence
Menacing in its green caul.

Anyone can hear, in this music, the perceptible turn between the first three sentences (variants on a single tune) and the fourth sentence, with its reticent irony at "For the time being." Just when Wright is being most biblical, the colloquial thrusts itself into the lines ("kicks on," "tumble us down," "and that's all right," "for the time being") and then something altogether unforeseeable—the "green caul" of the new—casts a ghastly light on the whole landscape.

If a reader wants more than the emotionally freighted image, more than the lift of a line, more than the heart's predicament between the snowy soul and the blooded body, then the poems by Wright that will linger most may be those that repeat religious promise in undoctrinal form. Here is the conclusion of Wright's Easter poem, at once biological and incandescent, borrowing its language from his earliest vocabulary for marvel, the Gospel resurrection:

Nubbly with enzymes,
The hardwoods gurgle and boil in their leathery sheaths.
Flame flicks the peony's fuse.
Out of the caves of their locked beings,
                              fluorescent shapes
Roll the darkness aside as they rise to enter the real world.

"We get no closer than next-to-it," Wright concedes, but he won't abandon the hope of propinquity to the invisible, the "definer of all things":

Something surrounds us we can't exemplify, something
Mindless and motherless,
                    dark as diction and twice told.
We hear it at night.
Flake by flake,
                    we taste it like tinfoil between our teeth.

Such an intuition is unprovable. Do we really hear it softly burying us, and taste it setting our teeth on edge, that unintelligible and aboriginal darkness? For those who do—who sense an enveloping and ethically burdening perplexity that is quite independent of personal tragedy, political evil or scientific ignorance—Wright's poems will appear as attempts to lift a curtain, to enlighten memory, to name the abandoned, to pierce into "the horned heart of the labyrinth," where "the unsayable has its say." Wright's Minotaur—more sinister than the original, because it is shapeless—awaits the reader.

In his generation, the generation of Ashbery, Rich, Ammons, Ginsberg, Plath and Merrill, Wright is perhaps closest to Plath in his intensity of the image, closest to Ammons in his sense of the sidereal. But he sounds like nobody else, and he has remained faithful to insights and intuitions—of darkness as of light—less than common in contemporary America.

DAVID BAKER

# *from* "On Restraint" (1996)

I am not concerned here with artistic timidity, moral constraint, or po-
lite decorum—that is, restraint as puritanic virtue—but rather with
tactics of restraint which allow us to gauge a poem's opposite pole, its
power and passion. Even Walt Whitman is at his most persuasive where his
enthusiasms are informed by subdued counter-pressures. In "Crossing
Brooklyn Ferry," those ominous, looming "dark patches," which accompany
his confessions of secular guilt, temper his later transcendental encourage-
ments to "flow on . . . with the flood-tide." The poem's polar forces—oblit-
eration and regeneration, liability and acceptance—hold themselves in a
kind of checks- and-balance. The result is precarious and powerful. Other
poets use different methods of restraint: Dickinson with her severe, compact
technique ("After great pain, a formal feeling comes—"); Bishop in her
very stance, what Jeredith Merrin calls an "enabling humility." Restraint can
ironize, enable, even sustain, a poet's great passions and wildness.

Charles Wright uses large, summary abstractions the way most poets use
images. His images alone sustain the oblique storylines of his poems.
These tactics are the reverse of most other poets. *Chickamagua* is an es-
sential collection of poetry from one of our most original poets, a lyric
master who continues to adjust and refine his complex poetic. Like most
of the other poets here considered, Wright is a Romantic, but he is more
expansive than Simic, more speculative than Kinnell, and more lavish
than Kelly. Readers of Wright's work will here rediscover his wide range
of influences and allusions: Southern idiom and landscape, Italian art and
culture, Continental surrealism, Oriental detail and clarity, as well as
jaunts into Vorticism, Imagism, and Futurism (as he quips in one poem
addressed to Charles Simic, those "who don't remember the Futurists are
condemned to repeat them").

Almost nothing ever happens in a Charles Wright poem. This is his
central act of restraint, a spiritualist's abstinence, where meditation is not
absence but an alternative to action and to linear, dramatic finality:

> Unlike a disease, whatever I've learned
> Is not communicable.
> A singular organism,
> It does its work in the dark.
>
> Anything that we think we've learned,
> we've learned in the dark.
> If there is one secret to this life, it is this life.

As here in "Mid-winter Snowfall in the Piazza Dante," Wright's speaker is nearly always physically static and rhetorically circular. He sits in his backyard "rubbing this tiny snail shell," he watches "the hills empurple and sky [go] nectarine," he eats "*gnocchi* and roast veal" at a *caffè* in Florence, and he ponders. We might understand something more of Wright's aesthetic by noticing that "sitting" and "reading" are the primary titular participles in the first sections of this book, while "waiting," "watching," and "looking" come at the end. In the middle (and all the way through) he is talking and talking. The eye becomes a voice. Even given his bounty of allusions and references, I think Wright's truest forebear is Emerson, whom he never mentions. In "Circles," perhaps his most difficult and lovely essay, Emerson could be prescribing Wright's revolving imagery and rhetorical stance: "Conversation is a game of circles. In conversation we pluck up the *termini* which bound the common of silence on every side." Wright's voice throughout *Chickamauga* is conversational—never lax, never dull, but also never spoken in the larger oratorical tone of Kinnell. If Wright seems continually to muse to an intimate friend, he also knows that the winding destination of language is also its extinction, that the real meanings—personal as well as historical—are ultimately "not communicable." Emerson in "Circles" concurs: "And yet here again see the swift circumscription! Good as is discourse, silence is better, and shames it."

There are precious few contemporary poets in whose work I find as much sheer wisdom as in Wright's. He is fearless in his use of grand generalities, as comfortable with "O we were abstract and true. / How could we know that grace would fall from us like shed skin, / That reality, our piebald dog, would hunt us down?" as with "Snip, snip goes wind through the autumn trees" ("Waiting for Tu Fu"). "Blaise Pascal Lip-syncs the Void" *begins* with the kind of summary realization at which most other poets' work strains to arrive: "It's not good to be complete. / It's not good to be concupiscent, / caught as we are / Between a the and a the, / Neither of which we know and neither of which knows us." Like Wallace Stevens, echoed in these lines, Wright treats the general (an "a") as a type of distinct particularity (a "the"). The abstract is as tangible and stimulating as any concrete detail. Emerson once more in "Circles": "Generalization is always a new influx of the divinity into the mind. Hence the thrill that attends it." Still, however thrilling, the operations of language ultimately persist in baffling Wright's desire for transcendence, as he says in "Looking Outside the Cabin Window, I Remember a Line by Li Po": "We who would see beyond seeing / see only language, that burning field."

Wright's affinity with Emerson is also apparent in his rhetoric. Emerson is invariably effective at the level of the sentence, but his paragraphs are often monuments to circular structure or to impressionistic meandering. That can be pretty damning for any essayist attempting philosophical stratagems, less troublesome for a poet of Wright's skill and orientation. Wright is indeed a master of the sentence, and his own circular movement in both the stanza and the section seems well-tuned to his thematic faith that "I remember the word and forget the word / although the word / Hovers in flame around me." Both Emerson and Wright glean considerable rhetorical power by varying the structure of their sentences, migrating with ease from the elongated compound-complex sentence to the clipped aphoristic kicker. I hear Emerson, and also Franklin, in pronouncements like these: "Ambition is such a small thing." "Prosodies rise and fall." "Words are wrong. / Structures are wrong." "This text is a shadow text." His diverse syntactic arrangements reinforce Wright's doubled persona, both ambitious and humble, and his very long lines are suited to contain his sentence variety. If Wright's language can seem too opulent or his line too thickened on occasion, veering toward the over-lavish, this quality is more frequent in *Zone Journals* than in the current volume. Far more often, the rich, flexible syntax is an apt partner for Wright's questing imagination.

I can, in fact, think of no other recent poet who can successfully deploy very long lines in such utterly non-narrative poems. In "Sprung Narratives," the book's longest poem at nine pages, Wright again refers to one of his masters as he alternately reveals and conceals his own strategy for story. Sprung rhythm, that endlessly weird and accurate self-description of Gerard Manley Hopkins's metric idiosyncracies, of course provides the trope for Wright's more extended application. Where Hopkins says that "the stresses come together," making a dense, nearly overlapping rhythmic pressure, Wright also suggests that memory is much less a narrative line than a series of bumping, elliptical shards, merging into and abandoning each other. The poem moves through many possible plots and settings—Wright's childhood, Italy in the 1960s, his seventeen years in Laguna Beach, his return "home" in Virginia—and yet, all along, Wright extinguishes story in favor of image, image in favor of abstraction: "Who knows what the story line / became. . . . The world is a language we never quite understand, / But think we catch the drift of." He urges himself toward a continued temperance, his deepest act of restraint: "Returned to the dwarf orchard, / Pilgrim, / Sit still and lengthen your lines, / Shorten your poems and listen to what the darkness says / With its mouthful of cold air." Wright's ascetic discipline is an instruction and an aesthetic. The whole world seems to orbit in a kind of meditative, slow circle around Wright's grave influence. That's the brilliant paradox throughout this big, powerful book. In a poetry where nothing ever happens, everything is possible.

JAMES LONGENBACH

*from* "Earned Weight" (1995)

" In living as in poetry," said James Merrill in "Overdue Pilgrimage to Nova Scotia," "your art / Refused to tip the scale of being human / By adding unearned weight." Even at a time when Elizabeth Bishop's light touch is fashionable, these lines remind us of how rarely a poet honors the circumscribed role that poetry plays in American culture. Poets have surely been on the defensive at least since the time of Plato. But more often than not, they have responded to an indifferent public by adding weight to what they do; Ezra Pound said that poets should be *acknowledged* legislators. Less common is a poet like Thomas Hardy, who turned from novels to poems (at least in part) because nobody paid any attention to poetry. "If Galileo had said in verse that the world moved," wrote the novelist weathering the publication of *Jude the Obscure*, "the Inquisition might have let him alone." Rather than exaggerating poetry's claim on our attentions, Hardy diminished it: by seeming to ask so little of themselves, his poems offer more than we could have imagined receiving. It's difficult to think of Hardy or Bishop or Merrill having any interest in the question *does poetry matter?* The danger of what Merrill called "unearned weight" looms in the language of any response.

I want to say much more about *A Scattering of Salts*, James Merrill's thirteenth and, following his death on February 6, final book of poems. But first I want to dwell on two other recent books, one by a poet reaching the midpoint of his career, the other by a poet who has nearly achieved the eminence that Merrill just left behind. Michael Collier and Charles Wright seem hardly to resemble Merrill (or each other); but like Merrill, they are extremely wary of unearned weight, especially when they find their own poems tipping the scale.

Charles Wright took on those challenges when he began writing the long-lined, meditative poems of *The Southern Cross*, published in 1981. As accomplished as Wright's earlier poems were, their precisions came to seem predictable. (It was Wright's diction that Robert Pinsky parodied in *The Situation of Poetry*. "The silence of my / blood eats fight like the / breath of future water.") Wright has never given up the image-freighted line, but throughout his past four books (collected in 1990 as *The World of the Ten Thousand Things*), he has written a much more ambitious kind of poetry—a poetry that no longer builds its precisions into artificially static structures. Paradoxically, these longer poems seem to honor "the world of the ten thousand things" more successfully than Wright's earlier, more modest productions: because they document not only the conclusions but the movements of thought, the poems earn their leaps from earthly things to metaphysical auras, and the words don't seem to strain against their own materiality. Taken in its entirety, *The World of the Ten Thousand Things* seems to me one of the great American long poems.

*Chickamauga* marks a new turning point in Wright's career. After Wallace Stevens completed the long poems of *The Auroras of Autumn*, he recognized that these sequences had become too tempting for him. He had lost the discipline of the short poem, and he set out in the last years of his life to curtail his hard-won extravagance. Over the past decade, Wright's poems have only become looser and longer (ultimately taking the form of poetic journals), and like Stevens's *The Rock, Chickamauga* is the result of a self-consciously imposed limitation. "Shorten your poems," Wright says to himself in "Sprung Narratives"; "I gaze at the sky and cut lines from my long poem," he says in "Broken English." Most of Wright's new poems fit neatly on one page, and, if anything, each poem seems more gorgeous than the one preceding it.

"East of the Blue Ridge, Our Tombs Are in the Dove's Throat" begins, as so many of Wright's poems do, with a figure in a landscape, waiting for "a sign of salvation." Rather than a world beyond, however, all Wright can see is the world of things:

> Five crows roust a yellow-tailed hawk from the hemlock tree next door,
> Black blood spots dipping and blown
> Across the relentless leeching
>              the sun pales out of the blue.
>
> We'd like to fly away ourselves, pushed
> Or pulled, into or out of our own bodies,
>                        into or out of the sky's mouth.
> We'd like to disappear into a windfall of light.
>
> But the numbers don't add up.
> Besides, a piece of jar glass
>              burns like a star at the street's edge,
> The elbows and knuckled limp joints of winter trees,
> Shellacked by the sunset, flash and fuse,
> Windows blaze
>              and earthly splendor roots our names to the ground.

One could almost think of this poem as "Anecdote of the Jar: Seventy-five Years Later." Like Stevens, Wright investigates the way in which a small, human-made thing portions out the landscape; but Wright's jar is broken, and however mundane, its power extends more plainly to an ethereal world.

Wright's turn toward smaller poems is the result of a metaphysical as well as formal dilemma. My use of the word *metaphysical*, which inevitably seems too weighty, is indicative of the dilemma: throughout the poems of *Chickamauga*, the word *small* is probably repeated more often than any other. "Better to concentrate on something close, something small," says Wright. The book opens with a meditation on a snail shell, and it closes with an inchworm. And in "Tennessee Line," Wright recalls a long journal he kept in 1958: his dissatisfaction with it sounds like a comment on his more recent journal-poems. "There's only the re-arrangement, the redescription / Of little and mortal things," he concludes. As much as Wright wants desperately to fly beyond the body, he distrusts his flights. And as a whole, *Chickamauga* seems to have been written out of a fear of unearned weight. "Ambition," Wright says in "Lines After Rereading T. S. Eliot," "is such a small thing."

Wright also registers dissatisfaction with his miniature world. Either explicitly or implicitly, many of the poems depend on a distinction between a static sense of the past (the mere recounting of events) and an animating sense of history (the mind's active re-creation of events). Wright wants to live "in history without living in the past"—to record not simply the life of things but the mind's constant reinvention of things. The signature quality of Wright's best poems is consequently their movement, embodying the process of thought: individual lines may seem hieratically still, but as one metaphor slides to another (each one more artfully improbable than the one before), the poems don't just record movement but make us feel it. "Sprung Narratives," perhaps the most stunning poem in the book, returns to several of Wright's familiar land-scapes (Tennessee, Italy, Laguna Beach), interweaving stories about the past with meditations on the process of memory. At its center, Wright re-calls an astonishing scene: a student priest, once a dancer, erupts into movement on the beach at Ostia.

> Spot, pivot and spin . . . Spot, pivot and spin . . .
>                                         Esposito breaks
> From the black-robed, black-cordovaned
> Body of student priests
>                     and feints down the wave-tongued sand
> Like a fabulous bird where the tide sifts out and in.
>
> His cassock billows and sighs
> As he sings a show tune this morning at Ostia,
> Rehearsing the steps and pirouettes
>                             he had known by heart once
> Last year in another life.

Remembering and reinventing the romantic topos of the dancer (Yeats is invoked here and elsewhere in *Chickamauga*), this scene is an emblem for Wright's own ambition: to be earthly and yet credibly transcendent, delightful and yet utterly serious, mindful of the past and yet constantly in motion.

I like Wright's poems best when he allows them to become a little an-
ecdotal—when he dirties the gorgeous surface with more homespun dic-
tion: not "Full moon, the eighth of March; clouds / Cull and disperse"
but "I've always liked the view from my mother-in-law's house at night."
One danger of Wright's style—one he recognizes—is that everything in
the world becomes an emblem. In sharp contrast to Michael Collier's
poems, Wright's are full of names but lacking in people, focused on land-
scapes but lacking a sense of place. How welcome, how necessary, are the
lines that end the book:

> Meanwhile, let's stick to business.
> Everything else does, the landscape, the absolute, the invisible.
> My job is yard work—
> I take this inchworm, for instance, and move it from here to there.

This self-deprecating humor is completely at home within the strategi-
cally circumscribed ambitions of *Chickamauga*, but the tone of the book
is far more often autumnal. Wright's head is full of the rhythms of the ode
"To Autumn": "City of masks and minor frightfulness." And if *small* is the
most commonly repeated word in the book, *again* must appear nearly as
often. "Looking Again at What I Looked At for Seventeen Years" is a typ-
ical title: Wright seems to feel that all he can do is spin new variations on
a limited number of subjects and scenes. This is without question the
source of his strength (as it was Stevens's), but I sometimes found myself
wishing that *Chickamauga* didn't seem quite so world-weary quite so
often. "How imperceptibly we become ourselves," says Wright, and he
seems aware, writing in the wake of *The World of the Ten Thousand Things*,
that he may have become too utterly, too completely himself.
*Chickamauga* is a beautiful book, bearably human yet in touch with the
sublime; I would not want to be deprived of any of its poems. But I can't
help wondering what Charles Wright—who must be thought of as one
of our living masters—could possibly do next.

CAROL MUSKE-DUKES

# Guided by Dark Stars (1997)

Autobiography is what Charles Wright has been writing—in poetic form—for over 30 years. It has been an uncommon kind of life accounting, and his new book, *Black Zodiac*, extends his oblique definition. For a life story, in Wright's terms, exists as much in what is not there as in what is. In *Black Zodiac*, as the title hints, Wright ruminates on the "dark stars" that guide our fates and provide the contrast that shapes us: the shadow, the photograph's negative, the mirror's reversals. He tracks the unspoken but heard, the unseen but sensed—the system of "signs" (including language itself) that creates us as surely as we believe we create it.

His emphasis on non-emphasis highlights a sharp division of perspective in contemporary poetry, one that has become increasingly politicized: the difference between poems concerned with the self's primacy (expressed traditionally by the narrative poem or, in more insistent form, by the poem of testimony or memoir-poem) and the so-called subjectless poem.

Wright is not unmindful of this controversy and its implications. (Not for nothing is the book's jacket a reproduction of the ideograms of the Tang Dynasty poet Huai Su's "Autobiographical Essay," surrounded by columns of dark scribbled "glyphs.") His response has been to eschew all poetic soapboxing and squabbles over turf and to concentrate on telling the "life story" of words themselves—by generating a hauntingly personal syntax. His contexts float like clouds, his startling impressions are "untied to incident," as one critic has observed. They imply the ultimate impossibility of a story yet somehow deliver, whole and integrated, a psyche, a poet's soul. His style is not to be confused with the meandering texts of theory groupies. Though he writes what appears to be shimmy-lined, loose-limbed scattershot topography—of narrative fragment, psalm drift and other musical scat, meditation, prayer, homage (to poets, visual artists, ancient philosophers, theologians), jokes and lyric graffiti—appearances dissemble. What mortars these jagged shards is the dead sure rhythms of a near-perfect ear. Wright combines an impeccable musical and prosodic sense with the kind of humility possessed by the masters (with the exception of Pound, to whose *Cantos* Wright is stylistically indebted). But it is, finally, Dante whom Wright most emulates in both spirit and substance—in his use of the lyrical demotic and his aspiration to the arc of knowledge informing his "trilogy" sequences. The echoes range from Montale to the Tang Dynasty's Tu Fu, yet Wright is most at home in his role as sly amanuensis, taking dictation as a shadow-scribe of language itself:

And my name? And your name?
>                      Where will we find them, in what pocket?
Wherever it is, better to keep them there not known—
Words speak for themselves, anonymity speaks for itself.

Words indeed speak for themselves in these poems—even if
"anonymity" does not. For all his iconoclasm, Wright is hardly unknown:
most contemporary poets could draw a bead on a Charles Wright line
after five words. He is steady author of a sprung-rhythm signature riff
that runs just east of the Blue Ridge and a little west of Gerard Manley
Hopkins:

>  Dogwood insidious in its constellations of part-charred cross points,
>  Spring's via Dolorosa
>                      flashed out in a dread profusion,
>  Nowhere to go but up, nowhere to turn, dead world-weight,
>
>  They've gone and done it again,
>                      dogwood,
>  Spring's sap-crippled, arthritic, winter-weathered, myth limb,
>  Whose roots are my mother's hair.

This rapid-fire riptide stanza turns and returns like a double mirror.
(Note how "dogwood" begins each half refrain and is then followed by
"Spring's.") The poet has counted every syllable, every stress. What is owed
to the psalm here is the long-line leitmotif, energized by each line's initial
hard stresses. What is owed to the extension and retraction of the reitera-
tive seven-syllable line is the dramatic sense of ascent, then descent, as the
eye climbs the tree and then moves down. What is owed to the visual
arrangement of the words on the page is a painterly accumulation of rich
and mirrored detail: the "constellations of part-charred cross points" turn-
ing the starlike blossoms of the dogwood into the Saviour's gibbet.
("Dogwood" flips to "godwood," another name for the crucifix; "dog" and
"god" is a favorite Wright reversal.) We see as well as hear the up and
down. We move from the flowering branches above, down to where the
tree's roots intertwine with the grave, the realm of the dead, with the un-
forgettable sight-and-sound shock of "my mother's hair."

Wright's ability to see in the dark in *Black Zodiac*, his "star-crossed,"
star-dark maps, have drawn him as close as he's ever come to an esthetic de-
fense. To quote from the same poem above, his own version (after Cardinal
Newman) of "Apologia Pro Vita Sua," which makes up the first of the
book's five sections:

>  Journal and landscape
>  —Discredited form, discredited subject matter—
>  I tried to resuscitate both, breath and blood,
>                      making them whole again.

Through language, strict attention—
*Verona mi fe', disfecemi Verona*, the song goes.
I've hummed it, I've bridged the break

To no avail.

The weariness and the lordiness of that passage (not to mention as
sacramental aspects) are not random; they demonstrate this poet's strug-
gle to stay humble. Wright, in his Father Hopkins collar and chasuble, can
occasionally sound like Jesus Christ crestfallen. But his sense of humor
usually intervenes to lighten up those heavy footfalls on the road to
Calvary:

The Unknown Master of the Pure Poem walks nightly among his roses,
The very garden his son laid out.
Every so often he sits down. Every so often he stands back up . . .

Yet his defense of poetry—its traditional models of learning that re-
quires "strict attention"—is dead serious. When he speaks of "journal and
landscape," he is not only reiterating his lifelong commitment to these
two disciplines, he is reaffirming the value of apprenticeship to the unre-
lenting standards of formal representation that are now "discredited." For
the fledgling artist or poet, as for the master, the elements of landscape
and life drawing, the systematic recovering of reverie and reflection in
daily notation, teach the same lesson: observe what is there and then how
it is not there. The diminishment of these lessons feels symptomatic to
Wright of our age:

*There's nothing out there but light,*
                              the would-be artist said,
As usual just half right:
There's also a touch of darkness, everyone knows, on both sides of both
    horizons. . . .
His small palette, however, won't hold that color.
                              though some have, and some still do.

or:

How Gyges of Lydia
Once saw his own shadow cast
                              by the light of a fire
And instantly drew his own outline on the wall with charcoal . . .
Learn to model before you learn how to finish things.

This stern warning to the neophyte from a seasoned artist hints at a
new voice for Wright, whose indifference to conventional autobiography
in no way prevents his donning of a dramatic persona. If he has now put
on the cloak of weathered sage, the "flashes" from his past illuminate a
hell-bent-for-leather youth in Tennessee:

> We're after deadbeats, delinquent note payers, in Carter's words.
> Cemetery plots—ten dollars a month until you die or pay up.
> In four months I'll enter the Army, right now I'm Dr. Death,
>
> Riding shotgun for Carter, bringing more misery to the miserable.
> Up-hollow and down-creek, shack after unelectrified shack—
> The worst job in the world, and we're the two worst people in it.

Beyond these minor indictments, the really persuasive part of his es-
thetic defense is his own "bridging of the break," his demonstration in
poem after poem—hardly "to no avail" as he says—that he is still riding
the thermals, negotiating the rapids with his characteristic grace and in-
vention. A young poet can look at these poems to see how it is done. In
"Disjecta Membra" (translated as "scattered parts," borrowed from Guido
Ceronetti's commonplace book, *The Science of the Body*) he walks his same
old lyric tightrope, but longs, as always, for landscape as a kind of thresh-
old leading toward death or insight:

> Acolyte at the altar of wind,
> I love the idleness of the pine tree,
>                                         the bright steps into the sky.
> I've always wanted to lie there, as though under earth,
> Blood drops like sapphires, the dark stations ahead of me
> Like postal stops on a deep journey.
> I long for that solitude,
>                         that rest,
> The bed-down and rearrangement of all the heart's threads.

Invisible forms resident in the visible (and illuminated by sources as
diverse as the Gnostic Gospels and Gertrude Stein) haunt the twenty
powerful poems of this book. Each of these poems reinstates the notion
of "inscape"—which Hopkins defined as the "soul" of objects and events
visible to the poet's inner eye—miraculously reproduced in poetic form.
"You've got to write it all down," Wright reminds himself in the title
poem. That is what he has done, recording "memory's handkerchief,
death's dream and automobile," and then refining that canvas as a great
painter refines: "Words and paint, black notes, white notes."

He has been an East Tennessee pilgrim, bard on the prowl in Italy,
worshiper of the Tang Dynasty, counter of stars on the southern
California coast (where his students called him Captain Dog), and now
the ageless Virginia sacerdotal poet. Yet each of these selves functions as
Hopkins conceived the word, as a verb—as in "Each mortal thing does
one thing and the same" it "selves." Charles Wright is that verb—and we
will never entirely define him.

DAVID YOUNG

# *from* "Looking for Landscapes" (1998)

W hy do I like landscape poems? What makes me hunt for them in new books, among poets familiar and unfamiliar? My rea-sons are manifold, not easily separated, but I'll attempt a sketchy list.

- Consider the painting analogy for a moment. A painter can't under-take a landscape without diminishing the scale of, and attention to, the human. If human figures are included—by no means a require-ment—their relative importance will have to be different than it would be in a portrait or a historical picture or a genre scene. They will be placed within a context that makes them less significant. If you compare the two accounts of Brueghel's *Landscape with the Fall of Icarus* by W. H. Auden and by William Carlos Williams, you will see that Williams understood this particular meaning and feature of landscape painting even more acutely than Auden did.
- Similarly, a poem that is set in a landscape tells me that the poet is trying in some way to look beyond the ego, beyond the communal and, indeed, beyond the human. Not to exclude these things, in most cases, but to place them in some sort of perspective, next to the larger creation they inhabit and interact with. This means the poem is less likely to be excessively personal, discursive, ideological, and anthropocentric. Since I think too much contemporary poetry suf-fers from these excesses, I can look to landscape poems for some re-lief.
- Interior and exterior are likely to cohabit in exciting ways in land-scape poems. If such poems are good, they won't—can't—com-pletely be one or the other. The exterior landscape will invoke memory, feeling, rumination, history, and large issues of conscious-ness, perception, even metaphysics. The interior one will at least be occupied with reifying and objectifying the perceiver's inner world in terms of the outer, mediating and qualifying self-absorption. The mix is surely healthy.
- I actually believe, perhaps quaintly, that poets can and should hope to function, still, in their most ancient role, that of the shaman, liv-ing out on the margin of the village, between the community and the larger creation, with all its mysteries, wonders and terrors. David Abram's book, *The Spell of the Sensuous*, has some useful things to say about this topic. As he points out, shamans, dwelling between nature and community, so to speak, can mediate between the needs and

interests of the community and the world that lies beyond, the plants, the animals, the ecosystem—indeed, the cosmos. We poets no longer get to practice magic, healing spells, and rituals, but we can and do still practice those old forms of mediation, in many, many ways.

- It is mediation between language and what lies beyond language too. When a poet writes a landscape poem, I know that he or she is apt to be working on that interface between the natural and human where so many important issues are confronted. Art and nature argue, dance, and turn into each other. "This is an art that nature makes" (Shakespeare). An old practice, but still a good one.

So I have been looking among new collections of poetry on our review shelf, for good landscape poems. Not all the books that were published this year got sent to us, so my research is by no means comprehensive.

Our past and present master of the landscape poem is probably Charles Wright, whose Italy, Tennessee, Laguna Beach and Charlottesville panoramas have come to inhabit our imaginations and shape our poetic sensibilities and vocabularies over nearly the span of a generation. To note that this is the twentieth anniversary of *China Trace*, in which this project was already well underway, and in which the landmark poem "Invisible Landscape" appeared, is to realize with a start how long and how consistently Wright has been turning out finely tuned and sharply etched studies of the natural world, charged always with the invisible world as well. The unanswerable question of how to reckon and understand our place within nature unfolds and then unfolds again within this enterprise, haunting the poet and his readers just as it has haunted humanity since we first came to consciousness. The newest collection, *Black Zodiac*, shows Wright still moving forward, building on his own achievement, using his expertise at landscape representation to layer tonalities and possibilities, teasing himself about the whole enterprise as he goes.

I have a friend who protests with dismay about what he calls "the new pretentiousness" in current American poetry (he especially instances Jorie Graham), and I have to admit to him that a lot of what we are seeing these days is pretty Baroque, or even Rococo, a little too pleased with itself to please anyone else for very long. But my friend is wrong to include Charles Wright in his blanket condemnation, because that reaction overlooks the humor and self-deprecation that attend Wright's undertaking at every turn. Knowledge of failure and wry mortification are part and parcel of each poem he produces, so that rather than giving us yet another dose of Southern gothic or Mandarin high talk, he is mocking such things, in himself and others, as he goes. Readers just tuning in may find themselves a little startled; those who have followed the project from its earlier stages to the present will have a better grasp of why and how these complicated poems came to be the way they are.

Here's an example:

## OCTOBER II

October in mission creep,
                        autumnal reprise and stand down.
The more reality takes shape, the more it loses intensity—
Synaptic uncertainty,
Electrical surge and quick lick of the minus sign,
Tightening of the force field
Wherein our forms are shaped and shapes formed,
                        wherein we pare ourselves to our attitudes . . .

Do not despair—one of the thieves was saved; do not presume—
        one of the thieves was damned,
Wrote Beckett, quoting St. Augustine.
It was the shape of the sentence he liked, the double iambic pentameter:
It is the shape that matters, he said.
Indeed, shape precludes shapelessness, as God precludes Godlessness.
Form is the absence of all things. Like sin. Yes, like sin.

It's the shape beneath the shape that summons us, the juice
That spreads the rose, the multifoliate spark
                        that drops the leaf
And darkens our entranceways,
The rush that transfigures the maple tree,
                the rush that transubstantiates our lives.
October, the season's signature and garnishee,
October, the exponential negative, the plus.

I spoke of Wright's "layering" of effects because that is how I see the as-
sembling of such different attitudes and utterances into a single whole.
We must react to the diction and imagery, as well as the movement, in
terms that take us outside our expectations for what belongs in one
place, and in a poem. "Mission creep," for example, is from military and
media parlance, along with "stand down." The "minus sign" and "expo-
nential negative" are math terminology, while "force field" belongs to
physics and "synaptic" to neuroscience. "Signature and garnishee" are ba-
sically lawyer talk. "Transubstantiates" is theological, and "iambic pen-
tameter," of course, is poetry lingo. All this coexists with Beckett and St.
Augustine doing hermeneutical turns with bits of the Bible. And with
the speaker's attempt to understand the relations of form and formless-
ness, shape and shapelessness, both in the ultimate sense and in the spe-
cific day and month around him. He senses that our sensing of the world
orders it but also distorts and disfigures it, but he doesn't know what to
do about that, other than notice it.
    The middle stanza may just be too abstruse for most folks, but I like
the way it both signals the limits of language, in paradox, and genuinely

bumps past them for a moment. It carries the double tone of amusement and ultimate seriousness that I tell my friend should disarm his accusations of pretentiousness.

I think the landscape design helps do that too. The speaker is in a specific place and time. He lets his mind and imagination wander, imperiling both place and time as present realities, but he reassures us by bringing us back, to the maple tree that starts in "mission creep" and ends in a rush of transfiguration, making the world the place where we can hope to learn about the ultimate mysteries. At the end, we find him trying, a little desperately, a little bemusedly, to characterize the month of October, to put an epithet on the month that will do it justice. I think he fails, and knows he fails, and means that we should know that too. The poem's success, in other words, lies in its acknowledged failures, the ways language and perception won't get at what they most want to witness and identify.

See if these ideas about Wright's emphases make sense when applied to the next selection:

CHINA MAIL

It's deep summer east of the Blue Ridge.
Temperatures over 90 for the twenty-fifth day in a row.
The sound of the asphalt trucks down Locust Avenue
Echoes between the limp trees.
                          Nothing's cool to the touch.

Since you have not come,
The way back will stay unknown to you.
And since you have not come,
                          I find I've become like you,
A cloud whose rain has all fallen, adrift and floating.

Walks in the great void are damp and sad.
Late middle age. With little or no work,
                          we return to formlessness,
The beginning of all things.
*Study the absolute*, your book says. But not too hard,

I add, just under my breath.
Cicadas ratchet their springs up to a full stop
                          in the green wings of the oaks.
This season is called white hair.
Like murdered moonlight, it keeps coming back from the dead.

Our lives will continue to turn unmet,
                          like Virgo and Scorpio.
Of immortality, there's nothing but old age and its aftermath.
It's better you never come.
How else would we keep in touch, tracing our words upon the air?

Will I startle readers if I say this is one of the funniest poems in *Black Zodiac*? It comes into focus gradually. When you reach the notes at the back, you find out, if you hadn't picked it up before, that it's a dialogue with Du Fu (Tu Fu), the great Chinese poet. His is the voice mixed in with the poet's, and the poem's weaving together of the two sensibilities teases our tendencies to want to encapsulate wisdom. Here it's not so much that assembling of different jargons and dictions by means of which "October II" unsettled its own solemn tone: it's more like outright self-parody, both by Du Fu and the poet.

Look at the opening of the second stanza. On one level, it's profound, or pseudo-profound, like a great deal of, say, *The Four Quartets*. On another, it's just plain funny, like Henry Reed's parody of Eliot, "Chard Whitlow." And look at the opening line of the third stanza. Is it possible to take that statement seriously? Ditto the close of that stanza, undercutting itself as Wright and Tu Fu both deprecate their own advice and seriousness.

The levels of tone and the range of reference are the special pleasures afforded by these expert poems. The Du Fu poem is funny but also touching, a tribute that is heartfelt as well as self-deprecating. The landscape effect, meanwhile, serves to emphasize the way that the speaker, stuck in a hot summer in Virginia, can't free himself enough to read his "China mail" without feeling sorry for himself, about the heat, about his current lack of inspiration, about the distance between past and present, mortality and immortality. All those Chinese poems in which one poet invites another to come visit, for the special pleasures of the place and season, lie behind this wicked self-parody, teasing itself about its own dark mood.

Wright understands how useful landscape is, and he also understands its limitations and pitfalls. He's creating a late-twentieth-century equivalent to that great Chinese tradition, and he's smuggling natural beauty and the value of the nonhuman as a check to our own self-infatuation as a species, back into poems where we thought it could no longer cohabit with our pains, anxieties, and over-refined responses. Here's how this wonderful collection ends, the last two sections of a thirteen-page poem called "Disjecta Membra":

Is *this* the life we long for,
                              to be at ease in the natural world,
Blue rise of Blue Ridge
Indented and absolute through the January oak limbs,
Turkey buzzard at work on road-kill opossum, up
And flapping each time
A car passes and coming back
                              huge and unfolded, a black bed sheet,
Crows fierce but out of focus high up in the ash tree,
Afternoon light from stage left
Low and listless, little birds

Darting soundlessly back and forth, hush, hush?

Well, yes, I think so.

———

Take a loose rein and a deep seat,

John, my father-in-law, would say

To someone starting out on a long journey, meaning, take it easy,
Relax, let what's taking you take you.
I think of landscape incessantly,

mountains and trees, lost lakes

Where sunsets festoon and override,
The scald of summer wheat fields, light-licked and
   poppy-smeared.
Sunlight surrounds me, and winter birds

doodle and peck in the dead grass,

I'm emptied, ready to go. Again
I tell myself what I've told myself for almost thirty years—
Listen to John, do what the clouds do.

★

I come to the end of this exploration of my pleasures with the handling of landscape in three new books of poetry dogged by that uneasy feeling which often shadows an emphatic use of terminology: I haven't really defined the particulars of "a landscape poem" in a way that firmly delineates a category or genre. Poetry is like that, I think. Borders exist so that they may shift, formulas are invented so they can be violated. If it isn't broken, break it.

Still, I think I have marked out some familiar and coherent territory. There's the matter of canny uses of perspectives, sizable and multiple. There's the practice of extending regard beyond the human sphere to permit an interaction with the nonhuman. There is inclusiveness and there is the kind of layering that allows radically different subjects and emotions to coexist harmoniously in a poem. I confess, as a reader, to a sympathetic response to poems that put me in a place where I can see and sense a lot, take in what I have sometimes called a panorama—*vista* is another word I might have used, echoing Whitman, among others.

I have found myself thinking of other poets—Eamon Grennan, Pattiann Rogers—whose use of "landscape" I would like to go back and explore. I've remembered with pleasure a reading from last fall, when Gary Snyder performed "The Mountain Spirit," a late section of *Mountains and Rivers Without End* that transforms and parodies elements of an ancient Japanese Nō play to create an encounter in the Sierras that has much of the same thrilling spirituality and playful humor that I've been admiring in Charles Wright. And I've remembered thereby to go back to an article by Bonnie Costello, in *The Point Where All Things Meet*, that deals with "Three Contemporary Landscape Poets."

Costello posits three kinds of landscape poet: the immanentist, the analogist, and the transcendentalist, with Snyder, Ammons and Wright exemplifying each category. She also summons Stevens (the first half of the article's title is "The Soil and Man's Intelligence") and Whitman as significant predecessors in an American tradition of landscape poems.

Terminology and categories do tend to beget more terminology and categories, and I think the jury is still out on whether those three classifications of hers are really all that helpful. But I certainly like what she says at the close of her discussion:

> One function of the poetry of our time (a function served by a variety of aesthetics) is to find a rhetoric in which description and abstraction are openly reciprocal, in which poetic authority thrives on an attachment to soil, artifice on realism, in which percept is not the master or object of thought but the source of its renewal.

Remembering that "percept" means "the meaningful impression of any object obtained by use of the senses," I can see, as she does, why American poets turn to the landscapes they inhabit and visit to create vistas of comprehension and association that will make poetry begin to do what Stevens says it ought to do: help us to live our lives.

# Appalachia (1999)

Charles Wright's last book, the Pulitzer Prize-winning *Black Zodiac*, ended with the admission that Wright was still "starting out on a long journey." With the publication of *Appalachia*, the journey has come to an end. Following *Chickamauga* and *Black Zodiac*, *Appalachia* completes not only a trilogy of books but a trilogy of trilogies—a Dantean cosmology that Wright has been pondering for thirty years. These days, when open-ended process has out-moded the well-wrought urn, Wright stands apart as a poet who insists that "what's at the road's end" is more important than the road. But since Wright is no slouch when it comes to openness (his *The World of the Ten Thousand Things* is an aleatory poetic journal) the compulsion to find the end—the absolute, the source—feels earned. *Appalachia* drives head-long into the end of things and does not shy away from the beauty it finds there.

Wright's first trilogy of books, later winnowed and collected in *Country Music* (1982), offers a highly compressed autobiography, tracing Wright's spiritual journey from the soil to the stars. In the next three books, gathered with a coda in *The World of the Ten Thousand Things* (1990), Wright adopts more wayward structures, his long lines reaching in countless directions at once. The trilogy which *Appalachia* concludes feels like a synthesis of the first two. Like *Country Music* it is dominated by short, often gnomic poems rather than sequences, but like *The World of the Ten Thousand Things* it feels expansive, journal-like. This complex effect is most fully achieved in *Appalachia*, whose forty-five poems are organized both temporally (unfolding in time) and spatially (following a predetermined pattern). While the poems appear in chronological order, tracing one soul's progress from February 1996 to August 1997, they are also divided into three sections—a trilogy in microcosm—each of which concludes with a poem called "Opus Posthumous." If we focus on the linear unfolding of the poems, *Appalachia* reads like a record of existential vicissitude, a traversing of the territory between spiritual plenitude and despair. If we focus on the book's tripartite structure, the book reads like a record of a pattern beneath experience, a foretelling that our lives will be made meaningful by the end towards which they move. "Hold on, old skeletal life," Wright intones in the first "Opus Posthumous," "there's more to come, if I hear right."

Wright was able to begin his life's work only when he glimpsed its end. "Light in the earth," he wrote long ago in an elegy for his mother, "the dead are brought / Back to us, piece by piece— / Under the sponged log, inside the stump." For thirty years Wright's subject has been the ghostly presences animating landscape, and now, at the end of the journey, he has named the landscape "appalachia"—a word that denotes simultaneously a particular place and a state of mind. Most of the poems of *Appalachia* take place in Wright's back yard in Charlottesville, Virginia: "This is our world. High privet hedge on two sides, half circle arborvitae." But even when the poems stray to Venice or Montana, they nonetheless constitute a page in what Wright calls "The Appalachian Book of the Dead." More precisely, the landscape itself is the page—riven with memories, arrested by metaphor. At times, this secret language stands beyond Wright's power of comprehension. More often, Wright recognizes that he himself is responsible for imagining the ghostly presences that elude him:

> I came to my senses with a pencil in my hand
> And a piece of paper in front of me.
> >                                   To the years
> Before the pencil, O, I was the resurrection.

Wright literally comes "to his senses"—comes to know the world—through the act of writing. And even if Wright does not assume that the power of metaphor necessarily provides him with a knowledge of destiny ("Still, who knows where the soul goes, / Up or down, after the light switch is turned off, who knows?"), there is no American poet who can match Wright's double-barrel mastery of visual description and aural delight. In lines like these, the back yard becomes a universe of possibility:

> Wick-end of August, wicked once-weight of summer's sink and sigh.

> Over the Blue Ridge, late March light annunciatory and visitational.

> Dogwood electrified and lit within by April afternoon late-light.

Each of these single lines constitutes a stanza in itself. Throughout his third trilogy Wright has written exclusively in self-contained stanzas of two to six lines, and in *Appalachia* this discipline is pushed to the extreme verge of possibility. *Appalachia* is Wright's least garrulous book since *China Trace* (the final book in the first trilogy), and renunciation is its key-note: "Abolish me, make me light." While Wright has often linked a fear of repeating himself to a dread of routine—the dailiness of work and the decay of the sexual body—all complaint has been banished from *Appalachia*. Wright's ascetic impulse is at times almost giddily austere: "The dream of reclusive life, a strict, essential solitude, / Is a younger hermit's dream." But the impulse infuses even the darkest moments of *Appalachia* with a quiet patience, a willingness to savor the beauty of each day's "minor Armageddon":

Jerusalem, I say quietly, Jerusalem,
The altar of evening starting to spread its black cloth
In the eastern apse of things—
    the soul that desires to return *home*, desires its own destruction.
We know, which never stopped anyone,
The fear of it and the dread of it on every inch of earth,
Though light's still lovely in the west
                  billowing, purple and scarlet-white.

As Wright's metaphors suggest, one sunset prepares us for each more harrowing Armageddon to come—the end of the season, the life, the work. The conclusion of thirty years of writing necessitates a confrontation with mortality and a perhaps even more harrowing appraisal of technique: "I cannot make it cohere," said Ezra Pound as the *Cantos* petered out. Given Wright's great strength—his ability to spin a universe of metaphor out of one small patch of grass—his greatest danger has been self-parody. But like Wallace Stevens more than any other modernist predecessor, Wright succeeds because he recognizes that repetition is both his curse and his salvation. His most beautiful poems exist on the hair-raising cusp between mastery and mannerism, between wholeness of vision and predictability of vision.

On the simplest level, repetition is described thematically in *Appalachia*: "love sees what the eye sees / Repeatedly." More profound are the intricate and manifold ways in which repetition determines the linguistic texture of the poems. Words are repeated within lines: "Green leaves. Clouds and sky. Green leaves. Clouds. Sky." Lines begin insistently with the same word: "Elsewhere . . . Elsewhere . . . Elsewhere." In "What Do You Write About, Where Do Your Ideas Come From" Wright repeats the phrase "never again," suggesting that what happens "never again" has been one of his lifelong preoccupations. But as the phrase recurs, the "never again" paradoxically recedes infinitely into the future. Each passing second of existence becomes a tiny apocalypse: "heart beat, / Never again and never again." And finally, only the "never again" itself is "never again" to be seen: "Everything up and running hard, everything under way, / Never again never again."

This variety of strategic repetitions transforms the possibility of dull routine into a ritualized metaphysical drama. While Wright notices with some impatience that "Children are playing their silly games / Behind the back yard," he discovers near the end of *Appalachia* that he loves "the sound of children's voices in unknown games." Routine becomes ritual when Wright sees himself—his own silly game—in the compulsively repeated games of childhood:

These things will come known to you,
                  these things make soft your shift,
Alliteration of lost light, aspirate hither-and-puff,
Afternoon undervoices starting to gather and lift off

In the dusk,
>Red Rover, Red Rover, let Billy come over,
Laughter and little squeals, a quick cry.

Listening and listening again, Wright discovers that the games we re-
peat, the poems we rewrite, are rehearsals for the final crossing: Red
Rover, Red Rover, let Charles come over.

Wright seems at every moment surprised to be alive. However
haunted, however elegiac, the work is buoyed by childlike wonder, and
even Wright's grandest effects are enabled by humility: the back yard be-
comes heaven on earth but never stops being "heartbreakingly suburban."
Coleridge defined the imagination as "a repetition in the finite mind of
the eternal act of creation in the infinite I AM." And in the most touch-
ing moment in *Appalachia*, Wright reverses this formulation, suggesting
that the creation of the infinite world is a repetition of the finite mind's
act of metaphor-making:

Wind lull, midmorning, tonight's sky
>light-shielded, monkish and grand
Behind the glare's iconostasis, yellow poppies
Like lip prints against the log wall, the dead sister's lunar words
Like lip prints against it, this is as far as it goes . . .

Wright's simile for the poppies ("Like lip prints") precedes and makes
possible the metaphor for the afterlife of Hildegarde Wright, to whose
memory *Appalachia* is dedicated.

She "lived there all her life," says Wright in the dedication, and no
matter how far he has traveled, so has Wright himself. Wright has been
mourning the dead for thirty years, surveying their landscape, wearing
their clothes, and his life's work is a record of possibility discovered
within persistence, of human limitation raised to the highest power.
Charles Wright's trilogy of trilogies—call it "The Appalachian Book of
the Dead"—is sure to be counted among the great long poems of the
century.

# Between Heaven and Earth (1999)

In Charles Wright's long career as a poet he has returned again and again to a few themes and subjects—the Appalachia where he grew up and the Italy where he has lived, personal and family history, favorite writers and painters. But the still center around which these themes whirl has always been Wright's metaphysical yearning, his desire for a mystical or religious transcendence that is seemingly impossible today. In *Appalachia*, Wright's thirteenth volume, that desire is more in evidence than ever. Despite the book's title, there is less here about Wright's native ground than in his previous work. The focus, rather, is on "God . . . the fire my feet are held to"; on the torment of wanting to believe and finding nothing that can secure belief.

The transcendence that Wright courts, and can never win, is left necessarily vague. His spiritual feeling is not Christian, though it is informed by Christianity, as well as by Eastern and Platonic ideas. It asks not for proof of any particular doctrine, but rather for a pre-theological affirmation that there is wholeness, beauty and meaning in the world and in our lives—"that pure grace / which is invisible and sure and clear." In search of such grace, Wright interrogates the heavens:

> The night sky is an ideogram,
> a code card punched with holes.
> It thinks it's the word of what's-to-come.
> It thinks this, but it's only The Library of Last Resort,
> The reflected light of The Great Misunderstanding.

And the earth:

> Roses and rhododendron wax glint
> Through dogwood and locust leaves,
> Flesh-colored, flesh-destined, spring in false flower . . .
>
> We haven't a clue as to what counts
> In the secret landscape behind the landscape we look at here.

But, as the lines acknowledge, what he is looking for lies in neither of these; grace is not in nature but beyond or behind it. And so it can only be described in symbols, of which light, for Wright as for Dante, is the most important:

All my life I've looked for this slow light, this smallish light
Starting to seep, coppery blue,
                                        out of the upper right-hand corner of things,
Down through the trees and off the back yard . . .

Until the clouds stop, and hush . . .
Until there is nothing else.

This fulfillment, however, remains always in the future tense, something to be wished for or despaired of, but never actually present. And so Wright's poetry is dialectical, asking and answering its own question, swaying back and forth between the moment of hope and the moment of realism:

The sacred is frightening to the astral body,
As is its absence.
                We have to choose which fear is our consolation.

Or, again:

We live in two landscapes, as Augustine might have said,
One that's eternal and divine,
and one that's just the back yard,
Dead leaves and dead grass in November, purple in spring.

Wright's poems, in their passionate hesitation, seem to be bowing down not to God but to the place where God used to be: a form of post-Nietzschean piety.

As might be expected, a spirit caught in this cul-de-sac, capable of neither true belief nor final resignation to unbelief, is a troubled one. Over the years, Wright has evolved a style that can communicate such a turbulent consciousness: the poems in *Appalachia* move in quick, jagged jumps, beginning with a dashed-off description or casual observation and then vaulting into the most elevated thoughts. His free-verse lines are loaded with compound words and heavy consonants, sometimes alliterative in the manner of Gerard Manley Hopkins, sometimes incantatory and repetitive like Sylvia Plath. And frequently those lines break into two shorter halves, as if to show us a caesura in the stream of consciousness.

Yet for all the agitation in Wright's style and mood, the poems in *Appalachia* have very little forward motion. Each of them returns to the same problem, the same dilemma, and comes away with the same frustration: Wright is "waiting for something to come—anything," but it never does. And while this monotony is not a defect, a sign of the poet's lack of skill, it is nonetheless a limitation.

It is a limitation that stems, ultimately, from Wright's very conception of what poetry should do. For Wright's spiritual dilemma itself—being trapped between the attractiveness of belief and its impossibility—is not a new one; we find much the same situation in Matthew Arnold, more than a century ago. The difference between them is that Arnold refused the completeness of spiritual conviction, but embraced the completeness of poetic form—the regularity and pattern that can make even the expression of doubt a confident, beautiful whole. Wright, like many serious poets today, refuses both kinds of completeness. He wants poetry to represent consciousness, to mirror the motions of the mind; and in this task, poetic form is not required, nor is extended, consecutive argument. These poems do not want to be made things, beautiful in their wholeness. They are, rather, faithfully incomplete, like the mind itself.

It is this refusal—the willingness to live without so much, both spiritually and poetically—that condemns the poems in *Appalachia* to turn continually upon themselves, allowing them neither sort of consummation. Yet it is also a product of Wright's particular integrity, and what makes his poetry such a significant and true reflection of our time.

# Ars Longa (1999)

Some long poems are born long; some achieve length; and some have length thrust upon them. In the beginning, there was an orderly sequence to a poet's career, from the lyric to the epic, and genres were steadied by tradition. In the nineteenth century, rigid categories and definitions loosened, and every stay or knot was next undone either by modernist poets or adventuresome readers. No one reads Whitman's *Leaves of Grass* as the long poem Whitman himself may have thought it, and some oddball critics have read a plot into Dickinson's discrete lyrics so they may be read as an epic. *The Waste Land* seems miniaturized next to, say, the *Idylls of a King*. Even so, it seems precision-tooled next to *The Cantos*, which Pound pursued as an epic—but did he ever have any idea where he was headed with that mishmash? *Paterson* too fizzled out. Hart Crane's *The Bridge* remains the purest and most successful example in our century of The Long Poem, grandly conceived, written at the pitch of epic elevation, its themes spanning centuries and continents.

It is more likely nowadays that our long poems become so after the fact. Berryman's *Dream Songs* began as a modest suite that over the years rose, as if by means of alcoholic yeast. Lowell's *History* took off in the two diaristic *Notebooks*, then climbed to the right altitude for the long traversal. Merrill's "Book of Ephraim," first part of another book, quadrupled in size on demand—the forces (i.e., his subject matter) insisting over the Ouija board that he sit not for witty conversations, as before, but for a series of complicated lessons. Other notable long poems, from Ted Hughes's *Crow* to Robert Pinsky's *An Explanation of America*, are really sequences of bite-sized lyrics or moral epistles, whereas a book-length poem like John Ashbery's *Flow Chart* just grows like Topsy.

With Charles Wright's new book, we are presented with an odder instance. The dust jacket of *Appalachia* states that "almost thirty years ago, Charles Wright began a poetic project of Dantean scope—a trilogy of trilogies . . . now brought to completion." The odd thing is this: the statement suggests that Wright had this idea in mind from the start, yet this is the very first mention of it. To emphasize the point, the page headed "Also by Charles Wright" for the first time forswears listing his previous individual volumes, as he had done in every earlier collection. Now he lists just his two most recent books and two compilations, *Country Music* (1982) and *The World of the Ten Thousand Things* (1990). It would seem that a Long Poem has been willed retrospectively into existence. Is it a ploy to inflate a body of work, or to be seen as a writer of larger ambitions? Or—this is more likely—is it only just now the poet has seen the figure in his carpet?

The symmetry is slightly askew for a "trilogy of trilogies." Both of the earlier compilations are distilled from four, not three, discrete volumes. *Country Music* corrals *The Grave of the Right Hand* (1970), *Hard Freight* (1973), *Bloodlines* (1975), and *China Trace* (1977). These books are not a single gesture slowly enacted over the arc of a decade. From his debut collection, *The Grave of the Right Hand*, he keeps only five of its thirty-two poems, and those five poems themselves constitute one of the book's five sections, the one called "Departures" (an aptly named starting point, but weaker than the more characteristic section called "American Landscape"), and are all written in prose. So *Country Music* begins with a recitative. It's a decision both perverse and practical. The impulse to dis-own one's apprentice work is natural enough, though Wright's prose is slightly more affected than his poetry in this book, and the "Departures" suite poses as exotic rapture, quite out of tune with the bulk of *Country Music*. I doubt most readers, given a poem from Wright's first book, would recognize it as his. Yes, smudged versions of later, more crisply drawn images are here ("Outside, in the night, a wind / Rises, clacking the dry fronds / Of the jacaranda tree."), but the lines are limp, the tone an echo of his training. My imaginary reader might have guessed young Mark Strand, for example, and there is a generic similarity between the two—at least at this stage. Strand went on to make larger versions of his early maquettes, ever more intimate and portentous, hollow and eerie. Wright slipped into a different set of singing robes; his voice cracked, and instead of a piping purity, his poems later sound like the crooning silki-ness of a mezzo, and his thematic range abandons the sardonic for the sublime. Strand has kept himself steadied by leaning on Stevens. Wright's more febrile imagination is a chariot pulled reluctantly toward the sun by Hopkins, Dickinson, Crane, and Montale. But all that only became ap-parent later on. By discarding his earliest poems from *Country Music*, Wright wants to keep the compass pointing ahead, and not be seen as merely spinning.

In its original edition, *Hard Freight* has forty poems; from them, Wright chose twenty-seven for *Country Music*. The poems of his second book print as positives what had in his first book been negatives. The focus is sharp, perspectives aligned, tone controlled. The elegantly expatriate sym-bolism, all cool surfaces and murky depths, yields to a more distinctive voice. It's a book that predicts this poet's bipolar affinities: Italy and America, the near and the remote. These are not only sites, but tempera-ments too. In a letter to his brother, Keats once claimed that "there are two distinct tempers of mind in which we judge of things—the worldly, theatrical and pantomimical; and the unearthly, spiritual and ethereal." The first half of the book is set in Italy—the enchanted Italy of the noble and sentimental pilgrim, as well as the fantastic Italy of the imagination, lacquered over with translucent texts by Dante or Piero. Later books re-turn compulsively to the Italian landscape, which for Wright is an ideal-ized field of memory, his virtual *paradiso*, spiritual and ethereal. But the

second half of *Hard Freight*, and the half he names the book for, is far su-
perior, worldly and theatrical, and the signal of his later refinements.
Beginning with "Dog Creek Mainline," he hovers over the rural South
of his childhood—also idealized, but in its primitive aspects. These poems
have all the emptiness, the grandeur, the loneliness of the American land-
scape, the sepia of old dreams, twang of banjo, and cry of loon. Wright's
next book, *Bloodlines, is* so clearly his breakthrough that it is no wonder
he reprints it entire in *Country Music*. First of all, the autobiographical
strain dominates. His sense of self is fraught, his sense of *home* darkly
ironic: "Home is what you lie in, or hang above, the house / Your father
made, or keeps on making." He's come to hold and be held by "all the
small things we used once / To push the twelve rings of the night back,"
and to evoke the land (mostly Tennessee) whose refrain is generation:

> The earth is what follows you,
> Tracing your footsteps, counting your teeth, father
> And son, father and grandson,
> A knife, a seed, each planted just deep enough.
> You start there.

He starts there, indeed, and tracks his memories and fantasies through
two extraordinary sequences of irregular sonnets, the appropriately
paired "Tattoos" and "Skins." Anecdotes and images from his past—prayer
meetings, sexual encounters, dreams—are conjured, the actual petals re-
served for footnotes to each, the attar in each sonnet's vial of a rare headi-
ness. These poems are suffused with remembered light, sometimes the
camera's flash, sometimes the moon's haze, which radiates into his gift:
"Inflamed like asparagus in the night field, / You try for the get-away by
the light of yourself." The getaway he recounts is not an angry one, only
haunted, especially by the deaths of his parents to whom he offers elo-
quent elegies in two long poems. The despair of loss is transformed into
an enduring wonder:

> And what does it come to, Pilgrim,
> This walking to and fro on the earth, knowing
> That nothing changes, or everything;
> And only, to tell it, these sad marks,
> Phrases half-parsed, ellipses and scratches across the dirt?
> It comes to a point. It comes and goes.

Here is Wright's mature voice, the rhetoric clipped, the tone wary. The
line, as Henry James would say, sits securely in the saddle. The phrases ac-
cumulate and solidify in order to celebrate, ruefully, evanescence.
Vanishing acts, the evidence of things not seen, the lamplit figure disap-
pearing through the door . . . these are the burden too of *China Trace*. (All
but three of its poems are included in *Country Music*.) This book is one
of Wright's finest, intense and seamless, the achievement at last of his

mature style, and home to some of his most acclaimed lyrics. (I would count "Snow," "Stone Canyon Nocturne," "Crystal Spider Ascension," and "Clear Night" not only stars of the book but among the great lyrics of the past half-century.) The marvelous plaiting of images, the cadence of phrases and clauses, the suppressed and enigmatic narratives, the meta-physical echoes, the self as emblem—here finally is *Charles Wright*. The late Seventies was a low point in civilization, but out of the pot-smoke and beads emerged this austerely beautiful breviary, this illuminated man-uscript. Nothing happens in these poems; there are no people. An eye slowly opens and closes. Everything transpires inside a sensibility. I don't "understand" many of these poems—which is to say they don't resemble poems I have learned to understand. The same is true for me of poems by Blake and Dickinson, Mallarmé and Auden. (On certain days I could add Frost or Bishop: there is nothing so sly as the Plain Style in the hands of a dark master.) When stumped, we call these poets or these poems "hermetic," sidle around them, and move on. Then, like Parthian horse-men, we turn to aim a shot of praise. But my admiration for these poems has only increased over the span of a quarter-century since I first read them, slack-jawed. They are the Buddha's smile, the dolphin's teeth, the galaxy's whirr, the coins on the eyes of the dead. And they're hunting for God, a stem principle and hot desire, both of which elude him.

> And here, where the swan hums in his socket, where bloodroot
> And belladonna insist on our comforting,
> Where the fox in the canyon wall empties our hands, ecstatic for more,
>
> Like a bead of clear oil the Healer revolves through the night wind,
> Part eye, part tear, unwilling to recognize us.

*The World of the Ten Thousand Things* also gathers together four earlier collections: *The Southern Cross* (1981), arguably Wright's finest single vol-ume, *The Other Side of the River* (1984), *Zone Journals* (1988), and a shorter group called "Xionia," which had been previously printed in a fine press limited edition. The dust jacket for the omnibus edition claims only a chronological coherence: that the gathering allows us "to see Wright's work of the past decade as, in essence, one long poem, a medi-tation on self, history, and the metaphysical." There is no linkage with *Country Music*, and it does make more sense to see this work of a decade as a more seamless group because, unlike his earliest books, these four books are so stylistically consistent.

*The Southern Cross* effects the shift from the shorter line Wright pre-ferred in earlier work to a long, often broken line. Or, not "broken," but trailing, a hemistich dropped both to extend and diminish what's pre-ceded it. It's the minor key of a dying fall, and the effect is of the mar-velous antiphonal echo of a Gabrieli chorale. It's also linked to the way memory trolls, dragging its nets along under the surface. There is in

Wright a Stevensian strain that wants to contrast the sufficiency of the world with our restless ideas about it:

> It's noon in the medlar tree, the sun
> Sifting its glitter across the powdery stems.
> It doesn't believe in God
> And still is absolved.
> It doesn't believe in God
> And seems to get by, going from here to there.

But generally he is after more. His poems are shifting panels—on one is an Italian landscape, on another a Montana outback, on a third his Charlottesville backyard, and so on—drawn back and forth across an ache, an eye, a desire for transcendence. It may be that all religious poets are poets of memory—the memory of something before or beyond. Certainly this is so for Wright. It allows him both his painterly emphasis and his philosophical stage directions. He is, above all, a decadent poet—if by decadent we refer to the writer who prefers the chapter to the book, the sentence to the chapter, the phrase to the sentence. As I write this I am listening to a new recording of Stravinsky's *Firebird*, conducted by Valery Gergiev, who takes the music at a much slower tempo than the composer's own recording. It's gorgeous, but as the hidden inner voices emerge, the arching line goes slack. This tendency works against what we think of as the epic thrust. Still, if God is in the details, that is where Wright looks for Him, that is his quest. No poet writing today has his lush musicality. He once defined his love of "the sound and weight and rub and glint of words" as the axis on which his work turns. He writes lines of a sable luxuriance you can run your fingers through. His jump-cutting is phrasal: words coalesce into phrases, phrases are strung into clauses. His poems accumulate themselves. (I wonder if in fifty years, readers will think of Charles Wright and Amy Clampitt and Jorie Graham as nearly identical poets, each with a philosophical turn of mind, but a penchant for the illuminating detail and detached phrase, each a poet of a decided floridity.) The way phrases link is itself the dreamwork of memory:

> It's linkage I'm talking about,
>                     and harmonies and structures
> And all the various things that lock our wrists to the past.
>
> Something infinite behind everything appears,
>                     and then disappears.
>
> It's all a matter of how
>                 you narrow the surfaces.
> It's all a matter of how you fit in the sky.

Wright wants to fit into the sky. He constantly worries about—no, worships—the God he doesn't believe in. There's more the pagan than the

Episcopalian about him, thank God. His gods are everywhere in the Ovidian landscape. And both *The Southern Cross* and *The Other Side of the River* plunge back to his childhood Tennessee, to the Italy of his young manhood: sacred sites which flicker in the halflight of his evocations, a golden bowl of images charged with mystery and possibility, with nostalgia and new knowledge. His descriptions of the natural world—and Wright looks at landscape not nature (that is to say, at a nature already composed by the hand or eye)—are as ravishingly exact and startling as any since Father Hopkins. But it is "the secret landscape behind the landscape" that draws him on, just as poetry is, as he recently told an interviewer, "a way to use language to get beyond language." A formidable task: to write about what isn't there in order to fall silent before it.

Is it an *epic* task? At times. *Zone Journals* is the question mark. The poems of this book, all haunted and haunting, each written with Wright's accustomed allure, pose as diary entries; each is dated. There's a slight prosy texture to some of them, but that's not the problem. I expect Wright was trying to loosen things up. But isn't there a contradiction between the journal squib and the epic? Between the casual and the sublime? This is not an easily decided question. Whitman's *Specimen Days*, for instance, is a text I have taught in a course on American Epic. But that is because it has an underlying structure clearly informed by all the reading aloud of Homer the young Whitman used to do on the beaches of Long Island. He is driving towards a theme—the doing and undoing of a nation, the call to battle and the refuge of nature—that overrides the format of the diary. But Wright is content to loaf and invite his soul. If he lacks the Homeric narrative line, he strikes instead what Auden called the *lacrimae rerum* note. The Virgilian *gravitas* is here, despite the hillbilly slang and *sotto voce* asides. A larger pattern is at work as well. If there were a myth all these poems enacted it would be that of Euridyce, the tale of death and redemption and the second loss, the moment of the fatal backward glance it the beloved: how we save what's lost in order then to lose what's been saved. Like Proust, Wright would say that the only true paradise is a lost paradise.

The next three books were published in quick succession: *Chickamauga* in 1995, *Black Zodiac* in 1997, and *Appalachia* one year later. One assumes that, as before, a further volume that gathers and re-titles these three will eventually be published. It would be a tighter and more balanced book than its two companions, because these three most recent collections spring from one impulse. *Chickamauga* appeared in the year of the poet's sixtieth birthday, and all three books are a sustained meditation on mortality. The last of them, *Appalachia*, continually evokes an Appalachian Book of the Dead, but in no sense are these books any sort of guide to the afterlife or anthology of spells for use by the newly dead to protect them in the next world. Rather, Wright's Book of the Dead is more of a directory. He has his guardian spirits, to be sure; these books function as a kind of commonplace book, filled with quotations from Wright's favorite authors, stationed along the way like talismanic milestones. But it is the ghosts, not saints, that preoccupy him; not the saved but the lost. They are the ghosts of friends and family, the ghost of his younger self, the ghost he is fated to become. All of them suffuse the landscapes described with an exquisite melancholy. "When I write to myself," he once told an interviewer, "I'm writing to the landscape, and the landscape is a personification of the people on the other side." It is, and always has been in Wright's work, a map of memories and a route to the dead. *Chickamauga* begins with a Keaton-esque image that sets the tone of controlled fear:

> The world is a handkerchief.
> Today I spread it across my knees.
> Tomorrow they'll fold it into my breast pocket,
> > white on my dark suit.

The steady, eroding roll of the surf sounds throughout the book. Its poems are set in ironic spring or hollow autumn. Its speaker is referred to as a "pilgrim," an acolyte of the Keatsian fullness that is death's predicate. The God, or God-principle, he sought before yields now to something more abstract and intimate.

> The book says, however,
> > time is not body's movement
> But memory of body's movement.
> Time is not water but the memory of water:
> We measure what isn't there.
> We measure the silence.
> > We measure the emptiness.

Sounding his most Eliotic, he has only fragments to shore against the accusations of emptiness, against the onrush of time:

> What have you done with your life,
> > you've asked me, as you've asked yourself.
> What has it come to,
> Carrying us like a barge toward the century's end
> And sheer drop-off into millennial history?
> I remember an organ chord one Sunday in North Carolina.
> I remember the smell of white pines,
> > Vitalis and lye soap.

In *Black Zodiac* too, every second thought is of death. The time is "shank of the afternoon, wan weight-light," and his life is "a loose knot in a short rope." Does the poet protest too much? Has he narrowed his focus too melodramatically, anointing his own forehead with holy oils against the end? If so, then it's as harrowing as any such set of reflections since Berryman. The taste of ashes, the bruised magnolia petal, the smog at sunrise, the purgatorial wait are the cards Wright deals, hand after hand.

It always amazes me
How landscape recalibrates the stations of the dead,
How what we see jacks up
           the odd quotient of what we don't see,
How God's breath reconstitutes our walking up and walking down.
First glimpse of autumn, stretched tight and snicked, a bad face lift,
Flicks in and flicks out,
           a virtual reality.
Time to begin the long division.

*Appalachia* now completes the meditation. (To emphasize its role in ringing down the curtain on a trilogy, its numerology is insistent. The book is divided into three sections.) Its pared-down spareness is announced on the opening page: "Renunciation, it's hard to learn, is now our ecstasy." Here is the *via negativa*, and Wright walks the line. His melancholy points an accusing finger at his muse in the midst of the shrine to her he has made of his study:

It's all so pitiful, really, the little photographs
Around the room of places I've been,
And me in them, the half-read books, the fetishes, this
Tiny arithmetic against the dark undazzle.
Who do we think we're kidding? . . .

Shrines to the woebegone, ex votos and reliquary sites
One comes in on one's knees to,
The country of *what was*, the country of *what we pretended to be*,
Cruxes and intersections of all we'd thought was fixed.
There is no guilt like the love of guilt.

The tone of these poems is more tentative in its consolations, more staccato in its advance, more assured in its capacity to live amidst uncertainties, mysteries and doubts without any irritable reaching after gaudy effects. His cry now, in fact and with reason, is, O for a Life of Thoughts rather than of Sensations! He is reluctant now to indulge in nostalgia, the ache for home: "the soul that desires to return home," he says, "desires its own destruction." But in looking ahead, he finds "an end without a story," the erasure of sequence and meaning on the margins of the void. Throughout his career—one of the truly splendid careers in contemporary American poetry—he has striven to write a body language, a style with an overt and seductive physicality, a style with spin on its gravity, a feather rising in the canyon, a riff on the old chants. But this is a book—no, the book—that lets go. The body is abjured. The language is dealt like a final hand.

When your answers have satisfied the forty-two gods,
When your heart's in balance with the weight of a feather,

When your soul is released like a sibyl from its cage,
Like a wind you'll cross over,
                            not knowing how, not knowing where,
Remembering nothing, unhappening, hand and foot.


The world's a glint on the window glass,
The landscape's a flash and fall,
                            sudden May like a sleet spill
On the tin roof, no angel, night dark.
Eternity puddles up.
And here's the Overseer, blue, and O he is blue . . .

That *blue*—for Wallace Stevens, the color of the imagination; for Billie
Holiday, something else again. The color dominates the final pages of the
book—or, of the trilogy. I suppose it is, finally, the blank sky at which we
gaze and from which we expect answers. Its emptiness is our American
sublime. Its unresponsive immensity is the bright slate on which we chalk
our questions, the alphabet of our yearnings. Let me quote the final page
of this enormous project. It starts with an overview out of MacLeish, and
swiftly rises, gathering up motifs from earlier poems.

Mid-August meltdown, Assurbanipal in the west,
Scorched cloud-towers, crumbling thrones—
The ancients knew to expect a balance at the end of things,
The burning heart against the burning feather of truth.
                                        Sweet-mouthed,
Big ibis-eyed, in the maple's hieroglyphs, I write it down.


All my life I've looked for this slow light, this smallish light
Starting to seep, coppery blue,
                            out of the upper right-hand corner of things,
Down through the trees and off the back yard,
Rising and falling at the same time, now rising, now falling,
Inside the lapis lazuli of late afternoon.


Until the clouds stop, and hush.
Until the left hedge and the right hedge,
                            the insects and short dogs,
The back porch and barn swallows grain-out and disappear.
Until the bypass is blown with silence, until the grass grieves.
Until there is nothing else.

So the long poem ends with the poet on the back porch, looking over
his suburban lawn, like a latter-day Thoreau. The effect should be our re-
alization that a leaf of grass is no less than the journey-work of the stars.
That grieving grass should alert us at once to Wright's affinity with
Whitman:

> I hear you whispering there O stars of heaven,
> O suns—O grass of graves—O perpetual transfers and promotions,
> If you do not say any thing how can I say any thing?

Perhaps now his publisher will publish a tome with selections from all eleven books, trimmed and shaped like a topiary, as The Definitive Edition. Or it may be that when Charles Wright has published three more collections, they will be sheaved together and talk will start of The Tetralogy. These sorts of designations—whatever: Long Poem, Epic, Trilogy—are in the end descriptions of how we want a poem to be read rather than descriptions of how it may have been conceived of or written out. By calling his eleven books a trilogy, Wright gives a quasi-Dantean shape to his project. Its installments, then, deal first with the past—his bloodlines and traces; the second, and most gorgeous, group deals with the present, the plenitude of his gift and the world, the conjunction of flesh and spirit; and this last installment has focused on the future—which is to say, on death, on the bitter hug of mortality. It has been a journey in three legs, from the autobiographical to the mythic to the mystic. The great long poems are about the founding of a city, and Wright has taken the rubble of his past to build the invisible city of the soul. But something nags at me when I read this book's flap. In the end, I prefer to read the trilogy in a less structured, more fluid manner. I can sense the underlying pattern and discuss it abstractly, but what I read is a twentieth-century *Song of Myself*, a mercurial and exhilarating and profoundly affecting account of one man's moods and imaginings. It flings my likeness after the rest and true as any on the shadow'd wilds.

RON SMITH

# An Enchanted, Diminished World (2000)

Charles Wright, artistic disciple of Dante Alighieri and Ezra Pound, has surpassed at least one of his masters. Line after line, page after page, Wright's poems exhibit a level of surface ingenuity, deep originality, and sheer verbal energy that Pound's hugely ambitious *Cantos* simply could not sustain. With *Country Music: Selected Early Poems* and *The World of Ten Thousand Things: Poems 1980-1990*, Wright's *Negative Blue* completes a skeptical homage to Pound and to Dante's tripartite *Divine Comedy*. Of course, the best this ex-Christian can hope for is "a small-time *paradiso*."

Wright's selected volumes present more than 280 poems culled from twelve earlier books. Few poets have dared to "select" so many poems from the first three decades of their career. But Wright's verbal inventiveness more than justifies keeping in print three different—sequential and separate—selected poems. In *Negative Blue* arresting images, startling figures of speech, and wry jokes are suspended in a kind of ether of meditation and observation. Performative riffs, syntactical surprises, deft use of repetition, delightfully functional assonance and alliteration and occasional rhyme, restless and witty shifts of diction and tone keep the mind moving, probing, re-evaluating.

This is definitely not poetry for readers impatient with the new or the difficult. Some fine (and not so fine) contemporary poets exploit well-worn techniques of fiction, film, and TV in order to give their readers more or less familiar experiences of narrative form or "realism." Charles Wright is not one of these. He is a poet's poet, specializing in interrogation and dazzlement. For lovers of contemporary poetry he is a thoroughly delightful, constantly challenging read.

This poet's poet is also a philosopher's poet, a theologian's poet, and one of the few genuine Nature poets now writing. In *Negative Blue* Wright wheels us through all the seasons of the year, giving each of the twelve months precise and loving attention, and always yearning "to be pierced by that / Occasional void through which the supernatural flows." Yet his philosophically hungry mind constantly flinches from its own pretensions: "*Study the absolute*," he tells us, "But not too hard." Sometimes the poems shrug in a way that reminds one of the deceptively serious Robert Frost.

Still, Wright's depiction of Nature is hardly Frostian. Wright aims not to represent the world but to apprehend it—which to a sensibility like his means to remake it as much as to receive it. For Wright, we never simply see or remember. To see or remember is always to create.

The 117 poems in *Negative Blue* certainly confirm what Wright has said are his subjects: "language, landscape, and the idea of God." There is a doggedness about Wright's treatment of these things that becomes, as the poems pile up, somehow both humble and heroic. The poems from the wonderful *Chickamauga* provide a kind of extended overture to the book's main sequence, the movement from fall to winter to spring to summer through the Pulitzer-winning *Black Zodiac* and then the even more impressive *Appalachia*. A handful of new poems at the end stands as a kind of brooding winter coda. *Negative Blue* is a great hymn to a divinity-deprived earth—and to the forms of language the mind shapes so gloriously and yet ultimately ineffectually to its shifting contours.

There are at least a dozen poems in *Negative Blue* that one feels the need to carry around whole in the mind. My favorites tend to be set in Wright's beloved Italy, poems such as "Midwinter Snowfall in the Plazza Dante," "Negatives II," and "Venexia I." But *Negative Blue*, like all of Wright's books, keeps moving us forward through a sharp, restless mind and an enchanted, diminished world, and most of the time we don't want to linger. His kinetic intelligence propels us through a vivid present that decays before our eyes into the past, a past that remakes itself into a vanishing present. And always the future looms, dark, where "The back porch and the barn swallows grain-out and disappear. / [Where] the bypass is blown with silence, [and] the grass grieves. / [And] there is nothing else."

# Part Two

# Essays

HELEN VENDLER

# The Transcendent "I" (1979)

> I was born on the 25th of August in 1935 . . . in Hardin County, Tennessee, in a place called Pickwick Dam. . . . My father worked for the TVA at the time as a civil engineer. . . . In the tenth grade I was sent to a school that had eight students. . . . My last two years of high school were at an Episcopal boarding school with the unlikely name of Christ School, in Arden, N.C.

This summary of the early career of the poet Charles Wright comes from an interview during a visit to Oberlin, transcribed and published in *FIELD* (Fall 1977). Wright went on to Davidson College ("four years of amnesia, as much my fault as theirs"), then spent four years in the Army (three of them in Italy) and two years at the University of Iowa. As he said to his audience, this represents "pretty much the biography of almost everyone here. . . . We all went through more or less the same things." The connections between that life lived in Tennessee and North Carolina and the poems that have issued from it— *The Grave of the Right Hand* (1970); *Hard Freight* (1973); *Bloodlines* (1975); *China Trace* (1977)—are intermittently evident, but the effort of the poetry is to render them tenuous, often invisible. Because Wright's poems, on the whole, are unanchored to incident, they resist description; because they are not narrative, they defy exposition. They cluster, aggregate, radiate, add layers like pearls. Often they stop in the middle, with a mixed yearning and premonition, instead of taking a resolute direction backward or forward. It may be from the Italian poet Eugenio Montale (1896-1981) that Wright learned this pause which looks before and after; Wright recently issued his translation, done in the sixties, of Montale's powerful 1956 volume entitled *La Bufera e altro* (*The Storm and Other Poems*).

The translation offers an occasion for a glance at both Montale and Wright; the conjunction helps to define what sort of poet Wright has become. Montale wrote *La Bufera* during the postwar years, and his pauses in the midst of event come as often as not in the midst of nightmare: "The Prisoner's Dream" shows a speaker imprisoned in a time of political purges, tempted, like everyone else, to "give in and sign," but instead waiting out the interminable trial, addressing from prison his fixed point of reference—a dreamed-of woman who represents beauty, justice, truth:

> And the blows go on, over and over . . . and the footsteps;
> and still I don't know, when the banquet is finally served,

if I shall be the eater or the eaten. The wait is long;
my dream of you is not yet over.

This poetry, though it implies a better past and an uncertain future, in-
corporates them in the burning-glass of the present. It renounces, as
forms of articulation, narrative, the succession of events, the sequence of
action and reaction. The spatial form, one of many in Montale, is for
Wright the most natural. It can be seen in "Spider Crystal Ascension," his
poem about the rise of the Milky Way at night. The galaxy, full of energy,
resembling a cosmic and eternal spider-web made of crystal, is watched,
as death might be watched, by the temporary inhabitants of an earthly
lake:

> The spider, juiced crystal and Milky Way, drifts on his web through the
>     night sky
> And looks down, waiting for us to ascend . . .
>
> At dawn he is still there, invisible, short of breath, mending his net.
>
> All morning we look for the white face to rise from the lake like a tiny
>     star.
> And when it does, we lie back in our watery hair and rock.

The spider looks, we look, he drifts through the sky, we rock in the lake,
his net is patient, we will be caught from our lake one day and ascend
with him, he is crystal, we are flesh, he can electrocute, we are mortal, the
end is foreseen but not yet accomplished. This arrested motion, this tak-
ing thought, though it is congenial to Wright, requires nevertheless cer-
tain sacrifices.

   The first sacrifice is autobiography. The autobiographical sequence
"Tattoos," which appeared in *Bloodlines*, solved the problem of reference
by appending, at the end of twenty poems, a single note on each one: a
sample note reads "Automobile wreck; hospital; Baltimore, Maryland."
Instead of a first-person narrative of the crash and its surgical aftermath,
Wright produces a montage of sensations:

> So that was it, the rush and the take-off,
> The oily glide of the cells
> Bringing it up—ripsurge, refraction,
> The inner spin
> Trailing into the cracked lights of oblivion.

In *Bloodlines* these verses are encountered with no title, no explanation;
the note is to be read later, and then the poem reread, from the crash to
the hospital:

> Re-entry is something else, blank, hard:
> Black stretcher straps; the peck, peck

> And click of a scalpel; glass shards
> Eased one by one from the flesh;
> Recisions; the long bite of the veins.

It is easy to see how interminable, predictable, and boring a plain narrative might appear after this "jump-cut" (Wright's words) monitoring of sensation. The problem of affixing closure to sensation and perception (since of themselves they have no closure but unconsciousness) has bothered Wright a good deal. The automobile wreck finds closure in sententious question-and-answer, with echoes of Williams and Berryman:

> And what do we do with this,
> Rechuted, reworked into our same lives, no one
> To answer to, no one to glimpse and sing,
> The cracked light flashing our names?
> We stand fast, friend, we stand fast.

The danger of this three-stanza form, as Wright realized, is that it is unduly "comfortable":

> Three stanzas is good because you can present something in the first, work around with it a bit in the second and then release it, refute it, untie it, set fire to it, whatever you want to, in the third. And that's its main problem for me. I felt I'd explored enough of what could be done, so I changed it for the next [long] poem.

The words Wright uses for the functions of that third stanza are all in some way linear, logical, causal: the problem can be "released," "refuted," "untied," torched. In any case, the problem goes away. The premise is that of syllogism in the realm of mind, action in the realm of morals. The premise, by extension, implies a world of meaning ranging from solutions to revolutions. The interesting thing about Wright's development is that he found he could no longer work within such a frame.

His next experiment, in the second sequence in *Bloodlines* (a wonderful poem called "Skins"), was to abandon the three equal pieces—presentation, complication, and conclusion—of "Tattoos" for a set of seamless meditations, each fourteen lines long. Though these have of course affinities with sonnets, they are sonnets that go nowhere, or end where they began: either the second half of the poem repeats the first, or the last line reenters the universe where the first line left it. Even the poems which seem to evolve in a linear way show only a moment in a life-cycle itself endlessly repeated; they are therefore more fated than free, as in the ease of the sixth and most beautiful meditation, about the metamorphosis of a mayfly:

> Then
> Emergence: leaf drift and detritus; skin split,
> The image forced from the self.

And rests, wings drying, eyes compressed,
Legs compressed, constricted
Beneath the dun and the watershine—
Incipient spinner, set for the take-off . . .
And does, in clean tear: imago rising out of herself
For the last time, slate-winged and many-eyed.
And joins, and drops to her destiny,
Flesh to the surface, wings flush on the slate film.

This is almost too ravishing in sound and sight, in its mimetic instability between the grotesque and the exquisite, to be thought about. The mind of the reader is delayed by the felicities of the slate wings on the slate water-film, by the dun detritus of chrysalis played off against the watershine, by the flesh flush on the surface, by the conjugation of drift and force, compression and incipience, and by the brief cycle of wings drying, rising, dropping. This sensual music precludes thought, almost; but the subject of metamorphosis is so old and so noble, the flesh as chrysalis so perennial a metaphor, that the conceptual words—image, self, imago, destiny—work their own subsidiary charm in the long run. In spite of the ephemeral nature of the cycle, Wright rescues by his vocabulary a form of transcendence. ("The nitty-gritty of my wishes . . . would be to be saved, but there's no such thing.")

Wright has talked about the "sparring match I had for about ten years with the Episcopal Church, in which I was raised, in which I was tremendously involved for a short amount of time and from which I fled and out of which I remain. But it had a huge effect on me":

> It's a very strange thing about being raised in a religious atmosphere. It alters you completely, one way or the other. It's made me what I am and I think it's okay. I can argue against it, but it has given me a sense of spirituality which I prize.

There are other names for this "sense of spirituality": it might just as well be named a sense of euphony, a sense for the Platonic or the seraphic. It is no doubt what attracted Wright to Montale. Montale preserved an exacerbated but inflexible fidelity to a principle itself exigent, even aggressive, in its purity and fierceness. This principle is figured in his absent "Clizia," named after the nymph who so loved the sun that she was metamorphosed into the sunflower forever faithful to radiance no matter how distant its path. Clizia burns through *The Storm* as a presence, even in absence, not to be put by, no less a Fury than an angel, sometimes rainbow, sometimes lightning-bolt, sometimes in tatters, sometimes in flames. The world is more often than not at odds with her: sometimes the ambience is vicious, sometimes simply obstructive. In "Hitler Spring," as Mussolini and Hitler appear together, Clizia must exist in the midst of "the sirens, the tolling bells / that call to the monsters in the twilight / of their

Pandemonium." In "The Eel," Clizia is sister to those ambitious swimmers into unpromising landscapes:

> The eel, whiplash, twisting torch,
> love's arrow on earth, which only
> our gullies and dried-out, burned-out streams
> can lead to the paradises of fecundity;
> green spirit that hunts for life
> only there, where drought and desolation gnaw,
> a spark that says everything starts
> where everything is charred, stumps buried.

The eel's world, full of momentum, is the paradoxical one of inception in extinction. The mystery of such motion defies linearity, and consequently allies itself with those Christian paradoxes of the dying grain and the lost life saved, antithetical to the prudential and the providential alike, since foresight and backward glances have nothing to do with illumination, conversion, metamorphosis.

Wright's aim in translating Montale has been to be idiomatic, within his own idiom as well as within Montale's. Robert Lowell's "imitation" of "The Eel" is more fluent and more condensed:

> The eel, a whipstock, a Roman candle,
> love's arrow on earth, which only
> reaches the paradise of fecundity
> through our gullies and fiery, charred streams;
> a green spirit, potent only
> where desolation and arson burn;
> a spark that says everything
> begins where everything is clinker.

Wright attempts greater fidelity, at the cost of some loss of naturalness (and, I have been told, of accuracy). Surely both Lowell and Wright, with their Italianate "paradise of fecundity," are themselves bettered by John Frederick Nims, who substitutes "edens of fertility." Montale—compressed, allusive, oblique, full of echoing sound—is relatively untranslatable; his poems swell awkwardly as they take on English under anyone's hands, and his infinitely manipulable Italian syntax begins to hobble, hampered by stiff English clauses. Wright's translations, as he says, taught him things:

> I feel I did learn . . . how to move a line, how to move an image from one stage to the next. How to create imaginary bridges between images and stanzas and then to cross them, making them real, image to image, block to block.

These are not—though they may appear to be—idle concerns. If conclusions are not the way to get from A to B, if discursiveness itself is a false mode of consciousness, if free-association in a surrealist mode (to offer the opposite extreme) seems as irresponsible as the solemn demonstrations of the discursive, what form of presentation can recreate the iconic form of the mind's invention? It is really this question that Wright takes up in *China Trace* and subsequent poems. Chinese poetry, as it entered twentieth-century literature through Waley and Pound, came to stand for an alien but immensely attractive combination of sensation and ethics, both refined from crudeness by their mutual interpenetration. Suggestion and juxtaposition seemed adequate to replace statement, as Pound's petal-faces on the Métro-bough would claim. Wright's trace—*vestigium*—of China is in part an homage to Pound, but it also pursues, yet once more, the problem of the potential complacency of stanzas, especially of repeated stanzas. Who is to say that today's poem, like yesterday's, should have three stanzas? or one stanza of fourteen lines? And yet to insist that every form is a nonce form—good for only one use and then to be discarded—is to falsify what we know of recurrences and rhythms in the mind's life.

For *China Trace*, says Wright,

> I decided, rather arbitrarily, that no poem was going to be longer than twelve lines. In the first section I wanted to have an example of each length of poem from one to twelve lines but I couldn't write a four line poem. It was the hardest thing. They always came out sounding like a stanza that needed another stanza, or two more stanzas.

This problem is less superficial than it may seem. Aside from light verse, gnomes, or riddles, poems in English often have either two or three stanzas, chiefly because thought and feeling often proceed either by comparison or antithesis (resulting in two stanzas) or by statement, complication or amplification, and resolution (yielding three stanzas or divisions). Perception, unsupported by reflection, tends to seem truncated, unfinished, uncommented upon. That analytic restlessness which causes the second, and even the third, stanzas to be written is absent in the Chinese lyrics—compact, single, coherent—favored by Waley, and hovering over *China Trace*. But in spite of Wright's deliberate variety of form, a principle of repetition has its way in the design of the book: each of its halves is prefaced by the same citation from Calvino's *Invisible Cities*, envisaging the day when, knowing all the emblems, one becomes an emblem among emblems. This Yeatsian notion stands side by side with a Chinese epigraph, about the ambition "to travel in ether by becoming a void" or, failing that, to make use of a landscape to calm the spirit and delight the heart. In these epigraphs Wright reveals his own disembodied ethereality in coexistence with his pure visual sense.

The poems in *China Trace* are frosty, clear, descriptive, seemingly dispassionate, wintry even in spring. Even in April,

[I] know I want less—

Divested of everything,
A downfall of light in the pine woods, motes in the rush,
Gold leaf through the undergrowth, and come back
As another name, water
Pooled in the black leaves and holding me there, to be
Released as a glint, as a flash, as a spark . . .

Throughout the volume Wright persistently imagines himself dead, dispersed, re-elemented into the natural order. ("And I am not talking about reincarnation at all. At all. At all.") In focusing on earth, in saying that "salvation doesn't exist except through the natural world," Wright approaches Cézanne's reverence for natural forms, geometrical and substantial ones alike. *China Trace* is meant to have "a journal-like, everyday quality," but its aphorisms resemble *pensées* more than diary jottings, just as its painters and poets (Morandi, Munch, Trakl, Nerval) represent the arrested, the composed, the final, rather than the provisional, the blurred, or the impressionistic. *China Trace* is in fact one long poem working its desolation by accretion; it suffers in excerpts. Its mourning echoes need to be heard like the complaint of doves—endless, reiterative, familiar, a twilight sound:

There is no light for us at the end of the light.
No one redeems the grass our shadows lie on.

Each night, in its handful of sleep, the mimosa blooms.
Each night the future forgives.
Inside us, albino roots are starting to take hold.

The entire life-cycle—light, dark, blooming, sleep, guilt, forgiveness, pallor, growth—takes place each night, and no phase is inextricable from its opposite. In a linear view, by inexorable necessity, the "first minute, after noon, is night" (Donne's version). Wright, in opposition, urges in "Noon" the extension of life, altered, into our perception of death:

Extension that one day will ease me on
In my slow rise through the dark toward the sweet wrists of the rose.

The "me" here defined is a biological, not a spiritual, entity:

The dirt is a comforting, and the night drafts from the sucker vines.
The grass is a warm thing, and the hollyhocks, and the bright bursts from
    the weeds.
But best of all is the noon, and its tiny horns,
When shadows imprint, and start
                        their gradual exhalation of the past.

Wright is not innocent of influence; one recognizes Whitman, Pound, and Stevens, as well as Berryman and Williams, among his predecessors. On the other hand, he is obsessed with sound rather more than they were. Sound adds to his poems that conclusiveness which logic and causality confer on the poetry of others: "Mostly I like the sound of words. The sound, the feel, the paint, the color of them. I like to hear what they can do with each other. I'm still trying to do whatever I can with sound." The tendency of sound to despotism does not go unrecognized. "Sometimes I think [Hopkins'] sound patterns are so strong that you miss what he is saying." Wright's poems would be endangered if they were constructed on a more casual base, but he seems to work with infrastructures which are powerfully organized; the one for "Skins," in all its twenty items, is spelled out in the interview in *FIELD*. These sub-scaffoldings may in the long run drop away, but they keep the poems from being at the mercy of whims of sound.

If *China Trace* can be criticized for an unrelenting elegiac fixity, nonetheless its consistency gives it incremental power. Its deliberateness, its care in motion, its slow placing of stone on stone, dictate our reading it as construction rather than as speech. It is not surprising that as a model Wright has chosen Cézanne, that most architectural of painters:

> I like layers of paint on the canvas. I also know after I'm tired of lots of layers on the canvas, I'm going to want just one layer of paint and some of the canvas showing through. . . . I've been trying to write poems . . . the way a painter might paint a picture . . . using stanzas in the way a painter will build up blocks of color, each disparate and often discrete, to make an overall representation that, taken in its pieces and slashes and dabs, seems to have no coherence, but seen in its totality, when it's finished, turns out to be a very recognizable landscape, or whatever. Cézanne is someone who does this, in his later work, to an almost magical perfection.

Wright's eight-poem sequence "Homage to Paul Cézanne" builds up, line by line, a sense of the omnipresent dead. Wright's unit here is the line rather than the stanza, and the resulting poem sounds rather like the antiphonal chanting of psalms: one can imagine faint opposing choruses singing the melismatic lines:

> The dead fall around us like rain.
> They come down from the last clouds in the late light for
>     the last time
> And slip through the sod.
> They lean uphill and face north.
>                         Like grass,
> They bend toward the sea, they break toward the setting sun.

Wright does this poetry of the declarative sentence very well, but many poets have learned this studied simplicity, even this poetry of the common noun. What is unusual in Wright is his oddity of imagery within the almost too-familiar conventions of quiet, depth, and profundity. As he layers on his elemental squares and blocks of color, the surprising shadow or interrupting boulder emerge as they might in a Cézanne:

> High in the night sky the mirror is hauled up and unsheeted.
> In it we twist like stars.

To Wright, death is as often ascent as burial; we become stars, like Romeo, after death, as often as roses. The modern unsheeted mirror reveals the Tennysonian twist of the constellations round the polestar, in this Shakespearean image of the posthumous—or so we might say if we look at Wright for his inheritances as well as for his originality.

Wright claims, like all poets, a return to original nature: the refusal to particularize his individual existence implies his utterance of universal experience, predicable of everyone. Everyone's dead are ubiquitous: we all "sit out on the earth and stretch our limbs, / Hoarding the little mounds of sorrow laid up in our hearts." On the other hand, the oracular mode sacrifices the conversational, and Wright evanesces under the touch in his wish to be dead (or saved), to enlarge the one inch of snowy rectitude in his living heart into the infinite ice of the tomb. In "Virginia Reel" he stands among family graves, in "the dirt their lives were made of, the dirt the world is, / Immeasurable emptiness of all things," and sees himself as a "bright bud on the branch of nothing's tree." A hand out of the air, like one of Montale's spirit-talons from an angel, touches his shoulder, and

> I want to fall to my knees, and keep on falling, here,
> Laid down by the articles that bear my names,
> The limestone and marble and locust wood.

The hunger for the purity of the dead grows, in these poems, almost to a lust. So far, as a poem quoting Dickinson's gravestone says, he has been "Called Back" by the bird songs and flowers of the world; but the ice-edged and starless cloak of night outshines his bougainvillea and apple blossoms. The eternal and elemental world is largely unrelieved, in *China Trace* and after, by the local, the social, the temporary, the accidental, the contingent. Some very good poetry has incorporated riotous, and occasionally ungovernable, irruptions of particularity; the "purer" voice of finely ascetic lyric has a genuine transmitter in Wright. His synoptic and panoramic vision, radiating out from a compositional center to a filled canvas, opposes itself to the anthropocentric, and consequently autobiographical or narrative, impetus of lyrics with a linear base. If there is nowhere to go but up from making the unsupported line your unit, the dead your measure of verity, and the blank canvas meticulously layered with single cubes of color your creative metaphor, Wright's poetry is bound to change. As it stands, it is engaged in a refutation of the seductions of logic, or religion, and of social roles. By its visionary language it assumes the priority of insight, solitude, and abstraction, while remaining beset by a mysterious loss of something that can be absorbed and reconstituted only in death.

The spiritual yearning in Wright is nowhere rewarded, as it sometimes is in Montale, by a certain faith in an absolute—damaged no doubt, elusive surely, disagreeable often, but always unquestioned and recoverable. The difference in part may be historical. Montale, who fought in World War I and saw the shambles of postwar Italy give rise to Mussolini, faced pressing social evils that demanded a choice of sides; he refused to join the Fascist party and lost his job in consequence. Virtue made visible by its denunciation of the evils of Pandemonium can appear emblematic, allegorical, winged, embattled. Without a historical convulsion, tones of poetry subside into perplexity, sadness, elegy. Wright's debt to Montale, attested to by original poems as well as by these early translations, is more than stylistic: the disciple exhibits that desire and hopelessness we associate with Montale at his most characteristic. Montale's description (in *Auto da Fé*, 1952) of the solitude of the artist can stand as a program for Wright:

> Man, insofar as he is an individual being, an empirical individual, is fatally alone. Social life is an addition, an aggregate, not a unity of individuals. The man who communicates is the transcendent "I" who is hidden in us and who recognizes himself in others. But the transcendent "I" is a lamp which lights up only the briefest strip of space before us, a light that bears us toward a condition which is not individual and consequently not human . . . The attempt to fix the ephemeral, to make the phenomenon non-phenomenal, the attempt to make the individual "I" articulate, as he is not by definition, the revolt, in brief, against the human condition (a revolt dictated by an impassioned *amor vitae*) is at the base of the artistic and philosophic pursuits of our era.

Wright's verse is the poetry of the transcendent "I" in revolt against the too easily articulate "I" of social engagement and social roles. Whether one "I" can address his word to other, hidden "I's" across the abyss of daily life without using the personal, transient, and social language of that life is the question Wright poses. Remembering Montale's eel venturing into the rocks and gullies of a scorched earth, I would hope to see in Wright's future poetry a more vivid sense of the social and familial landscape in which the soul struggles. "Life itself," Montale wrote, "seems like a monstrous work of art forever being destroyed and forever renewed." While Montale foresaw a popular art—utilitarian and almost playful—for the masses, he also predicted (and incarnated) a "true and proper art, not very different from the art of the past, and not easily reduced to cliché." The creators of this art—and for Montale, who translated Eliot, Eliot would be a case in point—though they may seem hermetic, isolated, and inaccessible, are not really such:

> It is these great isolated personalities who give a meaning to an era, and their isolation is more illusory than real. . . . In this sense, only the isolated speak, only the isolated communicate; the rest—the mass-communication men—repeat, give off echoes, vulgarize the poets' words.

In making Montale better known, Wright makes his own aims better understood, and his remote and severe writing more accessible.

# Tracing Charles Wright (1982)

Charles Wright, who longs to elude his too-local life, eludes you even when he isn't trying. He's trying on the cover of his third volume, *Bloodlines*, where reflected lights (irregular white patches like blotches on an abstract canvas) hide the eyes behind his sunglasses (eyes you know are looking at you). Haloed by a washtub hung on a cabin wall, he's a mock frontier-saint of purity—washed in the beyond, cleaned to blankness, bouncing back brilliance.

*Hard Freight* (1973), *Bloodlines* (1975), *China Trace* (1977), and *The Southern Cross* (1981) perpetuate with a horizon-pale passion what Yeats called "the inspired condition." Their often astonishingly beautiful lines seek to "pull that rib of pure light" that must still lie in language somewhere, it's such a solitary Adam. Not that Wright is occult; on the contrary, he would make the intangible stark. To him revelation came early and has remained unsparing: it is that the dead, who are superior to us, who know more and feel more, are always near us. He hails the super-human, writes of death-in-life and life-in-death.

To get into touch with this mystery Wright goes by his ear, which is subtler than any conscious understanding. Disallowing mufflings, it is one of the great precisionist instruments in the contemporary arts. Reading Wright you sometimes feel like Sylvia Plath's heroine squatting in the cornucopia of a colossus' ear, out of the wind, your hours married to shadow, counting at night "the red stars and those of plum-color."

It is all high church—reason's unease. You find yourself in somebody else's *Let us pray*. Liturgical rhythms, ritualistic repetitions, invocations, appeals for absolution abound. The four elements are everywhere, yet often in curious coalescences—as when "evening comes down / Its trellises one rose at a time." Very beautiful, but not quite of our world. The technique continually relates back to the metaphysics of death-in-life and life-in-death. Oxymorons and other reversals proliferate. As in the small poem "Death":

> I take you as I take the moon rising,
> Darkness, black moth the light burns up in.

This surprises at once with "I take you," again with "moon rising," again with "Darkness," and still again, climactically, with "black moth the light burns up in"—yet all is poised in an assured stance. Like dolphins, a Wright poem rises and re-plunges line by line, invoking a vast inhuman beauty. All is "procedure and process," "the one / Inalterable circulation."

Where does one stand in a circulation? It all "comes to a point," Wright said in the sequence "Skins" in *Bloodlines*—to this moment, this place. "It comes and it goes." Yeats held the "point" argumentatively, Dylan Thomas elegiacally; Wright, like a reed, bends along the river's flow, half here, half extended into the future, at right angles to himself, whispering "into a different ear." *China Trace*, particularly, pleads "for a second breath, / Great Wind, where everything's necessary / And every-thing rises," but always he is the poet of a deferred vitality, no swords-man, unless wishes can cut through life. "A wing brushes my left hand, ~ but it's not my wing"—that is his piercingly deprived note.[1] "The thing that is not left out always is what is missing," he said in *Hard Freight*, thus reversing the cloth of existence, placing being unsoiled on the other side.

A Christian upbringing iced his roots, the deaths of many loved ones have chilled them further. "Some things stay cold to exist: dry ice and the maimed child, / My hands, the nighttime and deep water. My hands." Wright is as one whose right to independent life was never ratified. Already in Kingsport, Tennessee, while sons danced "in their gold suits, / clapping their hands" mothers and fathers filled "With dust-dolls their long boxes." Guilt tries to coffin him up and ship him out before his time: "the crime is invisible / but it's there." "Will Charles look on hap-piness in this life?" Not if he seeks a comfortable place to lie among the dust-dolls.

"I write poems to untie myself, to do penance and disappear / Through the upper right-hand corner of things, to say grace." Yes; mostly by using landscape as a "Ouija board." In an interview in *Quarterly West* (Spring/Summer, 1981), Wright said:

> Lenny Michaels once said, "The great ones always speak from the other side." If that can be worked backwards, then you always try to talk from the other side. . . . That tends to be . . . the audience that I write to. When I write to myself, I'm writing to the landscape, and the landscape is a per-sonification of the people on the other side. That would be my ideal audi-ence. One writes for approval, in a strange way. And I'm trying to tell them that I understand and that I'm doing the best I can.

". . . in a way," he added, "I feel I'm speaking *for* them." But at times he knows he's just "jump-cut and Captain Dog," a child playing at being master, a fictitious character whose name could only be reversed to the superhuman on the other side. Meanwhile to appear to jump-cut from this side to the other one, in planes awry as Cézanne's, snicking into else-where, is his joy.

---

1. Here as throughout ~ indicates that the remaining portion of the line has been moved down a space in the text.

No one more medieval, more communal in his relation to the dead. In "Homage to Paul Cézanne" he says they "are with us to stay," says each year they "grow less dead, and nudge / Close to the surface of all things," says "They carry their colored threads and baskets of silk / To mend our clothes, making us look right." They need us—"Sometimes they lie in our beds with their gloves off / And touch our bodies"; "At night, in the fish-light of the moon, the dead wear our white shirts / To stay warm. . . ." But how much greater is our need for them. Indeed, they are our soul—our sadness, and our awareness. Our creativity is of them, from them: "We spread them with palette knives in broad blocks and planes . . . / Blue and a blue and a breath."

"I'm a nominal Pantheist," Wright said in *Quarterly West*. At best nominal, for God to this poet is remote. Even "God is the metaphor for metaphor" misses the gap. So figures of speech weep like willow's fall. The parents will lie dormant until lips say "what the lips in the west say / At evening"; only a "tomorrow" will start them "preening inside their graves, / A yearn for the natural hug, the quick kiss overhead." The father, especially, is far—the farthest nearness. The starry sky is his domain:

> I look up at the black bulge of the sky and its belt of stars,
> And know I can answer to nothing in all that shine,
> Desire being ash, and not remembered or brought back by the breath,
> Scattered beneath the willow's fall, a figure of speech . . .

At the end of *China Trace* the yearning "I" of the book turns to an achieved "He." Yes,

> Look for him high in the flat black of the northern Pacific sky,
> Released in his suit of lights,
>                 lifted and laid clear.

The son will be one with the father when he is all suit, all light, laid clear of flesh and desire.

Like a great white painting the Milky Way reflects Wright's varying postures of prayer (first in *The Grave of the Right Hand*, his apprentice volume). In "Spider Crystal Ascension" (in *China Trace*) it is a father-spider of terrible industry, patience, and beauty:

> The spider, juiced crystal and Milky Way, drifts on his web through the
>     night sky
> And looks down, waiting for us to ascend. . . .

> At dawn he is still there, invisible, short of breath, mending his net.

> All morning we look for the white face to rise from the lake like a tiny
>     star.
> And when it does, we lie back in our watery hair and rock.

This spider waits to devour us, to electrocute us ("juiced crystal"), and to redeem us ("crystal," "net," "ascend"). But we prefer the mother, the white imago that ascends from below, under-star and succorer—prefer to revert to the dreamy time of "watery hair." Between the starry host-spider severely maintaining his system (Wright's father engineered dams for the TVA) and the cradling maternal lake, between guilt and atonement, chilling distance and intimate union, this poet's metaphysics "quarter and spin."

"Spider Crystal Ascension" reveals his religious trust in metaphor, his flamey-icy otherness of figures and mind, and incidentally his recent skill at long lines descending like spiders on their own smoothly and rapidly played-out threads. Vitality of a kind, a "black hole" variety, there undoubtedly is. (Once compressed language "gets past a certain point," Wright said in an interview in the Fall 1977 issue of *FIELD*, it "goes out the other side and . . . expands.") The poetry stops your breath, questions it with its uncanny beauty. (How deaf it is to the tiny drum of the pulse. It races, races away.)

*China Trace* is a loose-leaf arrangement of poems ringed on a constant refusal: "If something is due me still . . . I give it back." But, flicked into the future like skip-stones of light, the poems fail to reach their goal. ("It's endless extinction," Wright said to me in conversation. "Isn't it? But I hope I'm wrong.")

The one-line poem "Bygones" epitomizes the book:

> The rain has stopped falling asleep on its crystal stems.

Of course the stems are not genuine crystal, they collapse; and of course there was no great awakening, only nodding. The single long line is an attempt at an aesthetic crystal stem, from which, however, the wish to be "singled out" ("I want to be strung up in a strong light and singled out") explodes like a watery flower and dies.

*China Trace* temporarily exhausted Wright's desire "to be bruised by God." Compression led to the need for expansion, the awesome hegemony of the "other side" to a renewal of interest (of search) in this one. Of course Wright will never be one to settle back in a wheelchair of earth, a metaphysical cripple like most other modern writers, his knees under a blanket of moths. His need for the dead is too fierce. But in *The Southern Cross* he discovers in his own natural affections a "loose Milky Way," to quote from *The Grave of the Right Hand*, "Gathering stars as it swarms / Deeper into the west."

"At 40, the apricot / Seems raised to a higher power, the fire ant and the weed." Bachelard's question as to how much world one must retain in order to be accessible to transcendency can be reversed, since transcendency, like a slipcover, may make us more mindful of the world. And Wright, who schooled his ear in Pound, has never been unmindful of it. Compared to the language of other poets attuned to "aethereal rumors"—T. S. Eliot's, or W. S. Merwin's—Wright's has always been bush-fragrant, dirt-loose.

Yet *The Southern Cross*—the long title poem especially—evokes what for Wright is a new haunting, the myth of the garden of earthly delights. The volume taps earlier strata of the heart, the senses' memory, the primal forest of desire, before desire was ash. Although Wright unremittingly hankers for the "Away-From-Here," at times it swings round to the past, as the hinter horizon. "How sweet the past is, no matter how wrong, or how sad"—have not Southerners been particularly quick to note this? "All things that are are lights," Wright said in *Hard Freight*, addressing his infant son, Luke: "The foothills of Tennessee / The mountains of North Carolina, / . . . Hiwassee and Cherokee . . . / Brindle and sing in your blood."

Still, the past is elusive and the title "The Southern Cross" (the constellation by that name cannot be seen even from the Southern United States) hints at its fabulousness. At the same time the title wittily characterizes a Southern upbringing: "The outline of 10 crosses," Wright said in *China Trace*, "still dampens and stains my childhood." Whether visible or invisible the past tugs at the long lines of the poem like a "kite at the end of its string."

"Places swim up and sink back, and days do." The poem observes no order, there can be no summing up in

> Overlay after overlay tumbled and brought back,
> As meaningless as the sea would be
> > if the sea could remember its waves . . .

The oceanic witlessness of random memory. The patternless observations of a lifetime. After "Gauze curtains blowing in and out of open windows all over the South" on to Garda, Venice, Laguna Beach, and other stations of the cross formed by the merciless right angle of time to space . . . the map gone.

"The landscape was always the best part." For "Time is the villain in most tales, / And here, too," and landscape is resistant to time: a bunched refusal. "Everything I can see knows just what to do, / Even the dragon-fly, hanging like lapis lazuli in the sun"—whereas time is all hesitancy and regret, the slippery cement of wishing and remembering. As Bergson argued in *Matter and Memory*, the spirit is of time, not space, and memory is a spiritual activity. It tries to hold on but "The lime, electric green of the April sea ~ off Ischia / Is just a thumb-rub on the window glass between here and there. . . ."

Sick Narcissus, memory finds in memories metaphors of memory. Everywhere it lingers over its own likenesses. For instance, "The clouds over Bardolino dragging the sky for the dead / Bodies of those who refuse to rise"; Venice "sunk to her knees in her own reflection"; "the way that Pound walked ~ across San Marco / At *passeggiata*, as though with no one, ~ his eyes on the long ago"; "the bog lilies [extinguishing] their mellow lamps"; "a brute bumblebee working the clover tops"; "the faint notes of piano music back in the woods."

"It's what we forget that defines us." Again, "Things that divine us we never touch." Deliverance thus lies in recollection. Yet

> I can't remember enough.

> How the hills, for instance, at dawn in Kingsport
> In late December in 1962 were black
> > against a sky
> The color of pale fish blood and water that ran to white
> As I got ready to leave home for the 100th time,
> My mother and father asleep,
> > my sister asleep,
> Carter's Valley as dark as the inside of a bone
> Below the ridge,
> > the 1st knobs of the Great Smokies
> Beginning to stick through the sunrise,
> The hard pull of a semi making the grade up US 11W,
> The cold with its metal teeth ticking against the window,
> The long sigh of the screen door stop,
> My headlights starting to disappear
> > in the day's new turning . . .

> I'll never be able to.[2]

What, then, is "enough"? To live at all is to lose ground ("The lilacs begin to bleed / In their new sleep . . .") and the only way to be defined, too divinely original to be subject, divined, is to push it all, every dispossession and dispersal of the soul, back to the beginning. Back to Pickwick Dam, which "was never the wind," and which "waits to be rediscovered":

> Somewhere in all that network of rivers and roads and silt hills,
> A city I'll never remember,
> > its walls the color of pure light,
> Lies in the August heat of 1935,
> In Tennessee, the bottom land slowly becoming a lake.
> It lies in a landscape that keeps my imprint

---

2. Although the verse is lovely and accomplished in its own way, there are echoes here of Theodore Roethke's "The Far Field." The passage harks back through *North American Sequence* to Walt Whitman. Wright said to me, "I always thought that what I wanted to be was Walt Whitman in Emily Dickinson's house, but now what I see I really want to do is be Emily Dickinson on Walt Whitman's road—that is, to have his length of line and expansiveness of life gusto with her intelligence walking along, and her preoccupations, which are my preoccupations."

> Forever,
>            and stays unchanged, and waits to be filled back in.
> Someday I'll find it out
> And enter my old outline as though for the 1st time,
>
> And lie down, and tell no one.

"Lies," "lie"—the refrain wants to give away the bravado. No matter, for the due repossession of original desire has been asserted with an irresistible passion and precision. To hold rewound in the hand, satiny and luxuriously self-bound, all that time had seized and run off with into the future would be the very apotheosis of narcissism. "And tell no one"; the life that can be told is not the eternal life.

   If you focus on the content, the poem feels multiple and fragmented ("No trace of a story line"). Oceanic, it is not borne up but heavy. Only the conclusion lifts it at all, in a brilliant ploy of asseveration. Yet in another view the poem is the non-longing for which memory longs. There is no strife in it, no effort at internal logic, no suspense, no self-memory, and no self-division. "Thirty spokes share the wheel's hub," comments Lao Tzu; "it is the center hole that makes it useful." In what Yeats called the "deliberate self-delighting happiness" of style, its "still unexpended energy . . . after the immediate end has been accomplished," in that self-completion, that prodigal self-reference, the poem itself provides (as all art does) a subtle model of joy. The form lays healing hands on the content and at length produces the small, emulative miracle of the close.

The five poems each entitled "Self Portrait" show almost a relenting toward "Charles," that troublesome odd-end and superfluity. Not, of course, an acceptance: a dissatisfaction, an edginess as of a spinning coin, a coin of light for which no slot has ever been devised, marks all this poet's work, save for his early sequence on his son. But gone, at any rate, is the punishing note of "Eyes thumbed, lips like pieces of cut glass . . . the shot unmistakable. / Take it, and be glad." Instead, we find

> Charles on the Trevisan, night bridge
> To the crystal, infinite alphabet of his past.
> Charles on the San Trovaso, earmarked,
> Holding the pages of a thrown-away book, dinghy the color of honey
> Under the pine boughs, the water east-flowing.

"The wind will edit him soon enough," he adds. "And why not?" Yet with that "crystal, infinite alphabet" the past draws him back. If he can lay his hands on it he can spell and spell in lasting blocks through which the sunlight must still be streaming. And the verbless poise of "Charles on the Trevisan, . . . Charles on the San Trovaso" weights the statements against the vagaries of the wind.

The trochaic tilt of these verbal photographs (enlarging on actual snapshots on his study wall) tells us that Wright is forward of those times, spilled out. While his eye marks a lastingness, his ear discovers an earliness. But back then, although already a book that life had read carefully enough to earmark, albeit essentially a throwaway, he had held on to the pages of a thrown-away book (as he has since held on to the snapshot) as if he himself wanted to last. The book was retained under enduring pines and in a dinghy the color of golden ripeness. The allusion is to Pound, who thought, then thought better, of throwing the proof sheets of *A Lume Spento* into the same canal. (Did Wright at that time feel like a book earmarked by Pound, whose ear his own had marked?) In homage to the master the end of the stanza catches the silken watermark of his phrasing—an homage that confirms the momentary anchoring in nostalgia.

All the same, not self-retrieval but self-purging is the project of the series: a sifting of the ashes for the indestructible, gold influences. The somewhat deceptive model is Francis Bacon's sequence of increasingly molten self-portraits. So "by the time you get to number five," Wright said to me, "the self-portrait series that started out strictly about me— 'Someday they'll find me out, and my lavish hands,' and so forth, which is the tip-off to how to find me by the time you get to number five—is completely altered, I trust." But Wright's image does not so much deliquesce as become an impure transparency: he himself is nothing, "Just red in the sky before the sun rises."

Even the first portrait, which Wright described as "fairly straightforward," is about his sense of indefiniteness and dispersal: "My features are sketched with black ink in a slow drag through the sky, / Waiting to be filled in." It closes with an appeal to his gift to define him: "Hand that lifted me once, lift me again, / Sort me and flesh me out, fix my eyes." But this sorting proves a kind of defleshing: "Angel of Mercy," he pleads by the fifth poem, "strip me down."

In the second and third poems he checks the "postcards and photographs" on his study walls for "evidence" (the third, quoting from Dickinson's letters, begins: "*The pictures in the air have few visitors*"). "Evidence," does he mean, of a crime? Have his "lavish" hands squandered too much, including others' words? Has he been wrong to pretend to be a source, he, a mere cloud-source, melting, derivative? The crisis of his existence: doubt of its separate validity.

Small wonder if in the fourth poem he first disappears into "place names in Italy." But then, returning to the scene of his crime, he is caught out when he names poets who "become places I've been to"—Dino Campana, Rimbaud, Hart Crane, and Dickinson.[3] (Combining place and art, Cézanne's *The Black Chateau* concludes the catalogue.) Now the jig

---

3. The major influence, the Pound of the early *Cantos*, peeps out from behind the Italian place names.

is up and in the last poem he pleads—he proves—unable to help himself. The three stanzas "have nothing to do with each other, other than having something to do with me." But he cannot hide in such a scatter. The first speaks of a "ghost-weight" that pinned him to a bed where two women had once been murdered—the dead proving once again more substantial than he. The second quotes from Donne, the third from Dickinson. "Donne and Dickinson are ghost-weights on your tongue?" "Yes." "Are you afraid that when you're found out you'll turn out to be other poets?" "We're all other poets. You're what you read, to a certain extent."

In all, a series remarkably original and subtle (and expectably elusive)—but then to begin to appreciate Wright is to expect nothing less from his oddly sorting, unfleshing hand. The originality, subtlety, and elusiveness alike lie in strategies of self-deliverance—skirling metaphorical substitutions and metonymies, dizzying jump-cuts, twists of oxymoron and parataxis.

In keeping with all this the poet goes one better and shuffles his series of self-portraits together with a counter series on death as a birth out of the self. ("After the first death, there is no other," as Wright's Vitalist parent, Dylan Thomas, instructed.) So "Mount Caribou at Night" finds "everything flowing and folding back / And starting again"; "Holy Thursday" sees "Children begin to move, an angle of phosphoresence / Along the ridge line"; "Virginia Reel" says

> . . . Just down the road, at Smithfield, the
>    last of the apple blossoms
> Fishtails to earth through the shot twilight,
> A little vowel for the future, a signal from us to them . . .

and "Called Back" ends: "When the oak tree and the Easter grass have taken my body, / I'll start to count out my days, beginning at 1."

The self-portraits concentrate on what weighed on Charles like evidence, the others on what Charles will one day fold back into (that day when the voices rising around him like mist and dew will no longer need to say, "*it's all right, it's all right, it's all right* . . ."). There is, then, in the intermingling of these groups an alternation (a "circulation") between guilty individuation and the counter-fate of a glorious dispersal, albeit this antithesis is qualified by the way his pitiless, magnifying gaze reduces even his individuality to isolated, impersonal specks.

What is it that Wright wants, to deliver the self or to escape it by dying, whether literally or figuratively? To effect the first you must break with the parents. This Wright is unwilling to do. In "The Southern Cross," to be sure, he erases them by going back to the starting point, the moment before the lungs first flapped with air. But at the cost, still, of infancy. That divine sinking in on the self—will he ever evoke it again? Distance from the self, star-distance, distance of "ashes and bits of char"; "spider love, undoer and rearranger of all things"—these are likely to remain his needs.

In the longest of the four divisions of the book (following "Homage to Paul Cézanne" and the section containing the selfportraits), Wright takes up a new technique for self-parting, one picked up from John Cage. At a concert Cage was asked, "What are you doing when you're up there fiddling with the score paper and twiddling your pencil?" Cage replied, "I'm giving myself instructions and carrying them out." "I thought that was a pretty interesting answer," Wright commented. "What I do in each one of these poems in the third section—and this should have no effect whatsoever on the reading—is give myself instructions and carry them out."

"A complete contortion," Wright said, explaining the title "Dog Yoga." The instruction: no verbs. "Yet to make it look as though it's effortless. And it does smooth on down the page, I think." It does:

> A spring day in the weeds.
> A thread of spittle across the sky, and a thread of ash.
> Mournful cadences from the clouds.
>
> Through the drives and the cypress beds,
> > 25 years of sad news.
>
> Mother of Thrushes, Our Lady of Crows,
> Brief as a handkerchief,
> > 25 years of sad news . . .

And so on for ten more lines and half-lines. And in the next poem, the reverse, "a verb in every line":

> At dawn the dove croons.
> The hawk hangs over the field.
> The liquidambar rinses its hundred hands.
>
> And the light comes on in the pepper trees.
> Under its flat surfaces horns and noises are starting up.
> The dew drops begin to shrink . . .

This goes on for nine more lines, each ending in a period, an additional artifice, raising the factor of difficulty. Both poems sound right and, moreover, like Wright. His themes—"We are what we have always been," "No sign of a story line," and so forth—accommodate both verblessness and a poking parataxis that with a threadless needle stitches and stitches the ungatherable moments.

Handed such instructions, the muse becomes thoughtful, self-watchful— she must keep one step ahead of herself. (Of course she must always have her wits about her but the technique helps exact what Eliot called "the continual extinction of the personality.") In "The Monastery at Vršac," for instance, she has to break off narrating and observing and suddenly base the poem "on a statement (something you really shouldn't do)," then follow it immediately with "another statement that becomes a new foundation." Nor can she decide in advance what the statements are going to be. She plays the game well—jump-cut and apogee are, after all, in her blood. It is only the initial narrative ("We've walked the grounds," etc.) that manacles her. It has her stupefied with conversation and "brandy-colored light."

Wright's turn for concentration amidst dispersal (for simultaneous being and not-being, hereness and thereness) assimilates the most difficult instructions. Take as a last example "Dead Color." The instruction: "No bobbin on which the whole poem is wound." This sounds anti-poem, but in a sense all Wright's poems are absences from themselves, the bobbin is always lost to the other side. (As he puts it in *China Trace*, "There's something I want to say, / But not here, stepped out and at large on the blurred hillside.") Almost all his lines express a waiting, and waiting is the bobbin-by-default on which "Dead Color" is wound. "Between the grey spiders and the orange spiders, / No voice comes on the wind. . . ." "Meanwhile" the usual cycles ("The lawn sprinklers rise and fall"; "Aphids munch on the sweet meat of the lemon trees"); the usual entropy ("The traffic begins to thin"); the usual promises ("the heavens assemble their dark map"; "Over my head, star-pieces dip in their yellow scarves toward their black desire"). This poem with "no point of reference" is effectively about having none—an unmistakable "Charles Wright."[4]

To all this esotericism of technique Wright's readers—such is the intention—remain a laity.[5] It does not concern them, it is his affair, his askesis, his self-extrication, his evasion (and not only of his readers but of the fleshpots of his art). The instructions are the ghost intelligences of his text; they constitute a secret order. Substitutes for the parental dead ("I have the feeling that the dead always know more than I do"), they sim-

---

4. Again, "Skins" had asserted that what "comes and . . . goes" nonetheless always "comes to a point." But this positivity, this heroic "point," is one that Wright's work, now lag-hearted, now leap-nerved, keeps missing or rejecting.

5. Secretiveness, writes Susan Sontag in her essay on Walter Benjamin, "Under the Sign of Saturn," appears a necessity to the melancholic: "He has complex, often veiled relations with others." Other Saturnine traits—among them the view of time as a "medium of constraint, inadequacy, repetition," the compulsion "to convert time into space," indecisiveness, a "self-conscious and unforgiving relation to the self"—are conspicuous in Wright's work.

ulate the instructions that are always pouring in, coded, from the other side: the side at once author and arbiter, giver and receiver, the beginning and end of the circle on which the poet is invariably at a point of exile, both departing and arriving, too far from and too near the "great ones" to be more than their torturingly eloquent trace.

Yet, to repeat, this complex, philosophically splayed volume contains more spadefuls of what Patrick Kavanagh called "the earth's healthy reality" than any of Wright's earlier volumes do, and the most conspicuous sign of this is its warm naming of real people and places. I return again to the fourth self-portrait:

> Marostica, Val di Ser. Bassano del Grappa.
> Madonna del Ortolo. San Giorgio, arc and stone.
> The foothills above the Piave.
>
> Places and things that caught my eye, Walt,
> In Italy. On foot, Great Cataloguer, some 20-odd years ago.
>
> San Zeno and Caffè Dante. Catullus' seat.
> Lake Garda. The Adige at Ponte Pietra
> —I still walk there, a shimmer across the bridge on hot days,
> The dust, for a little while, lying lightly along my sleeve . . .

However rapid, such naming is memory's sacrament. Charles, great cataloguer, is more passionately precise than Walt, who joyfully poured together the names of places that to him were more often signs than memories. Wright, too, chants, but at once more matter-of-factly and meticulously—memory getting it right.

At the same time the poet washes, as he said in *Bloodlines*, "in a water of odd names." In the first place, the names are objectified by their music. "Cactus, the mustard plants and the corn"—always the masterful selection and disposition. Where Emerson's "Bulkely, Hunt, Willard, Hosmer, Meriam, Flint" is (not undeliberately) cloddish and serial, Wright's "Woodburn and Cedar Hill, Smithfield, Auburn and North Hill" graciously drawls its geographical polyphony. Add to this the dulled romance of abstraction (the "other language" of "Wishes" in *China Trace*, in which the days are not "each nosed by the same dog"). Spiky "Marostica," valiant "Val di Ser," and so on, are freed from the capricious flux of phenomena, singled out by the strong light of the line. "Since I came to this abbey Hermit's Summons," wrote Meng Chiao, Wright's ancient Chinese alter ego, "For a while the dust weighs lightly on my cloak." Wright's own hermitage consists of a shimmering bridge of names.

Another master example of this ritual naming is "Bar Giamaica, 1959-60"—a verbal variation on a photograph by Ugo Mulas tacked to Wright's study wall. It begins:

> Grace is the focal point,
> >                         the tip ends of her loosed hair
> Like match fire in the back light,
> Her hands in a "Here's the church . . ."
> >                                         She's looking at Ugo Mulas,
> Who's looking at us.
>
> Ingrid is writing this all down, and glances up, and stares hard.
>
> This still isn't clear.
>
> I'm looking at Grace, and Goldstein and Borsuk and Dick Venezia
> Are looking at me.
> >                     Yola keeps reading her book.

And it closes:

> Summer arrives, and winter;
> >                         the snow falls and no one comes back
> Ever again,
> >             all of them gone through the star filter of memory,
> With its small gravel and metal tables and passers-by . . .

By this point the reader himself is mourning—the brisk process of the poem having suddenly closed in a beautifully managed pathos. Already in the simile of the match fire the present surface of the photograph is virtually aflame. The sanctifying and preserving power of art is hinted at only by a "Here's the church" formed by hands with a merely social wish to entertain. The "See all the people" follows. Then it's gainsaid, but not before Wright has conceded far more plenitude than usual to the first category of nouns (to persons as against places and things).

Ugo Mulas himself is included perhaps as a kind of muse and as the nominal photographer of Wright's own real or invented group (when "Ugo finishes . . . everyone goes away"). In a sense Ugo makes use of the group, after the alien manner of artists, like Ingrid who "is writing this all down, and glances up, and stares hard." Yola's reading, like the poet's later study of the photograph, completes the circuit of art, closing it back into the common world from which, in part, it sprang.

But greater than this subplot is the social moment of grace ("Grace" is indeed the focal point) among confirmed and easy friends. The cat's cradle of their glances is described, the equal emphasis on the individual and the group managed, in glad *allegro*. The camera position shifts frequently and democratically, is freely and lightly dollying. The many-angled and any-angled technique bespeaks a friendly trust in the group, a social togetherness harmonious with individual differences (Yola reads, Ingrid writes, etc.).

But the poem has the further, elegiac purpose of rescuing the heterogeneous names—those already quoted and "the rest of them: Susan and

Elena and Carl Glass, / And Thorp and Schimmel and Jim Gates, and Hobart and Schneeman"—from the still greater variance of dispersal and from the slow obliterations of time. It defies, before duly acknowledging, the snow that has fallen since that "afternoon in Milan in the late spring." Yet, despite the face value of the photograph (the one that enables the present tense), Wright is of course unable to rescue the group from the sad fate of being outlasted by small gravel and metal tables and anonymous passers-by.

In "Bar Giamaica" the spidery movement attempts to evade time through lightness and rapidity. Increasingly Wright has avoided stanzas ("I don't like blocks in poems," he said in the *FIELD* interview. "I like breathing space"). At his happiest he starts a flow that seems to circumvent time by escaping almost eagerly toward the freer future. He can run by a whole line of seventeen or nineteen syllables like a single ripple in the clear skin of a lake:

> The early blooms on the honeysuckle shine like maggots after the rain . . .

> Now the wisteria tendrils extend themselves like swan's necks under
>     Orion . . .

> I hope the island of reeds is as far away as I think it is . . .

Overcoming the dread of space, the contemplating I with a sweet energy identifies with renewing or self-extending or distant forms. Using long lines or slipped-down half lines, or variable line lengths, or polysyndeton, or enjambed stanzas, all inspired by the demand for deliverance, Wright can initiate a flow almost at will. In "Mount Caribou at Night," a poem about the first homesteaders in the region of Montana where the Wrights have a cabin, and about a final homestead in the universe itself, even the conservative appearance of the quatrains fails to dam the progress back to the inanimate—a progress itself, of course, profoundly conservative:

> Everything on the move, everything flowing and folding back
> And starting again,
> Star-slick, the flaking and crusting duff at my feet,
>
> Smoot and Runyan and August Binder
> Still in the black pulse of the earth, cloud-gouache
> Over the tree line, Mount Caribou
> Massive and on the rise and taking it in. And taking it back
>
> To the future we occupied, and will wake to again, ourselves
> And our children's children snug in our monk's robes,
> Pushing the cauly hoods back, ready to walk out
> Into the same night and the meadow grass, in step and on time.

I find these lines, indeed most of the book, enchanting. Sweet and strange, nearly everything in it is mesmerizingly in language. One might expect many casualties where each line is a cast into the uncanny; one might even resist their absence, which is itself uncanny. And a few lines do seem randomly afloat on the surface—"One lissome cheek a notch in the noontide's leash," for instance. But a very few. Wright's ear, again. . . . It is a highly developed, if peculiarly sensual, form of intelligence.

In addition to the hypnotic naming and the lithesome movement of the line and the absence of matte moments, there are graces of varying kinds. To begin with, telling metaphor: "The reindeer still file through the bronchial trees, / Holding their heads high"; "the brief and flushed / Fleshtones of memory." Grimacing wit: "I've made my overtures to the Black Dog, and backed off." Exact description: "Little tunnels of boat wash slipping back from the granite slabs / In front of Toio's, undulant ripples / Flattening out in small hisses, the oily rainbows regaining their loose shapes." Firm placings:

> Angels
> Are counting cadence, their skeletal songs
> What the hymns say, the first page and the last.

August but plainly worded imaginings, as of his brother "Winter on top of the Matterhorn":

> Behind him, the summer Alps
> Fall down and away, like hillocks of white on the noon sky
> Hiding their crosses, keeping the story straight.

Dantean archaisms: "Venus breaks clear in the third heaven." Imagist vividness: "Butterflies pump through the banked fires of late afternoon." Calliopean bursts of vowels: "Canticles rise in spate from the bleeding heart." And odd, compelling modulations:

> And towns that we lived in once,
> And who we were then, the roads we went back and forth on
> Returning ahead of us like rime
> In the moonlight's fall, and Jesus returning, and Stephen Martyr
> And St. Paul of the Sword . . .

In addition, there are audacious oxymorons: "I'll rise from this tired body, a blood-knot of light, / Ready to take the darkness in"; "My poems . . . / Little tablets of salt rubbed smooth by the wind." *Frissons* of the impossible stated, very simply, as possible: "And time to retrieve the yellow sunsuit and little shoes they took my picture in / in Knoxville, in 1938." Vivid illustrations: "Language can do just so much . . . / Flash and a halfglint as the headlights pass. . . ." Stunning tableaus: "Death never entered [Li Po's] poems, but rowed, with its hair down, far out on the lake,

/ Laughing and looking up at the sky." Unnerving interminglings: "man-tis paws / Craning out of the new wisteria; fruit smears in the west . . ."; "This is a lip of snow and a lip of blood." Above all the perfect pitch, the effect, always, of precision:

> Thinking of Dante, I think of La Pia,
> and Charles Martel
> And Cacciaguida inside the great flower of Paradise,
> And the thin stem of Purgatory
> rooted in Hell.

In all, Wright is a spellbinder of the first order. Needless to stress, his world is not especially various (most poets' are not); his few moods brush up against little besides landscapes. Yet his lines glow with a peculiar blue fire, part dusk, part sacred enkindling. He is never less than an exquisite poet of yearning for something elsewhere, something purer; and to this ancient hope and complaint he brings a finely calculated originality, a re-finement of sensual beauty, and an indomitable passion. The combination sets him high, I think, among the cold-quickened, cold-straitened artists of the age.

# Under the Sign of the Cross (1989)

I want to listen first to Charles Wright's "The Southern Cross," the title poem of his fifth collection, published in 1981. It is a long poem, in twenty-five sections of unequal length. In all his mature books, Wright has tended to cluster his short poems into sequences, lending each poem more weight by its collaboration with others. But "The Southern Cross" is a single, sustained poem. Its very title points to its effective origins: on the one hand, to the southern heritage he bears; and on the other, to Dante's *quattro stelle*, the sign over his purgatorial ascent. This helix of native and acquired resources—what the poet himself would probably call, after the titles of the two books that preceded *The Southern Cross*, his "bloodlines" and his "traces"—has been a crucial emphasis in Wright's poetry from the start, as often as not embodied in a diction that swerves from slang to grandiloquence.

The epigraph to *The Southern Cross* is also from Dante, the last seven lines of Canto XXI of the *Purgatorio*, where Statius kneels to embrace his teacher Virgil's feet, having just wished Dante that *his* great labor may come to good ("*Se tanto labore in bene assommi*"). Dante then startles the old poet by revealing that Virgil, the strength of both their poems, stands before him. The episode is a touching encounter, and a literal community of poets, master and pilgrim, across time. That same sense of community is one of Wright's burdens in "The Southern Cross," a poem that is above all the reconciliation of his two inheritances, of the natural and poetic, of Fate and Power. Wright has acknowledged the strong accents of others in his way of speaking, but he has singled out two masters: Ezra Pound and Eugenio Montale. Pound, I suspect it is proper to say, was Wright's instructor; Montale was an influence.

"I discovered poems in Verona," Wright once told an interviewer. (He was stationed there in the army, at twenty-three.) "I was given a book, *The Selected Poems of Ezra Pound*, and told to go out to Sirmione, on Lake Garda, where the Latin poet Catullus supposedly had a villa. . . . I read a poem that Pound had written about the place, about Sirmione being more beautiful than Paradise, and my life was changed forever."

The poem was Pound's gaslit "Blandula, Tenulla, Vagula," and its first line set Wright the question his subsequent career has sought to answer: "What hast thou, O my soul, with paradise?" That quest for the sublime, not only in "the impalpable / Mirrors unstill of the eternal change," but in an earthly paradise "wherein the sun / Lets drift in on us through the olive leaves / A liquid glory," has since been Wright's own. It has allowed him to gaze on both the gold leaf of his beloved Venice and the foliage of his native East Tennessee with equal wonder. Pound no doubt initiated Wright into modernism's "broken bundle of mirrors," taught him how to read a poem (for its rhythm and logopoeia) and where to find one ("only emotion endures"), prompted with a syllabus in cultural cross-referencing, and fixed his attention on the image. Wright was not alone in turning to Pound's work as the pattern for the image as that "instant when an outward and objective thing is transformed to a thing inward and subjective." Over the course of modernism and beyond, the image has been elevated from trope to genre. Every new dispensation from imagism itself to surrealism to the Writers' Workshop, has encouraged imagery to do the work of reason and music, physical description and emotional narration. Wright is one of the new contemporary poets with a sure command of the technique of images, whereby he can both epitomize and depart from a point in his poem.

Pound's example led to the identification of the image with the fragment, or series of phrasal units, and to that technique of dealing them out that Wright calls "jump-cutting." Pound taught Wright how to move through a poem by association rather than by narrative. I'd prefer to call this *linkage*. "It's linkage I'm talking about," he says in the title poem of *The Other Side of the River*, "and harmonies and structures / And all the various things that lock our wrists to the past." Linked images, then, are not just a means to structure a poem or harmonize its conflicting pressures; they are—as they were for Proust—the work of memory itself, and the way of spiritual enlightenment. These images are conceptual rather than exclusively visual, and from the beginning—it is important to remember—have been a way of listening. "Pound came to me aurally," he's said. "I really didn't know any of the background of the *Cantos*, so all I heard was the sound as I read it. . . . It just became a part of the way I hear things." (He also says he dreams this way—in vivid but dissociated fragments.) What this finally means is that Pound taught him to listen not to words, but to language; and less to language than to the *movement* of language, to those harmonies of sound that underlie the meanings of words.

He began writing, then, having read Pound. And having begun to write, he started translating Montale. "At such a formative time in my development," Wright has said, it "was a real gift—I was able to see the grooves and dovetailings, the suspensions and stresses and, in general, most of the physical ways he put poems together." Translation has always been a kind of classroom for a poet, where poems can be dismantled and reassembled. And few poets in this century put poems together better than Montale. The polyphony of his twenty-part *Motetti* is echoed in Wright's various sequences. In many other ways too Wright has seen to it that his work—everywhere his method, and sometimes his material—stands together with Montale's. What would have first attracted him? Certainly the interplay in Montale's lines between sound and silence; his complex analogies, especially between landscape and heartscape, and the

austere luxuriance of his language; his *eretismo*, a privatism at once inti-
mate and enigmatic, like a music heard at a great distance.

Of course there is other music to be heard in and behind Wright's
lines. Country music, for instance. That phrase itself is now the title of the
edition of his selected early poems. What Italian opera was for Whitman,
so for Wright are the rhythms and blues of Earl Scruggs, Lester Flatt, the
Carter family, Roy Acuff, and Merle Travis. Sometimes the echo is in-
tentional. Here are the last two lines from each of the three stanzas of
"Laguna Blues":

> Something's off-key in my mind.
> Whatever it is, it bothers me all the time.
>
> . . .
>
> I'm singing a little song.
> Whatever it is, it bothers me all the time.
>
> . . .
>
> Something's off-key and unkind.
> Whatever it is, it bothers me all the time.

The lines, especially taken out of context, are as flat as the refrains in the
standard villanelle. But put two guitars and a fiddle behind them. . . . The
influence, of course, is usually more subtle, and the subject matter of
country music—adultery, divorce, heartbreak, revenge, the soap opera of
love—is precisely what is *not* in Wright's work. What he has caught in-
stead are both the broader "lifey/deathy/afterlifey" themes of the songs,
and their sense of phrasing—the long, swelling strophes, the punched-out
refrains. He has listened for this music in poetry too, and hears it—maybe
he alone can hear this—in Emily Dickinson, whose work he wittily calls
"White Soul." Mention of her poems also brings to the mind's ear the
hymns he heard in church and on the radio during his childhood, the
rhythms of the catechism, the Bible, and the Book of Common Prayer.
Once asked to define his poetic voice, Wright said "it's some kind of
speech on the outside of the stained glass looking in." Often in his work
you hear the cadences of prayer. Here is a section of "Holy Thursday" (a
poem that also owes something to Blake's two poems of that same title):

> There's always a time for rust,
> For looking down at the earth and its lateral chains.
> There's always a time for the grass, teeming
> Its little four-cornered purple flowers,
>                                 tricked out in an oozy shine.
> There's always time for the dirt.
> Reprieve, reprieve, the flies drone, their wings
> Increasingly incandescent above the corn silk.

At other times, his lines may sound like the ejaculations of private prayer, or the steady catalogue of a litany or holy office. But more often, this measured, balanced tone can be heard. Much more than blank verse, these steady ecclesiastical rhythms are his contact with the rhetorical tradition. They are rhythms that invoke and celebrate a communal striving, and when they sound in a "personal" poem they give it greater dimensions. The high priests of modernism had a role too. The "freed" verse of T. S. Eliot and the pentameter of Wallace Stevens or Hart Crane (whose own "Southern Cross" is a register of Wright's) are undoubtedly part of it, but when Wright talks about his disdain for flat language and his love for a richly rhetorical art, it can be no accident that his metaphor comes from church: "I always like the organ in the background of a poem. I like those *profundo* notes, that swell." And it is his rhetoric, enriched and heightened, that distinguishes his work from that of poets he is usually associated with—Mark Strand, Charles Simic, and James Tate, the sound of whose work is more dead-pan or sardonic, more anecdotal and ordinary.

Wright dedicated *The Southern Cross* to H. W. Wilkinson—who is not anyone the poet knows. It just happens to be the name stenciled onto an old metal footlocker that Wright keeps near his desk, and in which he stores old family letters and documents and heirlooms, even a lock of Robert E. Lee's hair. Appropriately then, this book is dedicated to a voice box. The rhythms of family and region, so early imprinted, are a part of any poet's voice. This century's Southern poets, from Allen Tate and Robert Penn Warren to James Dickey and Dave Smith, have favored the orotund periods of preaching and the tale, and Wright too loves what he calls "the sound and weight and rub and glint of words," and likes stacking them. The Southern landscape that prompts these words is itself a kind of text. "When I write to myself," he told an interviewer, "I'm writing to the landscape, and the landscape is a personification of the people on the other side." It is, in other words, a map of memories and a route to the dead, his mother in particular. And, it is important to remember, he listens to their voices through the other texts he hears. The ritual of symbolism is one, and its repertory of charged images: stars, mirrors, crystals, wings, and silence itself. Other voices come to him in the bunched accents he has heard in Gerard Manley Hopkins, and in the speeded-up leaps of association of Rimbaud.

Even in his early poems, the hallmarks of Wright's style can be heard. Here is a brief description of the Arno in moonlight, a three-line stanza from the middle of "Nocturne":

> The Arno, glittering snake, touches
> The white cloister of flame, easing
> Its burden, the chill of its scales.

The perspective is as from a great distance. The tone is mysterious. Phrases interrupt, overlap, qualify. An internal network of sounds trembles with connections, whereby "glittering" and "chill," or "snake" and "flame" pull the lines together and bind the images. The bel canto of long, open vowels tends to slow down the line—"The *white cloi*ster of *flame, ea*sing"—and short consonantal bursts give it a snap. The pauses in the lines are variously distributed, twice near the end of the line to emphasize the action ("touches" and "easing"), and then earlier in the final line so that the image, which brings together the cold moonlight and the coldblooded snake, the backlit ripples and the monastic plainchant, is allowed its full resonance.

Or, to study the "movement" of a complete poem, here is "Snow," from *China Trace* (1977):

> If we, as we are, are dust, and dust, as it will, rises,
> Then we will rise, and recongregate
> In the wind, in the cloud, and be their issue,
>
> Things in a fall in a world of fall, and slip
> Through the spiked branches and snapped joints of the evergreens,
> White ants, white ants and the little ribs.

The poem is a single sentence, in two tercets. If the meter is unsteady, that is because the poem's rhetoric is its true binding agent. Its opening conditional sentence proposes a syllogism, and its rationalist logic is used to set up an improbable situation. In many poems, Wright alludes to the language of argument, or scatters bits of narrative, in order to invoke the energies of those kinds of discourse without lapsing into their rigors. The first stanza glides easily from legal to biblical terms—a "cold" diction—the better to prepare us for the surprises in the second stanza. Where before was resurrection, now is a miniature wasteland, the fallen world, threatening and disjointed. The first stanza ended with a birth, the second ends with a death. The snow we may have expected to cover or disguise the "world of fall" in fact reveals it, strips it to the bare bone. The snowflakes swarm and devour. Yet the tone seems one of acceptance; ours is "a world of fall," of process, of becoming and unbecoming. (The poem is preceded by one called "Childhood," and followed by one called "Self-Portrait in 2035.") And I think that tone is achieved by Wright's masterful control of pace and image. Each line of this second stanza has three blocks of sound and reference, three lapping waves. Their even distribution adds its own equanimity. The terms are strange, but the rhetorical pattern is familiar, nearly lulling. Wright's is a poetry of nouns and adjectives, of phenomena and qualifications, of metaphor—not of action and definition—and this lets his linked images create a marvelously fluent texture. The voice is depersonalized—literally drained of "personality," quirks, and traits. Its rhythms are musical and insistent; "most of my poems," he says, start "with a rhythm rather than a structure." And his rhythms tend to be primal—rising and falling—or formulaic. A good deal of ordinary material—exposition, transitions, explanation—has been deleted in the interests of a taut line, and the line itself is given an independence and prominence. It is as if each line bore the weight of the whole poem. As it is, the line for Wright is "the linchpin of the poem." "It is as though the lines," he says, "were each sections of the poem attached by invisible strings to the title, the way the various parts of a marionette are attached by strings to the control board." So in "Snow" we are directed back to and on by the control board, the dominant image.

But let me resume this discussion by turning now to "The Southern Cross" itself. Here is the opening section:

> Things that divine us we never touch:
>
> The black sounds of the night music,
> The Southern Cross, like a kite at the end of its string,
>
> And now this sunrise, and empty sleeve of a day,
> The rain just starting to fall, and then not fall,
>
> No trace of a story line.

The poem starts under the sign of the Cross. We begin with a premise, which the setting is then supposed to confirm; and we end with an observation which doubles back to the first line, and instructs us how to read the poem that follows. "Things that divine us"—and we then know what those "things" are, the sounds and sights and symbols of night turning into day. "Divine" means both to *understand* and to *foretell*; it can also mean to *make gods of.* "We never touch," on the other hand, means "We never contact" or "never violate." The poem opens, then, with a troubled transcendence. What knows us is unknown to us. What makes us more than human—that is, less ourselves—is something we can never wholly approach, a note we can't clearly strike. The aphoristic language seems affirmative, but its message is one of denial, reversal, absences.

When Wright says there is "no trace of a story line" to be found here, he is using an image that is linked with the earlier image of the constellation as a kite: there is no "line" that connects observer and heaven, poet and sublime. But he is also talking about his method in the whole poem—in all his work, really. His poems do not develop by a "story line," linearly or horizontally. They develop, let us say, vertically, lines and phrases overlaid on one another. Helen Vendler's description is apt: "They cluster, aggregate, radiate; they add layers like pearls." This technique, central to other latter-day imagists like James Wright or Galway Kinnell, is part of their surrender of voice. The effort is to have the poem write the poet. Its wise passivity represents the pure ascendancy of the poet's material, of spiritual analogies rather than intellectual analysis. This is the heritage of *epiphany*, whereby the familiar is revealed with new force; and it is our contemporary agency of *the sublime*, whereby the poet may be imbued with otherness, may transcend the self by erasing or expanding it. The next section of "The Southern Cross" drifts on its images, and treats the self as an object, insubstantial and evanescent:

> All day I've remembered a lake and a sudsy shoreline,
> Gauze curtains blowing in and out open windows all over the South.
>
> It's 1936, in Tennessee. I'm one
> And spraying the dead grass with a hose.
> The curtains blow in and out.
>
> And then it's not. And I'm not and they're not.
>
> Or it's 1941 in a brown suit, or '53 in its white shoes,
> Overlay after overlay tumbled and brought back,
> As meaningless as the sea would be
>                                   if the sea could remember its waves . . .

Nothing is sustained here; things come into focus only to fade again. The brief sections, with their one, two, or three line stanzas see to that. The lines pulse; their strong caesuras divide the line into two or three phrases; each phrase is a pair of terms, often a noun and adjective that may be both joined and contrasted. The poem is conjured rather than displayed. What is true for each section is true for the whole. "My poetic structures," Wright says in his notebook, "tend toward the condition of spider webs—tight in their parts but loose in the wholes." He prefers structure to form. That is to say, he works with a set of abstract ambitions and designs for the poem that evade many traditional formal assumptions and prescriptions.

Two sections later, we are given some classic Wright description:

> All day the ocean was like regret,
>                                   clearing its throat, brooding and self-absorbed.
>
> Now the wisteria tendrils extend themselves like swan's necks under
>     Orion.
>
> Now the small stars in the orange trees.

Water is the entire poem's dominant image. It is above all "the blank / Unruffled waters of memory"—amniotic fluid and developing solution. It washes through the poem, through the canals of Venice and into Lake Garda and the Adige and the California ocean. And throughout, as in the first line here, it is identified with the poet's own voice. It is a voice that seems to include its own echo. The dropped hemistich in the first line— and it is used all through the poem—functions antiphonally, as a sort of choral response to the first half of the line. One might even call it a sort of stichomythia. This is another of Wright's experiments with the line. At different times, he has stated his intentions differently. Sometimes he speaks of wanting to "relax" the line, to slacken the pentameter. Elsewhere he has spoken of wanting to lengthen the line "to see just how long I could make it and still have it be an imagistically oriented line and not a discursive, or narrative-based line: the extended, image-freighted line that doesn't implode or break under its own weight." Having cleared its throat, this sea-voice then speaks of the wisteria in such a way that its natural beauty is extended toward the sublime. I could imagine Whitman writing such a line. And he might also, like Wright, have then brought those same stars down to earth, as orange blossoms. The danger Wright runs is that he may miniaturize or aestheticize the sublime. He may do so to avoid the pressures of moralism or of history, but by "purifying" or essentializing his quest he sometimes falls short, underestimates its demands, refuses its power. This is a danger Wright largely avoids, however, and besides, it is his drive toward rather than his prolonged engagement with the sublime that matters, because it helps determine the underlying rhythms of his imagination. This upward urging of the beautiful toward the sublime counterbalances the lure back and downward of the elegiac note sounded everywhere in the poem as well. These shifts of tone and perspective give the poem its "sweet" but restless ambition, its weight and authority. Like the ebb and flow of water and wind, of memory itself, the voice of this poem moves through its "ghostly litany."

Away on waters, we move to Italy, where the clouds are "dragging the sky for the dead / Bodies of those who refuse to rise." This is another kind of divining: trying to raise the dead. As he searches the "river of sighs and forgetfulness" he realizes that "Dante and Can Grande once stood here," and before that Catullus, and "before that, God spoke in the rocks . . . / And now it's my turn to stand / Watching a different light do the same things on a different water." Boldly, Wright links himself with the great voices, the *original* voices. History is domesticated, and the self is aggrandized by its chosen company. His true parents then join these artistic parents. Valéry once remarked that one keeps in memory only what one has not understood. That is what is haunting about Wright's poem, and about his method of linkage.

> They're both ghosts now, haunting the chairs and the sugar chest.
>
> From time to time I hear their voices drifting like smoke through the living room,
> Touching the various things they owned once.
> Now they own nothing
>                and drift like smoke through the living room.

But in the poem's ebb and flow of the domestic and the sublime, these ghosts bring back Dante's, and at once another kind of divining occurs.

To remember is, figuratively, to embody again: "Thinking of Dante, I start to feel / What I think are wings beginning to push out from my shoulder blades, / And the firm pull of water under my feet." As if become a soul in Dante's poem, he envisions "the great flower of Paradise, / And the thin stem of Purgatory rooted in Hell." But as the *Commedia* implies, the vision of Paradise returns us to earth.

> Thinking of Dante is thinking about the other side,
> And the other side of the other side.
> It's thinking about the noon noise and the daily light.

Then follows, as the eleventh section, a long evocation of Venice, the most virtuosic in the poem. It is the Venice of cold pearl skies and mirror-of-steel canals. The only human figure is the aged Ezra Pound:

> I remember the way that Pound walked
> across San Marco
> At *passeggiata*, as though with no one,
> his eyes on the long ago.

It is worth pausing here to note how few people are present in Wright's poems. The epigraph to *Country Music* is from Hemingway: "The country was always better than the people." But it would be a mistake to think of Wright as merely a descriptive poet. People, he says, "become landscapes that I have loved in my life. Landscapes that have nourished me, landscapes that I have walked through, landscapes that have remained with me. Their works are landscapes." That is to say, landscape is a personification of both the dead (like his parents) and the poets. Places are either shrines or texts to "read," as well as a means to see and recover the self. For Wright, landscape is opposed to nature, but not entirely opposed to eternity. The landscape *speaks* to this poet. But the voices always trail off; are overlaid with others, or with silence:

> As always, silence will have the last word,
> And Venice will lie like silk
> at the edge of the sea and the night sky,
> Albescent under the moon.
>
> Everyone's life is the same life
> if you live long enough.

Venice *lies* because it does not have the last word. What does is the blank page on which the poem rests and shifts its weight. "The white space is really white sound," he explains, "sound the ear doesn't always pick up but which is always there, humming, backgrounding, like silences. It's what pulls the lines through the poem, gauging their weights and durations, even their distances. It is the larger sound out of which the more

measured and interruptable sounds of the line are cut." So the last word
is also the first music, the ground note from which melodies briefly arise.
The poet's task is how and when to break silence. As we look at the
*mise-en-page* of a poem by Charles Wright, we must realize that the
"white space" connects as it divides the lines. His is a poetry of pauses
and feints, as if his very reluctance to speak forced his extreme concision
and elegance. Silence too is a voice in the poem.

At its midpoint, the fourteenth section, after the long Venetian ca-
denza, the poem starts again, with a paraphrase of the opening:

> There is an otherness inside us
> We never touch,
>           no matter how far down our hands reach.
> It is the past,
>         with its good looks and *Anytime, Anywhere* . . .
> Our prayers go out to it, our arms go out to it
> Year after year,
> But who can ever remember enough?

One could link this with a later passage that speaks (like Cocteau) of
imagining "a mouth / Starting to open its blue lips / Inside me." *On
me dit.* The otherness within is not alien; it is both the past and the
voice that would speak of the past. But are memories enough to pro-
pitiate this otherness? "It's what we forget that defines us" is Wright's
answer.

"The Southern Cross" is a very American poem because it worries
about an old world and a new. But this is not the venerable polarity of
Europe and America. California and Montana, where the poem is being
written, constitute a present, while the Tennessee of his boyhood is the
past. Venice, Verona, and Rome have both an antiquity and a past (when
Wright lived there, a dozen years before the poem was written), and they
have a presence in his reading. The poem next casts a wide net over his
*Italienischereise.* This is not so much a man remembering as a man ob-
serving his memories. It is another way to efface himself, to let things
speak for themselves. His long catalogue of sense-memories, though, is an
odd erasure, denying what it includes, as here:

> I can't remember the colors I said I'd never forget
> On Via Giulia at sundown,
> The ochres and glazes and bright hennas of each house.

"Time is the villain," he concludes; it takes these details away, not just
from us but from the things themselves. And if we recall that "villain"
originally meant "one who lives in a city," then it's an appropriate term
for the process. The poem now leaves the city for the pastoral fields of
longer memory. Time itself is the landscape of this poem, and "its land-
scape is the resurrection of the word." As the poem moves toward

its conclusion, there is a literal race against time. It begins with a note of Keatsian plenitude: "I can't remember enough."

> How the hills, for instance, at dawn in Kingsport
> In late December in 1962 were black
>                                    against a sky
> The color of pale fish blood and water that ran to white
> As I got ready to leave home for the 100th time,
> My mother and father asleep,
>                              my sister asleep,
> Carter's Valley as dark as the inside of a bone
> Below the ridge,
>                   the 1st knobs of the Great Smokies
> Beginning to stick through the sunrise,
> The hard pull of a semi making the grade up US 11W,
> The cold with its metal teeth ticking against the window,
> The long sigh of the screen door stop,
> My headlights starting to disappear
>                                    in the day's new turning . . .

> I'll never be able to.

The finale is his resignation. Sitting on his step—as if it were a rung on the mount of the *Purgatorio*—the poet watches "a brute bumblebee working the clover tops." This Dickinsonian bee is Wright's thrush or nightingale. It goes about its sweet business; so do the lupin and bog lilies, and the wind signs a *Let-us-pray* and "the golden vestments of morning / Lift for a moment." We are back at the morning the poem opened with, but with the poet's realization that "everything has its work, everything written down." All the voices choir in harmony. And again, it subsides to a silence—the sound of the wind, of breath itself:

> The life of this world is wind.
> Wind-blown we come, and wind-blown we go away.
> All that we look on is windfall.
> All we remember is wind.

The liturgical cadences here can't disguise the puns. The tone is somber—as if we were meant to hear "dust and ashes" instead of wind—but the larger sense of process, and of the poet's resignation to it, gains by our participation in the moment: *we* look, *we* remember. A windfall is a sudden stroke of good fortune; and memory becomes inspiration itself. So the wind is destroyer and preserver both. Can we link it with Shelley's West Wind? "Be thou me," Shelley implores the wind, surrendering himself, his voice, "lift me as a wave, a leaf, a cloud . . . make me thy lyre."

"Pickwick was never the wind. . . ." So the last section begins, naming his birthplace. In a poem woven out of Proustian *intermittences du coeur*, it is only right that we return to his earliest memory now at the end. But this memory is not of a place, but of the idea of a place—and so Pickwick merges with Pound's paradisal city in *The Cantos*, and perhaps with Dante's Rose of Light as well. Again the poet alternates a memory and the scene of remembering, the past and a visionary future, activity and entropy, the human and the natural worlds—and above all, speech and silence. For this poet, who wants to make the world speak through him, whose lines are like beads for us to tell and to praise that world, to fall silent is to have accomplished his task.

> It's what we forget that defines us, and stays in the same place,
> And waits to be rediscovered.
> Somewhere in all that network of rivers and roads and silt hills,
> A city I'll never remember,
>                               its walls the color of pure light,
> Lies in the August heat of 1935,
> In Tennessee, the bottom land slowly becoming a lake.
> It lies in a landscape that keeps my imprint
> Forever,
>            and stays unchanged, and waits to be filled back in.
> Someday I'll find it out
> And enter my old outline as though for the 1st time,
>
> And lie down, and tell no one.

JAMES MCCORKLE

# "Things That Lock Our Wrists to the Past":
# Self-Portraiture and Autobiography in
# Charles Wright's Poetry (1989)

CÉZANNE: "I have my motif . . ." (He joins hands.)
GASQUET: "What?"
CÉZANNE: "Yes. . . ." (He repeats his gesture, spreads his hands, the ten fin-
gers open, brings them together slowly, slowly, then joins
them, squeezes them, clenches them, inserts them together.)
"There's what must be attained. . . . There must not be a sin-
gle link too loose, a hole through which the emotion, the light
or the truth may escape. . . . I bring together in the same spirit,
the same faith, all that is scattered. . . . I take from right, from
left, from here, there, everywhere, tones, colors, shades; I fix
them; I bring them together. . . . My canvas joins hands. It does
not vacillate."

("Interview," 1979)

It's linkage I'm talking about,
                and harmonies and structures
And all the various things that lock our wrists to the past.

("The Other Side of the River")

Charles Wright's poetry is an autobiography of energy and
transmutation, where the self's writing collaborates with the
natural world's writing. Writing extends our perception of the
natural world and, as such, writing forges interconnection through
the process of interpretation. Writing is the place of the transference of
the world's languages into our discourse; thus, writing mediates the
natural world and the self. Wright's poetics share G. M. Hopkins's
emphasis on syntax, music, and the natural world as the locus of medi-
tation as well as instructing us in the intimacies of nature and mortal-
ity. Writing on Hopkins, Gerald Bruns notes that Hopkins "figures
himself in terms of a hermeneutic relation to the created world, as to a
text or Book of Nature, whose 'compositions' are figures of energy that
enact, as forms of language do, events of differentiation—the 'running
instress,' in Hopkins's words, that 'unmistakably distinguishes and indi-
vidualises things.' To 'read' such compositions is an interpretive act, a
naming in the human language of signs of that which inscribes itself
('distinguishes and individualises' itself) in the natural language of

energy."[1] Unlike Hopkins, who privileged human speech as the evolutionary and doxological completion of the created world, Wright confronts a severed discourse where disclosure is never complete and presence is always provisional and stained by death. Nonetheless, Wright and Hopkins share a poetics in which writing and nature are thought of as an "energetic form" of a "continuity . . . shaped by the flow of energy, or energy made articulate in something visible and tangible."[2]

The idea of linkage encompasses Wright's concept of language, his use of the poetic line, the structure of the poem, and the conceptual order of his collections. Language itself is generated through the energies of connection; language, while generative, embodies its own elegy or its own death: "Something infinite behind everything appears, / and then disappears" (*OS* 24, "The Other Side of the River").[3] Writing and interconnection occur through the release of motion and energy; thus, writing is relational. Connection is the betweenness of the self and the other, the place of provisional mediation of subject and object:

> When the mind is loosened and borne up,
> The body is lightened
>         and feels it too could float in the wind,
> A bell-sound between here and sleep.
>
>                 (*OS* 56, "T'ang Notebook")

Within this configuration of energy, movement, linkage, and mortality, the consideration of autobiography must be included. Autobiography, here, is not meant as a purely confessional mode: instead of dictating personal experiences (however edited) into lyrics or narratives, Wright translates and transfers those experiences into meditations on mutability, memory, and generation. Autobiography becomes the convergence of the self and language; the poem self-reflexively comments on its own making and hence mirrors the poet's regard of the self:

---

1. Gerald Bruns, *Inventions: Writing, Textuality, and Understanding in Literary History* (New Haven: Yale University Press, 1982), 132-33.

2. Ibid., 136.

3. Charles Wright, *The Other Side of the River* (New York: Random House, 1984), 24. The following titles by Charles Wright are abbreviated, and citations for quotations from these works are provided in the text: *B—Bloodlines* (Middletown, Conn.: Wesleyan University Press, 1975); *CT—China Trace* (Middletown, Conn.: Wesleyan University Press, 1977); *G—The Grave of the Right Hand* (Middletown, Conn.: Wesleyan University Press, 1970); *HF—Hard Freight* (Middletown, Conn.: Wesleyan University Press, 1974); *OS—The Other Side of the River*; and *SC—The Southern Cross* (New York: Random House, 1981).

> It's all a matter of how
> > you narrow the surfaces.
> It's all a matter of how you fit in the sky.
> > > (OS 24, "The Other Side of the River")

The craft of perception and the making of the poem reflect the making of the self. By meditating on language and situating the self within the energies and erosions of language, Wright's autobiography records the making of the poem and the irreducible energy of mortality. Thus, his speculations propose that we live in a world of language. The heterogeneous forms of discourse—complete with tension, difference, and generation—mirror ourselves and inscribe our own mortality: to speak or write of ourselves is to speak or write about language and death.

The moment when the poet's mirrored self or imago is recognized and held in regard is an autobiographical moment, analogous to a painter's composition of a self-portrait. For both painters and poets, the creation of radical alterity through contemplation must not become self-objectification, for that would create a death mask instead of an interrogatory other. Self-portraiture is perhaps the most immediate and obvious form of autobiography, and it certainly suggests the formal and thematic correspondence of painting and poetry. In reference to his collection *Hard Freight,* Wright has remarked that he uses "stanzas in the way a painter will build up blocks of color, each disparate and often discrete, to make an overall representation";[4] however, his affinity with painting extends beyond this one collection of poems and beyond an analogous process of representation to include a similar process of self-definition. As William Howarth has argued, not only do autobiography and self-portraiture "suggest a double entity, expressed as a series of reciprocal transactions," but a self-portrait, unlike a portrait or biography, demands that "the artist-model must alternately pose and paint," for in "a mirror he studies reversed images, familiar to himself but not to others."[5]

Wright's explicit and self-announced "self-portraits" are "uniquely transactional" moments,[6] in Howarth's terms, which attempt and question re-presentation (the making present again). In each self-portrait, the fixity of image is in tension with the context, the transactional composition, and the duration of the regard of the artist and reader. In the autobiographical act, we confront the moment when the self clearly mirrors

---

4. Charles Wright, "Charles Wright at Oberlin," in *A FIELD Guide to Contemporary Poetry and Poetics,* ed. Stuart Friebert and David Young (New York: Longman, 1980), 268.

5. William Howarth, "Some Principles of Autobiography," in *Autobiography: Essays Theoretical and Critical,* ed. James Olney (Princeton: Princeton University Press, 1980), 85.

6. Ibid., 85.

itself, but at the same time the mirror clouds or reflects another image, so that we never return to the original. Though all writing is what John Ashbery calls the "leaving-out business,"[7] self-portraiture and autobiography constitute the most radical conjunction between writing and the self expressed through the dynamic energies of repression, selection, and revelation. Whether self-conscious or not, some detail is always included at the expense of another, and this repressed detail forms the silhouette of the original image seen in the mirror long ago. Wright attempts to recover the parts of the original imago, yet this turns to an exploration of the provisionality and fragmentation of self and narrative.

"Self-Portrait," in *The Grave of the Right Hand,* essentially quotes several of de Chirico's paintings from his metaphysical period: *Self-Portrait* (1913), *The Song of Love* (1914), *The Serenity of the Scholar* (1914), and *Portrait of Guillaume Apollinaire* (1914). Each stanza derives its imagery from de Chirico's iconography: the opening lines, "There is a street which runs / Slanting into a square" (G 57), fit any number of de Chirico's cityscapes, which typically play with the geometrics of perspective in Italian Renaissance paintings, generating a further interiorized quotation. Both Wright's poem and de Chirico's *Self-Portrait* (1913) contain fragments of classical statuary or the fragmentation of an idealized image; each self-portrait becomes a portrait of absence, or more precisely, the tangible memories of time's passage.

Wright's "Self-Portrait" emphasizes the distance between the self or the text and others—echoing John Ashbery's *artes poeticae* of self and text. Wright recognizes, not his own presence, but the fragments that lead toward another composition of another place, time, and hidden self. De Chirico's interest in reflexivity is easily illustrated in *Portrait of Guillaume Apollinaire*, which is alluded to in the second stanza of Wright's poem:

> There is a pair of glasses
> A statue also
> Casting a long shadow                                    (G 57)

In the painting a marble bust wears a pair of sunglasses, while in the background the silhouette of Apollinaire is glimpsed through an architectural construction in such a way that the bust and silhouette are almost back-to-back. The blinded, classical statue is isolated yet linked to the shadowy mannequinlike partial profile of Apollinaire, seen through the threshold: the past has become fixed and blinded; the present remains a mysterious shadow. The poem's final image, "Nailed to a door / There is a pair of gloves" (G 57), emblematizes the lack of presence: the hands that would fill the gloves are absent, and only the outer shell or lineament

---

7. John Ashbery, *Rivers and Mountains* (New York: Ecco Press, 1977), 39.

of that presence remains. Such images as gloves, shoes, and garments—comprising a contemporary iconography for poets like W. S. Merwin and Galway Kinnell—suggest traces of a past presence and the presence of a mysterious absence. The poem points to a nightmare of mere forms toward which language seems headed. Wright places himself into a particular poetic context in "Self-Portrait," yet his place is only provisional and can be understood only by examining what he has placed in it: the self is one of "the lost displays," Wright's apt title to this section of *The Grave of the Right Hand*.

De Chirico's use of facades and statuary creates a mysterious juxtaposition of the past and the industrialized present of locomotives and factories. Here, the signatory long shadows emerge as much from the enigma of memories as from the fragmented and scattered objects. Wright's self-portrait portrays not so much the self's presence as the presence of others. The poems of *The Grave of the Right Hand* appear to be fragments of a larger, fictive work, and thus self-reflexively point to themselves as texts that, like de Chirico's paintings, evoke an anticipated but disrupted order. The enigmatic unease of de Chirico's paintings is seized upon both to reinforce the anxiety of provisionality and to provide an anchor or iconic analogue offering stability, authority, and reference.

Wright's self-portrait in *China Trace* is again a version of himself absented. "Self-Portrait in 2035" depicts Wright in his hundredth year, buried and decomposing in the landscape:

> The root becomes him, the road ruts
> That are sift and grain in the powderlight
> Recast him. . . .                                            (*CT* 15)

As in the earlier self-portrait, assemblages and associative objects form the means of self-portraiture. The body sinks into the earth to be "recast" and thrown back into being in a new form. The transformative powers of such alliterations as "worm-waste," "dust-dangled," or "past pause" mirror and ground the force of organic decay; these mirrored sounds reveal the primacy of language as experience and mortality, rather than as an extracted significance.

The final couplet, "Darkness, erase these lines, forget these words. / Spider recite his one sin" (*CT* 15), points back at the poem, and in particular at the language of the poem. Like the body of the poet, which has disintegrated, the poem is about to disappear into darkness or the de-compositional monody of silence. The spider, left to recite the poet's one unnamed sin, maintains discourse—or metaphorically and allusively reopens with Arachne's challenge to weave more beautifully than Athena, to cast words as idealizations rather than as the segments of gossamer that they are. Whitman's noiseless spider, which casts its filaments into space to link with the other, also mirrors the challenge Wright seeks. Nevertheless, the speaker realizes that the other can be found only in the "sift and grain" or in the chaff and fruit. The spider of "Self-Portrait in 2035" recites the sin in the natural language of the web: a language from which the poet has fallen, becoming "Unlinked and laceless"; a language to which the poet can only return by being "recast"—thrown, molded, and given a new role—in the natural order.

Although the desire for the melding of the human into the natural world is apparent in the poem "Signature," its title points to the consideration of the paradox of presence and repetition. The poem becomes an ideogram of "Charles Wright," albeit transliterated into a linear form. As the most minimal of self-portraits, it is the signature that creates the presence of the self-portrait and not the painted and framed image. By it, we ascertain the "veracity" of a particular self-portrait, whether it be by "name" or by distinctive brushstrokes that make the signature a seal that authenticates and authorizes what it seals. The signature, and "Signature" itself, refers to the desire for presence:

> Live like a huge rock covered with moss,
> Rooted half under the earth
> > and anxious for no one.  (*CT* 52)

This Zen-like meditation demands a complete integration with the surroundings, where the self is a huge rock settled into the earth. In this state of presence in the landscape, there can be no change. To expect change as a condition for presence denies the corresponding immanence of self and spirit. The title, which suggests repetition, points to itself as writing and presents the impossibility of attaining presence anywhere outside the articulate and material energy of writing.

The self-portraits in *The Southern Cross* work equally as a group and as individual poems. The five self-portraits are contained in a single section of the collection; four longer poems punctuate the sequence. The self-portraits' symmetrical fifteen-line form—also used in the "Tattoos" sequence in *Bloodlines*—maintains a concise balance and interplay without the traditional rhetorical and argumentative demands of a sonnet. The self-portraits weave other poems into their fabric and formally mirror each other. Within the poems' common frame, the force of language discloses the imposed limitation of intentional form. The long lines quite literally explore the edge, the frame, and the boundary of self, language, and page; this active form tests and pushes against the margins of the page and against form itself:

> The wind will edit him soon enough,
> And squander his broken chords
> > in tiny striations above the air,
> No slatch in the undertow.  (*SC* 15)

The pressure of language against the containing walls of form describes an elemental tension in poetry. On the one hand, Wright has developed

an almost ecstatic and spiritual power for poetry through the contempla-
tion of mortality and the desired reintegration with nature. The poem
points to and belongs to a transcendental process in which nature unre-
lentingly repossesses the poet's corpus. The poet's place in a material and
organic world informs his spiritual understanding and strength. However,
there is the contrary tradition of self-reflexivity at work. The assertion
that the wind will "edit" the poet forms a complex trope; it not only sug-
gests the wind riffling the dust of the poet's bones and papers, but the
dispersion of his words, even on the page, the ironically failed voice, his
"broken chords."

The emblem of the poet's words dispersed into the air echoes W. S.
Merwin's poem "Sibyl."[8] Both Merwin and Wright recognize the ex-
treme dilemma of the lost efficacy of language when hollow words mir-
ror hollow men. Merwin, however, grounds his vision in the
mythological trace that, in turn, points to a different and lost conscious-
ness. Wright's vision always turns back to the intimacy of the self, the
poet, and the mirroring of the self in language. The turning inward fore-
grounds the poem's condition as a verbal construction in continual
mnemonic movement: a "night bridge / To the crystal, infinite alphabet
of his past" (SC 15).

The fourth "Self-Portrait" comes closest to what Wright describes as
the poems' central focus: his life and where and how he lives it. Even so;
the poem suggests only a nominal autobiographical quality, for the poem
consists, not of events, but of notations:

> Marostica, Val di Ser. Bassano del Grappa.
> Madonna del Ortolo. San Giorgio, arc and stone.
> The foothills above the Piave.                                    (SC 22)

The place has hardened into the minim of the name. The name holds in-
finite histories and narratives, but within the lyric what is important is the
music of the names and the hermeneutic energies of remembered names.
They are signposts, directions, signals of the eye-I's travels, "Places and
things that caught my eye, Walt, / In Italy. On foot, Great Cataloguer, some
20-odd years ago" (SC 22). Though Wright grounds himself in Whitman's
tradition of collecting and celebrating names and places, he distinguishes
himself from Whitman's vision by acknowledging that these names are of
public significance only in their music and that, as Calvin Bedient notes,
"such naming is memory's sacrament."[9] Copious yet having limitations,
lists and self-portraits are places where memory and current transactions
coincide in litany.

---

8. W. S. Merwin, *Writings to an Unfinished Accompaniment* (New York: Atheneum,
1976), 53.

9. Calvin Bedient, "Tracing Charles Wright," *Parnassus* 10, no. 2 (1982): 69.

Wright contemplates the self deferred, unaccounted for, only glimpsed through language, for any language we propose constitutes the self as another. The final line of the second "Self-Portrait," when "St. Augustine strik[es] the words out" (*SC* 15), rejects any privileging of the self. Though the autobiographer becomes a "'reader' of his own past," autobiography can be described as "'literally' the analysis of one's past discourses, of one's acts and utterances, insofar as they signify within a social and linguistic context."[10] Wright's autobiographical writings, while seeking to engage the language of the world or St. Augustine's book of nature, always turn back upon themselves; this turning back is in itself an attempt to erase the barrier between self and other. Yet any such visionary desire is undercut by the materiality of writing, be it the poet's or the phenomenal world's. Writing, however, provides only a posthumous presence, for Wright mock-elegiacally writes, "Someday they'll find me out, and my lavish hands, / . . . / My features are sketched with black ink in a slow drag through the sky, / Waiting to be filled in" (*SC* 13). Though self-portraiture and autobiography can be described as the "process of collaboration between an individual conscious and that Other which permeates it,"[11] in Wright's poetics self and other link without synthesis or transcendent unity in discourse's "process of collaboration" or in the space of language.

At the end of the first "Self-Portrait" in *The Southern Cross*, the poet offers a psalmlike prayer to save himself from the limitations and stasis imposed on and by language:

> Hand that lifted me once, lift me again,
> Sort me and flesh me out, fix my eyes.
> From the mulch and the undergrowth, protect me and pass me on.
> From my own words and my certainties,
> From the rose and the easy cheek, deliver me, pass me on.
>
> (*SC* 13)

Movement, synonymous with transformation, rescues the poet from stasis and death. The hand—that of inspiration that lifts the poet towards authentic language, of the poet himself casting with words towards some hoped-for permanence, of critics who will sift Wright's poetry, and of the celestial that offers salvation—will rescue the poet from complete dispersion and apocalypse in order to remake him, while "ashes and bits of char . . . will clear [his] name" (*SC* 13) of his primal sin. Language consists of the remains of a continent and its culture, debris and anonymous counters, all of which judge us. And what is the poet's "name" beside his

---

10. Candace Lang, "Autobiography in the Aftermath of Romanticism," *Diacritics* 12, no. 4 (1982): 11.

11. Ibid., 16.

"one sin" of "Self-Portrait in 2035"? Implied in these self-portraits is Michel Foucault's question, "What is an author?"[12] An author can only be a repository for influences and is subject to erosion. To be an author, Wright argues, is to seek some form of deliverance from the under-growth of signs, while committing the "one sin" of desiring an unnatural or hierarchic name. This is the hubris of writing that attempts to master and authorize the world.

The imposed form of the self-portraits in *The Southern Cross* creates an assurance of presence and memory in spite of the fragmentation and dispersal of the idea of the author. The repeated forms, furthermore, provide a counterpoint to the discontinuous and associative movement of language within the form's constraints:

> I see myself in a tight dissolve, and answer to no one.
> Self-traitor, I smuggle in
> The spider love, undoer and rearranger of all things.
> Angel of Mercy, strip me down.        (SC 24, "Self-Portrait")

Not only is the poet "in tight dissolve" (a vortex or a photograph still in the emulsion), but he betrays himself, for the writing immortalizes and deadens. Withal, the poet is reenvisioned as a producer of texts, an "undoer and rearranger of all things"; and as such, the poet's work parallels the spider's work, and reflects the spider's weaving of the poet's "one sin." Nevertheless, Wright implicitly hopes to recover his essential self: in spite of language's ability to overrun, there is some Angel of Mercy—a mysterious intervention of a Rilkean imaginative force—willing to "strip me down," or so the poet hopes, to essentiality. Yet such longing can only be nostalgic, recalling Blake's world of innocence—small, secure, distant, a place of tentative community:

> This world is a little place,
> Just red in the sky before the sun rises.
> Hold hands, hold hands
> That when the birds start, none of us is missing.
> Hold hands, hold hands.                      (SC 24)

Here, interconnection recalls childhood, community prayers, and the gathering of the souls in the early cantos of Dante's *Purgatorio*.

---

12. Michel Foucault's essay "What Is an Author?" in *Language, Counter-Memory, Practice* (trans. Donald F. Bouchard [Ithaca, N.Y.: Cornell University Press, 1977]), raises the question of authorship. Foucault substitutes "author-function" for "author" and suggests we look at a work in terms of its interactions, functions, and production, all of which could be subsumed into Wright's intertext and the idea of interconnection and linking.

Self-portraiture describes the confrontation with mortality and imma-
nence; salvation defers to the desire for presence:

> I've been writing this poem for weeks now
> With a pencil made of rain, smudging my face
> And my friend's face, making a language where nothing stays.
> The sunlight has no such desire.
> In the small pools of our words, its business is radiance.          (*SC* 38)

The poem doubles back upon itself to comment reflexively upon what is
written; thus, the writer's presence is known only through the presence
of other texts. The ironic title, "Portrait of the Artist with Hart Crane,"
indicates the poem's textual playfulness. In "Portrait of the Artist with Li
Po," Wright questions the possibility of defining presence only by conti-
nuity and not also by difference:

> Everyone knows the true story of how he would write his verses and float
> them,
> Like paper boats, downstream
> > just to watch them drift away.
> Death never entered his poems, but rowed, with its hair down, far out on
> the lake,
> Laughing and looking up at the sky.                      (*SC* 39)

For Wright, the confrontation with death—the knowledge of differ-
ence—is central; these two poems are homages to Crane and Li Po as well
as Wright's calling forth of their apparitions. Though Wright knows "The
distance between the dead and the living / is more than a heart beat and
a breath" (*SC* 39), he longs for continuity and interconnection. The rein-
scription, again another form of signature and re-presentation, of Li Po's
line "*The peach blossom follows the moving water*" suggests that the text,
whatever its status, has the efficacy to persist and to connect, regardless of
the dissolution of the self or the author. Writing itself transcends the anx-
iety of the provisionality of presence.

While maintaining a formal sensibility throughout, the spare early
poems of his first collection give way to the exploratory sequences of
poems in the triptych comprised of *Hard Freight*, *Bloodlines*, and *China
Trace*. While the self-portraits are experiments in the autobiographical
moment, the triptych collections, defined by their formal organization,
move diachronically and emphasize the autobiographical in geographical,
historical, familial, and generational terms. Wright's serially linked poems
are balanced and symmetrical groupings that elude closure by spatially
and temporally unfolding and infolding. The symmetry of each collection
reflects less the vision of an underlying whole than the architecture of
textuality. The poet, as architect, designs an artifice that inquires into the
order or repetitions within the natural world, and parallels the activity of
naming or the physical composition, brushstroke by brushstroke, of a

painting. Paradoxically, the intimation of completeness, implicit in sym-
metry, and the incomplete and undisclosed are held in tension. Wright's
use of symmetry is less intended to be "meaningful" than it is to be the
place of energized transactions. Resolution is elided; the architecture it-
self turns numinous.

*Hard Freight* is arranged to reveal the art of the book and to point to
itself, the book, as an object. The opening and closing sections, appropri-
ately titled "Homages" and "End-papers" respectively, bracket the title
section, "Hard Freight." *Bloodlines* creates a concentric and balanced
grouping of poems. The progress or pilgrimage of the reader moves from
the outer group of three poems, through the serial poem "Tattoos," to
reach the central group of two poems. The reader then moves outward,
from the serial poem "Skins" to the outer group of three poems. Such
symmetry demands that the collection be viewed as a whole and not as
a linear movement of diverse texts. Inside-outside, heart-body, or cen-
ter-frame are evoked, yet any separation of these seeming opposites is im-
possible, for one is defined by the other. The book itself illustrates
interconnection and movement. The book, too, atavistically mirrors the
world and inscribes a provisional order—evoking the Augustinian idea of
nature as book.

Each section of *China Trace* opens with the same quotation from Italo
Calvino's *Invisible Cities*. The quotations, like Calvino's book as a whole,
emphasize mirroring and the problematics of representation. *Invisible
Cities* consists of a dialogue between Marco Polo and the Kublai Khan,
in which Marco Polo recounts the cities he has seen; each city is an imag-
inary signifier, something desired yet always distant. Possession of the rep-
resentations of the other is impossible, for, as Calvino states, the Khan
would then be "an emblem among emblems."[13] Calvino, like Wright, ex-
amines the production of signs as the desire for the other that is always
alienated as well as being both telos and origin. *China Trace*, the final col-
lection of the triptych, moves away from the vision of the organic world
of *Hard Freight* and *Bloodlines* to view the universe as the movement of
signs puncturing silence and white space.

In *Hard Freight*, as the title makes clear, the poems travel back to past
places and events. The poems meditate on the ways in which our bodies
contain time and decay, while our names inscribe the past; thus the
poems' thematic and structural expressions of the dissolution of our
connections focus on mortality and a desire to forestall time.
"Primogeniture" ends with images of biological resurrection: "Rose of
the afterlife, black mulch we breathe, / Devolve and restore / . . .
Rechannel these tissues, hold these hands" (*HF* 54). By definition, pri-

---

13. Italo Calvino, *Invisible Cities*, trans. William Weaver (New York: Harcourt Brace
Jovanovich, 1974), 22-23.

mogeniture is the passing on of land or an inheritance to the firstborn son; yet it also indicates the bonds between generations represented through the land. The poem, an elegy for a primogenitor, a father, is also a poem about the passing on of life to another; thus, it is a companion poem to "Firstborn" and "Congenital." In the latter poem, Wright recognizes his ancestry in his own body:

> —These hands are my father's hands these eyes
> Excessively veined his eyes
> Unstill ever-turning
> The water the same song and the touch  (*HF* 58)

In the poem's first stanza, Wright locates his origins not only in his "father's hands" (one text) but also in the landscape where distinctions between things are diminished. The phenomenal world is suffused with presence, which is only recognized in the conjunction—the "hawk-light"—of being and language:

> Here is where it begins here
> In the hawk-light in the quiet
> The blue of the shag spruce
> Lumescent
>           night-rinsed and grand  (*HF* 58)

Like Elizabeth Bishop's "The Moose," the natural world is "grand" and otherworldly in its mysteriousness. For Bishop, such a moment occurs inadvertently; for Wright, the natural world translates into a spiritual moment that is potentially always near at hand. The poem's final word, "touch," hangs suspended, immanent, and immediate—"lumescent."

"Firstborn," a series of six symmetrical sections celebrating the birth of Wright's son, further develops the theme of genealogical interconnections: "We bring what we have to bring; / We give what we have to give" to "Welcome, sweet Luke, to your life" (*HF* 27). The past will be transmitted to the child, whose identity intermeshes with the world and mirrors the interconnectedness of the landscape:

> The bougainvillaea's redress
> Pulses throughout the hillside, its slow
> Network of vines
>
> Holding the earth together, giving it breath;
> Outside your window, hibiscus and columbine
> Tend to their various needs;
>
> The summer enlarges.  (*HF* 28)

The bougainvillaea's "network" of flowering vines, the "hibiscus and columbine" that "Tend to their various needs"—indeed, the whole fertile summer—parallels Luke's growth, "the new skin / Blossoming pink and clear." The metaphoric language of growth celebrates the possibility of life and connects the son to the flower-world outside his window. Furthermore, the father links himself with his son through the self-reflexivity of metaphoric language.

Language, however, has its own limitations: the mystery of the other overwhelms discourse and almost silences it:

> You lie here beside me now,
> Ineffable, elsewhere still.
> What should one say to a son?                                    (HF 29)

There is so much to say to one's son, yet neither "Emotions and points of view," nor the "Abstractions we like to think / We live by," nor "something immediate, / Descriptive" can serve as the means of address. The father realizes not only the "ineffable" quality of his son but the abyss between what he desires to say and what he is able to say. One can only "say" what one desires by stating its impossibility when confronted with the otherworldliness of the baby. Like W. S. Merwin, Wright finds that language can only be provisional; one may look for "those few felicitous vowels / Which expiate everything," but they are not to be found. Instead, they "remain in the dark, and will / Continue to glitter there. . . . No strategies, can now extract them" (HF 30).

Wright admits a certain exasperation with wrestling the angel of language and concedes, "What I am trying to say / Is this / . . . Indenture yourself to the land" (HF 31). Wright places himself in the mainstream of the tradition of American artists and thinkers concerned with the landscape and our places within it. He seldom refers to an urban setting; instead, the rural landscape retains mystery and interconnectedness that the urban landscape, for Wright, implicitly does not. Such distancing from the urban underscores his general disinclination to confront outright the political concerns constituted in language. Wright seems too accepting of male tradition, and even insists, particularly in this poem, on privileging male connections through genealogy. Wright essentially seeks to praise the natural world and our capacity for remembering it; however, he does not move to question his language in other than intimate terms. This is not to say that Wright's poetry slides into a pastoral mode or the solipsism of scenic poetry. Wright's poetry approaches being a phenomenological (a reverie of the world as writing) and theological poetry in the tradition of Hopkins. The natural world is the place of the other's language and energy that transform his perceptions into the poem's vectoring and traveling lines.

The fifth section of "Firstborn" ends with echoes of devotional hymns: "Surrender yourself, and be glad; / This is the law that endures" (HF 31). Wright anchors himself in the various traditions of Whitman, Faulkner, the Hudson River School of painters, American Transcendentalists, and

Native American teaching with this statement that affirms the primacy of the land. And through this statement he also enacts the continuation of this particular tradition's life and authority, for he passes it on—as it was passed to him—to his son and to his readers. To invoke and pass on the law of the father is to assure one, within discourse, of certain identity. Unlike Adrienne Rich and W. S. Merwin, who offer various critiques of the father (symbolic and autobiographical), Wright essentially celebrates the father as a symbol of generation, connection, and salvation. Language, for Wright, is less a subject for criticism than it is for Rich or Merwin, who emphasize the political and cultural corruption by and of language. In contrast, Wright envisions language, not as an arena of authority, but as the closest reach of the other. In the sixth and final section of "Firstborn," Wright names the sources of his vision of connection: "Nantahala, / Unaka and Unicoi," the Indian tribal names that "Brindle and sing in your blood; / Their sounds are the sounds you hear" (*HF* 32). Each name is a palimpsestic trace, hence a memory of previous traces. Luke's name is "like a new scar," something corporeal and, like a signature, identifiable and re-peatable. The name or the scar is the place where two edges fuse together, always marked and always re-membered.

Though "Firstborn" occupies a central place in Wright's work, the longer, meditative, and autobiographical poems of *Hard Freight* that de-scribe the landscape of his youth are the most stunning in their richness of language and point to the direction taken up in *Bloodlines*. The open-ing lines of "Dog Creek Mainline" reveal words stripped to their ener-gies of presence (nouns) and transformation (verbs):

> Dog Creek: cat track and bird splay,
> Spindrift and windfall; woodrot;
> Odor of muscadine, the blue creep
> Of kingsnake and copperhead;
> Nightweed; frog spit and floating heart,
> Backwash and snag pool: Dog Creek
> Starts in the leaf reach and shoal run of the blood;
> Starts in the falling light just back
> Of the fingertips; starts
> Forever in the black throat
> You ask redemption of, in wants
> You waken to, the odd door:
>
> Its sky, old empty valise,
> Stands open, departure in mind; its three streets,
> Y-shaped and brown,
> Go up the hills like a fever;
> Its houses link and deploy
> —This ointment, false flesh in another color.          (*HF* 43)

The landscape incorporates the poet's body; sounds generate new sounds; the colon opens new stanzas and creates a movement of growth and dehiscence.

Wright travels back into the past landscape of Hiwassee, North Carolina, and into his own childhood of 1941 and the outbreak of the Second World War. It is here that he confronts the body and the "black throat"—the always-present death within our bodies that gives us defini-tion. "Cross-tie by cross-tie" of "indigent spur" carrying "hard freight" takes Wright back to his beginnings, where he discovers loss:

> Dog Creek is on this line,
> Indigent spur; cross-tie by cross-tie it takes
> You back, the red wind
> Caught at your neck like a prize:
>
> (The heart is a hieroglyph;
> The fingers, like praying mantises, poise
> Over what they have once loved;
> The ear, cold cave, is an absence,
> Tapping its own thin wires;
> The eye turns in on itself.
>
> The tongue is a white water.
> In its slick ceremonies the light
> Gathers, and is refracted, and moves
> Outward, over the lips,
> Over the dry skin of the world.
> The tongue is a white water.).                                   (*HF* 44)

The eye or I "turns in on itself" to retrieve and renew memories of what was once loved. The parenthetically enclosed inward turn suggests the alienation of heart, fingers, ears, and eyes. Only the tongue, the metonym for the poet, remains undistanced and moving. From the tongue, like a river's source, language flows (ostensibly the poem above or beside the stanzas marked [off] by the parentheses) "over the dry skin of the world" and replenishes and reconnects the world with memories and names.

Landscape, like language, is, however, a topography created by rifts and abysses: "Half-bridge over nothingness, / White sky of the palette knife; blot orange, / Vertical blacks" (*HF* 51, "Northhanger Bridge"). And like the landscape, language can be "stripped of its meaning" (*HF* 51) and of its capacity for interconnection. These abysses signal the difficulty of au-tobiography and of representation. Wright writes over nothing—the blank page and death. Writing becomes a form of grace, and memory a spiritual activity.[14] The vocabulary consisting of "signatures," "emblems," "sentences," "nouns," "blue idiom," "pale semaphore," "inked-in valley," and "language of numerals" suggest that discourse penetrates everything so far as to be the medium of interconnection:

---

14. Bedient, "Tracing Charles Wright," 61.

> The past, wrecked accordion, plays on, its one tune
> My song, its one breath my breath,
> The square root, the indivisible cipher . . .

(HF 47, "Sky Valley Rider")

Walking along "the evening water," where he had once hunted unsuccessfully with his father, the writer in "Blackwater Mountain" startles a duck into a flight that

> shows me the way to you;
> He shows me the way to a different fire
> Where you, black moon, warm your hands.

(HF 49, "Blackwater Mountain")

The dark, absent moon—the absent father—is retrieved and conserved by the return to the place of previous union. Language is mysterious and material—its mysteriousness lies in its materiality.

The theme of linkage is further explored in Wright's third volume, *Bloodlines*; the collection's title itself emphasizes this pervasive theme. Though the birth of writing was "often linked to genealogical anxiety,"[15] bloodlines are genealogical exfoliations and the body's circulatory system, as well as the very lines of the poems in the book. The transposition of genealogy into poetic lines retains personal and familial voices while also decentering a vast cycle of flux, change, and reemergence:

> As we slide slide to the music, humming
> An old tune, knee touching knee,
> Step-two-three, step-two-three
> Under a hard hatful of leaves,
> The grass with its one good limb holding
> The beat, a hint of impending form.
> It gathers, it reaches back, it is caught up.

(B 75, "Link Chain")

Wright dances not only with his past childhood but with the cycle of life that "gathers," "reaches back," and "is caught up" in some intuited "impending form." The autumnal dance of life recollects past events: big sister's hair is "heaped like a fresh grave" and her "fingers [are] cool tubers" (*B* 74-75, "Link Chain"). In the midst of this harvest dance arises an awareness of mortality, but mortality must include life, for the dance never stops; nothing remains fixed in a particular form, but always metamorphoses into another, new form. The music of the poem transforms

---

15. Jacques Derrida, *Of Grammatology*, trans. Gayatri Chakravorty Spivak (Baltimore: Johns Hopkins University Press, 1976), 124-25.

the autobiographical moment into one of the steps of the dance of metaphors, "where all is a true turning, and all is growth" (*B* 69, "Skins").

The two most important poems of this collection are the paired and mirrored series "Tattoos" and "Skins." As their titles suggest, the tattoos inscribe events upon the skin, the body, and the poet without the possibility of erasure. The events, not to be celebrated in and of themselves, make up the partial alphabet of the poet. Tattoo, defined also as a rhythmic drumming, describes a form of signaling various events. Each poem of the series "Tattoos" is dated and carries a footnote identifying the place and the core autobiographical event alluded to, so that the notes further inscribe or tattoo the event. Each poem or tattoo is the inscription of an event on the poet's memory; the poem is a resurrection and "palm print, / The map that will take me there" (*B* 27). Memory and renewal work dialectically, for presence is stained by its other, death: "You stand in your shoes, two shiny graves / Dogging your footsteps" (*B* 38).

In the first poem of the sequence "Tattoos," the sight of camellias prompts Wright to propose the fusion of inspiration and redemption, while also questioning his memory and his song:

> So light the light that fires you
> —Petals of horn, scales of blood—,
> Where would you have me return?
> What songs would I sing,
> And the hymns . . . What garden of wax statues . . .  (*B* 19)

The provisional initiation of light and song opens the sequence. What follows are the songs he sings—about his parents' deaths, his sexual initiations, Italy, his childhood religious experiences. The poet enacts his Orphic role and sings the world into a provisional, mnemonic revival: "The dead grass whistles a tune, strangely familiar" (*B* 36). Nonetheless, Orphic dismemberment haunts these poems, in that the poems arise out of a severed past that must be readdressed and reinscribed:

> The hemlocks wedge in the wind.
> Their webs are forming something—questions:
> *Which shoe is the alter ego?*
> *Which glove inures the fallible hand?*
> *Why are the apple trees in draped black?*
>
> And I answer them. In words
> They will understand, I answer them:
> *The left shoe.*
> *The left glove.*
> *Someone is dead; someone who loved them is dead.*  (*B* 37)

In each of these sections, the poet emphasizes the salvational role of language. As a house of accumulated memories, language connects the poet with the discourses and actions of the natural world. The origin and inspiration—literally, the breathing in of life—remains unnamed, mysterious, and other. Inspiration, however, is made manifest in language, in the poet's fire-burnished syllables:

> Nameless, invisible, what spins out
> From this wall comes breath by breath,
> And pulls the vine, and the ringing tide,
> The scorched syllable from the moon's mouth.
> And what pulls them pulls me. (*B* 25)

Describing the effect of the rhetoric of composition in Piero della Francesca's "Resurrection," this poem transfers visual energy into linguistic energy, which is the movement of change and transformation resulting in the resurrection of language. Though Wright's conjunction of the personal vision and a larger, connective energy recalls romantic impulses, he continually displaces the self so that any romantic visionary union of the self and the other in language is vastly distant. Furthermore, language does not mirror or provide the vehicle to the other, but becomes the other, which can be known only as a provisional, ghostly trace.

In "Skins," Wright compresses long, chantlike lines, rich in assonance, alliteration, and imagery, into fourteen-line blocks. No stanza breaks or dropped half lines crack the tabletlike effect of these poems on the page. Each tabula rasa is fully impressed with the history of the self's intellectual past.[16] Like a pilgrim in an allegory structured as a dream, the speaker ascends and descends a ladder of knowledge that is symmetrically ordered and divided between fire, air, earth, and water. Like the skins, or "impermanent clothes" (*B* 51), we cover ourselves with interpretations—recalling Blake's bound and tattooed Albion, illuminated in plate 25 of *Jerusalem*. The compression of each poem demands language's release from abstraction. Energy, or the inherent potential of transformation and of transmutation, cannot remain in thrall. As a form of energy, language overruns and releases us from a single interpretation, intellectual design, and autobiographical moment. Wright distinguishes between the poem and the page's white space, which is "what the line lives in and breathes in, if it is to breathe at all."[17] The line, like Blake's line etched by burin and acid, is energy and presence—Blake's "eternal delight." The "white sound" of the page "pulls the lines through the poem, gauging their

---

16. Wright, "Charles Wright at Oberlin," in *A FIELD Guide* (251), describes the movement of "Skins" as a ladder; later (257-59), he provides thematic labels for each of the poem's sections: 1—Situation, Point A; 2—Beauty; 3—Truth; 4—Destruction of the Universe; 5—Organized Religion; 6—Metamorphosis; 7—Water; 8—Water/Earth; 9—Earth/Fire; 10—Aether; 11—Primitive magic; 12—Necromancy; 13—Black magic; 14—Alchemy; 15—Allegory; 16—Fire; 17—Air; 18—Water; 19—Earth; 20—Situation, Point A.

17. Wright, *A FIELD Guide*, 268.

weights and durations, even their distances," and it "is the larger sound out of which the more measured and interruptable sounds of the line are cut."[18] Language opens up a place where one recognizes, participates in, and is attentive to movement and transformation. To the writer's and reader's attention, writing draws forth interpretations and forms the liminal moment and place for continuing and participating in a dehiscent and semiotic world.

Particular concerns of each section of "Skins" form inside the music of the line; nonetheless, the music or energy is so strong that the words themselves gain a sonoral presence that overruns meaning, since language foregrounds movement and accumulation. Though interpretation does not cease to be meaningful, meaning loses its privileged status. Autobiography becomes an imago for the release, continuation, and conservation of poetic energies:

> Under the rock, in the sand and the gravel run;
> In muck bank and weed, at the heart of the river's edge:
> Instar; and again, instar,
> The wing cases visible. Then
> Emergence: leaf drift and detritus; skin split,
> The image forced from the self.
> And rests, wings drying, eyes compressed,
> Legs compressed, constricted
> Beneath the dun and the watershine—
> Incipient spinner, set for the take-off . . .                    (B 56)

The eye-I moves inward to "the heart of the river's edge" and is simultaneously emergent. "The image forced from the self" describes both the poem's emergence from memory and the mayfly or "imago rising out of herself." The poem, while casting back to Hopkins and Yeats, is not simply an epistemological meditation on poiesis; instead, the poem makes visible the dynamics of transformation found in the permeation of natural language and the poet's observation and recording of nature's signatures.

Wright yearns for a spiritual and transcendent engagement. With this desire, the poet becomes a solitary, a pilgrim, "one meandering man / . . . who looks for the willow's change" (B 69), knowing "There is a shine you move towards, the shine / Of water. . . . The river, rope of remembering, unbroken shoe, / The flushed and unwaivering mirror" (B 68). As Wright proclaimed in "Firstborn," the natural world holds us and is the one law to which we are responsible. In "Skins," this theme evolves from a father's didactic narrative to an embrace, in the poetic line and image, of a landscape and a field of sensations.

---

18. Wright, "Interview" in *Wright: A Profile* (Iowa City: Grilled Flowers Press, 1979), 38.

By ambitiously seeking the possibility of presence in language, Wright recalls Pound's interest in the energies housed in a Chinese ideogram, where, according to Fenollosa, "in all poetry a word is like a sun, with its corona and chromosphere; words crowd upon words, and enwrap each other in their luminous envelopes until sentences become clear continuous light bands."[19] Unlike Pound's and Fenollosa's enthusiasms for the potential of an archaeology of knowledge in a single sign, Wright understands that his language has limits and margins:

> And what does it come to, Pilgrim,
> This walking to and fro on the earth, knowing
> That nothing changes, or everything;
> And only, to tell it, these sad marks,
> Phrases half-parsed, ellipses and scratches across the dirt?
> It comes to a point. It comes and it goes.          (B 70)

In these concluding lines to "Skins," Wright emerges in the role of the pilgrim-writer, who turns his back upon his journey and realizes that its value can only be found in the dynamics and energies of the process, not in the completion or the expectation of completion. "Skins" thus asks us to turn back to what transpired, to look again at the signatures of language and its reinvention.

"Rural Route," the final poem of *Bloodlines*, addresses the issue of image and self found in the sixth section of "Skins," where the imago rises out of herself. Here, however, no transcendental and iridescent imago rises. Instead, the past persists:

> I back off, and the face stays.
> I leave the back yard, and the front yard, and the face stays.
> I am back on the West Coast, in my studio,
> My wife and my son asleep, and the face stays.          (B 78)

The mirror image of himself—doubly reflected as a twelve-year-old boy seeing his face (a self-portrait) framed in a dark windowpane and that reflection haunting Wright twenty-six years later—describes the impossibility of escaping one's past, the persistence and repression of the trace, and the failures of the past. The face "still looks in, still unaware of the willow, the boxwood / Or any light on any leaf. Or me" (B 77). This passage describes the pilgrim's progress: now he can see the light on the leaves; therefore, he can name the willow and boxwood and provide their scripts with signatures. The persistence of the face reminds Wright the Pilgrim of who he is and, like the final section of "Skins," of his limitations—thus comes his recognition of his own provisional self.

---

19. Ernest Fenollosa, *The Chinese Written Character as a Medium for Poetry*, ed. Ezra Pound (San Francisco: City Lights, n.d.), 32.

In *China Trace*, the final panel and stage of his triptych, Wright moves away from his past autobiography toward his future one. Wright attempts to free himself from the reflection of the face at the window; in fact, the opening poem of *China Trace*, "Childhood," answers the final poem of *Bloodlines*:

> You've followed me like a dog
> I see through at last, a window into Away-From-Here, a place
> I'm headed for, my tongue loosened, tracks
> Apparent, your beggar's-lice
> Bleaching to crystal along my britches leg:
>
> I'm going away now, goodbye.                                    (*CT* 13)

The poet joins his past to look at the vision of his future. There is a complete shedding of the past, its "names / Falling into the darkness, face / After face, like beads from a broken rosary" (*CT* 13). *China Trace* explores "one man's relationship to the endlessness, the ongoingness, the everlastingness of what's around him, and his relationship to it as he stands in the natural world"[20]: it is a book recording his yearning for salvation and recongregation in nature. Wright even considered "The Book of Yearning" as its title—and it suggests the difficulty of those yearnings: "the nitty-gritty of my wishes . . . would be to be saved, but there is no such thing."[21] To return to the congregation of dust and to issue again from that dust, forms Wright's vision of the only salvation one has to look forward to:

> If we, as we are, are dust, and dust, as it will, rises,
> Then we will rise, and recongregate
> In the wind, in the cloud, and be their issue . . .      (*CT* 14, "Snow")

The future tense and the repetition push language into greater motion to create the inexorable movement of time as it erodes presence. His is a pessimistic evolutionary vision coupled with the ideas of the conservation and ongoingness of poetic energy.

Wright states that writing is "the closest I got to 'salvation,' since salvation doesn't exist except through the natural world."[22] In "Reunion," which echoes W. S. Merwin's "For the Anniversary of My Death," Wright writes against death and toward death: "I write poems to untie myself, to do penance and disappear / Through the upper right-hand corner of things, to say grace" (*CT* 49). In this self-reflexive statement lies the paradox of the self asserting its presence with the pronoun "I," while desiring to relinquish his self-consciousness.

---

20. Wright, "Charles Wright at Oberlin," in *A FIELD Guide*, 260.
21. Ibid., 262.
22. Ibid., 266.

Wright intends to create a tracery of the self: "I wanted these [poems] to have a journal-like, everyday quality."[23] The collection must be read as a whole rather than as a collection of separate poems, for it works as a dynamic group of brushstrokes that are defined by each other's movements. The *poem* thus emphasizes that writing is a place of transference and translation of perceptions. Like a journal, the poems of *China Trace* mediate between the world-as-language and our later devisive interpretations: "The river stays shut, and writes my biography" (*CT* 21, "Quotidiana"). These poems are also mediations between a past and an elegiac present: "In some other language, / I walk by this same river, these same vowels in my throat" (*CT* 20, "Wishes").

The poems of *China Trace*, Wright comments, are like Chinese ideograms in that they are traces of Chinese poems without imitating them yet share the aesthetic of compression and transference between words.[24] In that each poem is an emblem, glance, or stroke, they constitute one larger emblem—the book as ideogram. This ideogram, though meaningful and the place of hermeneusis, nonetheless, is the site of the energies of movement, relation, and transformation: "I mimic the tongues of green flame in the grass" (*CT* 50, "Where Moth and Rust Doth Corrupt"). The desire for the self-contained ideogram, emblem, or symmetrically balanced and thus designed collection indicates a desire for an ideal form and a hope for a salvational closure. The ideal design would, in fact, de-sign itself by attesting the dynamic movements of language and hermeneusis. The self-reflexive, interlinking quality of language, however, subverts the attainment of this ideal. Through this subversion, the word and the self rejoin the world of things as things themselves:

> The wind harps its same song
> Through the steel tines of the trees.
>
> The river lies still, the jeweled drill in its teeth.
>
> I am glint on its fingernails.
> I am ground grains on its wheel. (*CT* 22, "At Zero")

In "At Zero," the self disappears into the frigid winter landscape, into the zero as origin and absence. The pilgrim, as a speck in time, is placed or inscribed on the "wheel" of fortune or a Tantric wheel of destiny. Appropriately, Fenollosa remarks that Chinese notation is "much more than arbitrary symbols" and "is based upon a vivid shorthand picture of the operations of nature" and that "in this process of compounding, two things added together do not produce a third thing but suggest some fundamental relation between them."[25]

---

23. Ibid.
24. Ibid., 262.
25. Fenollosa, *The Chinese Written Character*, 8–10.

Although Wright desires linkage and the fullness of emblems, he finds himself, like the sign, always already departing:

> I'm going away now, goodbye.
> Goodbye to the locust husk and the chairs;
> Goodbye to the genuflections. Goodbye to the clothes
> That circle beneath the earth, the names
> Falling into the darkness, face
> After face, like beads from a broken rosary . . .
>
> (*CT* 13, "Childhood")

*China Trace* commences with this litany of the relinquishment of childhood and one's past, and thus of the autobiographical. The cloak of childhood and belief is exchanged for one of spiritual loss: "And I turn in the wind, / Not knowing what sign to make, or where I should kneel" (*CT* 27, "1975"). Whatever we might expect or yearn for to save us ultimately rejects us and severs each link: "Like a bead of clear oil the Healer revolves through the night wind, / Part eye, part tear, unwilling to recognize us" (*CT* 47, "Stone Canyon Nocturne"). Throughout, the final isolation of the self resounds, as does the desire to return to a condition of belief where the poet "wait[s] for something immense and unspeakable to uncover its face" (*CT* 56, "Cloud River").

By the end of *China Trace*, presence and possibility of a sustained belief have shrunk. In "Sitting at Night on the Front Porch," Wright discovers "Everyone's gone / And I'm here, sizing the dark" (*CT* 63). In "Saturday 6 A.M.," he loses motion and speech:

> There's something I want to say,
>
> But not here, stepped out and at large on the blurred hillside.
> Over my shoulder, the great pane of the sunlight tilts toward the sea.
> I don't move. I let the wind speak.      (*CT* 64)

The wind, rustling through all these poems, intimates the everlastingness and interconnectedness of all things to which Wright accords salvation. What could be salvational lies beyond Wright's language and metaphor; because it escapes belief, Wright tries to listen or watch for its immanent traces. In the final poem, addressed to a transcendent other, the "I" vanishes and leaves the poem to instruct us to

> Look for him high in the flat black of the northern Pacific sky,
> Released in his suit of lights,
>                 lifted and laid clear.      (*CT* 65, "Him")

Wright's poetry, like so much of American autobiographical writing, is concerned with place and his relationship to a particular place. Through one geography he maps another, interior landscape. In *The Southern Cross* and *The Other Side of the River* Wright pursues a much more intimate and gestural poetry than in the earlier triptych and self-portraits. "The Southern Cross," "Lonesome Pine Special," "The Other Side of the River," "Italian Days," and "T'ang Notebook" form long notations and accretions of memories, geographies, sensations, and discrete harmonies. Suggestive of narratives—in that stories and anecdotes are offered but not pursued—each poem describes an intersection of pathways rather than one single highway. Radically supplanting and healing the division of signifier and signified, intersection and linking constitute Wright's vision of language.

In Wright's most recent collections, each poem becomes a "silvery alphabet" (*OS* 25, "The Other Side of the River"). In turn, the poems of *The Southern Cross* and those of *The Other Side of the River* construct jeweled nets, as in the Zenist Hua-yen doctrine, for the collection is formed of intertwined poems, each reflecting the others: "The ten thousand star-fish caught in the net of heaven / Flash at the sky's end" (*OS* 55, "T'ang Notebook"). The structure of each poem in *The Other Side of the River* consists of interwoven sections typographically set apart from each other, yet each forms a knot that ties together the entire fabric of the poem. Each section and each poem weave into one larger text, and thus into a larger shared memory. The texture of the overlay of lines and images corresponds to the overlay of recollected durations. One moment or one memory eclipses and calls forth, associatively, another. The extended lines, furthermore, suggest an inexorable movement: "There is no stopping the comings and goings in this world, / No stopping them, to and fro" (*OS* 36, "Italian Days").

In "The Southern Cross," Wright states that "No trace of a story line" (*SC* 49) exists; though stories arise, they are impossible to trace to their source or to complete. We find that memories, like stories, are compositions of places and scenes built upon an originary but unrecoverable moment:

> It's 1936, in Tennessee. I'm one
> And spraying the dead grass with a hose.
> The curtains blow in and out.
>
> And then it's not. And I'm not and they're not.
>
> Or it's 1941 in a brown suit, or '53 in its white shoes,
> Overlay after overlay tumbled and brought back,
> As meaningless as the sea would be
> > if the sea could remember its waves . . .      (*SC* 49)

These poems form palimpsestic "overlay after overlay," where brushstrokes and memory fuse together:

> The dead are a cadmium blue.
> We spread them with palette knives in broad blocks and planes.

We layer them stroke by stroke
In steps and ascending mass, in verticals raised from the earth.

We choose, and layer them in,
Blue and a blue and a breath,

Circle and smudge, cross-beak and buttonhook,
We layer them in. We squint hard and terrace them line by line.

And so we are come between, and cry out,
And stare up at the sky and its cloudy panes,

And finger the cypress twists.                                    (SC 6)

"Homage to Paul Cézanne" illustrates Wright's *ars poetica*: writing is seen as building textures of images and memory.[26] The painters Cézanne and Giorgio Morandi are Wright's closest visual analogues, and Cézanne's method of the accumulation of moments (and perspectives) parallels Wright's poetic craft. Yet the poetic line—not as structure, but as an ontological expression—parallels Morandi's line, which, Wright states, "is always on the point of disappearing, of not *seeming* to be there" traveling beyond the sense or notion of containment. Morandi's art is one of transference. Like a map, it offers, not discovery, but "affirmation: the voyage of discovery is ours now." Like his commentary on Morandi, Wright's own observations within his poems, "flicked off in a phrase," take on the weight of an entire life—"they are lifelines to the unseen."[27] Thus, what is lost or past converges with what is mysterious, primitive, and unseen.

Unlike the triptych, where language mediates the autobiographical narratives in such a way that the self is erased, "The Southern Cross" suggests that what is left of the self are myriad memories that mirror the otherness of ourselves. The litany of "I remember" creates an elegiac self-portrait and reveals the core of loss: the autobiographical impulse is an elegy for the self. All that Wright records reaffirms this elegiac chant:

Ebb and flow of the sunset past Sirmio,
                              flat voice of the waters
Retelling their story, again and again, as though to unburden itself

---

26. Wright comments that in "Homage to Paul Cézanne," the "sections aren't haphazard or substitutable, however, any more than certain layers or brushstrokes or colors are: They go in the order they have, which is, I hope, an accumulative order, but they are not numbered, hence they are not sections as we usually understand them in poems" (*Wright: A Profile*, 41).

27. Charles Wright, "Giorgio Morandi," *Antaeus* 54 (1985): 186–87.

Of an unforgotten guilt,
                              and not relieved
Under the soothing hand of the dark,

The clouds over Bardolino dragging the sky for the dead
Bodies of those who refuse to rise,
Their orange robes and flaming bodices trolling across the hills,

Nightwind by now in the olive trees,
No sound but the wind from anything
                              under the tired, Italian stars . . .

And the voice of the waters, starting its ghostly litany.          (*SC* 51)

Within these lines come the recovery and homage to Sirmio on Lake Garda, which is Pound's as well as Wright's magical place. Here Pound's Taoist vision fuses with Wright's "unforgotten guilt" and our "one sin" the spider recites in "Self-Portrait in 2035." Pound's influence is found throughout Wright's work, but it is certainly Pound's energy that is recalled in Wright's use of vectored lines; nonetheless, Wright seems to look toward the early, more elegiac Pound intent on what Hugh Kenner describes as "poiesis of loss."[28] Wright works from the aesthetic of seized glimpses that harden into worded moments—the ideogram of energy Pound developed throughout his writing.[29] Sirmio also mirrors the levels assigned to sinners in Dante's *Inferno*, who must be forever at their punishments; thereby their sins are metaphorically revealed and the interpretation of each sin forever remembered and reinscribed. Whoever gazes at Lake Garda must recognize and thus link with Pound, Dante, and the ebb and flow of daily life:

Everything has its work,
                              everything written down
In a second-hand grace of solitude and tall trees . . .          (*SC* 64)

As time's landscape is language, all writing traces an autobiography of what has been lost and accumulated.

Our search for our lost self, always and already an other, is finally limited, like language and time:

There is an otherness inside us
We never touch,
                              no matter how far down our hands reach.

---

28. Hugh Kenner, *The Pound Era* (Berkeley: University of California Press, 1973), 56.

29. Ibid., 71.

> It is the past,
> > with its good looks and *Anytime, Anywhere* . . .
> Our prayers go out to it, our arms go out to it
> Year after year,
> But who can ever remember enough?                    (*SC* 57)

The interminable process of remembering—forestalling silence and the last word—is paradoxically the unfulfilled reconstitution of the lost self. Thus, absence and a provisional presence coexist. The recovery of the imago or mirrored self occurs only at the last word—death—where we enter our "old outline as though for the 1st time, / And lie down, and tell no one" (*SC* 65). The full knowledge of the self occurs only at such thresholds; otherwise it remains unrecoverable:

> It's what we forget that defines us, and stays in the same place.
> And waits to be rediscovered.
> Somewhere in all that network of rivers and roads and silt hills,
> A city I'll never remember,
> > its walls the color of pure light,
> Lies in the August heat of 1935,
> In Tennessee, the bottom land slowly becoming a lake.
> It lies in a landscape that keeps my imprint
> Forever,
> > and stays unchanged, and waits to be filled back in.     (*SC* 65)

With overlay after overlay of memory, influence, and imagery, the hand that was dealt "blank, blank, blank, blank, blank" (*SC* 53) fills with luminous details and light. The palimpsestic overlay of autobiographical elements fills in the self's outline and links layer with layer: the "network of rivers and roads and silt hills" is a "landscape that keeps my imprint."

Wright's more recent poems could be said to resemble Theodore Roethke's "North American Sequence," for both poets explore the long, traveling lines that contain an organic and mnemonic world within them. Wright and Roethke search out communions with a natural landscape. Roethke, however, assumes the attainment of transcendence:

> Silence of water above a sunken tree:
> The pure serene of memory in one man—
> A ripple widening from a single stone
> Winding around the waters of the world.[30]

These final lines of "The Far Field" embrace a Zen conception of centeredness and focused contemplation that winds outward into the world,

---

30. Theodore Roethke, "North American Sequence," in his *Collected Poems* (Garden City, N.Y.: Doubleday, 1975), 195.

though always belonging to the world, and further into reflective nothingness. The "Silence of water" and "pure serene" celebrate Zen contemplation. Roethke, furthermore, sees the possibility of embracing the world, whereas Wright cannot assume such a stance spiritually because each link forged—transcendent as each link may be—remains provisional and at best only a suggestion of a larger harmony.

Wright also lacks the raw, open, raucous language that distinguishes Roethke's poetry. Instead, his poetry appears polished, refined, almost alchemically transmuted. A disturbing distance, however, checks our intimacy with Wright's language, though his poetry is in part the intimate process of remembering. The image—and self-reflexively the portrait and hence the self—always retreats deeper into an untranslated music. The intent is to plunge, not into silence, but into folds of music or layers of brushwork. Roethke moves us always to the concrete and discrete: the touchstone of Zen meditation and Zen poetry. Wright, distinctively, takes us away from the particular to the mnemonically mediated and to the abstraction of the particular image. The inherent distance found in abstraction evokes the difficulty of hermeneusis, self, and the very proposal of interconnection.

Wright's recent collection, *The Other Side of the River*, more persuasively proposes the provisional assemblages of the self than do his previous collections. To remember is to inform the self and is an act of self-portraiture:

> The poem is a self-portrait
> > always, no matter what mask
> You take off and put back on.
> As this one is, color of cream and a mouthful of air.
> Rome is like that, and we are,
> > taken off and put back on.
> > > (OS 46, "Roma II")

To remember is to revise and thus to craft one's own portrait. Remembering is also a means of survival, both in terms of the self and of history: "To speak of the dead is to make them live again: / We invent what we need" (*OS* 61). Memory is thus the force of invention, rising out of a deep need to pull ourselves from isolation into a world where "the frog-shrill and the insect-shrill" are "as palpable as a heartstring, / Whatever that was back then, always in memory" (*OS* 61, "Arkansas Traveller"). Memory holds the possibility of writing; in turn, writing retraces connections between the self and the world, defining the very craft of the poem:

> It's linkage I'm talking about,
> > and harmonies and structures
> And all the various things that lock our wrists to the past.
>
> Something infinite behind everything appears,
> > and then disappears.

> It's all a matter of how
>                          you narrow the surfaces.
> It's all a matter of how you fit in the sky.
>                          (*OS* 24, "The Other Side of the River")

To write is to mirror the world's writing, "To summon the spirits up and set the body to music" (*OS* 7, "Lost Souls"). Throughout *The Other Side of the River*, Wright maps the connections between Tennessee and Italy, the self and nature: "all the various things that lock our wrists to the past" (*OS* 24) or "the residue / Of all our illuminations and unnamed lives" (*OS* 9, "Lost Souls"). Names of places and friends rise out of bare narratives and anecdotes to claim some provisional presence. Wright, even in the brevity of a name and slight context, creates an intimate poetry: "you're part of my parts of speech. / Think of me now and then. I'll think of you" (*OS* 67, "To Giacomo Leopardi in the Sky"). The poetry is a process of self-definition and self-composition; yet, the possibility of composition or intimacy always has the shadow of time and loss passing over, which ultimately distances us from the other, be it text or human experience. Writing, by traveling to the pages' margins, attempts to recover presence, but in this act writing reinscribes loss:

> I have nothing to say about the way the sky tilts
> Toward the absolute,
>                          or why I live at the edge
> Of the black boundary,
>                          a continent where the waves
> Counsel my coming in and my going out.
>                          (*OS* 41, "Three Poems for the New Year")

Nonetheless, language remains luminous, fecund, transformative—and implicitly subject to decay. We yearn, Wright suggests, for some form of transcendence that comes from the possibility of the fullness of words and discourse:

> What language does light speak?
> Vowels hang down from the pepper tree
>                          in their green and their gold.
>                          (*OS* 51, "Cryopexy")

The possibility of a full language is always and already on the other side of the river. Rather than seeking something outside the self and language, as in the modernism of Eliot, Wright seeks to define the self with whatever bits and pieces of the world and the world-as-language can be found. He understands that the language of light—literal and metaphorical—is closed and divided from us. These poems thus mark our distance from our histories and landscapes; in this way, the language is transformational and alchemical: "Everything comes from fire" (*OS* 51, "Cryopexy"). Wright's quest, if we wish to call it that, is a search for presence—both of self and of world. Fire, then, is passion and transformation, as well as "The form inside the form inside" (*OS* 44, "Roma I"). Amidst time and the flux of self and world, Wright looks for some essential presence within himself and within what he sees:

> Weightlessness underwrites everything
> In the deep space of the eye,
>                     the wash and drift of oblivion
> Sifting the color out,
>                 polishing, still polishing
> Long after translucence comes.                  (*OS* 52, "Cyropexy")

We are recipients of the regard of others, which with light penetrates our consciousness "Into the endlessness behind the eye" (*OS* 52):

> Radiance comes through the eye
>                     and lodges like cut glass in the mind,
> Never vice versa,
> Somatic and self-contained.                  (*OS* 51, "Cryopexy")

Wright envisions the world as a book of signs, where each thing is an inscription we must interpret, and where such interpretation becomes increasingly difficult:

> These nights are like that,
> The silvery alphabet of the sea
>                     increasingly difficult to transcribe,
> And larger each year, everything farther away, and less clear,
> Than I want it to be,
>                 not enough time to do the job,
> And faint thunks in the earth,
> As though somewhere nearby a horse was nervously pawing the ground.
>                     (*OS* 25, "The Other Side of the River")

Indeed, there is some radiant utterance behind each thing, which can turn the sea into a "silvery alphabet"; each thing is, in fact, a figuration of "that luminous, nameless body whose flesh takes on / The mottoes we say we live by" (*OS* 5, "Lost Bodies"). Language—our Augustinian reading of the world as a book—describes both intimacy and difficulty, for any approach toward understanding is shadowed by a constant sliding away of what is desired.

In *The Other Side of the River*, the world is full of departures and mortalities. Indeed, Wright's central thematic concern throughout his poetry is the meditation on mortality:

> What other anagoge in this life but the self?
> What other ladder to Paradise
>                     but the smooth handholds of the rib cage?
> High in the palm tree the orioles twitter and grieve.

> We twitter and grieve, the spider twirls the honey bee,
> Who twitters and grieves, around in her net,
> > then draws it by one leg
> Up to the fishbone fern leaves inside the pepper tree
> > swaddled in silk
> And turns it again and again until it is shining.
> > (OS 71, "California Dreaming")

Refuting the opposition of life and death (while undercutting the high seriousness of the concern with the repeated phrase "twitter and grieve"), Wright confronts their interwoven immanence, which is apprehended only through the mediating energies of language. Each moment and object, in itself, marks the

> > point when everything starts to dust away
> More quickly than it appears,
> > > when what we have to comfort the dark
> Is just that dust, and just its going away.
> > (OS 25, "The Other Side of the River")

"It's not age," Wright states, but "It's discontinuity / . . . That sends us apart and keeps us there in a dread" (OS 21, "Two Stories"). The lines between silence and language or separation and connection blur; to write necessitates the venturing close to what Rilke in his sonnets called "the breath around nothing."[31]

The further Wright considers mortality, the more insistent is the place of language:

> Surely, as has been said, emptiness is the beginning of all things.
> Thus wind over water,
> > thus tide-pull and sand-sheen
> When the sea turns its lips back . . .       (OS 46, "Roma II")

The meditation on silence and emptiness becomes reinscribed through anecdotes and rhetoric. Nonetheless, language is as elusive as the making palpable of emptiness. The question of silence or the end, however, persists: "At the end of the last word, / When night comes walking across the lake on its hands, / And nothing appears in the mirror" (OS 38, "Italian

---

31. See Rainer Maria Rilke's Sonnet III in his *Sonnets to Orpheus*; the final stanza is "lerne / vergessen, dass du aufsangst. Das verrinnt. / In Wahrheit singen, ist ein andrer Hauch. / Ein Hauch um nichts. Ein Wehn im Gott. Ein Wind." *Ausgewählte Werke*, Vol. I (Leipzig: Insel-Verlag, 1938), 270. The English version: "learn / to forget that sudden music. It will end. / True singing is a different breath. / The breath around nothing. A gust inside the God. A wind."

Days"). What happens on the other side of the river when our self-portraits disappear? The loss of language will mean the loss of self-definition and interconnection. We "ask again if our first day in the dark / Is our comfort or signature" (*OS* 39, "Italian Days"). Do we write toward our death and away from our presence—where words are elegies of themselves and ourselves? Or does our signature, as at the end of a letter, insure our presence despite all distances?

Writing is our trace and afterlife: "What if inside the body another shape is waiting to come out" (*OS* 71, "California Dreaming"). The poems travel and build layer upon layer, so that there is always something that shines through a given pigment, informing the surface with depth, the past, and the measure of distance. Wright's meditations celebrate, for "What gifts there are are all here, in this world" (*OS* 40, "Italian Days"). Wright eloquently confronts our ends so as to turn back to this world, having discovered

> That all beauty depends upon disappearance,
> The bitten edges of things,
>               the gradual sliding away
> Into tissue and memory,
>              the uncertainty
> And dazzling impermanence of days we beg our meanings from,
> And their frayed loveliness.       (*OS* 15, "Lonesome Pine Special")

MICHAEL CHITWOOD

# Gospel Music: Charles Wright and the High Lonesome (1992)

> When I've sung my last song in the evening
> and the sun sets in the golden west,
> all the scenes of this world I'll be leaving.
> In the shadow of Clinch Mountain I will rest.
>
> —"In the Shadow of Clinch Mountain," A. P. Carter

Did you hear the one about the dyslexic atheist? He lies awake at night and worries that there might be a dog.

If you grew up in east Tennessee and western North Carolina in the 1940s, as Charles Wright did, and if you came of age on country gospel hits such as "I Am a Pilgrim," "Dust on the Bible," and "Farther On," as Charles Wright did, you wind up spending some sleepless nights listening to the barking in the neighborhood.

The barking worries a soul, and it's that worry that drives much of Wright's poetry; it's been, I think, a lifelong theme, born in the "white soul" music of Appalachia and considered in nine books of poetry, so far (*Halflife* 53). However, Wright's has not been a kind of worrying that makes for whining. It has, instead, inspired some of the most genuine spiritual poetry of the last several decades.

Wright has said of writing poetry that "if you can't sing, you better get out of the choir." Unlike many modern poets, he is not afraid to sing, and has become, for my money, the choirmaster of the modern hymn to the absolute. I think he came to this position by way of his Appalachian heritage, and yet there are probably few readers of modern poetry who would list him as an Appalachian writer. Because he's done time in Italy and California, he's often not thought of as even a Southern writer, but he is both Southern and Appalachian in his subjects and style—though that identity is not expressed in the usual way, which, of course, is his strength. He's like the early Louis Armstrong who would put a handkerchief over his hand so that other players couldn't see how he was getting the notes: Don't let 'em see what you're doing, he was saying, until you've put it in their ears.

I'm going to try in the next few pages to work a few old trails back into the shadow of Clinch Mountain. It's a deep shadow, full of the scenes of this world, and the next.

★

You won't find much 'shine-drinking, stump-jumping, hogkilling, Hee Haw hillbillying in Charles Wright's work. There's no old bluetick sleeping on the porch; however, the man seems dog-haunted, as is right and proper, I suppose, for someone born in Hardin County, Tennessee. In his book *China Trace*, you'll find the poems "Dog" and "Captain Dog," in *The Southern Cross* there's "Dog Yoga" and "Dog Day Vespers," in the poem "T'ang Notebook" from *The Other Side of the River*, he pledges his affections to the stars in the constellation Canis Major, and he started it off in *Hard Freight* with "Dog Creek Mainline," a poem he has said was a watershed where he became "very conscious of content" (*Halflife* 86).

Why all the dogs? Wright has explained it in this way: ". . . dog because a dog is a dog. . . . There is also the reverse spelling of dog" (*Halflife* 81). There's that barking in the night and the worrying. It's the theme of so many of the mountain gospel songs—"Are you right with Jesus?"

I'm only half-serious about the dog's life in Wright's poetry. He's much too serious to rely only on a trick like a reverse spelling to carry a major theme. No, it's deeper than that. Like A. P. Carter, Merle Travis, The Stanley Brothers and the other early hillbilly singers, Wright finds transformational meaning in the local landscape. None of these writers look around and see unicorns or griffins or a phoenix. What they see, however, is meaning in the everyday, the ordinary. In the wink of an eye, a dog can become a messenger of God and the Holston River is suddenly flowing with the Jordan's cold waters. Dog and river are big medicine, and the gospel singers, Charles Wright included, look out their back doors and glimpse eternity.

If you look to an early poem like "Dog Creek Mainline," the poem where Wright began focusing at least as much on content as technical matters, you see the importance the local landscape has for Wright.

> Dog Creek: cat track and bird splay,
> Spindrift and windfall; woodrot;
> Odor of muscadine, the blue creep
> Of kingsnake and copperhead;
> Nightweed; frog spit and floating heart,
> Backwash and snag pool: Dog Creek
>
> Starts in the leaf reach and shoal run of the blood;
> Starts in the falling light just back
> Of the fingertips; . . .

You hear the click of the mainline's cross-ties in the first stanza's spondees as the actual is enumerated with the intangible, a move Wright makes again and again. The locality is intimately felt, so much so that it is part of the speaker's body. Place can't be denied as essential in Appalachian sensibility, and the place is one with the speaker of this poem. The metaphor for heaven often used in the mountain gospel songs is home—"going up home to live in green pastures." In this world view, the streets of glory aren't paved with gold; it's the spindrift, windfall and woodrot.

The mystic journey into the landscape occupies the entire book *China Trace*, which completed the trilogy Wright began with *Hard Freight*. Early in the book, published in 1977, Wright in the poem "Self-Portrait in 2035" looks into the future: "The root becomes him, the road ruts / That are sift and grain in the powderlight / Recast him." Again the real and ethereal combine, and you can't help but hear echoes of Merle Travis' "Dark as a Dungeon," where the coalminer who knows he will die in a mine looks to the future and laments, "I pity the man digging my bones."

While there is lament in the pilgrim's progress in *China Trace*, the process is also celebratory in an Appalachian sense—the speaker works into the landscape and is thereby released. In the poem "April" the pilgrim says:

> . . . [I] know I want less—
>
> Divested of everything,
> A downfall of light in the pine woods, motes in the rush,
> Gold leaf through the undergrowth, and come back
> As another name, water
> Pooled in the black leaves and holding me there, to be
> Released as a glint, as a flash, as a spark . . .

And then, a little later, the poem "Going Home":

> The ides of a hangdog month.
> Dirt roads and small towns come forth
> And fall from the pepper tree,
>                           evening flashing their panes
> And stray flakes through a thin drizzle of darkness,
> Strikes in the dry fields of the past,
>                           bonesparks
> From the nailed feet that walk there.
>
> I ask for a second breath,
> Great Wind, where everything's necessary
> And everything rises,
>                           unburdened and borne away, where
> The flash from the setting sun
> Is more than a trick of light, where halflife
> Is more than just a watery glow,
>                           and everything's fire . . .

The "nailed feet that walk there," at home in the past, belong, I think, both to the crucified son of Man and the Appalachian locked to his landscape. The last poem in *China Trace* picks up on light imagery and raises it to the ultimate position. The poem chronicles the ascension of the pilgrim and ends this way: "Look for him high in the flat black of the northern Pacific sky, / Released in his suit of lights, / lifted and laid clear." I hear an Appalachian turn of phrase in the last line. Fruits and vegetables saved for the winter are said to be "laid by." Not only is that ending musically beautiful, the "l" sounds—*Look, flat black, lights, lifted, laid clear*—picking up speed and clustering at the end of the stanza, it is also a summation of the pilgrim's yearning toward the infinite.

Wright in his essay "A.P. and E.D." says the songs he grew up on were "God-haunted, salvation-minded and evangelical" (*Halflife* 53). He was pulling those songs in on his Zenith Trans-Oceanic portable radio and listening in the nights of his youth. He later attended a small Episcopal school called Sky Valley in the mountains of North Carolina. There, he got another gospel dose, as he explained in the February 1989 *Arts Journal*:

> Sky Valley was . . . very Episcopalian, very church-oriented. Mrs. Perry, who ran Sky Valley, was the daughter of Bishop Gary, the Episcopal bishop of South Carolina, and very much an evangelical.
>
> She ran a very tight evangelical ship there at Sky Valley, which settled into me, obviously. It mostly settled into me as something to fight against for the rest of my life, but it's in there. I fight against it, but I wouldn't change it for anything. Obviously it spoke to some part of my nature that I, even at the time, secretly felt was all right and that went begging during the years of my late teens and twenties. But I've come back to it over the last 20 years, and I write about it constantly. All my poems seem to be about the impossibility of salvation.

So firm a foundation, and yet "lifted and laid clear" and the "impossibility of salvation" don't quite seem to jibe. But that is the nature of the high lonesome. "Something's off-key in my mind. / Whatever it is, it bothers me all the time," Wright says in "Laguna Blues."

I have never seen "high lonesome" defined. Maybe it's like Louis Armstrong said when asked to define jazz: "Man, if you got to ask, you'll never know." I hear the high lonesome in the Carter Family and Merle Travis and Doc Watson and Charles Wright. It's a pitch, and it's a way of saying things that contains both the idea of salvation and its impossibility.

The old mountain hymns weren't the let's-all-feel-good-and-make-a-profit numbers of today's yuppie Christianity. Wright remembers the old songs and wants to know if, when the scenes of this life he is leaving, he will be released in his suit of light. It's a question that troubles the mind. It is the high lonesome and is, I think, what sets Wright apart from so many poets writing now; he has a serious subject that is not the tidal nature of the menstrual cycle or the drum-beating sensitivity of the '90s male. His subject is serious, and he must approach that subject in a fitting manner.

Wright has said that Form, capital F, is "everything to me. Content is nothing" (*Arts Journal* 12). I would suggest, however, that Wright's form and content, like the landscape and body in "Dog Creek Mainline," are one and inseparable. That, of course, is the mark of the true craftsman. If form and content are not intimately joined, you get the literary equivalent of Frank Sinatra singing the hits of Flatt and Scruggs.

Listen to how the tune and the words go together in "Dog Yoga."

> A spring day in the weeds.
> A thread of spittle across the sky, and a thread of ash.
> Mournful cadences from the clouds.
>
> Through the drives and the cypress beds,
>                                 twenty-five years of sad news.
>
> Mother of Thrushes, Our Lady of Crows,
> Brief as a handkerchief,
>                         twenty-five years of sad news.
>
> Later, stars and sea winds in and out of the open window.
>
> Later, and lonesome among the sleepers,
>                                 the day's thunder in hidden places,
> One lissome cheek a notch in the noontide's leash,
>
> A ghostly rain of sunlight among the ferns.
>
> Year in, year out, the same loom from the dark.
> Year in, year out, the same sound in the wind.
>
> Near dawn, the void in the heart,
> The last coat of lacquer along the leaves,
>                         the quench in the west.

If dogs meditate, I think this is the way they do it—a little sadly ("Mournful cadences from the clouds"), with minute observations ("A ghostly rain of sunlight among the ferns") and exquisite language, as if each word were tasted for its appropriateness and flavor ("The last coat of lacquer along the leaves, / the quench in the west").

I'm always floored by the skill that makes this poem move along, considering that it has no verbs, an omission that gives it the otherworldliness you need in a poem called "Dog Yoga." This poem also illustrates what I mean by Wright's approach. The loom in the dark and the sound in the wind are the ghosts of Mrs. Perry spooking the poem into a hyper-language that doesn't hyperventilate.

Thanks to Jimmy Swaggart, Jim and Tammy Faye Baker, and the rest of the con-men and celebrants of the Holy Temple of Big Folding Money, it gets harder and harder every year to sing a true, modern hymn. If singing such a hymn is your interest, you have to keep asking yourself, "How am I going to do it?"

It's Wright's question, and it gives his poems their yearning, their reach and their marvelous, strange music. "I want to sit by the bank of the river, / in the shade of the evergreen tree," he says in the title poem of his book *The Other Side of the River*, "And look in the face of whatever, / the whatever that's waiting for me." That's a nice riff that could easily have been lifted from one of those mountain gospel songs. It articulates Wright's quest nicely, but he usually employs a different tune, like this one from his poem "A Journal of English Days":

> There is no sickness of spirit like homesickness
> When what you are sick for
>                               has never been seen or heard
> In this world, or even remembered
>                               except as a smear of bleached light
> Opening, closing beyond any alphabet's
> Recall to witness and isolate . . .

The language pines beautifully. It's a language that says that if your sights are on the other side of the river, and you're still on this side, you better *keep* a worried mind.

I want to close with a scene that seems to me to capture so much of what Charles Wright does with his gospel music. In the fall of 1938, the Consolidated Royal Chemical Corporation of Chicago hired the Carter Family as one of several acts to be featured on Mexican border radio stations. The family traveled to Texas and spent the next several months broadcasting live shows.

I see them there, hymn writers and singers from the Appalachian Mountains, sending their pure, high lonesome across the line to the other side of the river.

JULIAN GITZEN

# Charles Wright and Presences in Absence (1994)

It is now over two decades since the appearance of *The Grave of the Right Hand* (1970), Charles Wright's first collection. In the years following he has shifted from the intense, metaphorically charged, syllabically measured lines of the early lyrics to the relaxed, conversational rhythms of lengthy verse meditations, the first of the latter being the title poem of *The Southern Cross* (1981). Despite striking changes in form and style, the passage of time has produced no corresponding alteration in his major subjects or themes, and these enduring concerns distinguish him as one of the few living American poets whose inward and outward gazes are steadily directed beyond the form and texture of the physical to the intangible and the spiritual.

While Wright's more recent long poems resemble *The Pisan Cantos* of his acknowledged mentor, Pound, his work inevitably suggests comparison with Wordsworth. Like much of Wordsworth's finest verse, Wright's poetry is heavily autobiographical, and, like *The Prelude*, much of it is devoted to recalling and assessing the significance of past events and actions. Like Wordsworth, Wright is temperamentally contemplative, and he is often inspired by landscapes, much as Wordsworth was moved by scenes of the Lake District and the views above Tintern Abbey. Most notably, perhaps, he shares a measure of Wordsworth's power to sense behind the outlines of the mortal and the finite the awesome presence of the immortal and the infinite. While Wright usually differs from the great Romantic in being somewhat diffident and ambivalent in his judgments, no such doubts or reservations weaken his implicit belief in the value and significance of the past and of the central importance of memory as an instrument for recalling that past and making it available to poetry.

Certainly Wordsworth also recognized that memory is valuable to the poet, for he believed that poetry originates in "emotion recollected in tranquility." Wright goes considerably further, founding his theory of composition on the operation of the memory. In his *Paris Review* interview he alters Eliot's formula of the Objective Correlative, describing memory as "the subjective correlative of the seen object." The task of the poet, he asserts, is to "turn the equation around, to make the unseen seen."[1] In that same interview Wright notes that fragments of the past may be

---

1. J. D. McClatchy, "The Art of Poetry XLI: Charles Wright," *The Paris Review* 113 (1989): 207.

recovered through Proustian associations, instancing from his own work the twenty-part sequence *Tattoos.* He explains that these remembered moments from his own past, spanning a period of some twenty-three years, were inspired by the sight of camellia blooms scattered on the ground in his yard in Laguna Beach, California. Studying the blossoms in the opening section of this poem, the poet pointedly inquires, "Where would you have me return?" It soon becomes apparent that the camellias have served as a reminder of the celebration of Mother's Day at the Episcopal Church of his childhood and thereby have led him into a series of reflections upon his frustrated efforts to experience spiritual feeling. The very title *Tattoos* bespeaks the power of memory, implying that the episodes recalled in that sequence have left a permanent mental impression.

While the camellia blossoms furnish an instance of spontaneous and unpremeditated association, Wright may deliberately evoke memories, as in "Blackwater Mountain" and "Virginia Reel," in both of which he has returned to sites from his past in order to refresh his memories. Occasionally too, as in "Link Chain," the occurrence of a holiday such as Palm Sunday triggers recollections of a former observance of that day. It should be emphasized, however, that the evocation of memory is a normal, and indeed fundamental step in composition for Wright; given space, solitude, and time in which to meditate, usually he can stir memories without the aid of associative foreground images. Rare occasions when he proves unable to do so, when "not a word is said that reminds [him] of anything," leave him desolate.

While reliant upon memory, Wright recognizes the limits of its powers. Inevitably as the past lengthens, events and emotions recede, "returning, diminished with each turn." Unable to recall details of several of his favorite landscapes or locales, the poet concludes despairingly, "I can't remember enough. . . . I'll never be able to." Furthermore, the shortcomings of memory prevent the writer from authentically recreating past experiences: "Nothing you write down is ever as true as you think it was." At least memory is likely to retain the most vivid of the thrilling features of any moment, and probably Wright's appreciation of this fact is behind the assertion that "Nothing's so beautiful as the memory of it." Furthermore, despite having faded in vividness, simply by virtue of being concluded, past events have acquired a distinctive form and significance. Some at least may be seen to have beginnings, middles, and ends, as well as causes and effects. The contemplation of them in their entirety may afford a pleasure comparable to that found in a work of art. The pains associated with past experiences also diminish in retrospect: "How sweet the past is, no matter how wrong, or how sad. / How sweet is yesterday's noise." Memories also constitute forms of possession, cherished images of what has been lost or abandoned. In "Lonesome Pine Special" Wright illustrates this point by taking the reader down a series of Montana back roads and wagon ruts which lead to a vacant log cabin, uninhabited for perhaps fifty years. Of that lonely and forgotten habitation he maintains:

> Whoever remembers that best owns all this now.
> And after him it belongs to the wind again,
>                        and the shivering bunchgrass, and the seed cones.

Whatever the limitations of memory and however inadequately it may encompass the past, Wright contends that the past itself endures and stands in a fixed and unalterable, intangible form. Like other presences of which he is conscious, the past lacks palpable texture and substance, but for him as for his predecessor Pound whatever has happened survives entire. Although he may have forgotten details of a youthful duck-hunting adventure, the experience in question retains its shape, and within it he and his companions will remain always as once they were:

>              . . . Churchill and I and Bill Ring
> Will still be chasing that same dead pintail duck
>                        down the same rapids in 1951
> Of the Holston River. And Ted Glynn
> Will be running too.
>              And 1951 will always be 1951.
>                                                      ("Lost Souls")

While the fixity of the past may offer some comfort, we must also accept that the past remains beyond our power to alter. At each recollection of the occasion, Wright is doomed to regret his failure to return home from Italy to attend his mother's funeral: "It was June again, and 1964 again, and I still wasn't there / As they laid her down and my father turned away." Perhaps most important, the past serves as a repository of those experiences which have shaped our identities. Could we but remember enough, the past could tell us who we are: "It's what we forget that defines us, and stays in the same place, / And waits to be rediscovered." Wright assumes that for all of us the past is endlessly fascinating and that we all share a frustrated yearning to recover it:

> Our prayers go out to it, our arms go out to it
> Year after year,
> But who can ever remember enough?          ("The Southern Cross")

Occasionally, as in "Driving Through Tennessee," Wright portrays himself as the dedicated poet of reverie:

> It's strange what the past brings back.
> Our parents, for instance, how ardently they still loom . . .
>
> And towns that we lived in once,
> And who we were then, the roads we went back and forth on . . .
>
> I am their music, . . .
> I put my mouth to the dust and sing their song.

As indicated in the above lines, in those poems which reassemble frag-
ments of the past, Wright frequently recalls beloved friends or relatives or
landscapes for which he holds a special regard. Often the people being
remembered are dead, and it is vital to understand the significance which
the poet attaches to the known dead and to death itself, which maintains
a steady though not necessarily ominous presence in his verse. If any-
thing, "The dead are with us to stay" is for him an understatement. With
help from Yeats, Calvin Bedient has correctly summed up one of Wright's
preoccupations: "He hails the superhuman, writes of death-in-life and
life-in-death."[2] Repeatedly, in poems such as "Anniversary," "Delta
Traveller," "Virginia Reel," and "Homage to Paul Cézanne," Wright in-
vokes the spirits of the dead and is comforted by their presence.
According to him, our dead continue to love and minister to us. Their
spirits hover round to "mend our clothes . . . hold us together." At times
they may go further by briefly drawing us far enough into their element
to allow us a rare transcendent moment of disembodied consciousness:

> Often they'll reach a hand down,
> Or offer a word, and ease us out of our bodies to join them in theirs.
>
> .   .   .
>
> We look back and we don't care and we go.
>
> And thus we become what we've longed for, past tense. . . .
>
> ("Homage to Paul Cézanne")

So strong is Wright's bond with the dead that, as in the lines above, he
looks forward to joining them. He repeatedly expresses an unmistakable
death-wish, and imagery of death is prominent in his lines, distinguished
by its own symbolism. Like numerous other poets, he persistently associ-
ates death with fire and wind, but he adds his personal touch by also link-
ing it with the color blue. Death is variously described as cadmium blue,
cobalt, plastic blue, and as a "blue idiom, blue embrace." The author visu-
alizes death as the ultimate mystery, of which the dead have acquired
knowledge; he assures the spirit of a dead relative, "There's only one se-
cret in this life that's worth knowing, / And you found it. / I'll find it too."
Wright's admiration for Dante may well stem in part from that poet's suc-
cessful imaginative journey through the realm of the dead, a pilgrimage
which Wright also yearns to make. In fantasy he transforms a bumble-bee
outside his window into the monster Geryon, upon whose shoulders he
longs to sit, in order to descend into "the hard Dantescan gloom," where

---

2. "Tracing Charles Wright," *Parnassus: Poetry in Review* 10 (Spring/ Summer
1982): 55.

he might converse with the dead. So intense is his anticipation of death
that he can assert:

> Each tree I look at contains my coffin,
> Each train brings it closer home.
> Each flower I cut, I cut for a plastic vase
> Askew on the red dirt. . . .
> Each root I uncover uncovers me.
>
> ("Link Chain")

Death is an especially obtrusive presence in *China Trace* (1977), perhaps
the most widely discussed of Wright's volumes. It is helpful to know (and
it might be less than clear in the reading) that he conceives of the three
volumes *Hard Freight* (1973), *Bloodlines* (1975), and *China Trace* as a tril-
ogy, "sort of a past, present, and future, an autobiography by fragmental
accretion."[3] Under these circumstances it is natural that death should
shadow the last volume, but it might be added that Wright's
death-haunted imagination is manifest in the very conception of a por-
tion of verse autobiography set in the future.

Evidently Wright looks forward to death in part because he imagines that
it will unite him with his unknown or forgotten past, making him complete
and allowing him full knowledge of himself:

> Soon it will be time for the long walk under the earth toward the sea.
>
> And time to retrieve the yellow sunsuit and little shoes
>                                              they took my picture in
> In Knoxville, in 1938.
>
> Time to gather the fire in its quartz bowl.
>
> ("Hawaii Dantesca")

In addition to its power of reconstruction, Wright hopes for even
more from death. He imagines that it will effect a transfiguration, alter-
ing the flesh into what he describes variously as "light," this being for
him perhaps the most precious phenomenon, beautiful in itself and nec-
essary to the expression of beauty. "Homage to Paul Cézanne" describes
the spirits of the dead as "little globules of light" which hover near the
ceiling, "thinking our thoughts." The poet dreams of being transformed
like them into "A BB, a disc of light." In "April," inspired by the bright-
ness of spring, he wishes himself "divested of everything" and released at
last as "a glint, as a flash, as a spark." A different season produces much the
same impulse in "October," which causes him to muse, "The transfigura-
tion will start like this, I think": red colors like leaves will fall from his

---

3. McClatchy 200.

hands, the air will grow cold, and the author will rise from his weary body, "a blood-knot of light."

Probably not since Roethke has an American poet of considerable stature and repute expressed such enthusiastic and unembarrassed spirituality. As he has repeatedly explained, however, "I would love to believe the world is Platonic—but I think it's Aristotelian."[4] Despite his doubts, he maintains that his poems form steps in a quest for ideal enlightenment: "A lot of what I want to say changes but the place I want to get to never changes. . . . I do want to get to that still, small, pinpoint of light at the center of the Universe, where all things come together and all things intersect."[5]

If each person's identity resides in his or her past, then locales as well as experiences have shaped that identity. "Sacred places" minister to Wright's sense of identity and supply cherished memories. His insistence that "the landscape was always the best part" rings with sincerity. While he has as yet supplied no detailed explanation of the reason for this feeling, it is likely that some indication of his own perceived need is expressed in the epigraph by T'u Lung which introduces *China Trace*:

> I would like to house my spirit within my body, to nourish my virtue by mildness, and to travel in ether by becoming a void. But I cannot do it yet . . . And so, being unable to find peace within myself, I made use of external surroundings to calm my spirit, and being unable to find delight within my heart, I borrowed a landscape to please it. Therefore strange were my travels.

Possibly Wright had in mind these words of T'u Lung when he observed, "My poems are mostly landscapes, both interior and exterior, and sometimes projected interiors. Psycho-transference of one landscape to a different kind of landscape. . . . One of the great contributions of the T'ang poets is to show us how to get personal emotions out of a real landscape. You transfer it to the landscape and then you get it back."[6]

Like the Chinese poet above, Wright has traveled extensively and has lived in various places, and a correspondingly wide range of landscapes appear in his poems, but the most numerous come from two areas: the region around the Holston River in Kingsport, Tennessee, his boyhood home, and a portion of northern Italy centered between Verona, where he was stationed with the Army, and Venice, where he also spent considerable time. While the influence upon Wright of both American and European scenes is abundantly evident in his poems, he has repeatedly emphasized that his introduction to the Italian landscape was profoundly moving and led indirectly to his decision to write poetry.

---

4. Elizabeth McBride, "Charles Wright: An Interview," *Ohio Review* 34 (1985):18.
5. McBride 16.
6. McBride 21.

Wright's verse-landscapes consist always of quick sketches, typically occupying a few lines, with mention of some half-dozen highlights. He does not verbally reconstruct scenes in detail. Furthermore, though he has composed a number of long poems, the first being "Tattoos" (1975), none of these extended works contains a lengthy and sustained descriptive or narrative section. Wright lays wry claim to being the only Southerner of his acquaintance with no skill as a storyteller. Instead, each of his long poems consists of a pastiche of brief, thematically related anecdotes, scenes, or events. The arrangement is nontransitional, consisting of what Wright refers to as "jump-cuts" or sudden shifts of scene. Among these long meditative poems the most recent, *Zone Journals* (1988), represents a significant departure in perspective. The distinguishing features of the poet's previous verse-landscapes were supplied from memory. As has been noted, he is painfully conscious of the weaknesses of memory, and, as if to avoid lapses in recall, *Zone Journals*, as its name implies, steps into the present and consists of diary-scenes drawn from on-the-spot observations, together with related commentaries.

Not surprisingly, Wright is a discriminating admirer of painting, who alludes frequently to Cézanne and to numerous other painters, particularly those noted for their landscapes. He brings to his own outdoor scenes the eye of a painter, singling out distinctive shapes, registering the degree and quality of light, and determining shades and blends of colors. The spectrum of his palette is broad and subtle. He describes Italian houses, for instance, as painted in "ochres . . . and bright hennas" or in "fuchsia and mauve and cyclamen" and speaks of a London sunset flaring "orange, / Tamarind, apricot" above "the slate slip" of the Thames. He resembles other painterly poets such as W. C. Williams and Charles Tomlinson in attending closely to effects of sunlight and shadow. He claims that his nearsightedness has served to make light all the more precious to him. For landscapes he prefers the more dramatic periods of daylight and darkness, often arranging his scenes at dawn, sunset, or twilight. Night scenes usually are illuminated by the moon or stars but also on occasion by artificial light, as in the case of remembered Venetian electric lights, which "Were played back, and rose and fell on the black canal / Like swamp flowers, shrinking and stretching, / Yellow and pale and iron-blue from the oil." Occasionally, as in the following lines from "A Journal of the Year of the Ox," Wright's interest in varied light effects produces an Impressionistic scene where increasing or diminishing light alters the definition of colors and shapes:

> —The sunset, Mannerist clouds
> > just shy of the Blue Ridge
> Gainsay the age before they lose their blush
> In the rising coagulation of five o'clock.
> Two dark, unidentifiable birds
> > swoop and climb

Out of the picture, the white-slatted, red-roofed Munch house
Gathering light as the evening begins to clot.
The trees dissolve in their plenitude
                      into a dark forest
And streetlights come on to stare like praying mantises down on us.

The final line above serves to illustrate the point that for all the scrupulous observation lavished by Wright upon his landscapes, it is the throng of metaphors, swelling here and there into a baroque luxuriance and complexity, which constitute perhaps the most distinctive feature of these verbal scenes. His imagination, which he describes as "metaphysical," like the imaginations of Donne and Marvell, frequently stretches the comparative boundaries of figures of speech in unexpected and startling directions. The heightened, occasionally surreal, qualities of these tropes caused Marjorie Perloff, writing in the St. James Press *Contemporary Poets*, to observe that though Wright might name Pound, Dante, and Montale as his chief influences, "perhaps his most immediate model" is George Trakl. Certain of the metaphorical effects produced by Wright recall the "deep image" poems of Bly, Merwin, and others of the previous generation.

As indicated by his practice in *The Grave of the Right Hand*, from the outset Wright evidently has assumed that metaphors contribute an essential ingredient of the intensity and denseness of expression common to his shorter poems. Characteristically, "Bygones," his sole experiment with a one-line poem, is chiefly remarkable for its bizarre combination of metaphors: "The rain has stopped falling asleep on its crystal stems." Amidst a multitude of apt and inventive points of comparison are a few purely whimsical images, such as the opening lines of "At Zero": "In the cold kitchen of heaven, / Daylight spoons out its cream-of-wheat." Occasionally also Wright's imagination throws up a metaphor too dazzlingly mixed to grace even his paradoxical vision, as when he declares:

> The breath inside my breath is the breath of the dream.
> I lick its charred heart, a piece of the same flaked sky
> The badger drags to his hole.            ("12 Lines at Midnight")

More typically, Wright's metaphors add fresh and vivid dimensions to commonplace scenes, as in "April":

> The plum tree breaks out in bees.
> A gull is locked like a ghost in the blue attic of heaven.
> The wind goes nattering on,
> Gossipy, ill at ease, in the damp rooms it will air.

While his recent long poems contain metaphors in abundance, the author acknowledges that following *The Southern Cross* metaphors have ceased to be in themselves a *raison d'etre* of his work or to function as self-sufficient statements. Whereas in a 1983 *Partisan Review* interview he was still insisting that the preeminence of tropes in his work was merely natural self-expression ("I think in metaphors"), six years later he discounted figurative language alone as "technique as a statement in itself" and argued instead that "Technique is half a statement in itself. It's a subject without a verb or object." He added, "My interest in technical matters, the 'how,' has not lessened, but my interest in what I am trying to say, the 'what,' has become more than equal to it."[7]

Particularly in *Zone Journals*, an important part of what Wright has recently been "trying to say" concerns technical or aesthetic issues. In drawing his verbal landscapes he is conscious that the establishment of a point of focus requires a massive act of exclusion. All features except those of the central image and its close associates must be omitted: "It's all a matter of how you narrow the surfaces. / It's all a matter of how you fit in the sky." Yet the very highlighting of certain forms or features by implication may direct the viewer's attention to what has been excluded. Despite the appearances of art, we know that nothing exists in isolation. Confronted by a painting, say, of a ruined barn or an unfamiliar street scene, we are immediately curious about both the subject's general location and its immediate surroundings. The imaginative eye of the viewer may supply images to complement the painting:

> . . . what's missing is what appears
> Most visible to the eye:
> the more luminous anything is,
> The more it subtracts what's around it, . . .
> making the unseen seen.
> ("Yard Journal")

Recognizing that his aesthetic theory is, to say the least, unconventional, Wright concedes that his friends remain skeptical that "what's outside / The picture is more important than what's in." Undeterred, he illustrates his point with this description of a Southern California shoreline:

> Turkey buzzards turn in their widening spins
> over the flint
> Ridged, flake-dried ground and kelp beds,
> Sway-winged and shadowless in the climbing air.
> Palm trees postcard the shoreline.
> Something is added as the birds disappear,
> something quite small
> And indistinct and palpable as a stain
> of saint light on a choir stall.
> ("A Journal of True Confessions")

---

7. McClatchy 201.

Whatever its merits, Wright's argument for the presence or visibility of the unseen is the fitting expression of a mind which broods upon and seeks evidence of the invisible, the intangible, the ideal. It may well be the Platonist in him which claims that "the obvious end of art" is "that grace / Beyond its reach." Similarly, he maintains, "In all beauty there lies / Something inhuman, something you can't know." Such aesthetic pronouncements focus attention upon "the absences" by which Wright is haunted and which he senses glimmering "at the edge of understanding." However patiently attentive he may be, glimpses into the center of being are all too brief: "Something infinite behind everything appears, and then disappears." In *The Paris Review* he described "the true purpose of poetry" as "the contemplation of the divine." When asked if he referred to "the textures of the world as well as an outline of the infinite," he replied, "The textures of the world *are* an outline of the infinite. Stevens said . . . the thing seen becomes the thing unseen. . . . Roethke wrote that all finite things reveal infinitude. . . . I'd say that to love the visible things in the visible world is to love their apokatastatic outline in the invisible next."[8] Wright's faith that an infinite power underlies and informs both the external world and its human inhabitants is expressed allegorically as follows:

> —We stand at the green gates,
> substitutes for the unseen
> Rising like water inside our bodies,
> Stand-ins against the invisible:
> It's the blank sky of the page
> —not the words it's never the words—
> That backgrounds our lives . . .
> The unknown repeats us, and quickens our in-between . . .
> Like the stone inside a rock,
> the stillness of form is the center of everything,
> Inalterable, always at ease.
>
> ("A Journal of the Year of the Ox")

In *Zone Journals* the poet makes a dedicated search of his favorite landscapes for evidence of the infinite behind or within the visible and finite, seeking proof that "what disappears is what stays." A supernatural aura arises in the brief appearance there of what is evidently the ghost of Dante, who counsels, "Concentrate, listen hard, / Look to the nature of all things."

---

8. McClatchy 220. Wright's imaginative joining of the visible and the invisible is related to and helps to explain his attachment to metaphors. Among the "Pensées" in his *Halflife: Improvisations and Interviews* (University of Michigan Press, 1988) is this declaration: "A metaphor is a link in the long chain which leads us to the invisible" (p. 30).

Left in solitude to act upon this enigmatic advice, Wright obediently listens intently to his surroundings but hears "no alphabet in the wind":

> Only this silence, the strict gospel of silence,
> 
> > to greet me,
> 
> Opened before me like a rare book.
> I turn the first page
> 
> > and then the next, but understand nothing,
> 
> The deepening twilight a vast vocabulary
> I've never heard of.
> I keep on turning, however:
> 
> > somewhere in here, I know, is my word.
> 
> > ("A Journal of the Year of the Ox")

At the poem's conclusion Wright wistfully inquires, "What is a life of contemplation worth in this world? / How far can you go if you concentrate, how far down?" While the answers to those questions must necessarily remain inconclusive, and while *Zone Journals* finds the poet as yet unable to decipher the message inscribed upon his surroundings, there can be little doubt that he will maintain his avid quest for the infinite and the absolute. It is a search which has often drawn him into the ghostly past to revive memories and to speak with the dead, which has led him to contemplate and even to welcome death as a form of completion and possible transfiguration, and which has caused him to survey land, sea, and sky with the rapt attention of one lured by an unseen but palpable presence, an invisible force manifest by its very absence.

STEPHEN CUSHMAN

# The Capabilities of Charles Wright (1992)

I begin with an anecdote. This past April I headed a committee which invited James Merrill to the University of Virginia for two days. On the second day of his visit, I arranged for Merrill to lunch with several graduate students, some from the M.F.A. program, some from the Ph.D. Charles Wright also attended. During the conversation, we began to talk about free verse, which Merrill, of course, does not usually write, but which he nevertheless claimed to admire in the work of certain poets.[1] In particular, he talked about free verse poets who carefully count syllables and stresses in order to avoid settling into a metrical pattern. Anyone familiar with Charles Wright's volume *Halflife* (1988) will recognize immediately this description of Wright's practice.[2] I shall turn later to an example of Wright's loose syllabic prosody, which he describes at one point as "a kind of bastardized quantitative measure" *(Halflife 163)*, but for the moment I would single out for consideration this general self-descriptive statement: "I write only in free verse, and I feel about free verse the way Frank Stella feels about abstract art: my life is dedicated to it. But formal issues involved in free verse are at the front of my consciousness at all times" *(Halflife 154)*.

No serious reader of Wright's poems could doubt the truth of this last statement, and no reader of his prose improvisations and interviews could fail to appreciate the relief I felt that, over the lunch I had organized, Merrill and Wright would find themselves in substantial agreement, at least about the demands of writing good free verse. But it was after Merrill had finished speaking that an unexpected lesson for the day came in the form of a casual, under-the-breath remark made by Wright, a remark no one else may have heard, much less might be able to dredge up under oath. Still, it was a remark which has given me a new perspective for this discussion: "Free verse is Negative Capability."

---

1. A notable exception is *The Changing Light at Sandover* (New York: Atheneum, 1982), in which Merrill, at the suggestion of Auden, has his angels speak in "NOTH-ING STRICT A CADENCE BREAKING THRU." Searching for an appropriate prosody, JM asks Michael, "Would the like you unmeasurable King / James inflections be perhaps the thing?" (p. 346).

2. See *Halflife: Improvisations and Interviews, 1977-87* (Ann Arbor: Univ. of Michigan Press, 1988), 84-86, 108, 163. Subsequent references to this edition will appear in the text as *Halflife*.

"Negative Capability." Since my discussion of Wright leans heavily on this famous phrase of Keats's, before it turns to consider the equal prominence of what we might call Wright's Positive Capability, let us recall its original setting. In a letter of December 1817, Keats is writing to his brothers, George and Tom:

> I had not a dispute but a disquisition with Dilke, on various subjects; several things dovetailed in my mind, & at once it struck me, what quality went to form a Man of Achievement especially in Literature & which Shakespeare pos[s]essed so enormously—I mean *Negative Capability*, that is when man is capable of being in uncertainties, Mysteries, doubts, without any irritable reaching after fact & reason—Coleridge, for instance, would let go by a fine isolated verisimilitude caught from the Penetralium of mystery, from being incapable of remaining content with half knowledge. This pursued through Volumes would perhaps take us no further than this, that with a great poet the sense of Beauty overcomes every other consideration, or rather obliterates all consideration.[3]

My main concern here is not to add to the mountains of commentary this passage has generated, but rather to use it to illuminate Wright's comment that free verse is, or involves, Negative Capability. If I understand him, I believe Wright means that the free verse poet, or rather the free verse poet who is mindful and self-conscious about technique, must be capable, with respect to the formal schemes of his or her poems, "of being in uncertainties, Mysteries, doubts, without any irritable reaching after fact & reason." When it comes to the arrangement of words into lines and lines into poems, free verse poets must be capable "of remaining content with half knowledge."

Fair enough, but what does this mean specifically? It means that because of their Negative Capability free verse poets do not reach for conventional metrical patterns to organize their lines, stanzas, and poems. If you ask James Merrill why he breaks a line where he does, he can give you a fact and a reason: Five iambic feet have passed and, since my meter is iambic pentameter, it's time to break the line. But if you ask Charles Wright why he breaks a line where he does, and Wright is outspoken on the subject of his line breaks (*Halflife* 3-5), he would not give you the same kind of empirically verifiable fact or reason. He might say, as he has said, "Each line should be a station of the cross" (*Halflife* 5), a compelling figure (and, incidentally, an iambic pentameter line) which combines Wright's devotion to form with his characteristic ecclesiastical idiom, a figure which I take to mean that each line of the poem should be both separate from and connected to the other lines around it. Or, to put it

---

3. *Letters of John Keats, 1814-1821*, ed. Hyder E. Rollins (Cambridge: Harvard Univ. Press, 1958), 1:193-94.

differently, the wholeness of individual lines should not be compromised and violated by persistent, compulsive enjambment. Furthermore, each line should have about it not only an autonomy or integrity but also a gravity or weightiness—a weightiness implied elsewhere by Wright's claim that he works with "a long image-freighted line" (*Halflife* 4)— which both reflects and inspires profound contemplation.

Obviously, a poet who believes each of his free verse lines should approach the condition of devotional meditation does not take the construction of those lines casually; and yet, in defending a given line break, he may be able to offer nothing more persuasive than "This is where I hear the break" or "This is where it felt right to break it." In other words, in Keats's terms both free verse poets and their readers often have no choice but to remain content with half knowledge of their techniques and procedures, despite many elaborate attempts of various critics of prosody to systematize exactly what they think free verse lines do.[4]

Two questions arise at this point. First, is it in fact true that in their formal practices, as well as in their explanations of those practices, free verse poets demonstrate Negative Capability more than metrical poets? Second, what are the implications and ramifications of this formal Negative Capability?

Although I believe Wright's statement tells us a great deal about him and his aesthetic ideology, which is the reason I'm dwelling on it, I don't think it necessarily describes American free verse poets in general. For example, Whitman and Williams are not at all content with half knowledge when it comes to explaining their free verse. Whitman insists that the construction of his verse represents the American difference from Great Britain, and Williams goes a step further, proclaiming that his free verse isn't free but actually bound directly to the auditory realities of the American idiom. To my mind, these two great poets are especially irritating in their reaching after fact and reason, particularly Williams, whose incapability of being in uncertainties, mysteries, and doubts about the nature and legitimacy of his own fine poetry led him into the fantastic fiction of the variable foot.[5]

---

4. A usually reliable introduction to free verse is Charles O. Hartman's *Free Verse: An Essay on Prosody* (Princeton: Princeton Univ. Press, 1980), although Hartman's argument wobbles when it turns to William Carlos Williams and the vexed subject of isochrony (see pp. 66 ff.). Tending more toward the elaborate and, to my mind, less persuasive is Antony Easthope's discussion of "Intonational Metre" in *Poetry as Discourse* (London: Methuen, 1983), 153–59. An earlier but still useful discussion is Benjamin Hrudhovski's "On Free Rhythms in Modern Poetry," *Style in Language*, ed. Thomas A. Sebeok (Cambridge: MIT Press, 1960), 173–92. See also Derek Attridge, "Poetry Unbound? Observations on Free Verse," *Proceedings of the British Academy* 73 (1987): 353–74.

5. I have treated Williams's fictions of "measure" at length in *William Carlos Williams and the Meanings of Measure* (New Haven: Yale Univ. Press, 1985).

But if Whitman and Williams are not good examples of Negative Capability, Charles Wright may be.[6] If we turn to the second question (What are the implications and ramifications of formal Negative Capability?), we find that in his case they are profound. Negative Capability does not merely describe Wright's ability to do without the reassuring certainties of metrical patterning; it also describes his attitude towards human existence itself. If this formulation sounds too dramatic, it should come as no surprise to readers of a poet who announces from the start that "Form is nothing more than a transubstantiation of content" (*Halflife* 3). This statement echoes and revises Robert Creeley's famous dictum that form is never more than an extension of content, but Wright's theological word "transubstantiation" improves on Creeley's nonchalant organicist slogan by introducing the elements of mystery and ritual.[7] Creeley would have us believe that the form of a poem emerges casually from, and is perpetually subordinate to, content. Conversely, Wright elevates the status of form by suggesting that form is to content as the body and blood of Christ are to the Eucharistic bread and wine. In this trope of communion, the poet is the celebrant, the reader is the communicant, and the transubstantiation which occurs changes poems built of long image-freighted lines into instances of what Wright calls "UFO—Ultimate Formal Organization":

> Larkin's comment was "Form means nothing to me. Content is everything." My comment would be that content means nothing to me. Form is everything. Which is to say, to me the most vital question in poetry is the question of form. Form lies at the heart of all poetical problems. I don't mean "forms"—I don't mean sonnets, sestinas, rondeaus, quatrains, triplets. I mean Form. UFO—Ultimate Formal Organization, if you wish. That may be extrapoetical in some sense. But I'm concerned with form and structures, the architecture of form. I'm one of those people who thinks that content has nothing to do with subject matter. I think there's form, there's subject matter, and then there's content. Content is what it all "means," somehow. Subject matter is what it's "about." Form is how you organize it. (*Halflife* 153-54)

With the felicitous phrase "Ultimate Formal Organization" Wright appears to be gesturing toward what the Greeks meant by the word *logos*, that is, the principle of order within the universe. This reading is confirmed as Wright continues:

---

6. Another free verse poet whose work provides good examples of Negative Capability on many levels is A. R. Ammons. See my "Stanzas, Organic Myth, and the Metaformalism of A. R. Ammons," *American Literature* 59 (December 1987): 513-27.

7. This statement is attributed to Creeley by Charles Olson in his essay "Projective Verse." See *Selected Writings of Charles Olson*, ed. Robert Creeley (New York: New Directions, 1966), 16.

The difference I'm making between "forms" as accepted traditional forms and Form is again one I can't explain really—but I feel it, I know it somehow. . . . The secret of the universe is Form, even if poems are not the secret of the universe. They're only clues to the secret of the universe. (*Halflife* 154)

In this excerpt we hear the rhetoric of Negative Capability coming through loud and clear: the transubstantiation of content into Ultimate Formal Organization is something Wright "can't explain really," but he "feels it," he "knows it somehow." Likewise, he makes no claim to knowing the secret of the universe, only to having access to certain clues to that secret. Wright's statement that content means nothing to him and form everything does not represent a glib posturing. Instead, if I follow his formulations about content, subject matter, and form, the real "content" of any poem, or at least any poem by Charles Wright, is the mystery of how the bread and wine of lines of verse become the body and blood of the universe. That one cannot explain—in fact, should not explain—this mystery is exactly the point, as well as the source of Wright's Negative Capability. But let us turn to a poem to see this mystery in action. This is "Saturday Morning Journal," originally published in *Antaeus* (1989), selected for *The Best American Poetry 1990*, and subsequently collected in the volume *The World of the Ten Thousand Things*:[8]

Nature, by nature, has no answers,
                    landscape the same.
Form tends toward its own dissolution.

There is an inaccessibility in the wind,
In the wind that taps the trees
With its white cane,
                  with its white cane and fingertips;
There is a twice-remove in the light
That falls,
          that falls like stained glass to the ground.

The world has been translated into a new language
Overnight, a constellation of signs and plain sense
I understand nothing of,
                local objects and false weather
Out of the inborn,
As though I had asked for them, as though I had been there.

---

8. *Antaeus* 62 (Spring 1989): 230; Jorie Graham, ed., *The Best American Poetry 1990* (New York: Collier Books, 1990), 234; *The World of the Ten Thousand Things: Poems 1980-1990* (New York: Farrar, Straus and Giroux, 1990), 208.

If we begin by considering the poem on the page, we notice four features of "Saturday Morning Journal" immediately. First, it consists of four sentences and three stanzas, all closed by periods. Second, as Wright insists on the integrity and autonomy of his stanzas, so he insists on the integrity and autonomy of his lines, his stations of the cross, by capitalizing the first word of each of the twelve lines, a convention discarded by many, if not most, free verse poets. Third, four times in the poem Wright employs what he calls the dropped line, or "low rider" (*Halflife* 52), splitting one of his twelve lines into two parts, so that four times the verse is suddenly aerated by shifts of blank space extending from the left margin. Fourth, the poem generates a strange typographic paradox: Since Wright insists that a "line" includes its detached, indented "low rider," the three stanzas consist of two, five, and five lines respectively; yet if we measure typographic length as would a typesetter (or an editor who is paying by the line), counting the dropped lines as separate, we get a stanzaic pattern of three lines, seven lines, and six lines. Depending on how we define a line, the central stanza is both equal to and longer than the final stanza.

The dropped line is an important part of Wright's technical repertoire, one which deserves more space than I can devote to it here. Although he did not invent this device, it has a special meaning in his work. Specifically, I would argue that the dropped line is to Charles Wright what the dash is to Emily Dickinson: It allows him to annotate various kinds of junctions within his lines at the same time that it enables him to maintain the left-to-right horizontal sweep of his lineation. Furthermore, for a poet who believes free verse is Negative Capability, the dropped line is appropriate, if not inevitable, for it calls into question the exact nature of a line. A line of verse which begins with a capital letter but suddenly turns split-level both is and is not a single line. How does Wright resolve this uncertainty? He doesn't, and in this instance his readers must remain content with half knowledge.

After making these four initial observations about the poem on the page, a curious reader must dig deeper into another typographic convention of Anglo-American verse, that of syllabism. In *Halflife*, Wright explains: "Well, I like to think I write in a kind of loose syllabics as opposed to, say, accentuals or something like that" (163). The patterns of accentual verse are accessible to the ear, those of syllabic verse only to the eye. If we count syllables per capitalized "line" in "Saturday Morning Journal," we get a pattern of 13-9 // 13-7-12-9-10 // 13-13-15-5-13. Obviously, there is no strict metrical pattern here, as there would be in the syllabics of Marianne Moore, but just as obviously, the number 13 recurs, if not regularly, frequently enough to suggest a general rhythmic patterning. These observations confirm Wright's own remarks: "I work with seven-, thirteen-, nineteen-, fifteen-, nine-syllable lines. Those are the five lines that I'm interested in. Especially the thirteen- syllable line, with four to five, usually five, stresses" (*Halflife* 108).

If fear of the number 13 is triskaidekaphobia, then Charles Wright is a triskaidekaphiliac.[9] One can justify this preference for a 13-syllable line prosodically, arguing that it gives a free verse poet the same number of stresses as the iambic pentameter, which often wavers between four and five prominent stresses, at the same time that it loosens the pentameter up with three extra syllables. But it is hard to escape all suspicion that Wright's triskaidekaphilia reflects some numerological significance the number 13 holds for him. Triskaidekaphobia, or superstition in general, has a complicated relationship to Negative Capability. On the one hand, it amounts to a compulsive reaching after certainty, fact, and reason: the number 13 is dangerous, and bad things necessarily follow from encounters with it. Superstition represents an attempt to know the unknowable, and therefore someone who surrenders to superstition lapses from Negative Capability. But on the other hand, superstition may be the last resort of someone who has forfeited all other forms of certainty. By returning regularly to this number, Wright consciously or unconsciously flirts with the power of its taboo. In the process, by a kind of prosodic homeopathy, he innoculates himself against paralysis by the emotion from which he believes he writes, the emotion always threatening someone in doubt, mystery, and uncertainty: "Fear" (*Halflife* 152).[10]

At any rate, an awareness of Wright's syllabic propensities reveals another layer of organization in "Saturday Morning Journal." If we look at the four dropped lines, we find that they have 4, 8, 8, and 8 syllables respectively. This patterning would appear to constitute both a pattern and a fable about pattern: The 8-syllable norm is not immediately present, but once it emerges, it persists. But consider the syntactic integrity of the four dropped lines. The first three are self-contained, closing with either a period or a semicolon, but the fourth ("local objects and false weather") is not, its syntax continuing into the next line, "Out of the inborn." If we combine "local objects and false weather" with "Out of the inborn" to complete the syntactic unit, we end up with—lo and behold—a 13-syllable unit broken across a line boundary. This return of the familiar unit is then clinched by the last line of the poem, which has 13 syllables.

---

9. A contemporary of Wright's who explores various schematic possibilities of the 13-syllable line is John Hollander. See his *Powers of Thirteen* (New York: Atheneum, 1983), especially pp. 87-93.

10. That Wright has some inclination towards superstition is evident when he knocks twice on the doorjamb of Poe's room at the University of Virginia, a ritual he repeats when visiting the last rooms occupied by Petrarch. See "A Journal of the Year of the Ox," *Zone Journals* (New York: Farrar, Straus and Giroux, 1988), 52-3, 66. This poem and volume are discussed more fully below. Page references to this edition will be identified in the text as *ZJ*. Notice, too, that Wright calls attention to the significance of Poe's address: "He lived, appropriately enough, at 13 West Range" (52).

In paying so much attention to the visual patterning of this poem, I have neglected its prominent auditory features, among them the constant repetition of words and phrases: "Nature, by nature"; "in the wind / In the wind"; "With its white cane, / with its white cane"; "There is . . . / There is"; "That falls, / that falls"; "As though I had . . . as though I had."[11] I have also spent no time with its tonal qualities (for example, the wry joke of "Nature, by nature"); its images, such as the personification of the wind as a blind person with a white cane; its characteristic ecclesiastical resnances, present in "stained glass" or the pun on "translated"; or its grammatical transformation (the conversion of the adjective phrase "twice-removed" into the substantive "twice-remove," which suggests a further estrangement compounding the "once-remove" of subject from object).

Instead, I have chosen to concentrate on the most prominent features of formal organization because, as I read it, this poem is remarkable for its congruence of what Wright would call content, subject matter, and form. All three converge in the third line: "Form tends toward its own dissolution." Not only is this what the poem is "about," on the level of subject matter; it is also what the poem "means," on the larger level of content transubstantiated into an instance of, or a clue to, Ultimate Formal Organization in the universe. Furthermore, the agent of this transubstantiation is the schematic organization of syllables into lines, both split and unsplit, because that organization shows a pattern, or form, dissolving, as the self-containment of the 8-syllable dropped lines ("with its white cane and fingertips" and "that falls like stained glass to the ground") suddenly dissolves in an 8-syllable dropped line which overflows syntactically into its successor.

But "Saturday Morning Journal" is not only about how form—whether prosodic form, natural form, or Ultimate Form—tends towards dissolution; it is also about how dissolved form is reconstituted or, in the phrasing of the poem, "translated into a new language." After the work-week of Monday through Friday, one awakes on Saturday morning with a sense that the usual patterns and forms of routine have dissolved; yet their dissolution has not simply left a void. Instead, they yield to a new "constellation of signs and plain sense," a new formal organization. Squinting into the strange, estranging Saturday morning light, one may not understand anything of this new arrangement, but, Wright is suggesting, such understanding is not the point. The point is that, when one form dissolves and another emerges, the subject or "I" has an uncanny sense of recognition, feeling that the change is not merely random but is a reflection of the subject's own volition and perception: "As though I

---

11. Notice that the usual notation for marking line divisions (/) is inadequate for Wright's verse, since it does not allow us to distinguish between two lines and two parts of a split-level line.

had asked for them, as though I had been there." At this revelatory or epiphanic moment, one experiences a connection between the external ("local objects and false weather") and the internal ("Out of the in-born"), a connection Wright deftly supports with the enjambment of the final detached 8-syllable line into its 5-syllable successor. In the poetry of Charles Wright, such moments and experiences ask to be considered religious, and perhaps he expects us to hear in the title "Saturday Morning Journal" an echo and revision of Stevens' "Sunday Morning."

In other words, this poem is an exercise in Negative Capability. No matter how much one craves them, "Nature, by nature, has no answers" to satisfy the hunger for fact, reason, and full knowledge. Furthermore, what nature does provide in the form of landscape, wind, light, objects, and weather leaves one admitting that these are things "I understand nothing of." Before turning to consider the Positive Capability of Charles Wright, I shall venture one last speculation about his attraction to Keats's notion of Negative Capability. Negative Capability does not come naturally to Wright. Instead, it represents a state or condition to be developed by discipline, much as a Buddhist frees himself or herself from suffering by means of a series of negatives: no-thought, non-assertion, non-attachment, non-attainment, non-duality, non-relying, not-self. In making this claim, I take my cue from several statements Wright has made in interviews, statements which both admit and reveal his compulsive orderliness:

> I am compulsively orderly. There is nothing out of place in my hotel room, for example. . . . I got that from my father. He was the same way. My shoes are lined up, the shirts hang the same way, the coats are on the same side. Everything is always that way. I like to think it has to do with my sense of structure, of architecture and form being carried over into my life in a ridiculous way. (*Halflife* 148)

Anyone who doubts that Wright pushes Stevens's blessed rage to order to Dantesque proportions need only review his explanation of the structure of "Skins," one of two long sequences in *Bloodlines* (1975; *Halflife* 74–77). Not only has Wright schernatized the sequence numerologically; he has planned—down to the smallest details—the architecture of the volume, as well as the sequence of volumes *Hard Freight* (1973), *Bloodlines*, and *China Trace* (1977). This same exhaustive planning characterizes Wright's later work as well.[12]

---

12. Consider, for example, the structure of *Zone Journals*, which has at the exact center of its central poem, "A Journal of the Year of the Ox," three 100-line sections written at Cà Paruta, a house in Vo, Italy (*ZJ* 54–69). The first section, dated July 9, narrates an encounter with Dante, for whom the number 100 also had architectural significance; the second, dated July 25, includes an ekphrastic reading of the 15th-century fresco in the Salon of the Months at the Palazzo Schifanoia near

My sense, then, is that for Charles Wright Negative Capability is a necessary antidote to his own compulsive orderliness. Without it, his irritable reaching after fact and reason could overwhelm him with signs and meanings that are overdetermined. If I am correct, we have come upon a paradox, both in the work of Charles Wright and in Keats's concept of Negative Capability. In the work of Charles Wright, the paradox is that the insistence on uncertainty or mystery situates itself in structures which are anything but uncertain or mysterious. In order to approach Negative Capability, Wright structures his poems according to an extreme form of Negative Incapability. Every element in a poem must be counted, ordered, and planned in order to reveal the limits of counting, ordering, and planning.

In turn, this paradox in Wright's work reflects an original paradox in Keats's concept of Negative Capability: A poet who was genuinely capable of living with uncertainty, mystery, doubt, and half knowledge would be incapable of making the choices necessary to construct a poem. No process is more burdened with the irritable reaching after fact and reason than the process of poetic composition. Why choose this word, this image, this phrasing, this meter, this line-length? In fact, Negative Capability, at least in its purest form, would preclude creativity altogether, since creation always involves the choice of one possibility over another, and any choice has hovering behind it the impulse toward knowledge or certainty. To make a good poem about Negative Capability, one must have considerable Positive Capability. One must be, to modify Stevens's description, a figure of positively capable imagination.

What are the techniques and strategies which best represent the Positive Capability of Charles Wright? In selecting my examples, I shall stick closely to the volume *Zone Journals* (1988), especially to its central (in several senses) poem, "A Journal of the Year of the Ox." In the space I have remaining, I can do little more than provide a descriptive inventory of three recurrent strategies or structures: the journal form, the interrogative mode, and the use of figurative language. However briefly, I hope to show that these are not only characteristic features of Wright's later work but also effective agents in his approach to Negative Capability.

The title "Saturday Morning Journal" is anticipated by the titles of the ten poems in *Zone Journals*, each of which attaches the word "journal" to a word or phrase which could otherwise stand alone: "Yard Journal," "A Journal of English Days," "March Journal," "A Journal of True Confessions," "Night Journal," "A Journal of the Year of the Ox," "Light

---

Ferrara; the third, dated August 3, meditates on Petrarch. For other statements about the structure of "A Journal of the Year of the Ox," see the interview with J. D. McClatchy, "The Art of Poetry XLI," *Paris Review* 113 (Winter 1989): 215. Here Wright describes his poem as "an American sprawl of a poem with a succession of succinct checks and balances."

Journal," "A Journal of One Significant Landscape," "Chinese Journal," "Night Journal II." Although a few of these titles suggest affiliations with a generic category which implies the daily recording of events, thoughts, and impressions over an extended period of time, many do not. For example, "Yard Journal" is an intriguing and puzzling title. What should one expect to find in a yard journal? A day-by-day record of how often the grass needs cutting? But the inaugural poem consists instead of association-provoking images from the poet's yard, images which have little or nothing to do with the linear passage of time.

In Wright's hands, the journal poem is a generic hybrid, one which crosses the lyric, in which time is often compressed, disrupted, or suspended, with the journal, in which the linear passage of time is preserved as the dominant structural principle. The word "journal" comes from the French word for "daily," but the dailiness of many of Wright's journals is beside the point. Instead, "journal" often resonates with the meaning of its cognate "journey" and suggests a kind of meditative travel which may begin in one time but move freely backward or forward. Also, Wright's titling a poem "X Journal" or "A Journal of Y" calls attention to the status of that poem as a written record of something. A poem called "Saturday Morning" is, on some level, about Saturday morning, but a poem called "Saturday Morning Journal" is about both Saturday morning and the written record of Saturday morning.

By contrast with the shorter journals, "A Journal of the Year of the Ox," as its title suggests, is closer to the conventional generic aspects of the journal. It covers the period from January to December 1985 and runs to forty-eight pages. Although the poem jumps freely in space and time from the present in Virginia or Italy to different zones in the past (Wright's earlier Army service in Italy or his youth in Tennessee along the Holston River or the first incursions of white men into territory held by the Cherokee along the Holston), it remains loyal to the passage of linear time. The poem has a distinct sense of monthliness, if not dailiness. This journal also suggests "journey," as the first few lines of the poem contemplate a pilgrimage to be undertaken in and by the poem: "Pity the poor pilgrim, the setter-forth, / Under a sweep so sure, / pity his going up and his going down" (*ZJ* 37).

Inevitably, the pilgrim's "going up and his going down" recall the ascents and descents of Dante's pilgrimage, and Dante is a large presence in "Journal of the Year of the Ox," appearing and speaking to the poet in July (*ZJ* 58–59).[13] But in sketching the genealogy of Wright's journal in

---

13. I also hear an echo of Satan's statement to God in the Book of Job: "And the Lord said unto Satan, Whence comest thou? Then Satan answered the Lord, and said, From going to and fro in the earth, and from walking up and down in it" (1:7). Hart Crane, a favorite of Wright's (see *Halflife* 176), uses Satan's reply as the epigraph to *The Bridge*.

order to describe the significance of his form, I would point elsewhere. In verse, one could look to other models in twentieth-century American poetry, such as Williams's "The Descent of Winter" (first published in 1928), Robert Lowell's *Notebook 1967-68* (1969), A. R. Ammons's *Tape for the Turn of the Year* (1965) and *The Snow Poems* (1977). One could also push back as far as Christopher Smart's *Jubilate Agno*, which for all its liturgical structuring reveals the day-by-day recording of events (as when Smart laments that a rat has bitten the throat of his cat Jeoffrey in one line and rejoices that Jeoffrey has recovered in the next). But more appropriate models are to be found in the prose journal. In particular, I am thinking of the journals of Emerson, described best by a sentence in "Self Reliance": "In this pleasing contrite wood-life which God allows me, let me record day by day my honest thought without prospect or retrospect, and, I cannot doubt, it will be found symmetrical, though I mean it not and see it not.[14]

This statement reveals two important features of Emerson's journal-keeping, features shared by Wright's "Journal of the Year of the Ox." The first and more obvious is that although Emerson's journals constitute a record of spiritual growth like *The Confessions* of Augustine (whose name appears three times in Wright's poem [*ZJ* 55, 67, 71]) or the *Personal Narrative* of Jonathan Edwards, they differ from these autobiographies by being day-by-day records "without prospect or retrospect." Augustine and Edwards tell their stories retrospectively; Emerson and Wright record their stories as they unfold. As a result, the second feature of Emerson's journals emerges and distinguishes his record from that of Augustine or Edwards. Since Augustine and Edwards narrate retrospectively, they already know where their narratives lead. But since Emerson records day by day, he cannot know where his narrative leads, and so he must possess significant Negative Capability: "it will be found symmetrical, though I mean it not and see it not."

In other words, in the hands of Emerson the journal is the generic form capable of the highest degree of Negative Capability, for in it pattern and symmetry are not imposed but rather discovered. According to Emerson, the journal, for all its apparent formlessness, will find an inevitable form, the form of the journal-keeper's "honest thought." Clearly, this aspect of the journals is attractive to Wright, but whereas Emerson exhibits calm confidence that form will emerge inevitably, Wright is more anxious, as we hear in this description of "Journal of the Year of the Ox":

> Part of my spatial theory of free verse is that structure resembles a giant spider web. It's endlessly expandable, but within a framework. The secret is to find the framework. To have found the framework for this journal has proven difficult. The year, obviously, is one reference. That's the skin

---

14. *The Complete Works of Ralph Waldo Emerson*, ed. Edward Waldo Emerson, Centenary Ed. (Boston: Houghton Mifflin, 1903-04), 2: 58.

structure of the poem. But you also have to make interior structuring devices so you know yourself you haven't just been vamping for a whole year—that there are three or four points the whole thing hangs on, that it does make a strange circular movement. I think art does try to be circular somehow. (*Halflife* 155-56)

Perhaps the difference between Emerson's trust in inevitable form and Wright's need for something beyond "the skin structure" of the year merely reflects a difference in two temperaments; or perhaps it reflects a difference between journals which don't particularly think of themselves as "art" and those which do. Whatever the truth, we hear in Wright's statement, particularly in his nervousness that he might only be "vamping" or enticing his readers with false appearances, the limits of his Negative Capability. On the one hand, he affirms the endless expandability of free verse journals; on the other, he insists on finding "three or four points the whole thing hangs on" in order to describe a circular pattern. This circular patterning represents an instance of Wright's Positive Capability, which enables him to construct poems that encompass uncertainty, mystery, doubt, and half knowledge. In an important moment, he confesses, "The more formal and the more disguised I can keep the organization, the happier I am" *(Halflife* 157). The ability to disguise his reachings after fact and reason, as he does in "A Journal of the Year of the Ox," is characteristic of Wright's Positive Capability.

The second structure or strategy which is especially prominent in "A Journal of the Year of the Ox" is Wright's use of the interrogative mode. The persistent question-asking begins with the ninth line of the poem:

> How shall we hold on, when everything bright falls away?
> How shall we know what calls us
>                   when what's past remains what's past
> And unredeemed, the crystal
> And wavering coefficient of what's ahead?        (ZJ 37)

In his illuminating discussion of the use of questions in poetry, John Hollander distinguishes between rhetorical questions, which anticipate specific answers and are therefore "closed," and poetic questions, which by their figurative nature perpetuate a process of questioning and are therefore "open." Somewhere between these poles, he locates philosophical questions, such as "What is knowledge?," questions which do not anticipate a specific answer but which nevertheless imply logical progress toward an answer.[15]

_____

15. See "Questions of Poetry" in *Melodious Guile* (New Haven: Yale Univ. Press, 1988), 18-40. As is usually the case with Hollander's essays, his discussion includes and subsumes major developments in the history of the discussion from Classical and Renaissance rhetoricians onward. Accordingly, those seeking a fuller bibliography on the subject should consult Hollander's notes.

Wright's question here, like many of the questions throughout "A Journal of the Year of the Ox," is at once rhetorical, philosophical, and poetic. "How shall we hold on, when everything bright falls away?" is a rhetorical question when we hear it as a version of "How shall we ever manage without water to drink?" The obvious answer in both cases would be "We can't and we won't." If everything bright falls away, so shall we. But the question turns philosophical if we assume that there may be a way of holding on amidst change, loss, and death, a way we don't know yet but in the course of the poem may discover. A Christian's answer to this philosophical question would be something on the order of "We shall hold on by means of our faith in Jesus Christ and the promise of everlasting life which He makes." One could argue that for a believer in Christ, the question is actually rhetorical, but for Charles Wright it is certainly an open one, although he may be approaching an answer when Dante advises him at Cà Paruta:

> Brother, remember the way it was
> In my time: nothing has changed:
> Penitents terrace the mountainside, the stars hang in their bright courses
> And darkness is still the dark:
> concentrate, listen hard,
> Look to the nature of all things . . . (ZJ 58)

Appropriately enough, the section in which Dante appears is itself framed by other questions asked by the poet: "Who is it here in the night garden . . .?" and "What *is* it these children chant about / In their games?" One could argue that the pilgrimage of "A Journal of the Year of the Ox" is a pilgrimage of philosophical questioning toward both this answer and the contemplation of the fresco at the Palazzo Schifanoia, a contemplation which exemplifies the kind of concentration Dante urges.[16]

But Dante's answer is not wholly adequate, since in fact something major has changed since his time: The Catholic Church and its world-view no longer exert the same explanatory power they did in medieval Europe. Uncertainty, mystery, doubt, and half knowledge have grown, at least for a poet estranged from the Episcopalianism of his Tennessee upbringing, and so the question "How shall we hold on?"

---

16. For background on the fresco, see Ranieri Varese, *Il Palazzo di Schifanoia* (Bologna: Specimen, 1983). Wright's reading of the fresco's three-layered structure as "Reality, symbol and ideal / tripartite and everlasting" (*ZJ* 61) corresponds to Varese's description (I quote from the English translation included in the booklet): "The Schifanoia cycle gives us an idea of contemporary life in the city, the orders from top to bottom [sic: actually bottom to top] corresponding to the everyday, the symbolic and the imaginary life of the city" (27).

becomes, at last, a poetic one, as its unanswerability turns into an image of ultimate unanswerability, the condition which demands Negative Capability.[17] As Hollander argues, poetic question-asking has a particular power for "a post-biblical and post-Homeric reader":

> But in a late—which is to say, a critical—age, a questioning voice seems to hold more authority than a propounding one. It is in this condition of thoughtful readership—the one we think of as being modern in that, for example, doubt seems to be a necessary and authenticating way station on the road to faith—that the poetic question hits home. It is in this way that the poem, rather than the orator, can better persuade by interrogation. (30)

Although Hollander does not appear to have Wright specifically in mind, his statement that "doubt seems to be a necessary and authenticating way station on the road to faith" aptly characterizes the credo of "A Journal of the Year of the Ox" and accounts for the authority of Wright's interrogative voice, an authority which is not easy to maintain amidst uncertainty, mystery, doubt, and half knowledge. As the poem opens with questioning, so it closes: "What is a life of contemplation worth in this world? / How far can you go if you concentrate, / how far down?" (*ZJ* 84). The unique texture of Wright's voice consists of what we might call the tonal chords he can play, as such questions sound simultaneously their rhetorical, philosophical, and poetic notes.

The third characteristic feature of Wright's Positive Capability is his use of figurative language. Of course, "A Journal of the Year of the Ox" does not have a monopoly on figurative language, nor does lyric poetry in general; and yet, in the context of Negative Capability, Wright's tropes perform special service. In "Saturday Morning Journal," we have already seen an example of his fondness for personification in the image of the wind as a blind person tapping the trees with a white cane. In discussing Wright's figurative language, one could produce numerous examples of personification from "A Journal of the Year of the Ox."[18] Alternatively, one could choose to concentrate on similes, which are omnipresent in the poem. Instead, however, I shall focus here on a figurative structure somewhat less familiar than personification or simile, that of the genitive-link metaphor:

---

17. The last entry of "A Journal of the Year of the Ox" is dated 25 December 1985. This final nod to the Christian calendar demonstrates the way Wright, like Dickinson before him, employs the vocabulary and symbology of Christianity to explore a private, and heterodox, spirituality.

18. In her brief discussion of *Zone Journals*, Helen Vendler considers instances of personification, as well as "the gorgeousness of [Wright's] descriptive equipment and his gift for the pathetic fallacy." See *The Music of What Happens: Poems, Poets, Critics* (Cambridge: Harvard Univ. Press, 1988), 389, 392.

the rising coagulation of five o'clock (*ZJ* 41)
the blank sky of the page (*ZJ* 42)
The slick bodice of sunlight (*ZJ* 50)
the sheer nightgown of daylight (*ZJ* 53)
the dog-sleep of late afternoon (*ZJ* 55)
A music of sure contrition (*ZJ* 59)
its marbled tear of light (*ZJ* 63)
the blue plate of the sky (*ZJ* 66)
Dead, stunned heart of summer (*ZJ* 66)
the strict gospel of silence (*ZJ* 68)
the slow snow of daylight (*ZJ* 73)
the cool suck of dusk (*ZJ* 73)
Shuffling the decks of the orchard leaves (*ZJ* 74)
the gray, cataracted eye / of a television set (*ZJ* 82)

Metaphor comes in many grammatical forms, most of which Wright employs at one time or another, but the form represented here is a favorite.[19] Its structure is "A of B," where B would be in the genitive case in an inflected language such as New Testament Greek. In the Book of Revelation, for example, John warns the church at Pergamos, which harbors Nicolaitans, "Repent; or else I will come unto thee quickly, and will fight against them with the sword of my mouth" (2:16; King James Version). In the Greek original, "the sword of my mouth" is *te hromphaia tou stomatos mou* (the sword of the mouth of me), where the possessive genitive could also have been translated "my mouth's sword," an echo of the "sharp two-edged sword" issuing from the mouth of Christ in the previous chapter (1:16). The metaphor here is glossed by a verse in Hebrews: "For the word of God is quick, and powerful, and sharper than any two-edged sword, piercing even to the dividing asunder of soul and spirit, and of the joints and marrow, and is a discerner of the thoughts and intents of the heart" (4:12; King James Version).

The tenor of John's metaphor "the sword of my mouth" is that when he speaks the Word of God (of course, "Word" is also figurative) to the Nicolaitans, what he says will cut or pierce their thoughts and hearts like a sword. In other words, what is swordlike is not his mouth, but the words his mouth speaks and wields like a weapon ("mouth" is a metonymy for speech). But in English the status of "of" in genitive-link constructions is ambiguous.[20] If I call an essay "The Capabilities of Charles Wright," it

---

19. For a usefully condensed introduction to metaphor, along with a relevant bibliography (now in need of updating), see George Whalley's entry "Metaphor" in the *Princeton Encyclopedia of Poetry and Poetics*, ed. Alex Preminger et al., enlarged ed. (Princeton: Princeton Univ. Press, 1974), 490-94.

20. See Randolph Quirk, Sidney Greenbaum, Geoffrey Leech, and Jan Svartvik, *A Grammar of Contemporary English* (London: Longman, 1972), 192–203, for descriptions of the *s*-genitive (inflected) and the *of*-genitive (periphrastic).

is obvious I mean Charles Wright's capabilities, or the capabilities possessed by Charles Wright. But if I threaten someone with the sword of my mouth, it is not exactly clear what I mean. Do I mean that what I have to say is wounding, or do I mean that my mouth is my sword and perhaps I shall bite him?

In favoring genitive-link metaphors, which come to him not only from the syntax of the King James translators but, closer to our own time, also from English translations of various twentieth-century poets grouped under the heading "surrealist," Wright skillfully exploits this ambiguity. In the phrase "Dead, stunned heart of summer," for example, does he mean that he has arrived at summer's "heart," that is, its core or middle? (This line comes, after all, in July near the "heart" of the poem.) Or does he mean that summer, in the strong Italian heat which makes one listless, is like an actual organ of the body, the dead, stunned heart of someone whose heart has suddenly stopped beating? Both possibilities involve personification, but the second one—that summer is a dead, stunned heart—is the bolder and more original.[21]

If we consider this example in isolation, both readings are possible, but in the group above, the pattern "A of B" tends, to varying degrees, toward the meaning "A is B" rather than "B's A": the sky is a blue plate, the page is a blank sky. The point is that metaphor, which is already an instrument of transformation, becomes even more powerful and complicated in this form. Not only does the genitive-link structure ring with the resonances of the King James translation, with all the scriptural authority these resonances retain (an authority for which Wright is inescapably nostalgic); this structure is also the one which represents most vividly the process of transubstantiation by metaphor. In following out the various possibilities of "of," a poet or reader witnesses the conversion of one object, phenomenon, or substance into another. To read "Dead, stunned heart of summer" as "summer's heart" is to limit and weaken the metaphor by subordinating one part of it to another; in the pattern "A of B," A becomes merely a part or feature of B. Rather than changing into A, B simply absorbs A. But to read "Dead, stunned heart of summer" as "summer is a dead, stunned heart" is to initiate the mystery of transubstantiation, as B turns wholly into A: in January five o'clock becomes a bloody coagulation in the sky; in September dusk is a cool suck.

It is no coincidence that so many of these genitive-link structures involve images of light at particular times of day in particular seasons. As the poem "Light Journal" makes clear, Wright has been studying light and its effects since his earliest attempts at poetry emerged in the 1950s

---

21. This second possibility is anticipated by an earlier poem, "Stone Canyon Nocturne," in *China Trace* (Middletown, CT: Wesleyan Univ. Press, 1977): "The moon, like a dead heart, cold and unstartable, hangs by a thread / At the earth's edge" (47).

(*ZJ* 87). By the process of photosynthesis, green plants convert light into chemical energy and nourishment. By the process of the genitive-link metaphor, Wright frequently converts light into a tangible substance. In turn, the conversion of light into something substantial is a conversion of the ephemeral into the abiding. This conversion, or the attempt at this conversion, is, I would argue, the largest aim of Wright's poetry. If the ephemeral cannot be changed into the abiding, then everything bright will fall away, and we shall be left tapping along with white canes like the wind in "Saturday Morning Journal." That he is able to make us believe in the possibility of such change is the most impressive of Charles Wright's capabilities.

BRUCE BOND

# Metaphysics of the Image in Charles Wright and Paul Cézanne (1994)

All my poems seem to be an ongoing argument with myself about the un-
likelihood of salvation.

—Charles Wright

In search of the absolute, Charles Wright finds himself in a world of
things, "the world of ten thousand things," as the title of his recent
poetry collection would have it. In spite of their longing for tran-
scendence, Charles Wright's poems remain forcefully visual, as if the
image were both bridge and barrier to the unseen, the most immediate
objects assuming a metaphysical inscrutability and allure. To quote
Wright's notebook, "If you look at it long enough, you won't recognize
it" (H, 30). Little wonder that Cézanne, with his ongoing struggle both
to penetrate and submit to the world of appearances, would suggest a
model for Wright's own conflicted sensibility. At the age of 67, Cézanne
saw his art as ever unsatisfactory, the forms of nature still hopelessly out
of reach. "Will I ever arrive at the goal, so intensely sought and so long
pursued?" he asked. "I am still learning from nature, and it seems to me
I am making slow progress" (in Merleau-Ponty, 9). His late paintings in
particular, those watercolors of increasing gaps and disintegrations born
paradoxically out of an impulse toward precision, inform much of
Wright's poetry, as the poetry itself is occasionally quick to note, so it
may come as small surprise that a pastoral scene from Cézanne's late pe-
riod greets us on the cover of Wright's recent retrospective volume. The
cover-painting, "Bend in the Road," conjuring as it does both the im-
manence of sensation and the seduction of the unseen, what lures us
around the bend, provides an emblem for the sacramental desire which
drives Wright's work. Likewise the book's opening poem, "Homage to
Paul Cézanne," in which all physical things take on a quality of depth and
disquiet, dramatizes the kind of skepticism and metaphysical longing
which reemerge throughout Wright's opus. Both vibrant and haunting,
his poems yoke imaginatively what reason cannot reconcile—namely, a
Platonic desire for access to wholly transcendent Forms and a late
Aristotelean disbelief in their existence. Wright's work thus thrives on a
deeply generative opposition between suspicion and wish. As he himself
states, "I would love to believe the world is Platonic, but I think it's
Aristotelean" (H, 130).

As further testament to their conflicted sensibilities, both Cézanne and Wright profess an elusive primitivism. "Primary force alone," writes Cézanne, "*id est* temperament, can bring a person to the end he must attain." The word "must" here leaves open the question of attainability, as does Wright's claim, "All great art tends toward the condition of the primitive" (H, 26). Just what constitutes "the primitive" remains vague, most often defined by what it is not, those mediating traces of culture which, even if they could disappear, would take with them our very language, let alone any so-called primitive art. Unlike the transcendent, the primitive is by definition a starting point rather than a point beyond. It comes first, either temporally or in the figurative sense as ground and condition—the way that sensation serves as a condition of consciousness. Unlike the transcendent, the primitive connotes an anchoring in concrete existence. But Wright's phrase, "tends toward the condition of the primitive," places primary conditions at an ever energizing, prospective distance. Since the primitive can never be clearly defined, we can never be too certain about the character of our aesthetic progress towards it. Even the efficacy of our spontaneity, like prayer, remains open to question.

Throughout Wright's "Homage to Paul Cézanne," the dead, as emissaries of the unseen, emerge incarnate in an archetypal, "primitive" world, unnervingly tangible, if only to make us increasingly aware of their unbridgeable distance. They inhabit our most intimate objects—shirts, shoes, our very beds—cling like dirt to our hands, coming as close as possible without quite dissolving their identity and ours:

> At night, in the fish-light of the moon, the dead wear our white shirts
> To stay warm, and litter the fields.
> We pick them up in the mornings, dewy pieces of paper and scraps of
>     cloth.
> Like us, they refract themselves. Like us,
> They keep on saying the same thing, trying to get it right.
> Like us, the water unsettles their names.
>
> Sometimes they lie like leaves in their little arks, and curl up at the edges.
> Sometimes they come inside, wearing our shoes, and walk
> From mirror to mirror.
> Or lie in our beds with the gloves off
> And touch our bodies. Or talk
> In a corner. Or wait like envelopes on a desk.
>                          (TWOTTT, 3, 1-11)

Wright's quiet directness, his declarative informality, as familiar as it is familiarizing, turns the poem itself into an intimate and inhabitable object for the dead. In spite of the implied auditor, the poem has the sparse, musing quality of interior speech. All the unmistakable strategies of heightening metaphysical tension—an elemental restlessness, the near ecstatic dissolution of identity, the transformative immersion into water—work by way of contrast with the ordinary thing and word: "shirts," "paper," "scraps of cloth."

These ordinary things, extraordinary in their suggestiveness, oneiric in their metamorphoses, quick to reflect an otherworldly light, provide Wright's landscape with white space, both literal and figurative, concrete and cryptic, and so resemble the patches of bare canvas so intriguing to Wright in Cézanne's later work:

> I like layers of paint on the canvas. I also know after I'm tired of lots of layers on the canvas, I'm going to want just one layer of paint and some of the canvas showing through . . . I've been trying to write poems . . . the way a painter might paint a picture . . . using stanzas in the way a painter will build up blocks of color, each disparate and often discrete, to make an overall representation that, taken in its pieces and slashes and dabs, seems to have no coherence, but seen in its totality, when it's finished, turns out to be a very recognizable landscape, or whatever. Cézanne is someone who does this, in his later work, to an almost magical perfection. (H, 66, 85)

What we see in the occasional white space is the implication of a larger story, *the* larger story as Wright would have it. The understated canvas stands like a Platonic shadow this side of its source and subject, or like a sacrament, the body of what we cannot see. In Wright's thinking, blank spaces serve not merely as barriers to a fuller knowledge but also as windows of access into the invisible:

> ". . . he regarded the colors as numinous essences, beyond which he 'knew' nothing, and the 'diamond zones of God' remained white . . ." (Cézanne). Change "colors" to "words" and "white" to "blank" and you have something I believe . . . (H, 37)

As "the diamond zones of God," empty spaces encourage our interpretive approach, charge their subject with desire, and so invite all the pleasures of doubt and speculation. In so doing, they vitalize their subject, or, more precisely, they "keep it alive," maintaining the dimension of possibility by respecting a distance. "Art tends toward the certainty of making connections," Wright states. "The artist's job is to keep it apart, thus giving it tension and keeping it alive, letting the synapse spark" (H, 22).

The quality of vitality and remoteness in Cézanne's work stems not only from his blank spaces, but also from a prioritizing of color over outline to imply shape and movement. The foregrounding of chromatic relationships accounts for a simultaneous myopic distortion and sensuous intimacy. Blues recede; yellows come forward; complementary colors vibrate—all by way of how colors touch. Wright's literal near-sightedness provides him with a similar sense of distance and heightened color-sensitivity:

> Their leaves lie in limes and tans
> Flocking the grass, vaguely pre-Cubist to me,
> And blurred, without my glasses, arranged
> In an almost-pattern of colors across the yard,
> The same colors Cézanne once used in the same way
>
> .   .   .
>
> Still these colors and pure arrangements
> Oozing out of the earth, dropping out of the sky
> > in memory of him each year.
> > ("A Journal of English Days," TWOTT, 127)

As if in a Platonic model of being, Wright's myopia makes the world of appearance seem incomplete, a teasing intimation of the real. But such distance becomes an end in itself, transmuted from failure into wonder. Light takes on a luxurious, animate quality, "oozing out of the earth," persuading in the terms of mere sensation. "Often 'light' becomes literary in poems," Wright states. "I like to think I think of light as light. When you are nearsighted as I am . . . light is where it's at, as they used to say" (H, 146).

To give words a similar concrete insistence, to layer them in "discrete blocks of color" as Wright claims he does, he needs a unit of color, some correlative to the brush stroke itself. According to Wright, these units are aural, created at the level of word, line, and stanza in harmonized patterns of balance and contrast:

> My poems are put together in tonal blocks, in tonal units that work off one another. Vide Cézanne's use of color and form. I try to do that in sound patterns within the line, in the line within the stanza, and the stanza within the poem. (H, 20)

Although there is a lot of cacophonous and spondaic grit in Wright's music which argues for the word as discrete unit, the poem "Homage" is most conspicuous and convincing in asserting the line as its brush stroke, something big enough to contain in itself an imagistic as well as a musical force:

> They reach up from the ice plant.
> They shuttle their messengers through the oat grass.
> Their answers rise like rust on the stalks and the spidery leaves.
>
> We rub them off our hands.                                    (13-16)

Wright's lines characteristically favor a monosyllabic percussiveness and emphatic finish, contributing to a heightened physicality. As each line here cadences on a crisp image, the overall pattern moves around the color wheel from greens to yellows to the rising oranges, from recessed cool shades outward toward the intimacies of our hands. Like the colors they wear, the dead "reach up" line by line, intent on perceptual resurrection.

The appeal of the transcendent in Wright's work lies largely in its power to disturb, to raise questions, invigorate an otherwise too certain world. Any imaginary reclaiming of the dead by way of sacramental union thus remains ephemeral. Unappeasable as the grief they inspire, they appear neither wholly dead nor alive but in a state of perpetual rising into our lives:

> Each year the dead grow less dead, and nudge
> Close to the surface of all things.
> They start to remember the silence that brought them there.
> They start to recount the gain in their soiled hands.          (17-20)

The dead, like us, "refract themselves," fragmenting into a picture of uncertainty and longing. They too are haunted by mere intimations and a prospective memory always just starting out toward the horizon of the past. They too approach "the surface of things" with anxiety and wonder, imagining the other side.

Through the dead's eyes, we are the transcendent. The project of the poem—or of all Wright's poems for that matter—is to see ourselves this way as well, made expansive and unfamiliar in the world mirror:

> High in the night sky the mirror is hauled up and unsheeted.
> In it we twist like stars.          (112-113)

Wright's poetry typically blurs and merges irreconcilable points of view, or plays them off one another like complementary colors. It testifies to his negative capability: how poem after poem, the dead see as the living, the living as the dead, the skeptic sees as the metaphysician, and so on—all in an effort to enlarge our range of feeling, to contain and be vitalized by contradiction.

Given his skepticism, Wright's nostalgia for an older metaphysics often expresses itself through acts of ventriloquism, by speaking through the sensibility of the dead, including such visionaries as Dante, Plato, and Cézanne. "Whose unction can intercede for the dead?" Wright's speaker asks in the final section of his "Homage." "Whose tongue is toothless enough to speak their piece?" (123-124). Clearly no one's, in spite of the fact that Wright has attempted just that and, if only momentarily, enjoyed the illusion of having succeeded:

> And thus we become what we've longed for,
>                                        past tense and otherwise,
> A BB, a disc of light,
>                          song without words.
> And refer to ourselves

In the third person, seeing that other arm
Still raised from the bed, fingers like licks and flames in the boned air.

Only to hear that it's not time.                                    (88-94)

The desire to pay homage to the dead, to speak their at best fragmentary piece, implies a longing not only to enlarge the self but also to redeem time, to become, by way of a multiplication of egos, "past tense and otherwise."

Though Wright's poem is deeply persuasive in creating a model of the object and character of Cézanne's obsessions, it likewise calls into question the final success of any such effort. Wright's instruments for redeeming time are the images of a riddling world in flux. In resisting the explicitly narrative conventions of the homage, Wright's "Homage to Paul Cézanne" focuses instead on what inspires and frustrates the narrative impulse. "*Remember me*," the dead chant, "*speak my name.*" And yet the only proper name here appears in the poem's title. The absence of identifiable people in the body of the poem not only encourages objects to bear the full burden of aesthetic affect, but also accentuates a simultaneous privacy and archetypal breadth, the sense of an introspective look into collective being, full of blank spaces, partial stories.

Though historical narrative appeals to the dead as a means of resurrection, Wright's poem turns on the irony that to bear up the dead is to bear up an absence. As the dead "take in" the meanings of favorite words, language appears as one more puzzling and intimate object:

They point to their favorite words
Growing around them, revealed as themselves for the first time:
They stand close to the meanings and take them in.          (24-27)

To say the dead are "revealed *as themselves*" is to imply the revelation of both their presence and their nature, which is to say their absence. Like the dead, language becomes something half-there, its meanings withdrawn into an otherworld of deferral and loss. The force of desire that drives words drives the ocean as it "explains itself, backing and filling / What spaces it can't avoid" (34-35). While, as Helen Vendler argues, the conservation of matter in Wright's work may offer its small consolations for a failure of faith, it is likewise the mirror of such failings, consigned to redundancy—the waves, like the dead, "saying the same thing, trying to get it right." In a world where language never gets to the bottom of anything, what we know of eternity is an eternal desire to know.

The mystique of the inexplicable allows for Wright's characteristic transmutation of despondency into wonder. In light of his frequent praise for inaccessibility and near-completedness in art, an aesthetic failure to fill the spaces of nature appears not merely inevitable but also desirable, encouraging the assertions of a reconstructive imagination. But this desire is met in Wright and Cézanne by a contrary one, intent on an un-likely mimesis. Both artists see themselves as simultaneously resisting and aspiring toward something larger than the individual imagination. "All great art is Neoplatonic," Wright claims, "you're always trying to make something that's the best replica of what it really is" (H, 35). For Cézanne, the mere fact that nature so often figures as the commanding starting point in his discussions of the aesthetic process complicates any notion of his work as freely subordinating natural form to individual expression:

> One cannot be too scrupulous, too sincere, too submissive to nature, but one is more or less master of one's model, and above all one's means. Penetrate that which is before you, and persevere to express it as logically as possible. (Bernard, 43)

Though there is a Platonic ring to Cézanne's metaphor of penetrating "that which is before" us, his emphasis on perceptual exactitude works against any metaphysical devaluation of appearances. It is as though the world of appearance itself, as ever elusive and humbling, took on a meta-physical dimension of depth.

In Wright's tribute, the omnipresent dead provide this dimension, charging natural forms with not only all the pathos attendant on human loss, but also the power of our need to participate more fully in being. In response to the question of who can intercede for the dead, Wright's speaker states:

> What we are given in dreams we write as blue paint,
> Or messages to the clouds.
> At evening we wait for the rain to fall and the sky to clear.
> Our words are words for the clay, uttered in undertones,
> Our gestures salve for the wind. (125-129)

Cézanne's parallel urge toward participation is key, for it sheds a possible light on the paradox of his later work, that paradox being, as Wright describes it, Cézanne's simultaneous disintegration of and attachment to natural form:

> The move toward a disintegration of the object in some of the most mem-orable works of a painter so passionately attached to objects is the attrac-tion and riddle of Cézanne's last phase. (11, 21)

One perspective on the riddle is to see the disintegration of the object, those refractions and gaps which beg our interpretive approach, as Cézanne's very expression for his attachment to it—or more precisely, for his ongoing desire to access it fully. As Merleau-Ponty claims,

> [Cézanne] did not want to separate the stable things which we see and the shifting way in which they appear; he wanted to depict matter as it takes on form, the birth of order through spontaneous organization. ("Cézanne's Doubt," 13)

According to Merleau-Ponty, Cézanne's objects are charged by the artist's longing to become involved ever more actively and intimately in the "primary force" of their existent being, their spontaneous coming into form.

Given his phenomenological orientation, Merleau-Ponty does not qualify the birth of order as the birth of perceptual order, since he will not go on to make claims as to a distinguishing form of order preceding perception. In a phenomenological model, attempting as it does to "bracket" phenomena off from transcendent conditions, the otherness of imagined objects stems from their intentional status—that is, the fact that they appear as the contents of consciousness without being identical to consciousness itself. When we say we are conscious *of* something, the barrier and bridge of the "of," which is to say the intentionality of consciousness, implies a distancing. According to Merleau-Ponty, sensation, as an absolute, an irreducible, primary condition of thought, precedes and resists the intentionality of consciousness. Cézanne's professed desire to realize sensation as art thus becomes for Merleau-Ponty a project of getting out of the way, of letting be, releasing meaning from objects rather than distancing them with the stylizations of imposed affect:

> The meaning Cézanne gave to objects and faces in his painting presented itself to him in the world as it appeared to him. Cézanne simply released this meaning. (CD, 21)

Through Merleau-Ponty's lens, Cézanne's representational liberties attempt not to abstract the physical but to resist abstraction, to wear thin the membrane between consciousness and its intentional object and so allow things to relinquish their delicate ontological light.

But Merleau-Ponty's statement is complicated by his mixed metaphors of meaning as both "presented to" and "given by" the artist. The immediacy of sensation appears not merely "realized," as Cézanne had hoped, but consciously endowed. Wright's "Homage" is far more explicit in asserting the role of artists as masters of their means:

> The dead are a cadmium blue.
> We spread them with palette knives in broad blocks and planes.
>
> We layer them stroke by stroke
> In steps and ascending mass, in verticals raised from the earth.
>
> We choose, and layer them in,
> Blue and a blue and a breath. (49-53)

Here the artist's powers of creative volition rival God's, raising the dead, supplying breath. Aesthetic form likewise rivals natural form, each giving shape to the ubiquitous dead. The mutual penetration of artist and nature blurs any clear distinction between the aesthetic and the natural. "Aren't nature and art different?" Emile Bernard once asked, to which Cézanne replied, "I want to make them the same" (Merleau-Ponty, 13). Of course art and nature, however similar, cannot be the same, any more than the speaker in "Homage" can intercede unequivocally for the dead. Even to see the natural as seamlessly continuous with human nature is to tame the inscrutable power and demand of nature's otherness. In short, Cézanne's and Wright's sensibilities thrive on the prospect of ever deferred unions.

The fact that natural form emerges as a new horizon of inaccessibility and command, as unrealizable and animating in consciousness as any divine ideal, testifies to the tenacity of metaphysical desire, its yearning to break the silence of things, to slip through the ontological white space. Even Merleau-Ponty's metaphor of meaning as "released from" objects invokes a stubbornly metaphysical model of secret and conditioning interiors. The notion of such interiors eroticizes being, encourages our intimacy, leads us on. Any aesthetic which professes a revolutionary commitment to mere immanence or surface, as sufficient to itself, free from the shadow of the ideal, faces a problem—that is, sufficiency breeds complacency. To adapt a claim from Merleau-Ponty, Cézanne and Wright are reluctant to separate stable things from our desiring perspectives through which they appear. The dead in Wright's "Homage" charge the visible world with not merely absence but lack, an impelling sense of inadequacy, of eros and grief. Much of the distinguishing power and immensity of Cézanne's and Wright's art lies in the way lack is transmuted into sacramental abundance, the way all things gesture toward a conditioning otherness—be it God or nature or being itself—which must be concealed to be revealed, inseparable as we know it from the way we long to know it, an otherness realized *as other* in the bold refractions of a loving eye.

### WORKS CITED

Bernard, Emile. "Paul Cézanne." *Cézanne in Perspective*. Ed. Judith Wechsler. Englewood Cliffs, NJ: Prentice Hall, 1975.

Merleau-Ponty, Maurice. "Cézanne's Doubt." *Sense and Non-Sense*. Evanston, IL: Northwestern University Press, 1964.

Rewald, John. *Cézanne*. New York: Abrams, 1986.

Vendler, Helen. *The Music of What Happens*. Cambridge, MA: Harvard University Press, 1988.

Wright, Charles. *Halflife*. Ann Arbor: University of Michigan Press, 1988.

Wright, Charles. *The World of the Ten Thousand Things: Poems 1980-1990*. New York: Farrar Straus Giroux, 1990.

PETER STITT

# Resurrecting the Baroque (1997)

Loosely speaking, the baroque impulse in contemporary American poetry is recognizable for the same reason the baroque has always been recognizable: its use of a style tending toward ornateness, even overdecoration. In art and architecture this style is characterized by ornamentation and curved rather than straight lines; in music it is characterized by embellished melodies and fugal or contrapuntal forms. In poetry it is characterized by lushness of both sound—the sort of stylistic complications chiefly of rhythm, internal harmony, and sentence structure favored by writers as diverse as Gerard Manley Hopkins and the early John Berryman—and image—an extravagant use of metaphor.

The baroque style is not a recent phenomenon; it was prominent among the British metaphysical poets of the early seventeenth century and has also been used in this country, both by such late-seventeenth-century writers as Edward Taylor and Anne Bradstreet and (albeit in a much watered-down form) by such early-twentieth-century writers as John Crowe Ransom and Richard Wilbur. In his standard work on the subject, *The Baroque Poem: A Comparative Study*, Harold Segel explains that baroque poets of the seventeenth century tended to favor the metaphor over other poetic devices:

> The metaphor allowed the poet a richer, more provocative use of his imagination, his *inventiveness*, and the metaphor, because it establishes *identity* rather than merely likeness, is bolder, more difficult, and potentially more successful poetically in view of its greater capacity to excite wonderment. Certainly no other feature of Baroque poetry stands out as sharply as the extensive use of metaphor; and it was this feature, above all others, that incurred the disfavor of later ages.[1]

What contemporary baroque poets primarily have in common with their ancestors is their extensive reliance upon the device of metaphor—though certainly they do not all use metaphor in the same way. It is in the area of subject matter that we will find the most difference between the early baroque poets and the contemporary baroque poets. In the seventeenth century, the baroque was a religious art form that used symbolism to express mystical concepts: "The usually clear, sharp division in mannerism between

---

1. Harold B. Segal, *The Baroque Poem: A Comparative Survey* (New York: E. P. Dutton, 1974), 104.

the spheres of earth and spirit faded before the Baroque vision of the indivisibility of man's world and God's."[2] Most contemporary poets who use the baroque style use it to secular ends; such is the case with Stanley Kunitz, though he does flirt at times with prehistoric, urmythic materials. Because of the vaguely spiritual questions raised in his work, however, Charles Wright is somewhat closer to the practice of the seventeenth-century writers.

In the contemporary baroque poem, then, we might expect to find these characteristics: ornamentation or a sensual richness of imagery; metaphor or a doubling of imagery; a rich and varied use of verbal effects; a tendency toward obscurity and fragmentation; a self-conscious interest on the writer's part in his art; suggestions of the mystical within the physical; intellectuality. The work of Wright embodies these characteristics to a considerable degree. Not only will we find a good bit of progression within the body of his work, but we will also find him reaching for the unseen world in subtle ways. Wright began his career with an interest in the possibilities of form—language, image, metaphor, cadence— and has become the contemporary American poet who most exemplifies the metaphysical dimension of the earlier versions of baroque poetry.

Wright is the author of eight separate, "major" volumes (all but one of them published by large, well-known publishers) in addition to several "minor" volumes (small press chapbooks). Wright has divided the major volumes into two groups of four by gathering them, respectively, into a selected and a collected volume. The first four books—The *Grave of the Right Hand* (1970), *Hard Freight* (1973), *Bloodlines* (1975), and *China Trace* (1977)—appear together, some of them partially, in *Country Music: Selected Early Poems* (1982), while the later four books—*The Southern Cross* (1981), *The Other Side of the River* (1984), *Zone Journals* (1988), and *Xionia* (1990)—appear together, all of them entirely, in *The World of the Ten Thousand Things* (1990). The attentiveness to form—specifically to the concept of balance—inherent in this publishing pattern is typical of Wright, as we shall see in detail as we look at his work and career.

Though clearly and emphatically a baroque poet, Wright is more conservative stylistically than Kunitz, and for a reason noticed by Harold Segal (the scope of whose discussion, of course, does not embrace Wright). To a greater degree than Kunitz, Wright uses "variety and ornament cumulatively in support of a central unity," seeking something akin to "the Baroque vision of the indivisibility of man's world and God's."[3] While occasionally using the baroque style to playful ends, Wright maintains a deep commitment to content and theme. Kunitz uses the metaphysical style primarily in honor of occasions—the one in which the speaker's girlfriend fails to call him on the phone, for example, or the one

---

2. Segal, 30.
3. Segal, 29, 30.

in which the powerful change of a season makes him want to change his life.

While Wright may have known what he wanted to write about from the start of his career, it took a lot of groping and experimentation before he was able fully to express his themes. As we shall see, form is—to an unusual degree—wedded to content in his work, and it was necessary for him to discover his own unique style and form before he could truly say what was on his mind. Thus, as he himself has explained, he began by concentrating almost entirely upon style and the mechanics of writing: "when I first started writing, I was interested in the tight weave of the surface only—technique as a statement in itself, so to speak."[4] The impulse to concentrate primarily upon style—which seems not only to have carried Wright completely through his first book and well into his second but also shows up significantly in his third—was noticed by Helen Vendler, who generalized while talking about Wright: "What above all distinguishes the true poet [is] his seeing words as things—things that make a shape on the page, things that lock together as though they had invisible hooks on them. . . . All this seeing is before and beyond any question of meaning."[5] It does indeed appear that, to discover a style that could appropriately express his subject matter, Wright first chose to experiment consciously with words, with the formal possibilities of language.

The verse in Wright's first two books seems dominated almost entirely by formal concerns; there is no readily apparent thematic continuity. The next two books, by contrast, seem to exhibit greater thematic depth and coherence. In making his selections for *Country Music*, Wright chose to republish only a few prose poems from *The Grave of the Right Hand*; each of them is distinguished by the same formal care that Hemingway is said to have lavished upon the prose experiments that make up his second book, the version of *in our time* that was issued privately in Paris in 1924. An ars poetica in Wright's second book, *Hard Freight*, indicates the almost complete exclusion of content, the singular orientation toward words, of the pieces in these first two volumes; "The New Poem" means to have little relevance to life—"It will not resemble the sea. / It will not have dirt on its thick hands"; "It will not attend our sorrow. / . . . / It will not be able to help us."

This process allowed Wright to create poems of great beauty, poems written primarily for the sake of their words, rhythms, and images. The first stanza of "White" for example—"Carafe, compotier, sea shell, vase: / Blank spaces, white objects; / Luminous knots along the black rope"—seems simply an accumulation of desirable and sometimes contrasting words and

---

4. J. D. McClatchy, "The Art of Poetry XLI: Charles Wright," *Paris Review* 113 (1989), 201.

5. Review of *Bloodlines, New York Times Book Review* (7 September 1975), 14.

images. Such writing is certainly beautiful; what is most impressive about these lines is their attention purely to technique, to rhythms, images, and words. Elsewhere—for example in the middle stanza of "Slides of Verona"—the reader's attention is captured by something more complex, a wedding of technique to meaning through a nascent use of metaphor: "Death with its long tongue licks / Mastino's hand affection he thinks / Such sweetness such loyalty."

Interest in content seems still greater in Wright's third volume, *Bloodlines*, though even here we still find many strictly verbal experiments. The book comprises the second installment in a trilogy that begins with *Hard Freight* and concludes with *China Trace*. Wright has explained that *Bloodlines* is meant to look both backward and forward; while *Hard Freight* deals with the past and *China Trace* with the future, *Bloodlines* deals with both of these and with the present. The three volumes are also meant to be formally distinct: "I was going to have a book of separate poems and I was going to have one of longer poems, and then I was going to have a full, book-length poem."[6] Even when he does attend to content in *Bloodlines*, Wright seems more interested in abstractions than in the concrete elements inherent in his subjects. The long poems are "Tattoos" and "Skins," each composed of twenty sections of, respectively, fifteen and fourteen lines. Though "Skins" anticipates one aspect of what is to come in Wright's work—an increased interest in metaphysics, the realm on "the other side of the river"—its relentless presentation of abstractions does not at all indicate the turn toward a specific and concrete use of imagery that Wright was also to make in his later poems.

Even "Tattoos," by far the more graphic of the two sequences, is so abstract that the reader would scarcely know what was going on were it not for the brief explanatory notes appended to the sequence. ("Skins" did not have such notes when first published, though Wright added them for the reprinting in *Country Music*.) Because the notes appear separately after the poems (which do not point to them with note numbers), the first-time reader does not have even what little help they provide. Number twelve is one of the more striking and accessible installments in "Tattoos":

> Oval oval oval oval push pull push pull . . .
> Words unroll from our fingers.
> A splash of leaves through the windowpanes,
> A smell of tar from the streets:
> Apple, arrival, the railroad, shoe.

---

6. Charles Wright, *Halflife: Improvisations and Interviews, 1977-87* (Ann Arbor: University of Michigan Press, 1988), 138.

> The words, like bees in a sweet ink, cluster and drone,
> Indifferent, indelible,
> A hum and a hum:
> Back stairsteps to God, ropes to the glass eye:
> Vineyard, informer, the chair, the throne.
>
> Mojo and numberless, breaths
> From the wet mountains and green mouths; rustlings,
> Sure sleights of hand,
> The news that arrives from nowhere:
> Angel, omega, silence, silence. . . .

The note for this section—"Handwriting class; Palmer Method; words as 'things'; Kingsport, Tennessee"—does make it clearer, though Wright was more generous with information when explaining the poem's occasion elsewhere:

> my real life began in the fifth grade under the all-seeing, all-knowing, all-powerful eye of Miss Grace Watkins, or "Granny Wildcat," as she was known to anyone under the age of twelve. Behind her back, of course. . . . [Her] little scholars labored to get their fingers to behave properly during penmanship lessons in the rigors of the Palmer Method. "Oval, oval, oval, oval, push, pull, push, pull" (pronounced "pursh, pull" in her solid cast Tennessee accent), "rolling toward the Borden Mill, purshing toward the Peggy Anne . . ." (two, to us, very recognizable landmarks in sight of Lincoln Elementary School, one a cotton mill, the other a coffee shop).[7]

Beyond its desire to record an incident from Wright's childhood, the poem functions as an ars poetica, indicating the poet's strong interest in both language and music. Language also serves to create truth in this poem, through the words that appear mysteriously from somewhere. Wondering where they come from leads us to the other subject of the poem, its religious concern, which appropriately seems to turn the poet back on himself, God having led only from "throne" to "silence."[8]

If *Bloodlines* is Wright's most explicitly autobiographical early book, then *China Trace* is his most metaphysical. It provides an appropriate

---

7. Charles Wright, *Contemporary Authors: Autobiography Series*, vol. 7, ed. Mark Zadrozny (Detroit: Gale Research, 1989), 291.

8. Two other critics have written about this poem, both of them largely in agreement with my perspective. Carol Muske sees the poem as "an object lesson, substantiating itself with the shapes of the developing calligraphy, abstraction made sensuous and morphous before our eyes" ("Ourselves as History," *Parnassus: Poetry in Review* 4.2 [1976], 117), while Kathleen Agena says: "the whole poem is about words, about the way they come to carry meaning, the dynamic that exists between words as signifiers and the things they signify, the guilt of words as opposed to the purity of silence" ("The Mad Sense of Language," *Partisan Review* 43 [1976], 627).

conclusion to the selected volume, for it is an unsettled book of changes, pointing as much to the future as *Bloodlines* points to the past. It is in *China Trace* that Wright comes to terms with the religious implications of the poem just quoted; as the original jacket notes for the book tell us, he investigates "identities, inherited beliefs, and assumptions once thought to be firmly acquired, that have dissolved and re-formed themselves, as rivers that change their courses alter the shape and nature of the land they nourish." Essentially what results from this process is a weakening of the religious beliefs he learned in his childhood in favor of a naturalistic humanism—though Wright's work will certainly never be free of sacramental undertones and questions, their language and imagery.

It would not be accurate to call Wright a strictly Christian poet in any of his guises, despite all the time he spent in childhood at a religiously oriented educational compound called Sky Valley ("At first, and on the outside, it was a summer camp. Later, it became a school, and all the while it was a workshop for the hammering out of little souls into the white gold of righteousness, ready for the Lord's work or the Lord's burden. . . . I spent three summers here and one entire year, in the tenth grade") and at Christ School (eleventh and twelfth grades).[9] The closest Wright comes to mentioning Christianity is when he carefully rejects rigid theologies—for example in "1975," from *China Trace*: "At 40, the apricot / Seems raised to a higher power, the fire ant and the weed. / And I turn in the wind, / Not knowing what sign to make, or where I should kneel." Having lost the ability to pray to an unseen and abstract God, Wright turns—as these lines also demonstrate—to the natural world.[10]

The abiding and sacramental affection that Wright came to invest in the landscape is anticipated by the important (and didactic) fifth section of "Firstborn," from *Hard Freight*:

> What I am trying to say
> Is this—I tell you, only, the thing
> That I have come to believe:

---

9. Wright, *Contemporary Authors*, 292.

10. Other critics have written on the role of religion in Wright's work. Helen Vendler, for example, contrasts Wright's strong sense of doubt with Montale's troubled certainty: "The spiritual yearning in Wright is nowhere rewarded, as it sometimes is in Montale, by a certain faith in an absolute—damaged no doubt, elusive surely, disagreeable often, but always unquestioned and recoverable" (*Part of Nature, Part of Us* [Cambridge: Harvard University Press, 1980], 287). George F. Butterick comes to a similar conclusion: "Each time [Wright] returns to this theme, his faith in nature is unshaken and, if anything, stronger than ever, while religion continues to appear extraneous" ("Charles Wright," *Dictionary of Literary Biography Yearbook: 1982* [Detroit: Gale Research, 1982], 399).

Indenture yourself to the land;
Imagine you touch its raw edges
In all weather, time and again;

Imagine its colors; try
To imitate, day by day,
The morning's growth and the dusk,

The movement of all their creatures;
Surrender yourself, and be glad;
This is the law that endures.

Wright manages to fulfill this injunction throughout his work, and he does it by locating the divine principle within nature rather than above it; as he says in "Invisible Landscape," from *China Trace*: "God is the sleight-of-hand in the fireweed, the lost / Moment that stopped to grieve and moved on."

The final poem of the volume completes this process by offering a full definition of its title character, "Him":

His sorrow hangs like a heart in the star-flowered boundary tree.
It mirrors the endless wind.

He feeds on the lunar differences and flies up at the dawn.

When he lies down, the waters will lie down with him,
And all that walks and all that stands still, and sleep through the thunder.

It's for him that the willow bleeds.

Look for him high in the flat black of the northern Pacific sky,
Released in his suit of lights,
                          lifted and laid clear.

As the poems and passages I have been quoting make clear, there is a restrained quality to the verse in Wright's early books. It is true that a good bit of beauty here results from his dual commitment to balance (two lines, one line, two lines, one line, two lines) and precision, but it is an almost minimalist beauty, reflecting the austerity of the plain free-verse style so many American poets favored in the sixties and seventies.

Where the baroque shows in Wright's early work is in his imagery, particularly in his use of metaphor, as we see in yet another poem perhaps defining God in *China Trace*, "Dog":

The fantailed dog of the end, the lights out,
Lopes in his sleep,
The moon's moan in the glassy fields.
Everything comes to him, stone

Pad prints extending like stars, tongue black
As a flag, saliva and thread, the needle's tooth,
Everything comes to him.

If I were a wind, which I am, if I
Were smoke, which I am, if I
Were the colorless leaves, the invisible grief,
Which I am, which I am,
He'd whistle me down, and down, but not yet.

It is no idle joke to point out that *dog* is *God* spelled backwards; the poem is a much-reduced, twentieth-century (and almost certainly unintentional) rewriting of Francis Thompson's "The Hound of Heaven." Among contemporary poets, Wright and Stephen Dobyns are by far the greatest practitioners of dog imagery, though to very different ends: Wright's divine and Dobyns' elemental.

Though "Dog" is baroque in its use of metaphor, it still appears restrained when viewed from the perspective of Wright's later work—not that we had long to wait for that more mature style to begin appearing. Even before the publication of *Country Music* Wright had already published his fifth volume, *The Southern Cross*, where we find the extraordinarily baroque, descriptive "Dog Day Vespers":

Sun like an orange mousse through the trees,
A snowfall of trumpet bells on the oleander;
                                        mantis paws
Craning out of the new wisteria; fruit smears in the west . . .
DeStael knifes a sail on the bay;
A mother's summons hangs like a towel on the dusk's hook.

Everything drips and spins
In the pepper trees, the pastel glide of the evening
Slowing to mother-of-pearl and the night sky.
Venus breaks clear in the third heaven.
Quickly the world is capped, and the seal turned.

I drag my chair to the deck's edge and the blue ferns.
I'm writing you now by flashlight,
The same news and the same story I've told you often before.
As the stag-stars begin to shine,
A wing brushes my left hand,
                            but it's not my wing.

How deeply and traditionally baroque this poem is is demonstrated in the fact that Harold Segal seems to have discussed—many years before Wright composed his poem—both its theme and its imagery in a general comment on the use of light in baroque poetry:

> In the Baroque . . . the light source is seldom bright sun but the warm or-
> ange-hued glow of later afternoon or the reddish sky of dawn or sunset;
> instead of coming from above diffusing all beneath it in a uniform bright-
> ness, as in the Renaissance, the light now enters from a side, leaving large
> areas obscured by darkness or semidarkness. This, complemented by an op-
> position of light and dark, suggested no longer the clear sense of certitude
> of Renaissance man but instead the Baroque cognizance of a spiritual
> realm yet inextricably bound up with the terrestrial, and the Baroque
> fondness for the dramatic.[11]

Often what a baroque poem describes is surprisingly simple, consider-
ing the amount of energy that is expended in the telling of it. "Dog Day
Vespers" really does little more than describe the onslaught of sunset as
viewed from a deck above Laguna Beach, California. The poem contains
images galore but is in no sense merely imagistic. Image is wound upon
image, simile upon simile, metaphor upon metaphor; nothing is given to
us straight, everything is doubled and tripled. At the end the poem takes
a final leap also mentioned by Segal; not only does the image of the wing
allude to Dante—Wright's favorite source of sacramental meaning—it
also expresses the speaker's baroque sense of a spiritual imminence lying
within the glory of the physical world.

Which would seem to be the most important thematic news presented
in Wright's books since *China Trace*, the volumes gathered in *The World of
the Ten Thousand Things*. These volumes are indeed closely related in terms
of theme, but they are even more closely related in terms of methodol-
ogy. In fact, in an important sense their theme is their methodology, or
vice versa—an idea that Wright has himself expressed in an only slightly
veiled and fragmented way. When Carol Ellis asked him about a statement
he had once made about Philip Larkin's concept of form, Wright said:
"Larkin's comment was 'Form means nothing to me. Content is every-
thing.' My comment would be that content means nothing to me. Form
is everything. Which is to say, to me the most vital question in poetry is
the question of form." Expanding upon this later in the interview, Wright
connected form to content at its deepest level: "As Roethke said, 'I long
for the quietness at the heart of form.' Well, he doesn't mean 'forms.' He
doesn't mean a sonnet. He means Form. Organization. The secret of the
universe is Form, even if poems are not the secret of the universe. They're
only clues to the secret of the universe."[12]

By expanding both the size of his poems and the length of his lines,
Wright took a quantum leap in *The Southern Cross* toward the kind of
form he seems always to have been pursuing. As he has told the story,
Wright found the solution to the fact that he "was never able to get a

---

11. Segal, 116.
12. Wright, *Halflife*, 153, 154.

grip on narrative (and still can't to this day)" in Ezra Pound's *Personae*: "the lyric poem that was structured associationally, not narratively."[13] Imagery is the element of poetry that is of most use to Wright in this type of poem for the way imagery allows him to expand the scope of his vision: "If one of the true functions of poetry is a contemplation of the divine, as I believe it is, and if writing poems is my way of doing that, as it comes increasingly to be, then my ability to think imagistically can turn out to be a great relief to me, rather than the grief I had previously thought it whenever I tried to tell a story."[14] Wright uses imagery to describe landscapes, to develop atmospheres, and to recount incidents and events from his own life, from history, and from literature.

Like *Bloodlines, The Southern Cross* is a book of memory. Time, its most pervasive concern, appears both in a preoccupation with death and in a preoccupation with memory and the burden of the past. Its best poems are the two long ones that open and close it. Each of the eight pages of "Homage to Paul Cézanne" contains an untitled and unnumbered section; all of them focus upon the dead and try to tell how the dead interact with the living and are present to us now—particularly through poems and paintings. In the fourth of these sections Wright most clearly connects the dead with the paintings of Cézanne:

> The dead are a cadmium blue.
> We spread them with palette knives in broad blocks and planes.
>
> We layer them stroke by stroke
> In steps and ascending mass, in verticals raised from the earth.
>
> We choose, and layer them in,
> Blue and a blue and a breath,
>
> Circle and smudge, cross-beak and buttonhook,
> We layer them in. We squint hard and terrace them line by line.
>
> And so we are come between, and cry out,
> And stare up at the sky and its cloudy panes,
>
> And finger the cypress twists.
> The dead understand all this, and keep in touch,
>
> Rustle of hand to hand in the lemon trees,
> Flags, and the great sifts of anger
>
> To powder and nothingness.
> The dead are a cadmium blue, and they understand.

---

13. Wright, *Contemporary Authors*, 293, 296.
14. Wright, *Halflife*, 184.

In the first section of the poem, Wright relates language and poetry to the dead by saying that "Like us, / They keep on saying the same thing, trying to get it right"; in the eighth and last section he ties Cézanne, poetry, language, and the dead together in images drawn from this fourth section:

> What we are given in dreams we write as blue paint,
> Or messages to the clouds.
> At evening we wait for the rain to fall and the sky to clear.
> Our words are words for the clay, uttered in undertones,
> Our gestures salve for the wind.

In section four it is the logic and progression of the images that is perhaps most interesting. The presentation of the dead through the action of painting is perfectly clear through the fifth line, though it does sound as though the clouds in this painting must be blue since the "cadmium blue" dead are described as having the shape of clouds. "Cross-beak and buttonhook" in line six are used associatively and metaphorically since they have nothing to do either with the act of painting or with clouds. In line seven, poetry is allied with painting as the dead are terraced "line by line." A neat connection is made when the speaker fingers "the cypress twists" and the dead "keep in touch" through the rustling of the leaves of the lemon trees, which seem to be comprised of their hands. The section is more oblique than precise, as befits its subject; it presents a feeling of the presence of the dead rather than actual knowledge of them.

When Dobyns writes of the dead in *Cemetery Nights* he treats them in strictly physical terms, as bodies gradually rotting and drying to dust. Though he does suggest that the presence of the dead may occasionally be felt in a gust of wind or in dust motes hanging in the air of a still room, these appearances are ascribed not to any vision of truth but to the imaginations of characters in the poems. Wright is also careful to locate his hints of the presence of the dead in natural phenomena, but he does not distance these hints from himself. While Dobyns, writing from his perspective of depressed realism, scorns any notion of an afterlife, Wright's baroque sensibility allows him to suggest, coyly and only through imagery and metaphor, a mingling of the here and the hereafter.[15]

---

15. Speaking of the many ghosts that people Wright's poems, George F. Butterick has said: "As [can] be seen throughout his work, there are presences in his imagination that the material world alone cannot explain" ("Charles Wright," 391). Calvin Bedient, in his radically disconnective and almost unreadable review of *The Southern Cross*, suggests that pursuing the dead is the sum of Wright's thematic quest in all his work: "Not that Wright is occult: on the contrary, he would make the intangible stark. To him revelation came early and has remained unsparing: it is that the dead, who are superior to us, who know more and feel more, are always near us. He hails the superhuman, writes of death-in-life and life-in-death" ("Tracing Charles Wright," *Parnassus: Poetry in Review* 10.1 [1982], 55).

The final and title poem of the volume, "The Southern Cross," is less concerned with death than with memory and the burdens of a personal past, just as the title refers less to the constellation than to the cherished burden of Wright's Tennessee heritage and his preoccupation with Italy (southern in a European context), both of which define him, establishing the "cross" he carries through his life. The poem is rich in image and incident, with interspersed passages of a more abstract nature. Wright has explained that for him the American South represents the fecundity of earth, a purely physical beauty, while Italy represents the spiritual: "Italy is metaphysical."[16] Like the entire book, this poem attempts to unite these two realms not just as parts of the poet's past, his memory, but also—and more importantly—as concepts. The poem ends with him wishing he could completely reinhabit the world of the South as it existed at the time of his birth:

> It's what we forget that defines us, and stays in the same place,
> And waits to be rediscovered.
> Somewhere in all that network of rivers and roads and silt hills,
> A city I'll never remember,
>                      its walls the color of pure light,
> Lies in the August heat of 1935,
> In Tennessee, the bottom land slowly becoming a lake.
> It lies in a landscape that keeps my imprint
> Forever,
>            and stays unchanged, and waits to be filled back in.
> Someday I'll find it out
> And enter my old outline as though for the 1st time,
>
> And lie down, and tell no one.

The odd promise to tell no one so hard-won a truth, were it to be discovered, has a profound rightness at the conclusion of this poem: throughout the poem and the book, it is not the finding that concerns Wright but the searching. We recall that the constellation, the Southern Cross, is a navigational aid to travelers, but of course it is not visible from the northern hemisphere. It seems clear, then, that Wright has structured this questing poem in a fundamentally uncertain way, so that it cannot arrive at its destination; his emphasis is consistently upon events and objects that are not at hand, that cannot quite be remembered.

*The Other Side of the River* continues the formal breakthrough toward expansive form achieved in *The Southern Cross*; most of the poems tend to run on for several pages each. *The Other Side of the River* makes use of four basic settings or locales. California is the setting of the present moment, the present tense, the time of actual speaking. Memory carries the

---

16. McClatchy, 192.

speaker into the past, which has two generalized settings—Italy and the American South. Desire carries him toward the future, into imagination or vision, the hint of salvation, whose domain is set across the river. The title Wright has chosen for this book seems intentionally to echo the title of one of James Wright's books, *Shall We Gather at the River*—in which a poem called "Willy Lyons" imagines the speaker's uncle as having achieved peace after his death by crossing the river—the River Styx masquerading as the Ohio River. In his title poem, Charles Wright's speaker expresses his wish in this way: "I want to sit by the bank of the river, / in the shade of the evergreen tree, / And look in the face of whatever, / the whatever that's waiting for me."[17] Perhaps it is the pat use of rhyme here that makes us doubt the ultimate truth of this vision; Charles Wright never explicitly accepts transcendence in his poems, however much otherworldly desire he expresses. As Bruce Bond has said, both the desire and the limitations are based on Wright's use of imagery: "In spite of their longing for transcendence, Wright's poems remain forcefully visual, as if the image were both bridge and barrier to the unseen, the most immediate objects assuming a metaphysical inscrutability and allure."[18]

Despite the fact that they contain elements that are clearly narrative, Wright's most characteristic poems are dominantly meditative and circular. Rather than tell stories, they incorporate incidents and events into imagistic structures that contemplate matters deserving of serious thought; the author or his speaker gradually circles in on the truth. In the words of Vendler: "[Wright's] synoptic and panoramic vision, radiating out from a compositional center to a filled canvas, opposes itself to the anthropocentric, and consequently autobiographical or narrative, impetus of lyrics with a linear base."[19] The opening poem of *The Other Side of the River* illustrates this meditative circularity; "Lost Bodies" is divided into seven unnumbered sections, each performing a specific function. The first section is introductory, much as the first sections of so many of Whitman's open-form poems are introductory. And just as Whitman so often does, Wright introduces all of the elements of his poem briefly at the start:

---

17. As Floyd Collins wrote in his review of *The World of the Ten Thousand Things*, after reading an earlier version of the present essay: "Wright's self-portraitures in *The Other Side of the River* increasingly depict incident and anecdote within the context of place—the present belonging to California, the past to Italy and the American South, the future to that mysterious river with one shore in the temporal world, the other in eternity" ("Metamorphosis within the Poetry of Charles Wright," *Gettysburg Review* 4 [1991], 470).

18. Bruce Bond, "Metaphysics of the Image in Charles Wright and Paul Cézanne," *Southern Review* 30.1 (1994), 116.

19. Vendler, *Part of Nature, Part of Us*, 287.

Last night I thought of Torri del Benaco again,
Its almond trees in blossom,
                      its cypresses clothed in their dark fire,

And the words carved on that concrete cross

I passed each day of my life
In Kingsport going to town
    GET RIGHT WITH GOD / JESUS IS COMING SOON.

If I had it all to do over again
                  I'd be a Medievalist.
I'd thoroughly purge my own floor.

Something's for sure in the clouds, but it's not for me,

Though all the while that light tips the fast-moving water,
East wind in a rush through the almond trees.

The first three lines introduce the Italian setting that forms the basis for one of the poem's patterns of memory; the next four lines introduce the setting in the American South that is the basis for the other pattern. The concluding six lines are thematic. The desire to be a medievalist seems like a wish for certainty, perhaps religious certainty. The something that is "for sure in the clouds" may suggest a spiritual possibility—the efficacy of which the speaker immediately denies but then just as quickly seems to grant, though in a different form: if he cannot find the spiritual in the clouds, perhaps he can find it in the more earthbound light on the water and wind in the trees.

The following six sections of the poem establish a regular and repetitive pattern: numbers two and five develop the memory of Tennessee; three and six develop the memory of Italy; four and seven develop the theme, the meanings of these memories. Charles Wright grew up in Tennessee; after college he lived in Italy while serving in the United States Army. The sense of spirituality that is developed in the Tennessee sections is earthy and Christian, the word emphatically made flesh: "the cross is still there, sunk deeper into the red clay / Than anyone could have set it." Wright has provided an indirect gloss on these passages in "Lonesome Pine Special," where he asserts: "In the world of dirt, each tactile thing / repeats the untouchable / In its own way, and in its own time."[20]

---

20. Mary Kinzie sees places as crucial in Wright's poems and also sees them at times as leading to the otherworldly: "Wright could be said to depend absolutely on place, to work from it, in his crucial journeys, traced in so many poems, from rest to intense engagement with ethereal thresholds, tints of light, floating gestures" ("Haunting," *American Poetry Review* 11.5 [September/October 1982], 40). Rather

Spirituality in the Italian sections is more evanescent, not so much inherent within material objects as dancingly associated with them; it exists in the interplay between wind, water, and vegetation:

> An east wind was blowing out toward the water . . .
>
> I remember the cypress nods in its warm breath.
> I remember the almond blossoms
> > > floating out on the waves, west to Salò.
> I remember the way they looked there,
> > > a small flotilla of matches.
>
> I remember their flash in the sun's flare.

The thematic sections are rational and intellectual rather than emotional and imagistic; though a desire for belief, for faith, seems expressed in them, it is overridden by the logic of doubt: "You've got to sign your name to something, it seems to me. / And so we rephrase the questions / Endlessly, / hoping the answer might somehow change." The answer the speaker wishes would change is that taught by the facts of everyday life:

> When you die, you fall down,
> > > you don't rise up
> Like a scrap of burnt paper into the everlasting.
> Each morning we learn this painfully,
> > > pulling our bodies up by the roots from their deep sleep.

No matter how hard he strives to make them suffice, the speaker of these poems ultimately cannot rest easy with the limited religious answers he considers.

Both the questions and the answers, the images and the statements, the doubts and the longings, however, are expressed in language, and language is always the underlying subject of Wright's poems. In "To Giacomo Leopardi in the Sky," Wright asserts the spiritual function of words while questioning their efficacy:

---

than seeing this progression as embodying Wright's peculiar strength as I do, however, Kinzie—who doesn't like Wright's poems—prefers to see it as another sign of his love simply for that which is insubstantial. Robert Pinsky takes a position close to mine when he points out how Wright links the concrete and the abstract, often through setting: "Repeatedly, Wright finds his most compelling voice when the described locale and the foliating poetic language are balanced by their relation to some moral abstraction—often an abstraction simultaneously hollow and powerful, like 'Salvation' in . . . lines about a childhood Bible camp" ("Description and the Virtuous Use of Words," *Parnassus: Poetry in Review* 3.2 [1975], 145).

Not one word has ever melted in glory not one.
We keep on sending them up, however,
As the sun rains down.
                          You did it yourself,
All those nights looking up at the sky, wanting to be there
Away from the grief of being here
In the wrong flesh.
They must look funny to you now,
Rising like smoke signals into the infinite,
The same letter over and over,
                          big o and little o.

If words cannot reach as far as heaven, then the solution Wright seeks in these poems must only exist as a component of poetry itself; somehow the form of the search is its own mysterious answer. Wright's thinking is circular indeed, as the search for an answer so often brings us and him back to the starting point at the end. Thus when he asserts what seems an ultimate answer in "California Dreaming," we end up back where we started: "What I know best is a little thing. / It sits on the far side of the simile, / the like that's like the like." The statement does not express belief in a settled truth; it establishes a path, a method, which might lead to some sense of truth—if spiritual certainty is to be found, that is, it will be discovered through the operations of something like metaphor or simile. The similarity of this to what we found to be the ultimate aim of Charles Simic's poetry—to touch the deepest element of *being* through the use of metaphor—is certainly striking. The two poets are close friends; their correspondence on the uses of imagery in poetry was published in the *Gettysburg Review* in 1995.[21]

Even more obviously to the point of Wright's work is a passage from the title poem in *The Other Side of the River*, where Wright comments directly upon the meditative, metaphorical, circular method of his long poems:

It's linkage I'm talking about,
                          and harmonies and structures
And all the various things that lock our wrists to the past.

Something infinite behind everything appears,
                          and then disappears.

It's all a matter of how
                          you narrow the surfaces.
It's all a matter of how you fit in the sky.

---

21. Charles Wright, "Improvisations: Narrative of the Image (A Correspondence with Charles Simic)," *Gettysburg Review* 8.1 (1995), 9-21.

Wright is talking neither about reality nor about settled truth here; his subject is the method of his poetry, the process whereby truth might someday be cajoled to reveal itself out of the confusing, the camouflaging, the byzantine fabric of the reality that conceals it.

The expansion of form that Wright began with *The Southern Cross* and continued with *The Other Side of the River* took another small leap forward in his next volume, *Zone Journals*. These journal poems are even less committed to tidy notions of structure than the poems that come before them. The new pattern is continued into *Xionia*, which contains another fifteen journal poems. Still, these two books are far more similar stylistically to the earlier books than they are dissimilar; in terms of theme we also find the latest poems similar to the ones immediately preceding them, as Wright continues to explore the relationship between the physical and the spiritual realms. And, again as before, his starting point and emphasis is with concrete images of reality; the holiness must trail after— like the shadow of a waving branch playing among fallen leaves.

In *Zone Journals* Wright is not particularly coy about what he is searching for; in the second poem he creates an image that lays out his theme:

> One of those weightless, effortless late September days
> As sycamore leaves
> tack down the unresisting air
> Onto the fire-knots of late roses
> Still pumping their petals of flame
> up from the English loam,
> And I suddenly recognize
> The difference between the spirit and flesh
> is finite, and slowly transgressable . . .

Wright wishes to demonstrate the presence of the spiritual within the realm of the real, and his approach is like that of the English rose: to grow from the soil, rich and real, to reach tentatively into the air, vague and insubstantial, and to produce a miracle of transubstantial beauty at the end of an extended stem. That's all.[22]

Nearly at the geographical center of this book we find a curious passage in which a departed, elder sage bestows upon the acolyte poet his sense of mission. The figurative imagery of Wright's framing is both entertaining and baroque:

> Who is it here in the night garden,
> gown a transparent rose

---

22. This way of handling death has been noticed as well by Helen Vendler: "To Wright, death is as often ascent as burial; we become stars, like Romeo, after death, as often as roses" (*Part of Nature, Part of Us*, 286).

Down to his ankles, great sleeves
Spreading the darkness around him wherever he steps,
Laurel corona encircling his red transparent headcap, . . .
                              voice like a slow rip through silk cloth
In disapproval? *Brother*, he says, pointing insistently,
A sound of voices starting to turn in the wind and then disappear as
    though
Orbiting us, *Brother, remember the way it was*
*In my time: nothing has changed:*
*Penitents terrace the mountainside, the stars hang in their bright courses*
*And darkness is still the dark:*
                              *concentrate, listen hard,*
*Look to the nature of all things.*

The insistent, fatherly saint—of course Dante, come to guide the younger poet as Virgil came to guide Dante—is himself a rose, growing from the soil of the grave. Look and listen, he says—look to the spiritual heart of "all things"; listen for the unutterable sound:

In the rings and after-chains,
In the great river of language that circles the universe,
Everything comes together, . . .
                    there is a word, one word,
For each of us, circling and holding fast
In all that cascade and light.
Said once, or said twice,
                    it gathers and waits its time to come back
To its true work:
                    concentrate, listen hard.

Wright will deal more fully with the subject of language in *Xionia*; here he prefers to concentrate upon objects—real, visible, audible. Moreover, he does not specify precisely the nature of the spiritual center that he seeks; in fact, his aesthetic requires that he *not* specify it. He speaks of "the obvious end of art" as being "that grace / Beyond its reach" and asserts that "what's outside / The picture is more important than what's in." Form and content thus correspond wonderfully to one another in *Zone Journals*, as each requires that there be an unspoken heart to the utterance. But because the spiritual is inherent within the physical and not separate from it, it does not subtract from what is here. Instead, it lies just beneath the surface or just off the page, energizing what we are given.

The baroque is present everywhere in these poems—in Wright's lush musicality, in his rich use of imagery and metaphor, and in the linkage of the invisible realm of spirit to the visible realm of reality. Thus the unseen adds energy to the seen, twisting it from its axis, enriching its colors and forms. Here is Wright describing the night in typical form:

The stars are fastening their big buckles
                                    and flashy night shoes,
Thunder chases its own tail down the sky,
My forty-ninth year, and all my Southern senses called to horn,
August night hanging like cobwebs around my shoulders:
How existential it all is, really,
                          the starting point always the starting point
And what's-to-come still being the What's-to-Come.
Some friends, like George, lurk in the memory like locusts,
                                    while others, flat one-sided fish
Looking up, handle themselves like sweet stuff:
                              look out for them, look out for them.

It is not just the oddness of the individual images here that is baroque but
the unharmonious profusion of odd images. Although Dr. Johnson recog-
nized that the metaphysical poets of the seventeenth century wished to
yoke "the most heterogeneous ideas . . . by violence together" through a
kind of *discordia concors*, he ended up finding more *discordia* than *concors*.[23]
So it is with this passage. When the speaker finds his senses "called to
horn," we suspect that he has been awakened to a fox hunt, or perhaps just
to another day in boot camp. These possibilities might be said to be rein-
forced by the first image, in which the nighttime revelers seem to be gath-
ering themselves for home. The description of the threatening morning
sky, however, is ornamental, as must be the concluding images—unless we
decide that the quarry of the speaker is not foxes but insects or fish. The
ultimate meaning of these lines remains mysterious, but not the impor-
tance of the search, the necessity that the speaker "look out for them."

Metaphysical and baroque poets have always been susceptible to the
charge of mixing their metaphors, and certainly Wright does not escape his
share of the guilt. Indeed, the very aspect of Wright's work that most obvi-
ously defines his style is—as we might expect—also the aspect of his work
that is most controversial among critics. Robert Pinsky, for example, sug-
gests that "Often Wright's style is so clotted with figures of speech . . . that
everything else tends to vanish."[24] X. J. Kennedy, a sympathetic reader of
Wright's poems, has pointed to extreme metaphors that he finds both suc-
cessful and unsuccessful: "As always, Wright has a rare way with a metaphor:
'Spring picks the locks of the wind,' 'The reindeer still file through the
bronchial trees.' Still, he is not always discriminate, as in lines about bears
(the constellations) 'serene as black coffee,' and about 'Sun like an orange
Mousse.'"[25] There are no laws where taste is concerned; Kennedy's last neg-
ative example has already appeared among my positive ones.

23. Samuel Johnson, "Life of Cowley," in his *Lives of the Poets*.
24. Pinsky, 143.
25. X. J. Kennedy, "A Tenth and Four Fifths," *Poetry* 141 (March 1983), 357.

Similarly, one of the metaphors praised by Kennedy is ridiculed in this comment made by Mary Kinzie: "Some of [Wright's] personifications are quite funny: 'Spring picks the locks of the wind'; 'spaces / In black shoes, their hands clasped'; 'The dead are constant in / The white lips of the sea.' Some of the stage props the dead must carry around are also awkwardly amusing: 'We filagree and we baste. / But what do the dead care for the fringe of words, / Safe in their suits of milk?'"[26] Calvin Bedient begins his critique of Wright's use of extreme metaphor by commenting on lines from the poem "Vesper Journal" ("petals fall like tiny skirts / From the dogwood tree next door, / last things in the last light"): "Charming as they may be, those 'tiny skirts' need to be shipped back to the warehouse; they're frivolous in the neighborhood of 'last things.' . . . Again, does it signify, in 'Language Journal,' that the light is 'cantaloupe-colored'? Is this any more than a 'pretty' detail? To call such luscious light 'Light of martyrs and solitaries' only makes matters worse, as does imagining it 'ladled' like 'a liquid' on the trees." Curiously, this is the same critic who begins his review with this praise of Wright's baroque sensibility: "Through his startling figures and, if less so, his eloquent rhythms, he has intimated an unthinkable glory of which life is otherwise bereft."[27] This last statement, of course, echoes my own thinking.

The ten poems that make up *Zone Journals* are geographically expansive, ranging from California to Italy to England, and with many scenes set in Virginia. The poems are linear in the way they handle time, with many of the sections in each dated and chronologically arranged. In terms of meaning, however, the poems are accretive, speculative, and ruminative; they do not move forward from a beginning to a middle and an end. The central poem, "A Journal of the Year of the Ox," proceeds entirely through 1985; the entry for May 15 is typical for the way it mixes concrete imagery of spring with thoughts on the nature of existence:

> —In the first inch of afternoon, under the peach trees,
> The constellations of sunlight
> Sifting along their courses among the posed limbs,
> It's hard to imagine the north wind
>                                   wishing us ill,
> Revealing nothing at all and wishing us ill
> In God's third face.
>                     The world is an ampersand,
> And I lie in sweet clover,
>                         bees like golden earrings
> Dangling and locked fast to its white heads,

---

26. Kinzie, 40.

27. Bedient, "Slide-Wheeling around the Curves," *Southern Review* 27.1 (Winter 1991), 230, 221.

> Watching the clouds move and the constellations of light move
> Through the trees, as they both will
> When the wind weathers them on their way,
> When the wind weathers them to that point
> > > where all things meet.

The goal of this volume is to speculate about that point, where the seen and the unseen might come together and reinforce one another. However, Wright still does not quite seem confident about where that occurs and how it might be achieved. Discovering and revealing that is the task he undertakes in *Xionia*.

Whereas the structure of *Zone Journals* is chronological and accretive, that of *Xionia* is symmetrical. Placed at the center of the fifteen poems in *Xionia* is the eighth of them, "Language Journal." Immediately preceding and following it are "Primitive Journal" and "Primitive Journal II," the latter of which answers the former. Similarly, poem ten, the optimistic "May Journal," answers poem six, the pessimistic "Georg Trakl Journal," and poem twelve, "A Journal of Southern Rivers," provides the thematic climax anticipated in poem four, "December Journal." The first three poems are introductory and the final three consolidate the gains made in number twelve. Finally, the poems alternate in length, with the odd num-bered poems being short and the even numbered poems being long. Wright has always favored balanced patterns; in interviews he is forever identifying the exact centers of poems, sequences, and books.

*Xionia* is both about truth and about poetry. Wright wishes to express wisdom about the nature of the universe, particularly how it integrates the spiritual and the physical, at the same time as he wishes to understand how this expression, this complicated use of words, can occur. Because of the way in which the two interact with one another, Wright is as inter-ested in the nature of language as he is in the substance of truth. Richard Jackson has commented on this aspect of Wright's work:

> In the context of an Idealistic Neo-Confucianism, Wright's world becomes one of presences that are inadequate substitutes for the absence he desires. As a result, the objects of his landscape aspire to the condition of language, our substitute, if we can trust the linguistic critics (Jacques Lacan, for ex-ample), for what we cannot fully possess, for what is missing. In a round-about way, he hopes language will bring him the void, will allow him to become, as another epigraph suggests, "an emblem among emblems."[28]

---

28. Richard Jackson, "Worlds Created, Worlds Perceived," *Michigan Quarterly Review* 17 (1978), 556. Kathleen Agena similarly noticed the commitment to lan-guage as subject in Wright's early work: "all three of his [early] books contain poems which, strictly speaking, refer only to words and their maneuverings" (626).

As is so often the case in his writings, Wright begins the sequence of poems that makes up *Xionia* with a kind of hypothesis:

Inaudible consonant, inaudible vowel
The word continues to fall
                                            in splendor around us
Window half shadow window half moon
                                            back yard like a book of snow
That holds nothing and that nothing holds
Immaculate text
                        not too prescient not too true.

Wright's two subjects—truth and articulation—are brought together here, as in the sequence as a whole, through an identification of nature with language. Wright suggests that the most crucial utterances may occur not only within poems but also within the sacred and visible world of nature.

In the central poem "Language Journal" Wright considers the relationship between language and reality. As is often his strategy, he first presents a false viewpoint—in this case the contention of "the theorists" that "everything comes from language": "Nothing means anything, the slip of phrase against phrase / Contains the real way our lives / Are graphed out and understood, / the transformation of adverb / To morpheme and phoneme is all we need answer to"—and then disagrees with it: "But I don't think so today." Wright goes on to assert that language is conduit, not creator, of truth: "Whatever it is, the language is only its moan. / Whatever it is, the self's trace / lingers along it." Abstraction is not truth; without the real to give it form and substance (concepts that together yield utterance), abstraction has no being.

"December Journal," the fourth poem in the sequence, uses the same strategy of false statement followed by a correction to nearly the same end, beginning:

God is not offered to the senses,
                                    St. Augustine tells us,
The artificer is not his work, but is his art:
Nothing is good if it can be better.
But all these oak trees look fine to me. . . .

Wright takes this occasion to praise the complexities of the physical world, which he is convinced embodies the abstractions within it:

I keep coming back to the visible.
                                    I keep coming back
To what it leads me into,
The hymn in the hymnal,
The object, sequence and consequence.
By being exactly what it is,

> It is that other, inviolate self we yearn for,
> Itself and more than itself,
>                                 the word inside the word.
> It is the tree and what the tree stands in for, the blank,
> The far side of the last equation.

In an interview, Wright commented upon the directness of his journal poems, how they allow him to say exactly what he thinks: "They are more didactic than other poems, perhaps, and more emotionally open. One tends to speak one's mind more nakedly in journals. One tends to say what is really troubling one's sleep."[29] Certainly in these lines, and throughout *Xionia*, Wright wants to be sure we understand his meaning.

Wright feels, most emphatically, the presence of the truth that he seeks within nature itself, which seems to *speak* to him. In "May Journal"—tenth in the series and the one corresponding to "December Journal"—he senses this truth most strongly, but is still unable fully to articulate it:

> What is it in all myth
>                         that brings us back from the dead?
> What is it that jump-starts in verisimilitude
> And ends up in ecstacy,
> That takes us by both hands
>                         from silence to speechlessness?
> What is it that brings us out of the rock with such pain,
> As though the sirens had something to say to us after all
> From their clover and green shore,
>                         the words of their one song
> Translatable, note by note?
> As though the inexpressible were made inexpressible.

It is in such a passage as this that Wright most resembles Robert Penn Warren. In his wonderful late volume *Being Here* (1980), as sporadically throughout his mature career, Warren also sought to understand the truth that he felt was being uttered by nature. His poem "Code Book Lost," for example, begins:

> What does the veery say, at dusk in shad-thicket?
> There must be some meaning, or why should your heart stop,
>
> As though, in the dark depth of water, Time held its breath,
> While the message spins on like a spool of silk thread fallen?

---

29. McClatchy, 204-205.

The uncertainty that Wright feels is echoed at the end of Warren's poem: "Yes, message on message, like wind or water, in light or in dark, / The whole world pours at us. But the code book, somehow, is lost."[30]

Wright comes to his answer in the twelfth poem of *Xionia*, "A Journal of Southern Rivers," which begins by positing a question—"*What hast thou, O my soul, with Paradise*"—we seem to have heard before. This is yet another way of asking, What is the ultimate relationship between the unseen and the seen, the spiritual and the physical? The answer comes in another passage that refers to a figure of authority, but this time a figure whose position is not undercut:

> If being is Being, as Martin Heidegger says,
> There is no other question,
>                       nothing to answer to,
> That's worth the trouble.
> In awe and astonishment we regain ourselves in this world.
> There is no other.

Since there is no other world, no spiritual realm that is separate from the physical realm in which we live our lives, then the poet can truly immerse himself in both realms by living fully in this one. Ultimately it is the ongoing process—of language, of poetry, of life—that captures his attention, rather than the finished product of a spiritual realm waiting at the end. Spirituality is to be found in poems.

Among contemporary American poets, Wright would seem to be the one who most fulfills the characteristics of the baroque mode. Not only does he write—musically, imagistically, and metaphorically—in the strikingly lush style that we call baroque, but he does so with real substance, habitually searching for signs of the spiritual within the physical, the unseen within the seen. It also happens that he is conscious of doing this, as is evident from a comment that he made almost offhandedly to J. D. McClatchy: "One more thing. Some years ago Octavio Paz called for what I seem to remember as a 'Baroque-abstract' in painting. A kind of Mannerism. A non-pejorative Mannerism. I think that has happened in the work, say, of Frank Stella. I think it is also happening, here and there, in poetry. One could name names—Ashbery, for instance. It is a position that interests me as well."[31]

Except for Stanley Kunitz, Wright is more different from the other poets considered in this book than he is similar to them. And yet there are areas of similarity. When he mentions John Ashbery in his comment

---

30. For a fuller discussion of this aspect of Robert Penn Warren's work, see my chapter on him in *The World's Hieroglyphic Beauty: Five American Poets* (Athens: University of Georgia Press, 1985).

31. McClatchy, 205.

on a nonpejorative mannerism just above, for example, Wright is point-
ing to one of these similarities: Ashbery and Wright both write their
poems at a far edge of contemporary style, the edge that favors floridness,
curlicues, and complicated thinking. With Charles Simic, Wright shares
an interest in extreme linkages of imagery, in far-ranging uses of
metaphor; indeed for both poets this type of figuration is crucial to
philosophical understanding. With Gerald Stern, Wright shares an inter-
est in the sacredness of things, the wonders of nature. With Stephen
Dobyns, however, he seems to share almost nothing, beyond the fact that
they are both contemporary American poets.

What makes Wright most unique within this group is his attitude, or
nonattitude, toward most aspects of life in the twentieth century: he
rarely if ever refers to politics; he does not describe massacres, atrocities,
drive-by shootings, muggings; he seems relatively unbothered by the
prospect of certain death. Though Ashbery is somewhat less grounded in
explicit details of twentieth-century life than Dobyns, Simic, or Stern,
Wright seems much less grounded in them than Ashbery. In almost every
way we can think of he is the least time-bound of these poets, the one
most comfortable with a style and way of thinking inherited from the
seventeenth century. And yet he still lacks the sense of certainty we see
in the earlier baroque artists; though he asks many of the same questions
as they, he arrives at no certain set of answers, no settled core of beliefs.
Rather, his questions lead him to shadows and hints, desires and longings,
evanescent scenarios more likely to have emanated from his own imagi-
nation than from the world of reality. Because of the relentlessly ques-
tioning nature of Wright's religious seeking, we can see working in him,
too, the principle of uncertainty.

LEE UPTON

# The Doubting Penitent: Charles Wright's Epiphanies of Abandonment (1998)

C harles Wright is one of our contemporary poets most willing to make self-characterizations for readers. Consider two statements from his prose assemblage "Bytes and Pieces":

> I write from the point of view of a monk in his cell. Sometimes I look at the stones, sometimes I look out the window.[1]

> I would like my poems to be like visionary frescoes on the walls of some out-of-the-way monastery.[2]

Surely Wright's presentation of a monk in his cell detailing his environment evokes an image of the poet as a solitary ascetic. In turn, his reference to the placement of his "visionary frescoes" indicates his fascination with the obscure and the hidden, the "out-of-the-way" phenomena that he believes will allow him to intuit spiritual presence. Throughout his career, Wright has been a self-described penitent, a pilgrim (a common persona in his poems) unvisited by the spiritual presences he seeks and unable to master his spiritual yearnings. He composes his poems with the stubborn will of a man intent on continuing his life's work without being understood by others.[3]

Wright's preoccupations are the traditional ones of the lyric poet: nature, mortality, and spiritual impulse. But he has taken these preoccupations and treated them in increasingly intricate ways; by the late 1970s he was widening and fanning out his poems as he questioned the stability of memory, identity, and language. What remains most significant in his prose writings and in oblique references within poems is his preoccupation with creating an autobiography. Such a goal is, in some ways, humble; autobiography, after all, professes to reveal primarily the limited life of its author, however well the author summons a cultural and historical situation. Yet

---

1. Charles Wright, "Bytes and Pieces," in *Quarter Notes: Improvisations and Interviews* (Ann Arbor: University of Michigan Press, 1995), p. 80.

2. Ibid., p. 81.

3. See ibid., pp. 81–82, in which the poet writes: "[My] subject (language, landscape, and the idea of God) is not of much interest now. But it will be again. How all three configure one's own face is important and must be addressed."

given Wright's belief in the inherent instability of memory and language, his project is ambitious: the one life revealed in the mutable medium of language may at least covertly reflect on the ways in which language represents many lives, and his compass points of meaning are no less than the great abstractions of language, nature, and God.

Composing poetry allows Wright the hope of abandoning the limited confines of the self and "unmastering" the known, including the recognizable status of both origin and identity that Maurice Blanchot alludes to in his essay "From Dread to Language": "Most of the time, to give oneself to language is to abandon oneself. One allows oneself to be carried away by a mechanism that takes upon itself all the responsibility of the act of writing."[4] As Wright, too, suggests, the act of writing, to which he repeatedly pledges his allegiance, cannot be ultimately controlled, and the process of composition reinforces and duplicates the contours of his spiritual longings, which, similarly, remain unmastered and unsatisfied. Wright's sense of his project connects with Blanchot's argument for the intractability of words as outlined in another essay: "The writer seems to be master of his pen, he can become capable of great mastery over words, over what he wants to make them express," Blanchot writes. "But this mastery only manages to put him in contact, keep him in contact, with a fundamental passivity in which the word, no longer anything beyond its own appearance, the shadow of a word, can never be mastered or even grasped; it remains impossible to grasp, impossible to relinquish, the unsettled moment of fascination."[5] For Wright, "unmastering" is linked to his wish to dissolve into what he suggestively frames as the oblivion of belief, an ultimate union with his desires that would evaporate the limiting boundaries of selfhood and its public identity. His obsessive focus on desires that cannot be met allows him to project a poetry that he can never master; the scope of his project mandates failure rather than authority over phenomena. Yet unmastering language, paradoxically, allows Wright intense pleasure, especially the pleasure of copious writing; error and incompletion make more writing possible, prompting rewriting.

Since his early career Wright has displayed a readiness for revelation and a near-religious commitment to aesthetic discipline. His poems are suffused with spiritual reference not only derived from his upbringing in the Episcopal Church ("from which I fled and out of which I remain"[6]) but from a temperamental yearning for transcendence. What we encounter in his poems are the principles and images of religious

---

4. Maurice Blanchot, "From Dread to Language," in *The Gaze of Orpheus and Other Literary Essays*, trans. Lydia Davis, ed. P. Adams Sitney (Barrytown, N.Y: Station Hill, 1981), p. 18.

5. Maurice Blanchot, "The Essential Solitude," in *Gaze of Orpheus*, p. 67.

6. Charles Wright, "Charles Wright at Oberlin," *FIELD* 17 (Fall 1997): 65.

supplication and transubstantiation put in the service of language. He has called language "the most sacred place of all,"[7] arguing that the "true purpose and result of poetry" is "a contemplation of the divine" through words.[8] He describes his poems as "little prayer wheels," "wafers," "sacraments," and "hymns."[9] Yet while Wright works in a reference area of spiritual imagery, suffusing his poems with religious terminology, he resists conversion to a stable point of view of the spirit or to any one system of belief. The forms of his poems evince his continual need to experiment with questions of belief as they may be intuited through language. Over the course of his career, he has "opened" the channels of his writing to stylistic change and to conflicting, often contradictory, meditations that unsettle belief in an otherworldly power. It is as if his entertaining of doubt—doubt of deity and of language's efficacy, self-doubt and doubt of the poem itself—performed as his essential spiritual practice.

In a sense, Wright's is a faith against faith, a resistance to his early indoctrination in the Episcopal Church but not a renunciation of religious strategies for seeking transcendent meaning. He stylizes his poems in the language and impulses associated with Christianity even while he escapes from the most consequential demands of faith in a higher power. It is not too much to claim that he has spiritualized doubt; in his poems, doubt becomes particular to spiritual aspiration, for he awaits illumination despite his skepticism, which seems, in much of his poetry, a manifestation of his asceticism. Apparently the poem for Wright is a means to secure religious feeling, to attain access to something akin to ecstasy and the sensation of dissolution, however momentarily, of the limited self. It appears that it is the sensations of religious conversion that he desires, but not the trappings of corporate religious life.

Given both Wright's spiritual themes and his references to his writing practices in interviews, his critics inevitably have viewed him in saintlike terms. Alluding to the photograph of Wright on the cover of *Bloodlines*, Calvin Bedient describes the poet as "a mock frontier-saint of purity—washed in the beyond, cleaned to blankness, bouncing back brilliance."[10] David St. John notes, "For his readers, Charles Wright's poetry often serves as a kind of prayer book, a kind of poetic hymnal or speculative

---

7. Charles Wright, "The Art of Poetry XLI: Charles Wright," interview by J. D. McClatchy, *Paris Review* 113 (1989): 195.

8. Charles Wright, "Improvisations on Form and Measure," *Ohio Review* 38 (1987): 23.

9. Charles Wright, "An Interview," interview by Elizabeth McBride, *Ohio Review* 34 (1985): 17.

10. Calvin Bedient, "Tracing Charles Wright," *Parnassus: Poetry in Review* 10, no. 1 (1982): 55.

field guide we might carry with us on our own metaphysical journeys."[11] While I do not wish to make Wright into a caricature of a saint of any sort, it is worth noting that his persona in poems, prose, and interviews conforms in part to characteristics that William James defines as saintly: "The saintly character is the character for which spiritual emotions are the habitual centre of the personal energy." The primary qualities of the saint include, James points out, "a feeling of being in a wider life than that of this world's selfish little interests; and a conviction, not merely intellectual, but as it were sensible, of the existence of the Ideal Power"[12]; "a sense of the friendly continuity of the ideal power with our own life, and a willing self-surrender to its control," "an immense elation and freedom, as the outlines of the confining selfhood melt down"; "a shifting of the emotional centre towards loving and harmonious affections."[13] Of these characteristics, Wright's frequent focus on divinity and his desire for self-surrender mark his endeavor as saintlike in James's terms. In addition, Wright is as willing as an ascetic to maintain a single-minded attention to his discipline, the discipline of probing toward intimation of divinity through experiments with language. He retains such alert mindfulness by refusing the comforts of distraction or of self-gratification and aiming for experiences linked to sainthood, particularly in terms of the disruption and dissolution of personality. His autobiographical poems in their distortions of point of view and their focus on a sketched outline of self are inflected with the contrary desire to disband selfhood entirely, in a way reminiscent of James's notion of sainthood: "Religious rapture, moral enthusiasm, ontological wonder, cosmic emotion, are all unifying states of mind, in which the sand and grit of the selfhood incline to disappear, and tenderness to rule."[14] As James sees it, this tendency toward obliteration of self-interest is paramount in sainthood: "abandonment of self-responsibility seems to be the fundamental act in specifically religious, as distinguished from moral[,] practice."[15] Sensations allied to such "abandonment" are sought repeatedly in Wright's poetry.

Inevitably, Wright's themes and vocabularies—his focus on salvation and transubstantiation, and his anticipation of impending divine presence—force his readers into a consideration of spirituality. But it is the autobiographically coded poems of an agonized speaker, a St. Sebastian punctured by the arrows of doubt, that allows for the near hagiography of some critical accounts about Wright. That is, while Wright salts his

---

11. David St. John, foreword to *County Music: Selected Early Poems*, by Charles Wright, 2d ed. (Hanover, N.H.: Wesleyan University Press, 1991), p. xiii.

12. William James, *The Varieties of Religious Experience: A Study in Human Nature* (New York: Collier, 1961), p. 220.

13. Ibid., p. 221.

14. Ibid., p. 225.

15. Ibid., p. 233.

poem with allusions to otherworldly presences, it is finally his own persona, "Charles," who seems to many of his readers to be the most afflicted and ultimately spiritualized amid his pantheon. His project takes its tensions from opposing pressures, pressures between, on the one hand, salvific yearning seemingly foreordained by the depth of his early religious instruction and, on the other, by empirical rationalism ingrained upon his mind by his experiences in a secular culture.

While Wright's poems suggest, as Bedient notes, "all high church—reason's unease,"[16] at the same time—and here's one of the most prominent paradoxes in this poet's work—they battle the religious transcendence that they would evoke, particularly in a frequent trope in which the longed-for spiritual or poetic forebear fails to appear. "God is the sleight-of-hand in the fireweed, the lost / Moment that stopped to grieve and moved on . . . ," he has written and rewritten in various forms in various poems.[17] This attitude of unrewarded receptivity manifested itself immediately in Wright's career. In "Aubade," the first poem collected in his early poems in *Country Music*, his speaker is depicted as "waiting—calmly, unquestioning—for Saint Spiridion of Holy Memory to arise . . . from his grove of miracles above the hill" (*CM*, 3). Wright's speakers assume postures of expectation, however acutely aware they may be of landscape and weather. As in another early poem, "Nocturne," his speaker is already a "strayed traveller, or some misguided pilgrim" (*CM*, 6). His speaker's anticipation, however, is crossed; even if the speaker is "waiting—calmly unquestioning—" the holy figure cannot emerge. Wright is the supplicant for whom no visitation entirely makes itself known but who finds even the lack of anticipated appearance a resonant sign of mystery. In other poems, if a strange figure does arrive with the semblance of a message, as in "Journal of the Year of the Ox," the message is unsatisfying nevertheless. More often "No one comes forth. Nothing steps / Into the underbrush or rises out of the frame," as in "Local Journal."[18]

Wright's imagination longs for divine visitations and divine interventions; yearning is a generative force in his poetry. The failure to be visited by any higher power practically achieves paradigmatic status in his work. His stopping short—his hesitancy, his refusal to release skepticism—is countered by his wish to be "battered" by God, as if only an

---

16. Bedient, "Tracing Charles Wright," p. 55.

17. Charles Wright, "Invisible Landscape," in *Country Music: Selected Early Poems*, 2d ed. (Hanover, N.H.: Wesleyan University Press, 1991), p. 134. Hereafter the title of this collection will be abbreviated as *CM*, and page numbers will be cited parenthetically in the text.

18. Charles Wright, "Local Journal," in *The World of the Ten Thousand Things: Poems 1980-1990* (New York: Farrar, Straus & Giroux, 1990), p. 229. Hereafter the title of this collection will be abbreviated as *WTT*, and page numbers will be cited parenthetically in the text.

extreme fleshly violation could release the self from doubt. His poems float above simple assertions, insisting on the inexplicable, while Wright cannot abandon himself to belief. That is, abandonment of self to God is a temptation that his poems resist—almost unsuccessfully. God in this scheme may seem a destroyer and Wright the penitent who wants to be "picked clean" by the divine. His characteristic wish for self-purification, even to the point of what appears to be self-obliteration (a desire that echoes John Donne and Gerard Manley Hopkins), is contrasted with Wright's secondary voice in "Clear Night." In this poem he would ask for a miracle, even while he finds himself stubbornly limited by rational imperative and material desire as in "T'ang Notebook": "Give me a sign, / show me the blessing pierced in my side" (*WTT*, 103). And yet, like Donne, he would be battered by his God in "Clear Night":

> I want to be bruised by God.
> I want to be strung up in a strong light and singled out.
> I want to be stretched, like music wrung from a dropped seed.
> I want to be entered and picked clean.
>
> And the wind says "What?" to me.
> And the castor beans, with their little earrings of death, say "What?" to me.
> And the stars start out on their cold slide through the dark.
> And the gears notch and the engines wheel.                    (*CM*, 152)

While the speaker wishes for a fleshly violation through the overwhelming energy of a higher power, the poem situates its spiritual cravings among natural emblems that in this context initially signal incredulity. Just the same, through the bemused question of the wind and the castor beans Wright suggests that the persona's desire is in some manner answered. His self-dispersal is put into effect at the moment of writing; his condition of existence is ultimately that of being "entered and picked clean" by forces of nature as they are energized by God's will and by the process of writing, which, for this poet, abrades certainty. For Wright, composing the poem proves a means to both record and act out the desire to be violated by divine force.

Perhaps precisely because of the destructive power that he attaches to deity, transcendence is feared by Wright, and perhaps even more feared than desired. A moment occurs in "A Journal of the Year of the Ox" that bespeaks a corollary anxiety to that of the anxiety that revolves for Wright around the failure of miraculous presence to emerge: that is, the poem registers horror at completion, a terror of being united with one's desires. In the twilight, with the voices of children near (a scene reminiscent of T. S. Eliot's "Little Gidding"), Wright's persona imagines ultimate transformation:

> The stone ball on the gate post, the snail shell in its still turning—
> Would burst into brilliance at my touch.

> But I sat still, and I touched nothing,
>
>                                   afraid that something might change
>
> And change me beyond my knowing. . . .

                                                   (*WTT*, 167)

He withdraws from a potentiality that threatens to absorb his identity. In this near visitation, the speaker is left with only the semblance of blazing attention. Such a scenario underscores the perceptions that we have entertained; yearning and yet doubtful, Wright prefers a posture betwixt and between the earthly and the transcendent. It is the pose to which he is accustomed and through which he most fully experiences the adventurous force of his own restless reverie.

What seems a near constant, despite or perhaps because of Wright's representations of desire for an ideal power, is his very attraction to images of disappearance. The image, for Wright, is of essential importance, and he has rightly been described by Charles Altieri as "a pure practitioner of the image."[19] Implicit in Wright's poetics of the image is a notion of the image's tenuousness: the image as revelatory of doubt, presence as paradoxical indicator of absence. "The image is always a mirror. Sometimes we see ourselves in it, and sometimes we don't." Although he has been allied with deep-image poetics, his aesthetic actually abrades the image, creating the effect of dissolving or dimming the visual field. His images hover between substance and immateriality. They are dominated by rippling or fading effects poising the images toward their own evaporation. Such images reflect his subject matter: "The image is always spiritual as it is beyond us, and analogous and seditious."[20] Unlike the deep-image poets, he does not rely on a battery of images that reflect a Jungian unconscious, but instead upon what Richard Tillinghast describes as "the dialectic between a philosophy that negates phenomena and a sensory keenness."[21] At times it is as if he is cutting free or burning his way through the rudimentary signals that lead us to establish any sort of primary visual ground. He is then a Penelope of the image, undoing what he has created and insisting on the radical instability of his images and, often enough, of the autobiographical self as reflected by images.

    The image as sign of time at work is particularly compelling to Wright. Aesthetically, he favors the glimpse of Eden, the paradise out of reach and thus hauntingly seductive. In many of his poems after the

---

19. Charles Altieri, *Self and Sensibility in Contemporary American Poetry* (Cambridge: Cambridge University Press, 1984), p. 49.

20. Charles Wright, "Halflife: A Commonplace Notebook," *FIELD* 36 (1987): 21.

21. Richard Tillinghast, "From 'An Elegist's New England, a Buddhist's Dante,'" in *The Point Where All Things Meet: Essays on Charles Wright,* ed. Tom Andrews (Oberlin, Ohio: Oberlin College Press, 1995), p. 197.

mid-1970s with their descending ladders of lines that allow for white space, slow turns or sudden descents, he reinforces through the poems' forms his thematic preoccupations with disintegrating natural and spiritual elements. He foils our notion of simple description, just as the voices in his lyric poems fluctuate between the earthly and the otherworldly, and embody his refusal to be "located" to the point where even his catalogs of landscape and weather, however meticulous, seem unearthly. "Wonder and awe must reside always in partial obscurity,"[22] he has written, and his attraction to descriptive opacity accounts for some of the challenge that his poems pose. Most often this challenge involves our registering evanescence in images that we are led in context to associate alternately with presence and absence. The poems forage in the past, haloed by loss and regret or—particularly in referring to Italy, site of Wright's "discovery" of poetry—a poignant nostalgia. His ruminations on such effects are infused with frequent sideways references to Asian philosophies and Asian poetry as well as to the vital significance of open space in painting:

> —Exclusion's the secret: what's missing is what appears
> Most visible to the eye:
> > the more luminous anything is,
> The more it subtracts what's around it. . . .
>
> > > > > > > > (*WTT*, 122)

In turn, the image of dust reappears frequently, an allusion to the biblical symbol of human ephemerality, but cast into contemporary scenes of desolation. In quoting Robert Hughes's discussion of the contemporary Italian painter Giorgio Morandi, Wright might have been describing his own aesthetic: "gradual permutations of experience, by insinuations that verge on monotony, as the color of dust will seem monotonous until you really look at it."[23]

A poet of changing optical effects, Wright connects the instability of images cast in words with images of light: "Looming and phosphorescent against the dark, / Words, always words" (*WTT*, 99). In "Cryopexy" (the title refers to "An operation to repair, by freezing with liquid Freon glass, a tear on the eye's retina"[24]) words are light and, in turn, selfhood is light-composed. Light and self, and the self composed of images in the poem, are jittery as cells under the microscope:

---

22. Charles Wright, "Improvisations on Pound," in *Halflife: Improvisations and Interviews, 1977-87* (Ann Arbor: University of Michigan Press, 1988), p. 15.

23. Charles Wright, "Giorgio Morandi," in *Halflife*, p. 7.

24. Charles Wright, "Notes," in *The Other Side of the River* (New York: Random House, 1984). Wright underwent this procedure in 1981, according to his *Quarter Notes*, p. 13.

One black, electric blot, blood-blown,
Vanishes like Eurydice
                    away from the light's mouth
And under the vitreous bulge of the eye's hill,
Down, O down, down . . .

(*WTT*, 100-101)

The lyric poet is thus an Orpheus who draws the Eurydice of the image toward the light, yet, no sooner than he looks back upon his work, must witness his images fading into darkness. The intractability of image and language—and self as language-composed—makes of the poem a Eurydice and each letter on the page, "one black, electric blot, blood-blown," and about to disappear. Blanchot is again suggestive in terms of Wright's preference for dissolving images in his poetry—particularly as his preference may prove resonant in connection with the myth of Orpheus and Eurydice:

> [I]f he [Orpheus] did not turn around to look at Eurydice, he still would be betraying, being disloyal to, the boundless and imprudent force of his impulse, which does not demand Eurydice in her diurnal truth and her everyday charm, but in her nocturnal darkness, in her distance, her body closed, her face sealed . . . not as the intimacy of a familiar life, but as the strangeness of that which excludes all intimacy; it does not want to make her live, but to have the fullness of her death living in her.[25]

Orpheus would play God; he would bring the dead to life again by means of his own miraculous powers to awaken sympathy and desire through his lyre. But Orpheus (and here we see one reason for Wright's favoring of the figure) fails; like so many of Wright's speakers he is fated to balance between life and death. While he works for the ultimate realization of his desires, Orpheus is destined to be denied, particularly through his impatience and lack of faith—and his anxious intellect that translates presence into absence.

The desire that Blanchot finds in the myth of Orpheus duplicates in a complex way Wright's desire for a death-inhabited poetry and for images, and self-portraits, that seemingly dissipate. Of the image, Blanchot suggestively argues: "Where there is nothing, that is where the image finds its condition, but disappears into it. The image requires the neutrality and the effacement of the world, it wants everything to return to the indifferent depth where nothing is affirmed, it inclines toward the intimacy of what still continues to exist in the void; its truth lies there."[26] In a manner that echoes Blanchot's formulation, Wright disrupts his own images, insisting on creating a sequence of images that are about to be

---

25. Maurice Blanchot, "The Gaze of Orpheus," in *Gaze of Orpheus*, p. 100.
26. Maurice Blanchot, "Two Versions of the Imaginary" in *Gaze of Orpheus*, p. 79.

released from materiality. His images of ascension and his common prac-
tice of using verbals that refer to rising actions are met almost relentlessly
with images of falls, dissipations, and dissolves. It is as if when Wright
turns to presence he is impelled, like Orpheus, to send what he has dis-
covered back into the underworld of the unconscious and to inculcate in
readers an obscure sense of loss.

Given the tendency of his poetry to create impressions of emptiness and
silence, what human presence could penetrate Wright's poetry? As many
of his readers observe, hardly so much as a single dominant human other
is fully cast as a complete living personality in his poetry. Wright's epi-
graph to *Country Music*—"The country was always better than the
people" (from Hemingway)—underscores his work as an unpeopled
poetry that favors its landscapes more than any potential for describing
human relationship. Persons pass through the poems anecdotally, often as
solitaries, as fellow alert observers, or as the mysterious dead. Frequently
they are engendered into a typology or apotheosized. The poems effect
an ultimate faith in language conducted with little human contact and
most often with attentiveness to catalogs of invented divines or veiled ab-
stractions—Sister of Mercies, Our Lady of Knoxville, Madonna of
Tenderness and Lady of Feints and Xs. Such names pinpoint irreality
more often than human presence. As in Wallace Stevens's poetry, place
conveys more meaning than any personality other than the poet's. As
such, Wright's musings are almost unrelievedly solitary. He passes along
the peripheries of relationship, and even his relationship with the reader,
which might seem more open to the suggestion of intimacy, is troubled
by the impression of solitude. For many readers, the experience of read-
ing Wright is like that of overhearing a lone mind ruminating to itself.
The work most often avoids presenting direct personal interchanges with
others. That is, Wright enacts a poetry of religious sentiment in which
any potential encounter with divinity is more sought after and reflected
upon than is mortal presence. Indeed, his poems may seem so often un-
peopled (even when listing names) in part because he prefers to pursue
underworld spirits and, in connection with them, intimations about land-
scape and language as they have been inherited from and channeled to us
by those who are now themselves dead. The dead form a "culture" of
sorts for him, a culture that affects current phenomena.

In their tropes, their very catalogs, on being and nonbeing, in the spiri-
tual lure of silence and darkness, Wright's poems bear an unmistakable sig-
nature. More often than most of his contemporaries, he is a poet of the list,
practicing a conjoining of things as if he were mounting evidence of some
sort. Unlike his contemporary James Tate, whose catalogs suggest spiraling
(even if sometimes comic) desperation, Wright composes sequences of im-
ages that point quietly to otherworldly forms. His accumulation of often
exquisite imagistic catalogs represents one of the most compelling in-
stances of a contemporary poet uniting his sense of autobiography with his

sense of language and, in turn, with his facility with the image. His fluent, seductive, mysterious images that hover as if about to evaporate reflect Wright's need to escape identity in the quixotic processes of writing: "I write poems to untie myself, to do penance and disappear" (*CM*, 141).

Wright has been referred to as a particularly difficult poet to paraphrase or describe, as Helen Vendler observes: "Because Wright's poems, on the whole, are unanchored to incident, they resist description; because they are not narrative, they defy exposition. They cluster, aggregate, radiate, add layers like pearls."[27] We may note that in Vendler's description, Wright's poems are essentially cumulative. We should note however, that the poems, as we have seen, also "shed," discarding what they gather and pursuing, in Wallace Stevens's terms, "Nothing that is not there and the nothing that is." Indeed, at times, images of divesting become nearly prescriptive.

Despite Wright's imagistic and thematic focus on shedding preconceptions and on "unlearning," he emphasizes the necessity of repeating his questions about the nature of divinity, as in "Dog Day Vespers": "I'm writing you now by flashlight, / The same news and the same story I've told you often before" (*WTT*, 32). Or more comically elsewhere: "There is so little to say, and so much time to say it in" (*WTT*, 72). Repetition of many sorts—of images, scenarios, statements and questions—is not only a signature device, an identifiable stylistic and conceptual element in his poetry, but, to literalize the term, repetition appears imagistically as self-inscription: "You've got to sign your name to something, it seems to me. / And so we rephrase the questions / Endlessly, / hoping the answer might somehow change" (*WTT*, 60).

In his eagerness to repeat essential scenarios, Wright's poems revisit the seductions of his introduction to poetry. He has written often of his initial encounter with poetry in spring 1959 as a twenty-four-year-old serviceman who read Ezra Pound's verse at Lake Garda while stationed in Italy. His textual "encounter" is a meeting not only with poetry but with nature, setting in motion his later preoccupation with the relationship between word and nature—and with Pound as poetic influence. By detailing Pound's influence on his own work in interviews, essays, and poems, Wright recaptures the first enchantments of his discovery of poetry and focuses on his preference for moving abruptly between luminous images, a preference reflecting not only the impact of his early close reading of *The Pisan Cantos* but his first perceptions of the Italian landscape. After his discovery of Pound (a discovery of poetry as Pound, poetry as Italy, poetry as Italy-and-Pound) he attempted for two years "to

---

27. Helen Vendler, "Charles Wright: The Transcendent 'I,'" *Part of Nature, Part of Us: Modern American Poets* (Cambridge: Harvard University Press, 1980), p. 277.

rewrite" *The Cantos*.[28] His attempt is telling, evoking a neophyte's urge for imitation and his immense youthful confidence.

Surely his desire to retrace and reassess Pound as a poetic father must have been both dangerous and ideal. Dangerous because of Pound's fanatical ideology, his acknowledged megalomania, his late silences. And certainly Pound's forbidding edifice of knowledge and linguistic training must have seemed intimidating. And yet ideal, perhaps for precisely some of those same reasons: Pound not only offered an aesthetic method for emulation, a method that makes capacious use of allusion and language fragmentation, but his seemingly endless lacunae—part of the very fabric of *The Cantos*—presented an enabling strategy that amounted to an echo of Wright's imminent spiritual practices. In turn, Pound's aesthetic technique of assembling fragments, including diverse voices, is duplicated by Wright in his approach to self-identity as well as in his approach to the text; Wright avoids Pound's tragically corrupting political and social certainties by extending fragmentation to representations of his own personae. Doubt of authorial mastery plagues—and humbles—Wright. "Sometimes I erase so much I tear a hole in the paper" he notes in an interview in which he remarks on Pound's influence on his work.[29] His observation about his own vigorous erasing is recounted with both humor and pride, reflecting self-revision and continuing ambition. The act of tearing a hole in paper by erasing becomes analogous to an effect he seeks through words; he would break through a tissue of language and of materiality itself to suggest that which escapes language. He would insinuate that whatever resists material inscription resists critical accommodation.

In Wright's early poetry, Pound is cast as the "cold-blooded father of light." Like his Odysseus of *The Cantos*, Pound awaits his "voyage" into death, a voyage much like many that Wright will situate at his poems' borders:

> Here is your caul and caustic,
> Here is your garment,
> Cold-blooded father of light—
> Rise and be whole again.        (*CM*, 12)

Surely here is Wright's wish for the psychic resurrection of Pound, employed in the poem as a strategy of closure that works off the trope of

---

28. Wright, "An Interview with Charles Wright," interview by Sherod Santos, *Missouri Review* 10.1 (1987): 75.

29. Charles Wright, "Metaphysics of the Quotidian: A Conversation with Charles Wright," in *The Post-Confessionals: Conversations with American Poets of the Eighties*, ed. Earl G. Ingersoll, Judith Kitchen, and Stan Sanvel Rubin (Rutherford, N.J.: Fairleigh Dickinson University Press, 1989), p. 35.

ascension. Yet it is telling that the poem's symbolic natural forces speak against the desire of the speaker, for natural orders in the poem are undergoing disruption and dissolution, marking as such Wright's ambivalence.

Perhaps what attracted Wright to Pound was not only Pound's bold assemblage of materials and brisk movement without ligature between images, although Wright is more cohesive than Pound and limits his range of references, but his own perception of silence in Pound as much as speech. In "Improvisations on Pound," Wright narrates an anecdote that he heard from the critic David Kalstone. The anecdote may shed light on Wright's reasons for focusing so often on Pound as influence (Pound's name is tied to virtually all of Wright's self-accounts regarding his development as a poet):

> The only light seemed to gather on Pound's hands, he [Kalstone] said, everything else and everyone else in a kind of elusive, watery darkness, and throughout the time they sat there—while Pound apparently spoke, but inaudibly, his comments being repeated each time by Olga Rudge—Pound kept scratching at the back of one hand with the nails of the other, clawing almost, over and over, as though to rid himself of something: only the hands obsessively scratching in the artificial light, the voice inaudible and sibylline.[30]

In retelling Kalstone's story, Wright makes Pound a figure of the sibyl or prophet, failed but portentous. Pound is "inaudible," and yet his body confesses feeling, his gestures, perhaps at least in conventional terms, revealing a desire to purify or to "erase." Thus Wright gives Pound a curious ritualistic and divinatory status, a sort of aged unreality, as if the elder poet were the Sibyl of Cumae evoked in Eliot's epigraph to *The Waste Land*. Here Wright affords Pound the elaborate trappings of mysticism, trappings that seem more appropriate to Eliot than to Pound. (Eliot's issues—among them, the path between flesh and spirit and their point of possible meeting—are more clearly Wright's own than are Pound's historical and economic themes.) But perhaps it is the late Pound's silences and even his errors (Wright views *The Cantos* as "the most interesting failure of the century") that make him ultimately fascinating for Wright, and something of a renewable resource. Wright views Pound as a mysterious figure who cannot ultimately be known. Such a characterization is deeply attractive, for it echoes Wright's own conception of the elusive transcendent. And tracking the elusive transcendent has been the most generative pursuit for Wright as a poet. Indeed, Pound's practice of omission and Pound's status, for Wright, as an "omission" of sorts—an obscured figure of large gestures—are provocative. The elder poet's scope and ambition are

---

30. Wright, "Improvisations on Pound," p. 19.

certainly of great interest to Wright, who himself is ambitious and prolific, with a wide-ranging intelligence and a readerly sensibility. Of *The Cantos*, Wright observes, "[Pound] never finished the poem, it was abandoned"[31] —a statement that might reflect Wright's recognition of the inevitably un-completable nature of his own project.

Beyond Pound, Wright's influences are numerous and he points to them readily. He has absorbed some of Dante and the influence of such figures as Hopkins, Yeats, Hart Crane, and Montale (whom he has translated) to the point that no one influence predominated even by his early midca-reer. Complicating the issue of influence, Wright frequently has noted his affinity with Emily Dickinson, whom he makes rather an inhuman fig-ure—somewhat as he does Pound. "One has to imagine that Emily Dickinson was inhabited. How else could she know those things?" he asks.[32] While Wright's tendency is to somewhat laboriously render Pound as a quasi mystic, Dickinson comes more conveniently as a nearly ready-made mystic of sorts. In a "Journal of the Year of the Ox" he de-scribes his visit to the Dickinson mansion in Amherst, Massachusetts. In the poem, his persona looks through a window as he assumes Dickinson must have, noting details of weather and landscape, an isolated activity of observation that is familiar to us from many of Wright's poems. Although the speaker wishes that it would appear, the ghost of Dickinson does not make itself known. But the speaker registers an affection for the place where she lived, and he nearly ascertains a Dickinson-like presence until his name is called, apparently by his friends who have been waiting for him in the downstairs hallway. The quiet activities detailed in the poem are Wright's passions: intense observation and listening, a fruitless (but somehow nearly rapturous) waiting for a sign of sorts. As this scenario suggests, it may be as profitable an exercise to consider his affinities to Dickinson as to Pound, in that his poems, like Dickinson's, experiment with spiritual belief. Both Wright and Dickinson's metaphysical questions focus on much the same provisions, and both reveal an urge toward tran-scendence coupled with skepticism. His approach, similar to Dickinson's, is that of an investigatory doubter steeped in the language of religious ritual and yet passionate for the diurnal. Both poets are grounded in a keen sense of place and view paradox as endemic to language. For Wright, as his poems enclosing the figures of Pound or Dickinson sug-gest, any literary forebear is a compressed visual notation figured as a light source—a source of illumination within language. Each literary fig-ure (for whom Pound and Dickinson serve as essential prototypes) is

---

31. Ibid., p. 15.

32. Wright, "Halflife: A Commonplace Notebook," p. 28.

nevertheless finally "unreachable," a sort of departing light from which he might finally detect only faint traces of the otherworldly. With his "divines," literary or otherwise, any approximation of salvation lies in approach rather than in arrival, as in "Homage to Arthur Rimbaud":

> —Desperate to attempt
> An entrance, to touch that light
> Which buoys you like a flame, . . .
>
> We cluster about your death
> As though it were reachable.                        (*CM*, 13)

Most often the summoned literary representative is already "risen" in this poetry, and literature is imaged as a possible means of ascension into a realm beyond suffering and loss. Yet the trope in this work is that of rising toward disappearance, an ascension out of sight, in a phosphorescent after-image or after-path. The literary figure is not only one who disappears but one who leaves behind in his or her poems emblems of absence.

In interviews and essays Wright is forthcoming about his aesthetic techniques. For Wright, the "odd marriage" of Dickinson and Whitman, the leisurely breadth of Whitman melded with the gnomic, imagistic units of Dickinson, must be conjoined.[33] His lines are built progressively, but each is meant to detain the reader, creating a discrete moment of intensity within the greater event of the poem. The line is most often speculative, pulling language forward into ever-widening conjectures. As such, the poet defeats the premature impulse toward closure:

> if one of the primary urges of a work of art is to become circular and come to a completion, then one of the real jobs of the artist is to keep the closure from happening so he can work in the synapse, the spark before the end.[34]

Such a forfeiture of "arrival," refusing a collapse into readily accessible meaning, echoes the deferred spiritual meetings that his speakers undergo. An imagistic openness, a renunciation of firm coloring-in and, often, of narrative continuity, is characteristic of his aesthetic. Similarly, his poems would be stripped of connectives, exfoliating gradually in a way that Wright has connected to his heritage as a Southerner: "A

---

33. See Wright's comments about the influence of Emily Dickinson and Walt Whitman on his work: "Improvisations on Form and Measure," p. 21.
34. Wright, "Improvisations on Pound," p. 15.

tendency toward the romantic, an identification with language as opposed to what we think of as nature, a desire to subtract rather than add, a liking for lushness in a spare context."[35]

It may be our impression of Wright's poems as emptying out or un-folding themselves, bearing wavering traces of meaning, that is peculiarly affecting. His change of style in the late 1970s occurs as a form of spatializing, an extension of the poem's boundaries as if they were the body's boundaries—as if even his self-representations would radiate outward eventually to occupy the place of his longed-for ideal. That is, the hide-and-seek with God enacted in so many of his poems is also a hide-and-seek with selfhood and identity, as reflected in the poems' spatial structures, which allow for delayed completion and "empty" white space. Wright structures his poems through definition by negation, un-doing or reversing effects he has laboriously set up. He favors paradox and logical reversals ("I find myself in my own image, and am neither and both" [WTT, 168]), rhetorical devices that are prominent in both his prose and his poetry.

For Wright, a change in style reflects a change in the imagination of selfhood. In one of the most convincing arguments about Wright's poetry, James McCorkle calls Wright's work "an autobiography of energy and transmutation, where the self's writing collaborates with the natural world's writing."[36] With McCorkle's words in mind, it is instructive to compare Wright's emblematic natural images to those of Louise Glück. In her fifth book, The Wild Iris (1992), Glück gives voice to nature to represent human vulnerability and bafflement. Wright, in opposition, makes nature a voiceless accompaniment whose "actions"—the movement of foliage in wind, any natural response to seasonal change—resonate with his own philosophic musings. Wright composes the parable of the pepper tree or the oleander as nature's reflection of what the poems relentlessly state: destruction accompanies the appearance of order. Yet when symbols of nature counter a death instinct in the work, they do so only peripherally and momentarily. One of the curious effects of this work is that particulars of the natural world, however seemingly in close focus, dissipate amid the meditations that Wright outlines. Nature is beaded, worked over, and references to it are drawn from art, particularly from painting and music, as if Wright's nature is illustrated. He conveys physical relationship and movement in artful "unworldliness," moving the natural into the realms of art and the supernatural.

The Southern Cross (1981) retains its special status in Wright's work, embodying conflicting pressures most intensely. It is marked by traces of

---

35. Wright, "An Interview with Charles Wright" (Santos), p. 90.

36. James McCorkle, The Still Performance: Writing, Self, and Interconnection in Five Postmodern American Poets (Charlottesville: University Press of Virginia, 1989), p. 172.

some of the blocklike imagistic density that he perfected in his previous four books. In addition, it reveals, with all the viscerality of discovery, an emerging aesthetic as he restructures his poems, particularly by loosening syntax and rhythms and extending line lengths. In *The Southern Cross* he infuses his poems with more casual moments than in his earlier books, creating a recognizable first person and narrative sequences that encompass a varied rhetorical range. The associations we bring to the book's title, conjuring not only the constellation but Wright's birthplace in Tennessee and his partial allegiance to a Southern Christian sensibility, announce that the astronomical and the salvific—and the torture of the cross—authorize the volume. But the book also allows us to make associations with the cross as a meeting point, and the cross as exit and bar, denying entry. The cross reflects his historical position, "crossed," in his metaphor, by the Episcopalianism of big youth, by a propensity for the Southern tall tale, and by a dearly acquired worldliness that threatens to cast spiritual belief as simple superstition.

The book opens with the eight-page paean "Homage to Paul Cézanne," composed as if to a ghost identity. The poem poses the questions: What can we do with the dead, and what can the dead do with us? The dead for Wright become an artistic medium, almost wholly aestheticized, just as the self for Wright turns into an artifact of writing. The dead are figured as paintlike or textual, revealing something to us of the future, as if writing were this poet's Ouija board with which he contacts the spirits of his own departed: "They point to their favorite words / Growing around them, revealed as themselves for the first time" (*WTT*, 4). The dead "dust over" nature with their dry essences and rise to request remembrance, even as Wright refers to them as artful materials, moving them into color, to "spread them," "layer them," "[c]ircle and smudge, cross-beak and buttonhook" them (*WTT*, 6). The dead in the opening section of *The Southern Cross* are aesthetic stand-ins; what they assume, the writer assumes:

> Like us, they refract themselves. Like us,
> They keep on saying the same thing, trying to get it right.
> Like us, the water unsettles their names.
>
> (*WTT*, 3)

However gently, the dead also camouflage and violate their living hosts. As Bruce Bond provocatively asserts of the poem, "Through the dead's eyes, we are the transcendent." "Homage to Paul Cézanne" and many other of Wright's poems aim to allow us to "see ourselves this way as well, made expansive and unfamiliar in the world mirror."[37] This

---

37. Bruce Bond, "Metaphysics of the Image in Charles Wright and Paul Cézanne," *Southern Review* 30, no. 2 (1994): 121.

conceptual move noted by Bond is fascinating; Wright would have us view ourselves as the dead might: as suddenly strange, as "transcendent" in Bond's formulation—a formulation that makes palpable the very uncanniness of the way this poet inhabits and deploys language. As David St. John notes: "It is as if many of Wright's poems keep seeking some ideogrammatic form"[38]—and spatializing their arguments, it seems to me, by conveying the auditory quality of poetry into the visual field.

In "Tracing Charles Wright" Calvin Bedient notes that for Wright "revelation came early and has remained unsparing: it is that the dead, who are superior to us, who know more and feel more, are always near us."[39] Of Wright, Bedient says, "No one more medieval, more communal in his relation to the dead."[40] Wright's position over time has become increasingly ambivalent, registering a desire for the presence of the dead and nevertheless an obtrusive disbelief in regard to their presence. The self-extinction that menaces his personae is mirrored in his fear of total extinction of not only physical life but spiritual intimations.

"Homage to Paul Cézanne" prefaces a series of self-portraits in *The Southern Cross* that further suggest, as we shall see, Wright's sense of life-forms as being inhabited by death. His self-portraits tend to emphasize mortality, and they make the self "strange" to the self. His most focused renderings of the self-portrait in *The Southern Cross* were preceded early in his career by "Dog Creek Mainline" from *Hard Freight*, a poem that Wright credits with teaching him the possibilities inherent in autobiographical poems. "Dog Creek Mainline" opens with a visual and olfactory catalog. A sense of place widens in memory and allows Wright to reenvision and requestion stages of identity as the self is inevitably surrounded and defined by place. Places take on bodily meaning, a blood knowledge, and each part of the body that is mentioned in the poem—heart, ear, eye, and tongue—is mirrored in the environment. Certainly the experience of writing the poem taught Wright that autobiography could be flexibly cast through elements of landscape that intimate spiritual desire in the abstract. The natural world is translated for spiritual notation, and the self not only identifies with nature but is made into an element of nature. In consequence, the self is not "confessed," not personalized in daily action, but consecrated by the poet's observant sensibility ranging over his natural environment. In an interview, Wright cautions about the factual references of his seemingly autobiographical poems: "[M]ost all of the stories that come out in my poems are things that not necessarily happened to me but I would like to have had

---

38. St. John, Foreword to *County Music*, p. xviii.
39. Bedient, "Tracing Charles Wright," p. 55.
40. Ibid., p. 58.

happen to me."[41] For a poet so deeply—indeed, almost obsessively—attracted to transformation, he fears that the actual self may be stubbornly untransformative:

> It just suddenly occurred to me that there is a moment when what you are is what you're going to be. You will not be able to alter yourself. You have already made yourself into what you are. That time comes at different ages for everyone. Mine came in the fifth grade when I realized that I was the onlooker. . . . I was the person who was always doing the observing. This has continued in my life to this day.[42]

Despite his references to personal transformation in many of his poems, Wright suggests that there is no escape from the self. Certainly some of his poems attend to faith in a polyspiritual web of nature, even as his spiritual hunt for meaning erases conceptual origins; for Wright, reality seems to evade any vision of a founding moment or a central source of meaning. Yet he sees himself as a poet haunted by the limited, unconvertible, unchanging self, a self that relentlessly observes itself: "The past is the one mirror that never releases its images. Layer and overlay, year after year, wherever you look, however you look, whenever you look, it's always your own face you see there. All those years, and it's still your own face."[43]

Before *The Southern Cross* Wright had dealt with the autobiographical impulse almost systematically by centering on isolated incidents that defined key aspects of his past. In "Tattoos," from *Bloodlines*, events inscribed deeply upon his psyche are crystallized through images dense with implications. Such spiritualized and aestheticized blocks of memory deal with the death of his mother and father, religious ceremonies, and encounters in Italian cities. His ultimate objective in this series seems to be to project psychological condensations rather than psychological confessions. The series of twenty poems, largely cast in present tense, is ordered in a way that allows him to mark, to make an imprint upon, the language as he himself was deeply affected by each event. In such poems, the past is seductive but only illusorily capturable. At best it may be evoked, for instance, through a sequence of place names, and thus the self, which Wright fears may be limited and static, is rendered suggestively elusive.

Wright's desire to recall the past and to trace the outlines of a self is countered by another strain in his poems: he would unsettle a localized

---

41. Charles Wright, quoted in Joseph Parisi, "Charles Wright," in *Poets in Person: A Listener's Guide* (Chicago: Modern Poetry Association, 1992), p. 149.

42. Ibid., p. 151.

43. Charles Wright, "Bytes and Pieces," in *Quarter Notes*, p. 83.

self, unmastering identity in language by writing toward the transcendent (just as God, whether approached through language, or landscape, is similarly "not in place"). His poems' instability, insisting that no one meaning be settled upon and refusing closure, would oppose the paralyzed and limited self. For Wright, while the same known face greets his in the mirror daily, ultimately self-representation is an impossibility of sorts—which may account, oddly enough, for his attraction to poems professing self-portraiture; he has always been a poet attracted to the impossible. Echoing Jorge Luis Borges, he writes by way of preface to *Country Music*:

> It has been suggested that all forms possess their virtue in themselves and not in any conjectural content. I don't entirely agree with this, but I do believe such a statement contains more truth than falsehood. It has also been suggested—again by Jorge Luis Borges—that everything a man writes, in the end, traces the outlines of his own face. I find it has been that way with me.[44]

Wright consciously aims toward a tracery of the self, an outline, rather than filled-in portraiture, as if "Form tends toward its own dissolution" (*WTT*, 208), including the dissolution of the autobiographical center.

Given his fondness for peripheral and fleeting images and his preference for abbreviated anecdotes about the self, it is perhaps surprising that few contemporary poets have placed the self-portrait under such sustained and yet ironic focus. "The poem is a self-portrait / always, no matter what mask / You take off and put back on" (*WTT*, 97). If every poem is a self-portrait, poems actually titled self-portraits reflexively point to lyric selfhood as plural and shifting, and capable of continual reframing. In another context he refers to autobiography as "a kind of minus tide that runs just under everything and adds by subtraction."[45] He has proven attentive to the project of presenting a self not only aware of mortality but given to the rehearsal of its own death—as if to dislodge threatening conceptions of an overly defined, limited self, harnessed by its recognizable social identity. Notably, the lyric poet is a "self-traitor" to one voice; the lyric self must "smuggle in" devices that affront simplicity (*WTT*, 21). The self-portrait by Wright enacts an identification between self and language: the self's insufficiencies and the language's, yes, but also the proliferating energy of language that may be discovered by contemplating selfhood.

In his midcareer Wright draws increasing attention to the lyrical first person, self-referentially language-made, for he recognizes poetry as his integral route of knowing. Poetry "is the one boat . . . that's going to get

---

44. Charles Wright, Preface to *Country Music*, p. xxiii.
45. Charles Wright, "The Art of Poetry XLI," p. 205.

me across the river," he told Elizabeth McBride.[46] He remains less distrustful of images cast in language than enamored of the multiplicity of meaning that they make possible. He asks for "A little vowel for the future, a signal from us to them" (*WTT*, 18). In another turn, "Language can do just so much, / a flurry of prayers, / A chatter of glass beside the road's edge, / Flash and a half-glint as the headlights pass" (*WTT*, 20). In such tropes, language is likened to the scene of an accident; words appears to us in sudden, brief, and puzzlingly partial illuminations. Nevertheless, this "just so much" remains a great deal, for the ephemerality of effects, the referential slide of language, its "flurry," "chatter," and "flash," become the motions he chooses most consistently to describe, the visual incidents that he finds most appealing and that most closely approximate his experience of being.

Five forays into a way of saying "I" in the second section of *The Southern Cross* suggest that Wright hopes to make the first-person pronoun excessive, transcending physical and cultural limits. For this poet, the language of poetry is a way of both making and unmaking selfhood, a means of singing selves into and out of being, of assembling bits of memory and abandoning preconceptions about their meaning. His five fifteen-line poems titled "Self-Portrait" in *The Southern Cross* attempt to make the self estranged to the self through repetition; that is, like a familiar word that has been repeated until it seems odd to us, the self-portraits in this series attempt a defamiliarizing perspective. That the poems are interrupted by longer, more anecdotal pieces further intensifies our awareness of discontinuous identities. Wright offers his characteristic devices of self-examination—lists of places, photographs, landscapes, prayers, and lyric poets—to move toward a self inhabited by "the ghost-weight" of the once-forgotten dead. He reemphasizes the nature of language as his ostensible subject, for the portrait in words becomes a portrait of words.

Wright's first self-portrait in *The Southern Cross* prefigures his last in formulating a prayer of deliverance from a simple stable self in favor of a self capable of enlarging its sympathy. In Wright's series the self would be a fugitive from certainty, about to be "rearranged":

> From the mulch and the undergrowth, protect me and pass me on.
> From my own words and my certainties,
> From the rose and the easy cheek, deliver me, pass me on.

The first portrait is unremittingly self-focused; its speaker, being "found out," will "hum to [him]self," meditating on the present moment, the

---

46. Charles Wright, "An Interview" (McBride), p. 129.

passivity of plants, and the place he occupies. But this contemplation of nature is interrupted by Wright's characteristic prayerlike plea: a petition against self-complacency, against the sort of vegetal passivities that lie in wait for him, against, that is, what seem to be his instincts for preserving his own ego. "The ashes and bits of char that will clear my name" (*WTT*, 11) not only suggest the extinction of identity in death, but insinuate that death is a release from the limitation of being and from an initially unspecified sin. This unnamed sin seems, in context, to be that of complacency, indifference, and self-satisfaction. Wright thus opens the series by expressing the hope to be "unfixed" and absolved of blame.

In the second self-portrait the self and textuality are united, yet being and writing make absence curiously almost tangible. Investigating the self as if it were a text, Wright looks with detachment at this "Charles," this "infinite alphabet of his past." "The wind will edit him soon enough," he predicts of his "earmarked" persona. His speaker, "Holding the pages of a thrownaway book" (*WTT*, 13), is ever aware of his own transience as a creature of words and redaction, and he would seem to fade into his own text.

From verbal images, Wright moves on to photographic images. His third self-portrait reflects "camera range" in images of Wright's father and brother. Of course, the future of the photographer's subjects is known by the one holding the photograph. And in this small act of holding the photograph and knowing the fate of its subjects, it is possible for the speaker to feel (at least momentarily) almost a God-like foreknowledge. Wright sharpens the irony of assuming such inflated knowledge by insisting on ignorance of his own future. Static representations are "evidence" that Wright regards only as suggestive pointers:

> Checking the evidence, the postcards and the photographs,
> O'Grady's finger pointing me out . . .
>
> Madonna of Tenderness, Lady of Feints and Xs, you point too.
>
> (*WTT*, 16)

He juxtaposes the human specificity of O'Grady with the otherworldly divines of woe and ephemeral effects. Two pointings, O'Grady's and the Madonna of Tenderness's, earthly and otherworldly, must be engaged if life and death, earth and spirit, are to form a more complete iconography.

Furthering his investigation, the fourth self-portrait calls up lyric poets of the past. Whitman is engaged at the poem's start, along with a list of places and dead literary figures. This self-portrait makes memory elastic, moving back in time by two decades and projecting a self as dust and evaporate, a ghostlier self than has so far appeared in his self-portrait series. At the poem's conclusion, Wright supplicates a literary pantheon: "Dino Campana, Arthur Rimbaud. / Hart Crane and Emily Dickinson.

The Black Château" (*WTT*, 19). While we think of catalogs as most fre-
quently centering on presence, Wright introduces his own sequence of
names of dead literary figures to point up spiritual absences.

Each of the self-portraits in *The Southern Cross* that we have discussed
provides an account that is explicitly partial, preparing for and augment-
ing the fifth self-portrait as it extends from a localized persona's early past
toward communal impulse. What begins as the most rooted of portraits
and the most straightforward in syntax moves toward the language of
communal need. In the final portrait in this series, Wright depicts a spir-
itual presence as an "undoer and rearranger." Moreover, this persona is
further inhabited, "the ghost-weight of a past life in my arms, / A life not
mine." The self is inhabited by the dead, here a feminine imploring fig-
ure of ill fortune. This counterself, an interior ghost, is herself engaged in
Wright's characteristic pose of expectancy, "still waiting to rise." The
speaker's self is permeable, inhabited by the dead and by the "evening
[that] becomes us." The dead figure seems like a lover, yet Wright wishes
for a note of commonality toward the living: "Hold hands, hold hands /
That when the birds start, none of us is missing. / Hold hands, hold
hands" (*WTT*, 21). The series ends as a lyric evocation for contact before
absolute loss. The final cry, "hold hands," enacts a new patterning; to hold
hands is to make a physical human design. The lyric "I" comes closer to
a "we," a communal singing.

According to Northrop Frye, "The lyric is the genre in which the
poet, like the ironic writer, turns his back on his audience."[47] Wright
seems to have had his back to readers in this series of self-portraits, and
yet finally and surprisingly moves away from the solitary meditative
mode to create the illusion of emerging before an audience. Breaking out
of his meditation, he suddenly assumes communion with the invitation
"Hold hands."

What, then, is the self-portrait for Wright? Representations of self-
hood become ways of questioning traditional means of saying "I" and as-
suming social identity by insisting on nonbeing, a "ghost-weight," the
perception of immateriality in selfhood. The lyric poet is like that per-
sonage whom the poet calls "the spider love," an "undoer and re-
arranger," making a network of presence and absence. Inevitably no
self-portrait is adequate, for the project of representing an ultimate inte-
gral self in language must elude us. To compose such a self-portrait in
words is eventually to make a cry not only outward toward a gallery of
spiritual guides but finally, however tentatively, to a human community
united by awareness of death. The "I" emerges as a simile of sorts, a bridge
toward other presences, those ghosts of nonbeing as well as those

---

47. Northrop Frye, *Anatomy of Criticism: Four Essays* (Princeton: Princeton
University Press, 1957), p. 271.

O'Gradys of the flesh. As Wright suggests, "The 'I' persona that I often use in my poems is not, I hope, the 'merely personal' I of so many poems that one sees. I hope it does go through a kind of sea-change into the richness of the impersonal, where the true and touchable personal actually lives."[48]

Throughout a poetry that examines the lyric first person as a precarious text of sorts, Wright enacts his awareness of the difficulty for the contemporary poet who writes in the first person. That he does so has been an occasion for discomfort for some critics, a discomfort that X. J. Kennedy voiced in reviewing Wright: "He is serious, unafraid, and a master of intelligent music. Perhaps theme, and Tennessee, will yet weight him and steady him down."[49] Kennedy's is an eloquent wish, but one that ignores Wright's essential project, which disavows a "weighted" self or central wholeness in favor of selves that move between extremes. Wright prefers to flicker imagistically between Tennessee and Italy, the natural and the artificial, rising and falling, the living and the dead, rather than to alight and "steady" himself. For Wright, to make a self-portrait in "a language where nothing stays" is to ride, however disconcertingly, upon a wavelike knowledge of appearance and disappearance.

That Wright's self-portrait series finally broadens, even if briefly, toward the suggestion of communal chant suggests the permeability of his lyric selves as well as a recognition of his audience. "No one is listening," Wright concludes section 9 of an early series of poems. That someone now might indeed be listening Wright seems to presume within the more intimate tone of his work after *China Trace*. Helen Vendler, writing of his early work, describes Wright's as "the poetry of the transcendent 'I' in revolt against the too easily articulate 'I' of social engagement and social roles. Whether one 'I' can address his word to other hidden 'I's' across the abyss of daily life without using the personal, transient, and social language of that life is the question Wright poses."[50] In work after the late 1970s, however, he presents the self less as the transcendent "I" and more as an "I" willing to rehearse death even while scaling various ranges of selfhood. The recording of transience has clearly become his project. He acknowledges a way of writing selves into and out of being, crossing gaps, executing self-portraits as testing measures of identity. "It's synaptical here, / And rearranged" (*WTT*, 114), he tells us of his poems, in which abandonments and disappearances are cast in a vocabulary of ascents and descents. This lyric mode liquefies boundaries between past and present and being and nonbeing. The first-person inconclusive, a

48. Wright, "An Interview with Charles Wright" (Santos), p. 85.

49. X. J. Kennedy, "A Tenth and Four Fifths," review of *The Southern Cross*, by Charles Wright, *Poetry* 141 (1983): 358.

50. Vendler, *Part of Nature, Part of Us*, p. 288.

"traitor" to simple identity, becomes the first-person plural in Wright. Posing both evaporations and new gatherings, these self-portraits would allow us to imagine the projected loss of any singular identity, as Wright reimagines selfhood as unfinished and "lavish."

Wright further defines his position in "Gate City Breakdown," a poem unusual for Wright, for it is more openly conversational, less narratively "rearranged" than many of his lyrics of the same period. His speaker describes speeding in a car with other Tennessee boys. As a self-portrait, the poem makes certain claims on us even while seeming to efface its speaker:

> Jesus, it's so ridiculous, and full of self-love,
> The way we remember ourselves,
>
>                     and the dust we leave . . .
>
> Remember me as you will, but remember me once
> Slide-wheeling around the curves,
>
>            letting it out on the other side of the line.
>
>                                 (*WTT*, 40)

By "letting it out on the other side of the line," Wright focuses in the vernacular on his fluency with the line break (he is surely one of our contemporary masters) and, more important, suggests that he would present himself as a poet escaping the universal sheriff of law and order, running his aesthetic "moonshine" across the borders of poetic convention.

The prominence of vertical motion throughout Wright's work bears further on this issue of establishing and dissolving private selfhood and public identity through language. Wright charts a self in continual motion or in irreal suspension between dramatic alternatives. Ascending, descending, rising, falling: these participles appear frequently in Wright's work, early and late. It seems clear that his focus on descent is not simply a conventional metaphor for the human fall from a realm of grace; the fall he writes of depicts being itself as dynamically moving toward nonbeing.

In *The Other Side of the River* (1984), Wright adopts a more leisurely inclusion of anecdotes than in his previous poetry, particularly anecdotes of near falls that echo the highly charged patterns of imagery throughout his work. He narrates incidents of suspension or descent in which survival appears contingent. In "Lonesome Pine Special," for instance, the persona's car has "spun out" with "one front wheel on a rock, / and the other on air, / Hundreds of feet of air down the mountainside" (*WTT*, 72). The speaker must balance there, close to extinction. Similarly, in "Italian Days" a helicopter engine has stopped "And we began to slide sideways down the air, / As quietly as a snowflake" (*WTT*, 87). The irreality of the moment, its strange delicacy and silence, duplicates in narrative form Wright's conceptual emphasis upon the provisional nature of selfhood: if there are many representations of selves that Wright longs to deploy in language, none of them are less liable to extinction. In "Two

Stories" (*WTT*, 75-77) Wright tells first of his speaker as a boy camper who has sleepwalked to the edge of a drop-off and wakes to face both the drop-off and a bear. The child is granted a miraculous reprieve and returns to his tent unscathed. In the second story, a rattlesnake, several hours dead, bruises a man's wrist; the "stump" of the snake strikes. Similar to tall tales, such narratives illustrate the closeness of death to the living in ways that Wright has always presented imagistically in his work. Rather than a departure, the frequent inclusion of such anecdotes in *The Other Side of the River* underscores his characteristic concern with unusual physical and psychic states.

As Wright has it, his work becomes "this business I waste my heart on. // And nothing stops that" (*WTT*, 38); the desire to make poems, making selves out of language, comes closest to certainty for him. Wright is clearly a poet who cannot entertain complacency and punishes himself if he lapses even momentarily into any relaxation of his aesthetic and spiritual pursuits. As a number of his readers have noted, his poetry is characterized by melancholy rather than anger, a tonal quality that is alien to the zeal of much neo-surrealist practice and that depends upon confessionalism's legacy of ruthless self-examination. "Whatever it is, it bothers me all the time" is Wright's refrain, uttered three times in the five-line stanzas of "Laguna Blues," progressing from the riddle in the mind, to the riddle in the song/poem, to whatever's "off-key and unkind" (*WTT*, 23). The refrain might be his signature piece with its light humor and its conceptual repetition. "Whatever it is," "the unknown and unknowable" does not leave him alone.

While Wright's dilemma initially may seem ahistorical, it is, in greater measure, a cultural and even a generational one. As Norman Finkelstein notes: "The absence of the sublime may offer relief to many 'radical' Postmodernists, who perceive the sublime as nothing more than an exhausted mode of bourgeois literary discourse, but its absence provides a devastating tension for these poets who experience it first-hand."[51] Julia Kristeva, for one, speculates about the inescapability of melancholy for any creative imagination: "[T]here is no imagination that is not, overtly or secretly, melancholy."[52] Wright surely would seem to express an intensification of his generation's melancholy. Both Bedient and Pinsky note such a strain in Wright. Bedient observes: "A jubilant melancholic, this poet—like every poet—leads a second life (it may feel like the only one) of figures, rhythms, and meanings, exalted and artificial, eloquent and to-be-continued."[53] Bedient further draws upon Susan Sontag's

---

51. Norman Finkelstein, *The Utopian Moment in Contemporary American Poetry* (Lewisburg, Pa.: Bucknell University Press, 1988), p. 47.

52. Julia Kristeva, *Black Sun: Depression and Melancholia*, trans. Leon S. Roudiez (New York: Columbia University Press, 1989), p. 6.

53. Calvin Bedient, "Slide-Wheeling Around the Curves," in Andrews, ed., *Point Where All Things Meet*, p. 39.

speculations about Walter Benjamin's melancholia to support his assertion about Wright as melancholic: "'He has complex, often veiled relations with others.' Other Saturnine traits—among them the view of time as a 'medium of constraint, inadequacy, repetition,' the compulsion 'to convert time into space,' indecisiveness, a 'self-conscious and unforgiving relation to the self'—are conspicuous in Wright's work."[54] Robert Pinsky notes the same propensity in depicting Wright's sensibility as melancholic: "It is as though the constant, unrelaxing stream of dense poetic language is the only way to relieve the painful memories and bad foreboding which are Wright's characteristic materials."[55]

Wright's poetry grows perhaps increasingly melancholic in its regard for contemporary culture. In their ruminations, Wright's poems bear the mark of his resistance to much of contemporary Western culture and its superficial innovation and frenetic consumerism. The poems insist on the ephemerality of the material (even as Wright casts affectionate attention on nature, he shades natural phenomena with references to silence and absence) and bespeak an oppositional cultural position in late-twentieth-century America. Moreover, the poems reflect a difference from culture in their melancholy near ennui, their desire to purify their speakers of egoism, their antimaterialism, and even their refusal of haste. He would oppose other contemporary conditions, including a climate of therapeutic cheer and a wholesale cultural embrace of technological innovation that encourages heterogeneous but shallow desires.

Perhaps it is not surprising, then, that visions of contemporary apocalypse are close to this poet, a fact that the poems confront in outward rhetoric and disparate images. In the final poem of *The Other Side of the River* Wright presents one of his more devastating indictments of a future. His landscape in "California Dreaming" glitters with the ultimate destruction of any vestige of self or selves. We have not arrived at the other side of the river but rather at Lethe and a surrounding landscape of Darvon and Valium. He creates a particularized environment in which the inner life has been reduced as his speaker finds himself adrift in a testing ground: a California of sorts that seems be a state of spiritual inertia. The poem details anesthetized self-unraveling, beginning with the projected extinction of both identity and world, all orchestrated to a superficially inconsequential voice humming a popular song:

> Piece by small piece the world falls away from us like spores
> From a milkweed pod,
> > and everything we have known,

---

54. Ibid., p. 68.

55. Robert Pinsky, *The Situation of Poetry: Contemporary Poetry and its Traditions* (Princeton: Princeton University Press, 1976), p. 112.

> And everyone we have known,
> Is taken away by the wind to forgetfulness,
> Somebody always humming,
> > California dreaming . . .
>
> > (*WTT*, 118)

Calypsoed in this strange California of the soul, Wright chooses earlier in the poem to send out a chain of similes by which to travel:

> What I know best is a little thing.
> It sits on the far side of the simile,
> > the like that's like the like.
>
> > (*WTT*, 116)

He must look warily for signs of immanence, attending with concentrated discipline to his environment.

"For over a half century I've waited in vain" (*WTT*, 229), Wright notes elsewhere. His poems are willfully repetitious as if they are what he has called the "worry beads" of a man who has abandoned a prescribed faith. Just the same, it would be a mistake to think of his notations as acknowledgments of defeat. However abandoned by his divinity, or absolute meaning, it is the melancholy art of tense expectation that sustains this poetry into a future.

Almost never lost in these poems is the depiction of a first person as a realm of desires, desires to discover the next poem in "a language where nothing stays" (*WTT*, 33). In Wright's returns to Italy, to Laguna Beach, to the landscapes of his Southern childhood, to the inner life of quiet contemplation, he would call up a necessary language. While this attentive pursuit in language is akin to belief, it is a belief that cannot wholly suffice—and thus prompts Wright to compose the next poem as a means for discovering the elusive epiphany.

The title of Wright's eleventh book, *Chickamauga*, refers to the battlefield where the poet's great-grandfather and namesake, a Confederate captain, was shot in the mouth. After the battle of Chickamauga, Wright's great-grandfather was captured and for two years confined at Rock Island. "And came back to Little Rock and *began his career*." He was dead at sixty-six, "a ticket to Cuba stored flat in his jacket pocket" (*WTT*, 106). The story of Wright's great-grandfather is not only that of a mouth wound (with all the resonance such a wound evokes for a poet) but also a narrative of restlessness and action in the public world. The name of the battlefield in which Wright's forebear fought is thus talismanic, suggesting Wright's own psychic battlefield.

The book's first section is titled "Aftermath," directing attention to Wright's interest in exploring endings and outcomes. At the same time, the section title plays on assessing life as a form of mathematics, alluding to Wright's customary search for "equations" of meaning. "Sitting Outside at the End of Autumn" rehearses a number of Wright's characteristic gestures by relating his earnest effort to create, even to force, meaning from the daily particulars of his life. He centers on the landscape as a way to apprehend an innerspace or soulscape. In this, the first poem of *Chickamauga*, Wright expresses immediate failure; his grand project of determining autobiographical meaning has not been fulfilled. In the autumn of later middle age the speaker thumbs a snail shell. "I rub it clockwise and counterclockwise, hoping for anything / Resplendent in its vocabulary or disguise." He refers to Lao Tzu to pose a conundrum, to make a figure, "looking to calculate" his life's meaning.[56]

As his final poem in the collection, "Yard Work," indicates, the poet's business is to measure space and time through deployment of the line on the page and, by extension, to measure his own spiritual and aesthetic nature within the actual physical space that nature affords him. "My job is yard work— / I take this inchworm, for instance, and move it from here to there" (*C*, 92). As the poem suggests, in his quiet way Wright is a poet of puns, confident in using the terms of our grammar—the sentence, the line, the measure—to disport on nature, ethics, and, self-reflexively, his own poetic. "The invisible" and "the absolute," referred to individually in the first and second stanza of the poem, are brought together in the third stanza as if to emphasize that Wright's aesthetic is founded on a virtual mill of words.

Ultimately in this collection Wright would ask that the limits of the self and its reliance on a publicly sanctioned identity be abandoned, as in "Looking Across Laguna Canyon at Dusk, West-by-Northwest":

> Like others, I want to pour myself into the veins of the invisible
> At times like this,
>              becoming all that's liquid and moist.
> Like Dionysus, I'd enter the atmosphere, spread and abandon—. . . .
>
>                                     (*C*, 88)

This poem insinuates that the self made of words enacts its own disappearance in Wright's poems of his later career. Even more than wishing for presence, such poems further rehearse an abandonment of identity, an active self-annihilation, a paean to invisibilities as the poet yearns for a loss of secure identity boundaries. Through such an imagined merging with nature and godhead, Wright desires and verges on, but never quite entirely allows for, ecstatic self-abandon. His portraits of spiritualized desires give us, as Wright has said, the "outline" of a face. In an age of ever more heated confessions in mass communications, he announces and defends obscure sensations allied to the private even as the private in his poetry turns out to be made of ethers and implosions.

---

56. Charles Wright, "Sitting Outside at the End of Autumn," in *Chickamauga* (New York: Farrar, Straus & Giroux, 1995), p. 3. Hereafter the title of this collection will be abbreviated as *C*, and page numbers will be cited parenthetically in the text.

In "Lives of the Saints," in *Black Zodiac*, Wright contemplates two of his key themes: mortality and the yearning for God. Amid reminders of contemporary despair and violence in the poem—pimps and prostitutes and drive-by shootings—he pronounces his own wariness as a "lookout and listener."[57] Yet his evocation of Zen at the poem's close carries little conviction:

> Contemplative, cloistered, tongue-tied,
>                                         Zen says, watch your front.
> Zen says, wherever you are is a monastery.

It is the final two lines that utter a deeper resolve: "The lives of the saints become our lives. / God says, watch your back."[58]

"Lives of the Saints" laments the failure to arrive at "the new and negotiable, / The undiscovered snapshot"[59] even as the middle-aged poet ponders his life's work as evasive substance over style, as, that is, elusive religious transformation: "We believe in belief but don't believe, / for which we shall be judged."[60] His skepticism, inevitably, keeps him from too easily assuming an oracular mantle. Wright has stated that his poems resemble "prayers," but more often one sees the poems as what he calls "unanswered prayers." They are framed repeatedly as if Wright can hardly help himself; he cannot avoid, that is, locating his aesthetic in the terms of spiritual feeling in which, like a saint, he too emerges for his readers as iconic, his essence unknowable.

Despite the bulking threat of mortality, Wright commends disciplined yearning for the divine and perpetual aesthetic alertness even as he suffers toward an assumption of belief. Such habits, characteristic of "the lives of the saints," become less a mark of individual distinction than of what he sees as a common path. To watch one's back, as he tells us God advises, is to watch for death and loss, an attentiveness that Wright seemed predisposed toward from early in his career. "Happiness happens, like sainthood, in spite of ourselves" (*WTT*, 193), he acknowledges. But, then, giving the lie to our hopes of settling upon and reaching our desires, in another poem he remarks: "Sadness is truer than happiness" (*WTT*, 141).

---

57. Charles Wright, "Lives of the Saints," in *Black Zodiac* (New York: Farrar, Straus & Giroux, 1997), p. 42.

58. Ibid., p. 45.

59. Ibid., p. 42.

60. Ibid., p. 43.

CHRISTOPHER R. MILLER

# Poetic Standard Time:
# The Zones of Charles Wright (1998)

In the first poem of *Black Zodiac* (1997), Charles Wright seems to bid farewell to an idea that has sustained most of his career. He has tried, he says, to "resuscitate" journal and landscape—"Discredited form, discredited subject matter"—to no avail. This declaration, from "Apologia Pro Vita Sua," may surprise readers who have come to know Wright through his strange territories of memory and experience: the hypertrophic green backdrops of his Tennessee youth; the Italian *paesaggio* of his army service and Fulbright travels; the Pacific of his seventeen-year residence in Laguna Beach; and, most recently, his Charlottesville backyard, a sort of suburban cloister for his daily meditations, Wright's dismissal of the journal might also seem too harsh: though the exhausting vigil of "A Journal of the Year of the Ox" doesn't beg to be repeated, the poet *has* successfully preserved vestiges of the form up to the present.

Discredited or not, landscape and journal still structure his poems. "Apologia" begins with the blooming of April dogwood and ends in the summertime profusion of honeysuckle and poison ivy, and its seasons progress in installments of description and meditation. Wright's brief plaint might, then, be read as a diary entry in a dark mood: a bad day to be superseded, without comment, by better ones. Even on a dull afternoon, Wright can reanimate himself in the natural world with descriptive tenacity. Over the years he has given lasting illumination to Emerson's belief that "the whole of nature is a metaphor for the human mind." Now, as he passes what he ruefully calls "the back brink of my sixth decade," it is a fine moment to appraise his contribution—voiced regrets notwithstanding—to American poetry.

If Wright expresses frustration with his chosen form and subject matter, it is partly because he's always been wryly suspicious of his own eloquence. Landscape poetry lies open to the charge of sybaritism, of immersion in rich atmospherics for their own sake; even if it aspires to the philosophical, it risks the show-and-tell seesaw between thoughts and appearances. Increasingly conscious of his aesthetic, Wright in his most recent work often seeks to justify poetic description, to crystallize the ways that the visible world opens avenues to other realms. In the title poem of *Black Zodiac*, he writes, quoting Stevens, "*Description's an element, like air or water*"; and in *Chickamauga* (1995), he enlists Bishop's aid in the defense—proceeding, almost reflexively, with more description:

It's just description," she said,
                              "they're all just description."
Meaning her poems . . . Mine, too,
The walleye of morning's glare
                              lancing the landscape,
The dogwood berries as red as cinnamon drops in the trees,
Sunday, the twenty-ninth of September, 1991.
                    ("Miles Davis and Elizabeth Bishop Fake the Break")

In Wright's characteristic syntax, the look of the day and the precise date serve as subordinate clauses to the poet's thought. Ever since *China Trace* (1977), Wright has been fascinated by dates, the oddity of marking in a Heraclitean stream a spot to which you can never return. Almost inevitably, these impulses coalesced into the *Zone Journals* (1988); and though he has abandoned the explicit form of the journal, Wright continues, as in this passage in "Apologia Pro Vita Sua," to be haunted by the calendar:

My parents' 60th wedding anniversary
Were they still alive,
                    5th of June, 1994.
It's hard to imagine, I think, your own children grown older than you ever
    were, I can't.

I sit in one of the knock-off Brown-Jordan deck chairs we brought from
    California,
Next to the bearded grandson my mother never saw.
Some afternoon, or noon, it will all be over. Not this one.

Past and present intersect in the abstract marker of a number, while the mind slides from temporal specificity to the vague futurity of death. It would be sobering enough to say "Some afternoon, it will all be over," to align this afternoon with a yet-to-be-determined one; but to inject the revisionary afterthought "or noon" is to give chilling exactness to the day of one's death, to imagine it as an event that happens, when it happens, at a specific time. And the postscript, typical of Wright's sardonic compression, registers a subtle spectrum of feeling: cautious celebration, stubborn defiance, stoic blankness.

For recording such stabs of consciousness, Wright has perfected a syntax that deftly balances dates, description, and introspection. Despite his misgivings, it is at the crossroads of landscape and journal that Wright has found his most distinctive voice; here, he can mediate between space and time, between the impersonal and the personal. Landscape offers a "lever of transcendence," a way of imagining himself under a similar sky in a different time; it also means what he calls, thinking of Cézanne and Rothko, utter "lonesomeness"—vast space devoid of any other perceiver. The journal-entry form, meanwhile, tethers him to the present, to changeable moods and transitory details.

For all his mystical leanings, Wright cannot help explicitly locating himself in time and place. In this way his descriptive element differs from that of Stevens, with whom he shares a tendency toward abstraction. Stevens once explained of "Notes Toward a Supreme Fiction" that "The weather as described is the weather that was about me as I wrote this. There is a constant reference to the real, to and fro." Wright could (much less surprisingly) say the same about his own meteorology; he anchors even his most gnomic perceptions in the personal. He has given us a memorable vocabulary and syntax for saying how a particular day looks and feels.

It's easy to pick from Wright's work favorite days, all of which seem to begin with a proposition and then to accrete detail. In a happy moment, you might say to yourself, "Today is sweet stuff on the tongue," as Wright does in a mid-'80s poem, "California Dreaming":

> Today is sweet stuff on the tongue.
> The question of how we should live our lives in this world
> Will find no answer from us
>                     this morning,
> Sunflick, the ocean humping its back
> Beneath us, shivering out
>                   wave after wave we fall from
> And cut through in a white scar of healed waters,
> Our wet suits glossed slick as seals,
>                  our boards grown sharp as cries.
> We rise and fall like the sun.

Like Whitman's vicarious twenty-ninth bather in "Song of Myself," Wright imaginatively projects himself into a flotilla of surfers. As often happens in his poetry, the declarative mode yields to the kinetic energy of phenomena. The subject of the second sentence—the "question of how we should live our lives"—sinks in a current of subordination; reflecting the transfer of force from sea to surfers, the first clause ("the ocean . . . shivering out / wave after wave") engenders a second ("we fall from / And cut through"). In describing tidal motion, the constant sparkle of things rising and subsiding, Wright moves from the present participles of the ocean ("humping," "shivering") to the past participles of the forms that momentarily float on its surface ("glossed," "grown"). Perhaps the most arresting of these is "healed," not only for its theological resonance in a poem that alludes to Easter and "Sunday prayer-light," but also for the ephemeral event it describes: the water endlessly closing up the gashes the surfboards momentarily carve. We might not expect these flickering motions to be compared with the rise and fall of the sun, but Wright's simile aptly suggests the visionary dimension of what has been no ordinary day at the beach.

Reviewers have often called Wright's poetry "visionary"; and overused though the word may be, it accurately defines the element of the extraordinary in his verse. If you gesture to an ideal realm in order to find this world wanting, you're practicing a form of irony, and if you find the ideal in the real, you're living in an idyll; but Wright hovers between these poles, a pragmatic dreamer. If he is visited by a revelatory vision, it usually has a mundane explanation. "I've had these for forty years," he says in "Apologia Pro Vita Sua," "light-prints and shifting screed, / Feckless illuminations. / St. John of the Cross, Julian of Norwich, lead me home." He is talking about migraines, not séances. Elsewhere in *Black Zodiac*, in "Meditation on Summer and Shapelessness," he refers to a less painful illusion: "Without my glasses, the light around the window shade / Throbs like an aura, so faint / At first, then luminous with its broken promises— / Feckless icon, dark reliquary." In both visitations, Wright seizes on the sharp word *feckless*, a term of intellectual judgment amid the verbal haze of auras and light-prints.

Wright once said in an interview that he lacks a "logical, sorting-out type of mind," and it's true his imagination eschews strict dialectics: the visionary dwells in, or alongside, the everyday. His method might be termed juxtaposition or collage, and his artistic development can be seen in the way he has put his fragments together. It's especially interesting to note how his representation of memory has changed. In the early sequence "Tattoos," from *Bloodlines* (1975), memory consists of discrete episodes of hallucinatory immediacy: a fainting spell the poet suffered as a young acolyte, a childhood bout of blood poisoning, an auto accident, a grammar-school handwriting lesson. Beginning with the title poem of *The Southern Cross* (1981), however, Wright found a more complex form for his memory—a series of blocks separated by little horizontal lines. This patchwork allowed him to alternate between recollection and observation, between backward and forward yearnings. Rather than framing one distinct memory, these later poems create an atmosphere of disconsolate remembrance, a process rather than a result.

In light of later work, "Tattoos" might strike us now as almost naively confident in recapturing the past, but the results are frequently arresting. Each poem—a spot of time without the assurance of narrative—brings the reader, *in medias res*, to a bewildering sensory world. Wright renders his tattoos with the aural gusto of a poet in the first flush of his powers, as in this tug of vowels in the blood-poisoning episode:

> Skyhooked above the floor, sucked
> And mummied by salt towels, my left arm
> Hangs in the darkness, bloodwood, black gauze,
> The slow circle of poison
> Coming and going through the same hole . . .

"Skyhooked" modulates into "sucked"; "arm" fades into "darkness"; and the "slow circle of poison" flows through one "hole"—either the original puncture wound or, more unsettlingly, the heart itself. And the immobile arm, frozen into a basketball shot, hangs syntactically between present and past participles, like the buoyant surfers in "California Dreaming."

Without helpful endnotes, we would not know for sure that Wright was retailing a recovery from blood poisoning. The notes offer a compromise: they keep narrative out of the poem itself but verify that these were real events in Wright's life. This is juxtaposition in *extremis*, a strange poetry of vision balanced with prose explanations of everyday life. The car accident in "Tattoos," with its aeronautic metaphor of "take-off" and "re-entry," dramatizes this tension between the uncanny and the familiar:

> So that was it, the rush and the take-off,
> The oily glide of the cells
> Bringing it up—ripsurge, refraction,
> The inner spin
> Trailing into the cracked lights of oblivion . . .
>
> Re-entry is something else, blank, hard:
> Black stretcher straps; the peck, peck
> And click of a scalpel; glass shards
> Eased one by one from the flesh;
> Recisions; the long bite of the veins . . .
>
> And what do we do with this,
> Rechuted, reworked into our same lives, no one
> To answer to, no one to glimpse and sing,
> The cracked light flashing our names?
> We stand fast, friend, we stand fast.

At the risk of generic familiarity, we might call this a soul-body poem. With its "oily glide of cells," the body shares the stuff of the automobile, while the soul hovers as the mysterious physical vector of "inner spin," the ghost in a literal machine. Soul temporarily takes leave of body at the ellipsis-trail of the first stanza, reunites to feel the consonantal abrasion of glass and scalpel in the second, and triumphantly emerges in the third to deliver a postscript. Where does soul go in the first? Those "cracked lights of oblivion" suggest some astral projection, the tunnel-end of proverbial near-death experiences; and yet, back on earth, they simply denote damaged headlights or the glittering remnants of a windshield. Nostalgic for the celestial cracked lights, Wright feels a strange melancholy of anticlimax about being "reworked" into his "same" life; and we, too, might feel betrayed by the sententious stoicism of the conclusion. Is this the wisdom of the resurrected—*we stand fast?* The last line seems purposely trite, as if to suggest that nothing worthwhile can be retrieved from such experiences other than an art in which they're recreated.

Wright's tendencies toward the abstract and the biographical merge in "Homage to Paul Cézanne," the opening poem of *The Southern Cross.*

Having mourned the deaths of his parents in separate poems in *Bloodlines*, Wright achieves in "Homage" a crystallization—stoically purged of particularity, yet unmistakably full of feeling. It surely ranks as one of the most peculiar elegies in American poetry, in that it replaces the vertical scale of underworld descent and apotheosis with a horizontal landscape of Lucretian dispersal. This is the essential territory Wright has visited ever since, saying in various ways that we remain in the landscape forever. As he starkly and rather awkwardly puts it in "Apologia Pro Vita Sua": "Like any visible thing. / I'm always attracted downward, and soon to be killed and assimilated."

"Homage," Wright has explained, grew out of a nocturnal glimpse of white rectangles on his lawn, which turned out, next morning, to be loose leaves of notebook paper: "At night, in the fish-light of the moon, the dead wear our white shirts / To stay warm, and litter the fields. / We pick them up in the mornings, dewy pieces of paper and scraps of cloth." With this premise, the bare truth behind the illusion is exposed, a truth that turns with tantalizing ambiguity on the fulcrum of *litter*: if it's a transitive verb, the dead are leaving wanton scraps from their midnight gathering; if intransitive, the dead revert to particles in the landscape, and the spell is broken. Poised between these possibilities, the poem suggests how momentary shivers of the uncanny can become comforting presences, the way the dead might be caught through peripheral vision, in light glimmering on a chair or a shadow moving, across the floor.

The poem pays homage not directly but through a visual conceit. Its lines are brushstrokes, restrained elegiac increments that correspond to Cézanne's crisp planes of color:

> The dead are a cadmium blue.
> We spread them with palette knives in broad blocks and planes.
>
> We layer them stroke by stroke
> In steps and ascending mass, in verticals raised from the earth.

If lines of poetry do indeed compare with painterly lines, then Wright might implicitly be justifying the static quality of his syntax—unrelieved by variable phrasing, the dead do such-and-such and we do thus-and-so. This plain style echoes the terse subject-verb cadence in the poems of *China Trace*, which, for all its imagistic originality, can be dull on the ears, a sort of strained haiku. Yet in "Homage," Wright's syntactic monotony provides a neutral background against which he arrays the protean shapes of the dead: ghosts in the house who "lie in our beds with their gloves off / And touch our bodies," Puckish sprites who "shuttle their messengers through the oat grass," empty spaces the tide fills in, "globules of light," droplets of rain.

When the spell of this litany is broken in the last section, we feel it as a strangely moving loss—so lulled have we become by the constant propositions about the dead. There is no more "they," only a solitary, disconsolate "we":

We're out here, our feet in the soil, our heads craned up at the sky,
The stars streaming and bursting behind the trees.

At dawn, as the clouds gather, we watch
The mountain glide from the east on the valley floor,
Coming together in starts and jumps.
Behind their curtain, the bears
Amble across the heavens, serene as black coffee . . .

In this elegy for no one in particular, we mourn the passing of a noun. This is what Wright might call "re-entry": no longer part of the poet's fantasy, the world of clouds, stars, and wind reverts to what it always was, its serenity marvelously reflected in the animal nonchalances of Ursa Major and Ursa Minor creeping slowly across the sky. Like Keats's knight-at-arms in "La Belle Dame Sans Merci," Wright has been enthralled by a vision only to be deserted on a cold hillside, and he ends "Homage" with a shivering vigil: "We sit out on the earth and stretch our limbs, / Hoarding the little mounds of sorrow laid up in our hearts."

Wright has continually revisited the landscape of "Homage" but has largely abandoned its abstraction; some element of the personal—often in the form of memory—must give substance to his meditations. The photograph, with its beguiling visual exactness, has long fascinated him as both an ideal of recollection and a naive arresting of time—most memorably in "Bar Giamaica, 1959-60," from *The Southern Cross*, in which he revised a Ugo Mulas photo called "Bar Giamaica, 1953-1954." Wright substitutes his own friends (with whom he frequented the same Milanese bar) for Mulas's subjects and changes the date. Not satisfied with the stop-action of earlier memory poems, Wright crosses photographic stasis with cinematic movement, image with process:

Grace is the focal point,
                    the tip ends of her loosed hair
Like match fire in the back light,
Her hands in a "Here's the church . . ."
                        She's looking at Ugo Mulas,

Who's looking at us.

Ingrid is writing this all down, and glances up, and stares hard.

This still isn't clear.

I'm looking at Grace, and Goldstein and Borsuk and Dick Venezia
Are looking at me.
              Yola keeps reading her book.

And that leaves the rest of them: Susan and Elena and Carl Glass.
And Thorp and Schimmel and Jim Gates,
                              and Hobart and Schneeman

One afternoon in Milan in the late spring.

The poem has the wide panorama of lines and half-lines that have be-come Wright's trademark. No mere stylistic quirk, the lineation here makes a seismic graph of restlessness; it suits the chaotic sightlines and captures the struggle of a photographer getting everyone into the picture, or of a poet trying to hold memory still. Starting with the language of technical mastery ("Grace is the focal point"), the poet grows less sure of his grip on the past ("This still isn't clear") and ends up with a roll call of names yet to be filled in. It is an unlyrical task, recording those names, but the longer line accommodates the burden.

The names mean nothing to us, of course; they share the anonymity of the people in Mulas's photograph, and have perhaps become as much ghosts to Wright as they are to us. Characteristically, Wright resumes the flow of time after the freeze-frame: the party breaks up, and the photog-rapher, a casual Prospero, drinks his coffee and leaves the stage props be-hind. Ugo stands in for the poet himself, who, after everyone has left, lingers in memory, sparely marking the passage of seasons. Wright regis-ters the cold finality of departure in a drop through white space into the bereft line "Ever again." The poem ends with a disappearance, one of his favorite kinds of conclusion; here it takes the form of a fadeout through an odd "star filter of memory."

Wright's obsession with memory and forgetfulness participates in a larger and more sublime sense of appearances and vanishings in the world, things passing through filters into somewhere else. In *The World of the Ten Thousand Things*, the collection of his poems from the '80s, we see this literally from one end to the other—from "Homage to Paul Cézanne" to the curt "Last Journal," in which the poet offers a variation on the Buddhist fire-sermon of decay:

Soon enough we will forget the world.
                    And soon enough the world will forget us.

The breath of our lives, passing from this one to that one,
Is what the wind says, its single word
                    being the earth's delight.

Reading chronologically through this decade of Wright's career, we can't help feeling some disappointment in this last poem, a pinched and wrung-out result of what the poet has called in *Chickamauga* an aesthetic of "subtraction." "Last Journal" contains the merest prose-skeleton of an idea, too close to the bare bones of its own paraphrase; it lacks the flesh he had given with such sensual generosity in earlier work. If Wright's

talent lies in the shock of juxtapositions, then this poem falls far short of
his best. It represents, we might say, the inverse of "Tattoos"—not the
pure presence of memories, but their absolute negation.

Wright has been perfecting his poetry of juxtaposition ever since the
title poem of *The Southern Cross*. The blocks of that poem represent what
he was later to call "zones": here, they include the Italy of his early adult-
hood, the Tennessee wilderness of his youth, and a Montana cabin of the
present. He establishes his characteristic structure: a shuttling between
memory and observation, between the sifting of old images and sensa-
tions and the present view through a window. After Wright's raid on his
mental attic for stored souvenirs, the outward vista promises a momen-
tary gust of spring cleaning. Wright, who's often professed an aversion to
linear narrative, admires the caprices of the weather not only as emblems
of human consciousness but as alternatives to it: "The rain just starting to
fall, and then not fall, / No trace of a story line." The poem, it turns out,
also lacks storyline; in fact, many recollections echo the flat binary syn-
tax of the rain—the rhythm of falling and suddenly not falling:

> It's 1936, in Tennessee. I'm one
> And spraying the dead grass with a hose.
> The curtains blow in and out.
>
> And then it's not. And I'm not and they're not.

Wright's memories often appear in this penumbral way, like glimpses
through billowing curtains. If, to borrow a phrase from Tennyson, these
poetic blocks are short swallow-flights, then some never really get off the
ground: but fortunately, not all are earthbound. The straitened, dead-pan
notation of "China Trace" and "Homage" alternates with more extended
lyricism, as when Wright recalls time spent in Venice:

> After 12 years it's hard to recall
> That defining sound the canal made at sundown, slap
> Of tide swill on the church steps,
> Little runnels of boat wash slipping back from the granite slabs
> In front of Toio's, undulant ripples
> Flattening out in small hisses, the oily rainbows regaining their loose
>     shapes
> Silently, mewling and quick yelps of the gulls
> Wheeling from shadow into the pink and grey light over the Zattere,
> Lapping and rocking of water endlessly,
> At last like a low drone in the dark shell of the ear
> As the night lifted like mist from the Ogni Santi
> And San Sebastiano
>                     into the cold pearl of the sky . . .

The attempt to recapture one sound yields a radiant accretion of other
layers of experience: opalescent colors, place-names, the cries of gulls.

Even as he laments the difficulty of recalling the canal's "defining sound," those echoing liquids and labials—*slap, slipping, slabs, ripples, lapping*—say otherwise. The ear, Blake said, is a whirlpool fierce to draw creations in, and here Wright synesthetically imagines it as a dark shell to hold the pearl of the sky, a reliquary akin to memory itself.

On the inadequacy of memory, we may think the poet protests too much, as when he writes, "I can't remember the colors I said I'd never forget / On Via Giulia at sundown. / The ochres and glazes and bright hennas of each house." Hasn't he invoked the precise shades of the artist's palette? But no: they form only a generalized Mediterranean postcard, a loose approximation of what that street looked like on a certain day and hour. The kaleidoscopic sensations of Wright's time in Italy remain inextricably a part of the past, "an otherness inside us / We never touch," a pearl that can't be pried from the shell. Whatever onomatopoeia the poet applies to the Venetian canal can only be a pale surrogate of the original moment: it was Wright, as Stevens would say, and not the canal we heard.

Stevens, of course, exulted in the breach between imaginative language and experience; but Wright has never felt such confidence, partly because he's striven to represent his past in a way that Stevens never did. Over the years, Wright's attempts have often come attached to a caveat about language—as pale shadow, residue, proximate marker for vanished things. In such moments the poet gives us eloquence with one hand and takes it away with a dismissive wave of the other. Scholars of the elegy call this the "inexpressibility topos," but we, after repeated exposure, might call it merely a tiresome habit. In much of his finest work, Wright forgets to lament his limitations, as at the end of "The Southern Cross," where he transforms the empty spaces of the irrecoverable and inaccessible into a place of exquisite yearning:

> It's what we forget that defines us, and stays in the same place,
> And waits to be rediscovered.
> Somewhere in all that network of rivers and roads and silt hills,
> A city I'll never remember,
>                            its walls the color of pure light,
> Lies in the August heat of 1935,
> In Tennessee, the bottom land slowly becoming a lake.
> It lies in a landscape that keeps my imprint
> Forever,
>              and stays unchanged, and waits to be filled back in.
> Someday I'll find it out
> And enter my old outline as though for the 1st time,
>
> And lie down, and tell no one.

Forgetfulness here takes on a broader significance, encompassing not only the gaps in Wright's memory but also the things he could *never* have known. Rather than assigning himself something (the sound of a Venetian canal) to recall, he imagines a place that existed on the day of his birth, but of which he could have no consciousness. After starting with a memory of himself at age one, Wright presses further back, to the horizon of his existence. Like Keats's embowered niche in "Ode to a Nightingale," the imprint in the Tennessee landscape is both bed and grave; it links Wright's first year to the hour of his death, as well as to a pastoral beyond that shimmers with a light that never was on sea or land.

By now such landscapes are immediately recognizable as Wright's, not only for their language but for their appearance on the page: the airy amplitude of white space, the outrider-lines drifting eastward like clouds. From a long line of cartographic intricacy ("Somewhere in all that network of rivers and roads and silt hills"), the eye moves to a short line of yearning ("A city I'll never remember") to an outrider of dreamlike fragility ("its walls the color of pure light"). Why is this last line set adrift? Imagine it incorporated into the preceding one, or capitalized and moved to the left margin: its fugitive unreality would be diminished.

Wright's lineation, then, marks a kind of conceptual zoning. In "To Giacomo Leopardi in the Sky," from *The Other Side of the River* (1984), the eighteenth-century poet hovers as a constellated patron saint while Wright marks time below:

> I know you're up there, hiding behind the noon light
> And the crystal of space.
>                     Down here,
> In the lurch and gasp the day makes as it waits for you
> In your black suit and mother-of-pearl,
> The mail comes, the garbage goes,
>                             the paired butterflies
> Dip and swoop in formation,
> Bees trail their tongues
>                 and tiptoe around the circumferences
> Of the melaleuca puffs,
> Sucking the sweetness up, July 27th,
> The hummingbird asleep on her branch,
>                      the spider drawn up in flame.

The indented "Down here" literalizes Leopardi's drop from the firmament, but Wright's earthly gaze nonetheless pulls us into a comforting place, containing the cheerful in-out cycle of mail and garbage, the acrobatics of butterflies, the tropical specificity of melaleuca. Often in Wright's poems of the '80s and '90s, it is impossible to quote just a few lines, so irresistible is the rhythm of his observation—the opposite of the halting sentence-units of his earlier work. "Sucking the sweetness up, July 27th" may not be astonishing in itself, but it takes part in a larger mosaic of notation. Here he takes a bemused pleasure in the sheer arbitrariness of dates, in the sense that neither the celestial Leopardi nor the buzzing bees care a fig for July 27; only Wright, caught between them, does. In his manner of juxtaposition, he places two poets—one living, one dead—on either side of a veil. But the real interest of such symbolic zoning lies in the way Wright makes the realms of life and death overlap, to reach a new sense that, as Frost put it, earth's a fine place for living.

Other poems from this volume have strong Christian overtones, in the familiar Wrightian effort to see tokens of the sacred in the ordinary. Set on Easter Sunday, a frequent seasonal touchstone for him, the title poem cheekily refers to the "purple joy" of a Chevrolet, and it compellingly connects vernal nourishment with the rite of communion in the epithet "Easter with all its little mouths open into the rain." "Lost Bodies" is a meditation organized around the axis of a remembered hilltop crucifix in Tennessee, a beacon that impassively watches over sordid motel liaisons and the dilapidation of tourist cabins along a forgotten stretch of road. Introducing a technique he will repeat in *Zone Journals*, Wright inter-leaves all this with memories of Lake Garda. Italy, a "sacred place" in his mythology, shines through the drearily opaque landscape in glimpses of almond blossoms and cypresses. These halcyon memories might intimate a promise of salvation, but they don't end the poem; instead, we return to the cold hillside and Christ on the cross, in a vision far bleaker than the conclusion of "Homage":

> All things that come to him come under his feet
> In a glorious body,
>                          they say. And why not?
> It beats the alternative, the mighty working
> Set to subdue the celestial flesh.
>
> And does so, letting the grass grow stiff, and the needles brown,
>
> Letting the dirt take over. This is as far as it goes,
> Where deer browse the understory and jays
>                          leap through the trees,
>
> Where chainsaws
> Whittle away at the darkness, and diesel rigs
> Carry our deaths all night through the endless rain.

After the biological and astronomical sublime of "Homage" and "Giacomo Leopardi," the brief theological excursus in "Lost Bodies" jars us; we don't really need a prose commentary on the crucifix. But Wright interrupts him-self with such startling abruptness that we forgive his exposition: "And does so . . ." And *what* does so? It takes a moment to realize that this is the Wordsworthian "mighty working," a coiled energy that unspools itself in in-exorable clauses to the poem's end. "Homage," by contrast, lingered in the enchantment of the benign black-coffee bears—a starry afterimage. In the edgier, less fanciful "Lost Bodies," Wright reduces his metaphor of divine "working" to the tireless human machinery of chainsaws and diesel rigs.

Despite the seeming jumble of perceptions in "Giacomo Leopardi" and "Lost Bodies," both poems have strong conceptual organizations: sky versus earth, cross versus highway. The diary form Wright adopted a few years later in *Zone Journals* simply gave more room for his predilections: the juxtaposition of places, the fascination with dates, the dislocations of travel and nostalgia, the variations on a theme of weather. In a sense the journals respond to the elegiac note of earlier memory poems like "The Southern Cross." If you can't return to the past, at least you can resolve to do a better job of recording the present—a task anticipated in "Bar Giamaica" by Wright's friend Ingrid, who is conscientiously "writing this all down."

Yet to write it all down, even if that were possible, wouldn't make much of a poem; and Wright acknowledged in a 1985 interview that he would need for his journals a principle of design that went beyond just the calendar. The act of keeping a journal does, of course, imply certain alignments: to write a date on a clean sheet of paper is to connect it to earlier dates in one's life, as well as to milestones in history. In Wright's imagination, times become further associated with spatial zones—symbolic places from both personal and official history. In various pilgrimages in "A Journal of the Year of the Ox"—to a Cherokee burial ground, to the homes of Dickinson and Poe, to the town where Petrarch died—Wright's attempts to envision the past's richness jar against the present's impoverished commemorations, such as the tourist-trap frescoes advertising Petrarch's poetry and a heartbreaking sign that scrupulously marks the "3.61 Acres Returned" to the Cherokee nation. Remembering the Verona stadium where he used to have reveries about Catullus, Wright calibrates the limits of his search for lost time in a physical gesture of straining:

> Catullus's seat—VALERI—was carved on top of the left-hand wing.
> I used to try to imagine—delicious impossibility—
> What it must have been like to be him,
> > his vowels and consonants
> The color of bee wings in the bee-colored afternoons.
> An iron-spiked and barbed-wire jut-out and overhang loomed
> Just to my left.
> > I always sat as close to it as I could.

To quote "Lost Bodies," this is as far as it goes. Wright's longing for the honeyed hives of Roman poetry runs into the fences of the present; yet those "bee-colored afternoons" seem, for a moment, to encompass both eras. Stadiums might crumble, but the weather is forever; and Wright uses the color of skies as a transcendent backdrop that squares his calendar with the grander time-line. When he refers to skies as "pre-Columbian" or "Mannerist," he is not merely engaging in aesthetic free association but thinking about the periods they represent and what Stevens called "the look of things," then and now. "A Journal of the Year of the Ox" begins in the gray opacity of January clouds and ends with Wright scanning the winter skies for Halley's comet, so that the sky becomes a kind of crystal ball for the year. "How far can you go if you concentrate," he asks, "how far down?"

Whereas "Year of the Ox" pledges itself to 1985, come what may, "A Journal of English Days" is devoted to the experience of a country, and to a deliberate vision of it. The poem is patterned by daytrips; but behind this to-and-fro, Wright is always aware of the larger motions of a world suspended in unimaginable space, amidst a cosmic wind "[t]hat blows continuously under our feet / Holding up everything." In an account of Sunday train rides, Wright's impressionistic sketch of the passing stations gives way to a larger sense of motion:

> Sadness of platforms, black umbrellas
> Doleful on benches, half-opened, damp,
> Tedious sense
> Of expectation, the clouds
> Continuing on for days past our destinations . . .

Of course clouds move on; it is only the temporary frame of a train window, the visual equivalent of a journal date, that makes weather seem part of a bounded picture. One's travels, Wright reminds us, are a tiny subset of larger migrations.

"English Days" closes with a flashback to a Sunday in September when the poet sat in the courtyard of the Victoria & Albert Museum gazing at a bronze Buddha. In a playful circuit of imitation, Wright resembles the stranger who appears at the poem's beginning sitting in the lotus position on a "weightless, effortless" day in Kensington Gardens; he has become a buddha contemplating the Buddha. In the finale, Wright gathers all the flickers of light and currents of air into one splendid metaphor:

> Weightlessness of the world's skin
>                         undulating like a balloon
> Losing its air around us, down drifting down
> Through the faint hiss of eternity
> Emptying somewhere else
>                         O emptying elsewhere
> This afternoon, skin
> That recovers me and slides me in like a hand
> As I unclench and spread
>                         finger by finger inside the Buddha's eye . . .

It seems like a fantastic yogic exercise—to imagine the sky as a membrane that sinks to re-cover you in twilight after the day's restless peregrinations. Wright's undulating balloon suggests the world of illusion that Buddhists call *maya*; and its deflation is both cosmic and intimate—the "faint hiss of eternity" and the breath of someone meditating. Nirvana, as Wright probably knows, comes from the Sanskrit for "a blowing-out."

If Wright expresses a philosophy in "English Days," he does so in this allusive, imagistic way. We catch him, as Whitman might phrase it, in "drifts." Yet sometimes the drift comes attached to more overt summary, as in this gorgeous description of a rose garden:

> One of those weightless, effortless late September days
> As sycamore leaves
>                     tack down the unresisting air
> Onto the fire-knots of late roses
> Still pumping their petals of flame
>                     up from the English loam,
> And I suddenly recognize
> The difference between the spirit and flesh
>                     is finite, and slowly transgressable . . .

We may be suspicious of this "suddenly": surely Wright had this thought in some of his earliest poems. It isn't the familiar moral that's sudden, but rather the way he comes to it—transplanted to England, the lotus-in-the-mud of Buddhist iconography becomes a demure rose-in-the-loam.

Lately Wright has reversed this stratagem: rather than looking at a rose and then thinking about mind-body dualism, he is more likely to read Descartes and then apply it to the things in his backyard. The tendency is especially strong in "Xionia," the final sequence in *The World of the Ten Thousand Things*, and in *Chickamauga*. Books replace the pilgrimages and milestones of the journal-poems. In the past Wright thrived on the friction between the visionary and the real, pictorial and verbal, eternal and diurnal; lately, in poems that invoke Eliot, Celan, Richard Rorty, Plutarch, St. Augustine, and John the Solitary, he has been testing literature on the pulse of life. These poems often bear such humorously prolix titles as "After Reading Tu Fu, I Go Outside to the Dwarf Orchard." Such titles shed any pretense of spontaneous response to nature; clearly literature has come first, echoing in the poet's mind like snatches of music. "Blaise Pascal Lip-syncs the Void," from *Chickamauga*, provides a template for Wright's recent form:

> There's change and succession in all things, Pascal contends,
> But inconstancy, boredom and anxiety condition our days.
> Neither will wash for him, though,
>                     since nature is corrupt.
> That's why we love it.
>                     That's why we take it, unwinnowed,
> Willingly into our hearts.
>
> December. 4 p.m.
>                     Chardonnay-colored light-slant
> Lug weight in the boned trees.
>                     Squirrel dead on the Tarmac.

Boom-boxing Big Foot pickup trucks
Hustle down Locust,
                    light pomegranate pink grapefruit then blood.
    We take it into our hearts.


"Once you start thinking in sentences and ideas," Wright said in 1985, "you're working toward prose," and he seems to have inched perilously close. These snippets of books might be compared with his earlier insertion of remembered vignettes, but it is trickier to paste in prose fragments than to integrate one's own memories. The demon of quotation plagues "Blaise Pascal" and newspaper articles alike: what synonym for "said"? Wright settles on "contends," but the verb seems too stridently rhetorical for the *penseur*. The colloquial phrase "wash for" offers a softer alternative, its folksiness bringing Pascal into the orbit of Wright's self-deprecating idiom. In the second phase of Wright's pattern, earthy particulars contrast with quoted abstraction—here, the insistent modernity of brand names, the specificity of his neighborhood, and the grotesquery of a flattened squirrel. Wright's chromatic transcription of twice-flattened roadkill nicely demonstrates his point about the human capacity to absorb the world in all its shapes, no matter how ugly.

And yet it's hard not to think that Pascal has been made to serve as a philosophical straight man, a foil to Wright's pagan, imperfect, messy "we"—the collective persona that embraces all accidents, imperfections, ambiguities. By now, Wright's bibliographic citation takes on a recognizable pattern:

God is not offered to the senses,
                        St. Augustine tells us,
The artificer is not his work, but his art:
Nothing is good if it can be better.
But all these oak trees look fine to me . . .
                    ("December Journal")

As Kafka has told us,
                sin always comes openly:
It walks on its roots and doesn't have to be torn out.

How easily it absolves itself in the senses,
However, in Indian summer . . .
                    ("Peccatology")


In these examples the Wrightian half-line serves the new purpose of lightening the load of philosophical quotation, of clipping a line that verges on prose. These passages function as baselines to be quarreled with or confirmed by experience; in moments of disagreement, as in the drubbing of Augustine, Wright's reaction recalls Samuel Johnson's kicking of a stone to make his point about idealist philosophy: "I refute it thus."

Quotation need not be a stone to kick, of course. In "Cicada," from *Chickamauga*, the awkwardness of borrowing disappears because the poem convincingly dramatizes the act of reading and reflection. The world of the poem comprises two zones, the confinement of a study and the outdoors of a rainy day:

> All morning I've walked about,
> >               opening books and closing books,
> Sitting in this chair and that chair.
> Steady drip on the skylight,
> >               steady hum of regret.
> Who listens to anyone?
> Across the room, bookcases,
> >               across the street, summer trees.

In the syntactic and visual rhythm of fretful pacing, Wright suggests an impasse, the immeasurable gap between the books he's been reading and the world beyond his window. Venturing a quotation from Augustine on resisting "the allurements of the eye," as if to see if it will solve his dilemma, he substitutes the stimuli of the ear—the counterpoint of a cicada's drone against September rain. As he listens, Wright muses on another Augustinian passage, about the elusiveness of sound:

> If time is water, appearing and disappearing
> In one heliotropic cycle,
> >               this rain
> That sluices as through an hourglass
> Outside the window into the gutter and downspout,
> Measures our nature
> >               and moves the body to music.

> The book says, however,
> >               time is not body's movement
> But memory of body's movement.
> Time is not water but the memory of water:
> We measure what isn't there.
> We measure the silence.
> >               We measure the emptiness.

If you compare the length of two syllables, Augustine wrote in the *Confessions*, you must keep the memory of the first in your mind even as you utter the second, while both waft away into the past. As John Hollander pointed out in *Vision and Resonance*, Augustine's example implicates poetry as a ritualized marker of time, a ghostly index of vanishings. Wright finds a memorable image for the belatedness of human perception in the shed husk of a cicada left "in the dark tree of the self." The poem's last section finds an eloquent correspondence

between literature and life: first, Wright offers the lovely triangular anal-
ogy among time, rainwater, and bodily movement; then, corrected by
Augustine, he adds his melancholy qualification and subsides into silence.
Here, philosophy is not to be confirmed or denied, but poetically
enacted.

Wright succeeds most signally when his descriptions both invite and
elude philosophical paraphrase. If made to summarize the invigorating
"Easter 1989" from *Chickamauga*, we might say something about the su-
perposition of the biological on the religious; but this can't keep pace
with the physical gusto of Wright's version of resurrection—a heady
brew of cells, membranes, and enzymes mixed with the ceremonial trap-
pings of habits, cowls, and cassocks. This landscape is tinted with the pa-
thetic fallacy, but not in the expected way. It bristles with hidden
assassins: the willow "[m]enacing in its green caul," the full moon "gun-
ning under the cloud's cassock," and the "power that kicks on / the cells
in the lilac bush," undoing us by a sort of electrocution. Wright has often
written about the breach between official landmarks, like New Year's, and
the way he feels; here, Easter resurrection becomes the disorientation of
waking up in his middle-aged body—reworked, as he put it in "Tattoos,"
into his same life:

> We are what we've always thought we were—
> Peeling the membrane back,
>                           amazed, like the jonquil's yellow head
> Butting the nothingness—
>                      in the wrong place, in the wrong body.

Butting the nothingness: in the exuberant aural collision of words,
Wright gets inside the jonquil's assertive stem with Keatsian energy. So
dazzled are we by this felicity that the next verse-paragraph, a cabalistic
aphorism from Pseudo-Dionysus ("The definer of all things / cannot be
spoken of"), passes as the merest blur.

Visiting luminaries like Pseudo-Dionysus sometimes seem like inter-
lopers in Wright's landscapes, but in another poem from *Chickamauga*, a
line from Li Po ("The river winds through the wilderness") actually sets
the Milky Way in prospective motion:

> Sunlight reloads and ricochets off the window glass.
> Behind the cloud scuts,
>                    inside the blue aorta of the sky,
> The River of Heaven flows
> With its barge of stars,
>                     waiting for darkness and a place to shine.
>
> We who would see beyond seeing
>                        see only language, that burning field.

The scene pulses with life as alluvial star-clusters flow through an aerial heart. Who would have thought to call the sky an aorta? Behind the metaphor we see the Greek verb meaning *to lift up*, hear the faint syllable of *air*, remember the naming of earthly thoroughfares as *arteries*. We "see only language," indeed. Wright can't help adding the appositive kick of "that burning field," which turns the invisible concept of "language" back into a metaphor, the sun-dazzled meadow in which he started. And yet this last sentence breaks the spell of Wright's fine images; it adds an opaque gloss to the radiant translucence of the words. The heavenly river barge, the sun's artillery, the sky-blue aorta—all threaten to vanish under a self-conscious sermon to the converted. Such generalization is perhaps the unavoidable residue of a poetry that aspires to both descriptive particularity and philosophical presentation. Yet finally we don't need to be reminded that we're seeing only language; if we have been reading Charles Wright, we have been grateful for it all along.

BONNIE COSTELLO

# Charles Wright, Giorgio Morandi, and the Metaphysics of the Line (2002)

The relation between drawing and poetry begins before a single mark has been made. "I came to my senses with a pencil in my hand and a piece of paper in front of me," puns Charles Wright (b. 1935). He is quite aware that this statement could describe him as an artist rather than a writer *(Negative* 158). Putting down lines on flat white space, and thus giving it depth, becomes the artist's gesture of mediation between nothing and something, even before the line performs any encoded function. Furthermore, Wright's comment identifies the artist's vision with his compositional activity. Perception arises within the creative environment. "*True* description is enactment; [. . .] what is being described is part of the process" (*Quarter* 77, emph. Wright's). Wright's model of artistic agency has been the modern painter, who has led him not only to painterly images and metaphors but also to a conception of the poetic line as having spatial integrity. The line is not only the verbal register of stimuli or the encoding of voice, but it is also a direct visual mark in a spatial pattern of such marks. Yet, for Wright, the line is ultimately metaphysical in its import. Like synesthesia, the convergence of the arts (and the reciprocity between visual and phonological elements) points away from the senses. The artistic design and the description emerging from the writer's formal and imaginative "enactment" probe and project an ineffable, spectral, order.

Most comparisons between literature and the visual arts involve considerations of the organization and quality of the images, and Wright frequently draws analogies on these terms. Wright's descriptions, which employ a visual-art vocabulary of brush stroke, vanishing point, and frame, remind us of our role in producing what we see. While matters of imagery and representation bring poetry and painting together, discussions of prosody most often seek analogy with music. But in Wright's work the influence of the visual arts carries over from image to the line. Indeed, in Wright, the line emerges at an alignment of oral and visual impact, and the visual page becomes encoded with visionary themes.

The work of Giorgio Morandi has been central in Wright's development of this dynamic, in which the visual page shapes the sense of the line and becomes associated with the poem's abstract meaning. "Basic Dialogue" begins:

> The transformation of objects in space,
> 
> > or objects in time,
> 
> To objects outside either, but tactile, still precise . . .
> It's always the same problem—
> Nothing's more abstract, more unreal,
> 
> > than what we actually see.
> 
> The job is to make it otherwise. (*Negative* 147)

Wright does not acknowledge the source of the middle lines, but he no doubt knows that he has here a citation from Morandi. Karen Wilkin quotes this remark of Morandi's in her study of the artist: "I believe that nothing can be more abstract, more unreal, than what we actually see. We know that all we can see of the objective world, as human beings, never really exists as we see and understand it. Matter exists, of course, but has no intrinsic meaning of its own, such as the meanings we attach to it. We can know only that a cup is a cup, that a tree is a tree" (qtd. in Wilkin 122). In his search for this elusive knowledge, the artist works to strip away rather than add on meanings. He has studied those shallow, biplanar spaces ("two-ply air" [Wright, *World* 199]) with their perpendicular shapes and profiles, where the functional life of objects has almost vanished into abstraction. The bottles may have contained something, but what they suggest in Morandi is the form of an absence, the hollowed-out quality of the substantial world and its disembodied outline. Morandi's lines have inspired Wright not only in his treatment of the image but also in his handling of the visual page. The text, for Wright, creates a mental space that transforms objects in space and time to "objects outside either," but it also creates an optical space where lines carve into the white surface. In Wright, the "problem" of representation slips over into the "problem" of inscription. The mental images and the story of abstraction that they tell become directly related to the immediate optical configuration of the page and its "transformation" to a map of the invisible. Postmodern poetry often breaks the mimetic ties of word and image, but the space of artifice may be refigured in metaphysical terms.

As Renée Riese Hubert suggests in "The Postmodern Line and the Postmodern Page," many contemporary visual artists—Sol LeWitt, Jasper Johns, Cy Twombly, for instance—have minimized the distinction between graphic and verbal arts, creating a "dynamic performance of lines" (136) that evokes literary and visual values at once. It is for this reason, presumably, that Wright chose Twombly's deliberately untitled scribble drawing for the cover of his volume *Zone Journals*. He may indeed be "reading" Morandi's work in just this way: as inscription rather than pictorial representation. Conversely, writers have been fascinated by the sense that writing is a kind of drawing. Paul Valery's manuscripts, for instance, often cross the boundary between one graphic medium and the other as he leaps toward the revelation of thought in image (Bourjea 136). The concept of writing as drawing suggests a greater immediacy of the text's material production. Something of this idea is present in what Martine Reid, in her introduction to the special issue of *Yale French Studies* entitled *Boundaries: Writing and Drawing*, has called "textual genetics": "Textual genetics reasserts the value of the active, fluid process that is the textual production of the writer 'at work,' the evolution of the writing towards its final form" (4). This return to compositional origins, for Reid, breaks down the boundary between writing and drawing, the legible and the visible, and thus participates in the larger modern project of undoing "the old imperatives of differentiation" (5).

My emphasis on the visual text might seem to align Wright with the materialist aesthetic that Jerome McGann describes in *Black Riders: The Visible Language of Modernism*. McGann observes a turn in modernism, initiated by the "Renaissance of Printing," away from a correspondence or mimetic theory of meaning (in which poetry participates in a system of symbolic exchange) toward a phenomenology of images arising in the encounter with the material text. "The work forces us to attend to its immediate and iconic condition, as if the words were images or objects in themselves, as if they were *values* in themselves (rather than vehicles for delivering some further value or meaning)" (75, emph. McGann's). Yet Wright does insist on something "beyond" the line and its "face value," even as he draws attention to the page. McGann would deconstruct this "beyond" as a subordination of the materiality of the text to an existing "patriarchal order of symbolic value" (75). For him, the materiality of the line ought to be obdurate with respect to such values. But, for Wright, the artist's production is a sounding and a mapping of the infinite, or what Justus Lawler, in his Stevensian title, calls "celestial pantomime." In this sense, the most material element of the work, through formal patterning, can direct us to its most abstract meaning. Like Wallace Stevens, Wright defers questions of whether the invisible exists outside poetic enactment. Calvin Bedient is right to note that the poet is "defiantly un-Derrida'd" ("Slide-Wheeling" 47). Nor does he engage in any ideological scrutiny of his transcendental formalism. This question aside, my interest here is in analyzing the role of free verse in Wright's understanding of his own and Morandi's artistic ambition. Whether we accept Wright's visionary project or not, we might consider how his interest in the material condition of the line (its spatial and aural integrity, and this relation to grammar and syntax) works to reinforce his metaphysics.

Wright's feeling for Morandi's work grew out of a prior and lasting love of Italian landscape and art inspired when he served in the Army Intelligence Service in Verona from 1957 to 1961. This formative passion combined with his attachment to the scenes of his childhood in Tennessee and North Carolina to produce a unique blend of the visionary and the local. Wright's poems constantly evoke Italian landscapes, savoring their names, their light, and their associations. Italian writers—Dante and Leopardi, as well as those Wright has translated—provide companionable points of view as he moves through even American spaces (e.g., "Laguna Dantesca" [*World* 311]). The influence of Eugenio Montale's transcendentalism has been particularly lasting. (Like Montale, Wright composes his volumes as trilogies; Wright's *Xionia* recalls Montale's *Xenia*, as if to mark a shift from the homey to the eschatological.) In Montale he found a commitment to modernism that retained the Romantic passion (especially Leopardi's) for the infinite. But Montale pursues a music that Wright never adopted, either in his English translations or in his own poems.

Wright absorbed Ezra Pound's influence more superficially, but at the same time more broadly. Pound was the inevitable poet to inspire a young American discovering his art in Italy. Pound also introduced Wright to Chinese poetry, with which he has sustained a long dialogue. He may have inspired Wright's early compression and disjunction, and especially his insistence on the formal integrity of free verse. But Wright's line differs from Pound's, especially after *China Trace*. Since Wright is a meditative poet, one might expect him to turn to Wallace Stevens, whose phrases reverberate throughout Wright's poetry. Instead, for a formal model, he turned to the visual arts. He states: "I began to look closely at Cézanne and Morandi, two painters who used space and structure in ways that appealed to me. I've tried to carry some of those ideas over into my poems. So, structural considerations, architecture of the poem, the use of space, design" (*Quarter* 106).

Wright chose a landscape drawing by Morandi for the cover of his collected early poems, *Country Music*, a volume that includes a poem entitled "Morandi." He has since written several other poems about the artist and mentions him frequently in interviews. In Morandi, Wright found an imagination akin to his own, interested in "the metaphysics of the quotidian" (*Halflife* 22) and drawn to the everyday for the sense of mystery it arouses. He traces disappearances to awaken a sense of what's not there. For both artist and poet, a tension develops between the particular, referential world of description and a universal, absolute Platonic world of structure. This creative play "between the speculative and the decorative," as Sidney Tillim said of Morandi (Wilkin 118), takes place most profoundly in the line, where substance enters form and form enters composition, and where the particular meets the abstract. But what most attracts Wright is the way the line both breaks and evokes the emptiness of the page, creating a haunting dialectic of presence and absence. Morandi's silhouetted bottles and minimally sketched landscapes maximize negative space. "There's a kind of spatial negation," Wright observes, "a visual power in absence that painters understand and employ, and which I'm interested in poetically. It's a sort of white hole that has a kinetic draw to it that the lines of the poem float and resist" (*Quarter* 173). Wright instinctually associates Morandi's line with the poetic line, a poetic line with a spatial pattern spun out in time: "Morandi's line is always on the point of disappearing, of not *seeming* to be there. And it takes so few of them to get the structure right. Again Montale. Or the spider and her web" (*Halflife* 8, emph. Wright's). The practical aesthetics of the page in poetry may be musical or conceptual (he does not experiment much with typography), but the line is visual in its dialectic with space and in its ability to evoke an invisible order. The textual page is a map, not an image, on the one hand, or a score, on the other. Like a visual artist, the poet covers the white surface with dark lines. For the poet, syntax rather than geometry forms the logic of the line. Individual lines also form a relational dynamic with other lines, just as they do for the visual artist. For Wright, the line gives the page a depth that evokes a metaphysical dimension. Wright understands form as "style." As he puts it in an early interview, "Morandi is a stylist I much admire. His line in his drawings and *incisioni* is the kind of line I would like to have in my poems" (124). But individual style, for Wright, as for Morandi, pursues an ultimate structure. Not satisfied with the ambitions of a formalist, he aims for the revelation of form.

Wright's painterly, non-narrative conception of the line ("the line works best for me, a series of building blocks, or strokes, or layers that tend to accrue rather than be directed" [*Quarter* 172]) distinguishes him from other contemporary poets. He states: "I want people to be able to look at the poem on the page, read it and say, as though they had seen a painting on the wall, 'This is Charles Wright'" (104). Henry Sayre and Marjorie Perloff have both suggested that William Carlos Williams's line is essentially visual rather than aural, but they do not develop a metaphysics of this aesthetic patterning, nor do they understand the relation of this visual patterning to the thematic content of the poem (Perloff 89-117). For Williams, visual patterning objectifies verbal art. For other free-verse poets, the line is organic, a means of enhancing the sense of natural speech, defining an intimate voice, or developing the drama or local meanings of a poem. Wright's expressive theory applies to a general prosodic scheme for each poem, not just to local effects. He might call it constructive or reconstructive theory. "Composition by line has always been my game," he insists (*Quarter* 172). For a long time, Wright associated the unit of the line with the unit of language producing a mental image. But Wright's recent work is far less image-dominant. The declarative statement, the startling paradox, the confident aphorism, have become governing units, though one could argue that they function like images and that their rhetorical and syntactic form is more important than their ideational content. Again these utterances are "constructed line by line" rather than carried over several lines as a discursive communication, so that one feels the force of the line rather than the pressure of the line break. Wright relies more on symmetry than on counterpoint in his handling of syntax in relation to line. But, while the line seems to objectify the image or rhetorical shape, it may be more accurate to see these as governed by a principle of lineation. The line is a compositional unit determining voice rather than an expedience of voice.

The cover of Charles Wright's *Country Music*,
published by Wesleyan University Press, Middletown, CT, 1982

And Wright's sense of the line is not only "in the integrity of the writer's ear." The visual power of the line works more directly. The poems he has written since 1982 take up more of the page and build in more white space. As Wright sought a way out of the confines of free verse, "spatially tight and formally loose," he has conceptualized the poetic line as plastic design: "What we could use a bit more of is the poem that is spatially loose and formally tight, where the line is rib and bone and object, where the line is a thing, tactile and unrepentant" (*Halflife* 5). Wright has taken a route opposite but parallel to that of George Oppen, whose poems are spatially *and* formally tight, controlled, as Perloff has shown, in terms of the coalescence of sound, yet syntactically and semantically jagged, removed from ordinary discourse, and bent on turning desire toward hard fact. Wright's line is increasingly coordinated to phrase, directing desire toward the infinite rather than the discrete. For Wright, that "unrepentant[ly]" material design marks out the desire for incarnate meaning: "Each line should be a station of the cross" (*Halflife* 5). Wright identifies art and religion, reifying negative space and vanishing point as "The Unseen." Wright's "tactility," not only in the sharpness of his images but also in the visual integrity of his form, gives "The Unseen" a sacramental vigor.

These remarks about the line appear in "Improvisations on Form and Measure," which introduces Wright's prose collection, *Halflife: Improvisations and Interviews*. Yet Wright's insistence on the importance of poetic form, and especially "the line" as a route to form, has received little comment from critics, perhaps because prosodic matters in general are neglected in the discussion of modern poetry. But form is the ultimate content of poetry. Apparently minor decisions about syntax, grammar, and line become ways for writers to dramatize the relation between the finite and the infinite, the many and the one. All poetry, in this sense, is essentially abstract, whatever its subject matter or representational values. Wright understands this when he remarks, "Form is nothing more than the transubstantiation of content" (*Halflife* 3). This is the opposite to a mimetic theory of form, since Wright's content is "the idea of God." When Wright declares his subject as "language, landscape and the idea of God" (*Quarter* 135), he does not presume the existence of God. On the contrary, he locates God as an idea arising within a system of representation and a perceptual frame, without prejudice (though with profound interest) as to whether that idea establishes a transcendent meaning. The "idea" gains tremendous rhetorical power from the endowment and reification in the line.

Most readers attend to Wright's themes without considering their formal embodiment. While his metaphysical imagery and metaphoric capacity have been much noted, few have attended to his line, except to note that it has grown longer and looser. Only Stephen Cushman, in his excellent essay entitled "The Capabilities of Charles Wright," has provided a detailed analysis of Wright's free verse in terms of the fictions the poet constructs to produce it. Cushman follows out a remark Wright made in conversation, that "free verse is Negative Capability" (222). Why a line ends on a certain word rather than another is, for Wright, something neither premeditated nor arbitrary, but is felt and intuited according to an idea of metaphysical pattern, what the poet only half jokingly calls UFO, or "ultimate formal organization" (225). For Wright, the "secret of the universe" is formal in nature, and the poet's lines pursue this secret. Cushman rightly introduces a practical scrutiny into this rather mystical claim and documents Wright's tendency to "loose syllabics." (And we might note that syllabic verse in English is more visual than aural.) Cushman observes how Wright's insistent capitalization of first words makes the line emphatic, whereas what the poet names his "dropped line or low rider" (*Halflife* 52) calls the nature of the line into question. Cushman turns from Wright's negative to his "positive capability," relocating the poet's poetics in the actual work of poetry. Here he moves to matters of genre, figuration, and rhetoric, as a means of "conversion of the ephemeral into the abiding" (238). But clearly that phrase applies equally to Wright's transmission of voice as line. I wish to extend Cushman's discussion, relocating matters of lineation in relation to the visual arts.

The visual arts have, of course, provided Wright with images and metaphors as well as prosodic principles. That is, they have provided him with images of a way of seeing. Writings of Cézanne, Monet, Braque, Stella, Giacometti, and others dominate Wright's commonplace books. Modern painting has provided Wright with his primary genres, which often merge in his work: landscape, still life, and self-portraiture. More importantly, modern painting models the tension and integration between seeing and forming. Objects (or what Wright calls "subject matter") dramatize perception, serving as foci where will and world intersect. With painters, Wright strives for a condition of phenomenal truth emerging in this encounter. Even Wright's self-portraits are not psychological or autobiographical; they are meditations on the self as perceiver and pilgrim of the aesthetic ideal. Charles Altieri's notion of "aesthetic idealism" (in *Painterly Abstraction in Modernist American Poetry*), with its emphasis on the semantic force of the performative and the exemplariness of the constructive will in art, might take us some way in appreciating Wright's abstraction. But the poet's insistence on a negative metaphysics, and on landscape, as a source of this metaphysics, remains at odds with Altieri's emphasis on agency and abstraction. Landscape is Wright's primary genre because it is a site in which "nature" and "imagination" intersect. The world in Wright's poems often seems a canvas. In such poems as "Yard Journal" and throughout the poems in Wright's middle volume, *The World of the Ten Thousand Things*, the poet composes an image from experience and then reflects on the meaning of what he has composed. "My landscapes have always been imaginary, invented and reconstructed," he says. "I look and I impose and then I decompose them and then recompose them. In taking apart and putting back together, the emotional glue—the cement of abstractions that hold reality together—gets worked in and, I hope, becomes an integral part of the reconstruction" (*Halflife* 181). Words on the page are not transparent vehicles for creating a mental picture of this play between perception and landscape. Sentences have been "recomposed" spatially on the page so that one sees and hears clausal units and responds to the piling up of thoughts and images. One is aware of the poet working the language, creating balance and opposition in the verbal plane as a painter works the plastic surface of art.

This approach to composition derives from Cézanne. Wright states: "[Cézanne] breaks down and reassembles the landscape the way I like to think, when I'm working at my desk, I break down and reassemble what I'm looking at and put it back into a poem to recreate it, to reconstruct it. I like the idea that in fact he is very much of a realist although up close everything looks abstract. But once you get the right perspective, he is showing you just what's out there. I like to think I'm showing you just what's out there, but as I see it" (*Quarter* 135). Cézanne is the resident artist of *The World of the Ten Thousand Things*, and Wright often seems to be working alongside him. Bruce Bond has written thoughtfully about Wright's connection to Cézanne in "Metaphysics of the Image in Charles Wright and Paul Cézanne," where he follows out ideas from Claude Merleau-Ponty's "Cézanne's Doubt" and applies them to Wright's "Homage to Paul Cézanne" (*World* 3-10). Both artists, Bond argues, create a metaphysical depth in their quest for the real, since the primitive is always an object of desire and future attainment. Bond's discussion remains thematic, however, and does not provide much analysis of technique. But Wright tries to relate Cézanne's visual model not only to image and landscape but also to the line. Comparing his technique to Cézanne's, Wright states: "Change colors to words and white to blanks and you have something, I believe" (*Halflife* 37). This visual analogy alternates with a sensory crossing: "My poems are put together in tonal blocks, in tonal units that work off one another. While Cézanne's are color and form. I try to do that in sound; patterns within the line, in the line within the stanza, and the stanza within the poem" (20).

Morandi provided a more lasting example for Wright, especially as the poet's attention has shifted from an image-centered to a gnomic, contemplative line. With Morandi, he discovered a coincidental rather than a strictly analogical relation between the arts. Wright's sense of structure now involves more chiaroscuro than blocks of color (or, in verbal terms, with positives and negatives rather than with a spectrum of metaphors and images or tonal variety) and his sense of truth involves the absence that construction discloses. He discovers form through outline and disappearances rather than through a struggle with substance and sculptural modeling. When Wright now mentions Cézanne, it is the late Cézanne, the artist of form: "Cézanne became a great painter when he deserted forms and discovered structure. [Cézanne] had gotten down to the essence of his art" (*Quarter* 134). Morandi also studied late Cézanne obsessively. He was the first Italian artist to recognize Cézanne's importance, and his early landscapes expose the influence. But, while Cézanne works in the tension between perception and construction, Morandi, at least as Wright understands him, works in the tension between what's there and what's not, between form and disappearance. "I like Morandi because he's very little known and Morandi's aim, his program, was different from everybody else's around him at the time. He sat there and he painted bottles and flowers and landscape. When your subject matter in 1991 is language, landscape, and the idea of God, your aims are different from everybody else's. You're sitting there painting landscapes, flowers, and the edges of houses while everybody else is, you know, at the Super Bowl or whatever. So there's another reason I like him. Because he stuck with it, all his life" (135-36).

Morandi's objects do not excite the senses or engage the viewer in the delightful plenitude of the "world of the ten thousand things." Like Wright, he is interested in the ephemeral world as it reveals eternal principles. As Emily Braun writes, "Of subject matter, there is none, since the bottles and bowls exist as mere armatures for the articulation of the picture plane and the play with spatial illusion" (8). Morandi's indifferent, homely bottles were famously covered in dust and seem to dissolve under its weight. Wilkin notes the "thick, unifying layer of dust" conveyed on the canvas. The subtle differences from one canvas to the next record a myopic struggle to see things as they verge on disappearance and expose the outline of something eternal. Wright works increasingly on this boundary. He has given up the rich palette of "Yard Journal" for a spare, abstract rendering of a few obsessive themes and images. "Back yard, dry flower half-border, unpeopled landscape / Stripped of embellishment and anecdotal concern" (*Negative* 129).

Morandi offered Wright the example of an Italian artist, almost contemporary, committed to the modern but deeply tied to tradition, going back to Giotto and Caravaggio. Morandi first appeared with the Futurists, exhibiting with Boccioni and Severini at the Hotel Baglioni in 1914. He broke ranks with this group (while remaining close to individuals) because their rage against tradition was purely negative, subverting every rule of vision and object recognition. Wright seems to have a similar relationship to radical movements. He remarks in "With Simic and Marinetti at the Guibbe Rosse," "Those who don't remember the Futurists are condemned to repeat them" (*Negative* 48). Morandi learned a great deal from the Cubism of Braque and Picasso, but in Italy this movement went beyond questions of perception; it sought to "mean more." The artist was briefly associated with the movement called "Metaphysical Painting" and remained friends with its other major proponents, Giorgio de Chirico and Carlo Carra (who anticipate Magritte and Cornell). This tradition remains important to Elizabeth Bishop,

Charles Simic, Mark Strand, John Ashbery, and other American poets. But where de Chirico and Carra suggest radically reinvented geometries that remove objects from observed and natural spaces, making the scene a metaphysical theatre, Morandi preferred to discover the metaphysical in the elemental forms of appearance. The job of the artist is not to make objects mean more by transposing them to a surreal landscape. Rather, the artist must make us discover the infinite in the appearance of things. In this endeavor, Morandi was aided by the Italian poet Giacomo Leopardi, whose volume he kept always at his bedside.

Wright includes a poem to Morandi in his last book, *Appalachia*. Again, in "Giorgio Morandi and the Talking Eternity Blues," the poet imagines the older artist out of the *spiritus mundi*:

> Late April in January, seventy-some-odd degrees.
> The entry of Giorgio Morandi in The Appalachian Book of the Dead
> Begins here, without text, without dates—
> A photograph of the master contemplating four of his objects,
> His glasses pushed high on his forehead,
>                         his gaze replaced and pitiless. (*Negative* 167)

The photograph that Wright refers to provides the frontispiece to Rizzoli's *catalogue raisonné* of Morandi. It presents a half torso, Morandi seated behind a table with his objects laid before him. He could be a mirror image of the writer at his desk. The word *replaced* where we expect the Yeatsian *blank* suggests indeed that Wright has no real communion with the dead, only with himself through their representation. Morandi's glasses point heavenward; his gaze remains fixed on objects. The poet contemplates the gap. And, indeed, from this opening, Wright moves back to his situation, on this side, where the mourning doves coo. Morandi is unmoved by the doves' lament, which the poet clearly feels. "Giorgio Morandi doesn't blink an eye / As sunlight showers like sulphur grains across his face" (167). Sunlight *is* sulphur grains when rendered in photography. The poet, whose wife is a photographer, knows this well. But, by making the literal metaphoric, Wright can invoke a reality of "eternity" beyond representation. The play of the transient against the eternal is again figured in the landscape, where "clouds moving south to north along the Alleghenies" awaken him to the substanceless "rock and hard ground" of Eternity (167).

The poem's mourning and longing ends in the final stanza, where Wright seems implicitly to be thinking of Morandi's still lifes, those bottles that bear witness to ideal form:

> Now starless, Madonnaless, Morandi
> Seems oddly comforted by the lack of comforting
> A proper thing in its proper place,

Giorgio Morandi. Photograph by Herbert List.
Reproduced by permission of the Herbert List estate.

> Landscape subsumed, language subsumed,
>                                   the shadow of God
> Liquid and indistinguishable.                    (*Negative* 167)

How different the form of this final passage is from the one that began the poem! It is the difference, perhaps, between near-prose and poetry, between the reportorial and the meditative, between talking temporality and talking eternity. The opening of the poem anticipates this end, of course. To find "late April in January" is to disturb temporal sequence (the *a* sound fusing the seasons), and the third line, with its repetition "without text, without dates" both speaks and sings of something working beyond temporal drift. But most of the lines stretch out across the page, descriptive in their function and subtle in their cadence. A tense dynamic is set off when the lifting *a*'s of line 1 meet the *d*'s of "odd degrees." And the stanza as a whole seems clipped by the *p* sounds in *pushed*, *replaced*, and *pitiless*. The sense of these lines is not extension but finitude. By contrast, the last stanza lulls us with its assonance and alliteration, its gracefully rocking rhythms, accomplished by caesuras and phonemic echoes. The sense is not of an unfolding description but of an established balance of syllables and thoughts in each line. "A proper thing in its proper place" does what it says, but the technique here is not narrowly or locally mimetic. There is a prosodic scheme for the whole. And any risk of confining repetition, of "rock and hard ground," is released in the beautifully fluid closing phrases: "the shadow of God / Liquid and indistinguishable" (167). The poem is almost without metaphors; (the one simile, we have seen, is a false simile). It nearly gives up the sensuous image, or rather replaces it with the sensuous idea in the form of the shapely and sonorous line. Its shape is musical and linguistic, drawn to evoke the expressiveness of Morandi's visual line. But it would be wrong to understand the link only analogically. Sound here reinforces the graphic integrity of the line. The two work together. Wright avoids enjambment without simply yielding to the dictates of the discursive utterance. His objective seems to be to let the optical and tonal units support each other while loosening the hold of the discursive or mimetic to evoke an abstract aesthetic order. The possibilities for such integration are many and suggest just how malleable the notion of the poetic "line" in free verse really is.

In the mid-1980s, Wright published two short prose pieces on Morandi, which he later brought together in *Halflife* (7–8). In juxtaposition, they outline the paradox that fascinates Wright: the artist's line is a precise rendering of what is there, and yet it draws attention to the unseen; loving attention to the humble and common awakens our desire for an invisible absolute. Part 1 of Wright's essay (published in 1987) focuses, with aid from an article by art critic Robert Hughes, on the artist of "persistent and continuous inspection," of "things as they are." Like Cézanne, Morandi is a "rescuer as well as a reconstructor" (7) of the real. In this version, Morandi is devoted to "the gradual permutations of experience." But Part 2, published earlier, emphasizes the late Morandi's abstraction, his "Platonic drawings," and his confident assertion of abstract vision:

> Morandi's drawings, toward the end of his life, resemble the poems of certain masters of style: each line tends to be a statement, self-sufficient, self-contained, where no elaboration is needed: the entire weight of their lives seems flicked off in a phrase, an observation. [ . . . ] The famous bottles and compote dishes begin to be drawn back into the paper, becoming larger the more they dissemble. It's almost as though they are drawn on the air, that masterly, and in that instant starting to be borne away, the statement having been made, the design now lodged in memory, tactile and unremovable.[ . . . ] These drawings [ . . . ] are maps, trail markings, sand sketches from an absolute, [ . . . ] lifelines to the unseen.
>
> (8-9)

Norman Bryson has also noticed Morandi's penchant for "seeking solid in void and void in solid" (98). Wright's early conception of his own line, which transforms Celan's famous phrase by connecting it to Edvard Munch, reverberates: "Notes in a bottle, our lines the ink from the full moon" (*Country* 127).

As the elegy and these prose remarks make clear, Wright's relation to Morandi's line is improvisatory, varied, and intuitive. It wavers between analogy and affinity. We can begin to plot the shifts in this relation by looking at three poems explicitly connected to Morandi, each from one of the poet's major collections. Inspired by Dante, Wright has collected his work into three separate trilogies, which together, and individually, suggest past, present, and future in ontological terms that shift from self, to world, to God. In each of these poems —"Morandi" (*Country* 114); "Chinese Journal" (*World* 199); "Still Life with Stick and Word" (*Negative* 60)—we find poetic versions of the dialectic of concrete and abstract, presence and absence, form and forms, which fascinate him in Morandi. These poems map out changes in Wright's style as he reapplies Morandi's example of the metaphysics of the line to his own developing aesthetics.

In *China Trace*, the last volume in his collected early work entitled *Country Music*, Wright includes his poem "Morandi." Significantly, this is the only two-line-stanza poem in the entire collection, which includes most of Wright's second, third, and fourth volumes, as well as a few poems from his first. All the other poems are written in sonnet-like blocks, longer stanzas, or stanzas of variable length. Morandi's lean, precise line seems to inform Wright's lineation here, but it develops more fully into Wright's signature style in later books.

> I'm talking about stillness, the hush
> Of a porcelain center bowl, tear vase, a jug.

I'm talking about space, which is one-sided,
Unanswered, and left to dry.

I'm talking about paint, about shape, about the void
These objects sentry for, and rise from.

I'm talking about sin, red drop, white drop,
Its warp and curve, which is blue.

I'm talking about bottles, and ruin,
And what we flash at the darkness, and what for . . .

(*Country* 114)

*China Trace* as a volume is rapturously driven toward the void, pursuing disappearances, divestitures, "names falling into the darkness" (*Country* 111). The lines of this poem work as emphatic, discrete thrusts into silence; white space paradoxically dramatizes the darkness to which the poem refers. Wright's lines present discrete "flashes at the darkness." Since each stanza is one two-line sentence, the second line tends to feel like an extension of the first, part of one long thrust. Wright had not yet invented the "dropped line" that characterizes later work, and in fact the effect is different here. One feels the second line of each stanza as a comeback, the completion through a second try at the silence. The anaphora exaggerates the sense of the two-line stanza as a discrete unit, and it also brings the stanzas into relation with one another. End words also do important work here, in creating that "kinetic energy" with the white space. "Hush," "sided," "void," "drop," "ruin" not only mark off the line aurally but also make it self-referential, investing the white space with meaning. "You keep the composition apart just a little to let this energy in and out, and to let the poem in and out of the energy generated by this emptiness" (*Quarter* 173). The second lines of each stanza (which complete each sentence) seem to let the energy out, beginning with unimportant words and prefixes such as "of," "un," "these," "its," and "and," and ending with phrases that defy the closure of the sentence such as: a list—"bowl, tear vase, jug"; an abandonment—"left to dry"; an emergence—"rise from"; an ambiguity—"which is blue"; an ellipsis—"what for. . . ." Wright is perhaps thinking of the relationships in Morandi's drawings, where some lines seem definitive and structural, pulling together the composition, while others dissolve into the paper's undefined boundary and open up the composition to indeterminacy. While lineation enhances the paratactic structure of "Morandi," the words develop a complex relation between image and abstraction. As the ekphrastic poem, the presence/absence dialectic emerges in the paradox of silence and speech that opens the poem.

Wright returns to Morandi in *The World of the Ten Thousand Things.* These poems, as the title of his second trilogy suggests, involve textures, objects, and events in the world around him and in memory. The poems are descriptive, journalistic, and discursive by comparison with the compressed metaphors, enigmas, and visionary intensity of earlier work. Bedient expressed discontent with this collection, particularly its last section, *Zone Journals.* He complains of a "discursive normalization," which leaves the visionary impulse subject to "niggardly disagreement," whereas the "raptorial," Dickinsonian quality of *China Trace* "threatened to swallow language" in visionary metaphor and thus left such disagreement far behind ("Slide-Wheeling"). As compressed metaphor has yielded to anecdote and commentary for Bedient, so the looser line has shown a "tendency to disintegrate" into "American sprawl" (44). (This is Wright's phrase, which Bedient turns on him.) But the Father of American sprawl is Whitman, and, like Wright, he associated that black effusion across the white page with the spider who casts his line across the void. Whereas earlier, Wright followed Pound and Williams in breaking the line into symmetrical units of two or three, his aim now is to keep the line whole. "One of the purposes (one of several) of writing the two-step line I have used on and off since 1978, the low-rider, whatever you want to call it, was to be able to keep the line from breaking under its own weight" (*Quarter* 79). The dropped line also creates pattern (aural and visual) in breaking against the white space and thus making the latter palpable as a space of resistance even as the poet continues sending out his filament. What looks like sprawl close up, full of debris, may at a distance reveal a careful design. Bedient's criticism of Wright is thoughtful and serious, provoked within an overall approval of Wright's aesthetic ambitions and a profound admiration for past and even current achievements. But we must test it against Wright's own explanation of his change in style: "Like a spider's web that is tight in its individual parts, but expandable in its larger structure, the entire poem trembles when any area is touched" (*Quarter* 103). Does Wright, as Bedient suggests, give up form in his thematic search for the UFO of form? Has discourse overtaken prosody in the way Bedient says it has overtaken metaphor? Or is it latent even in these "looser" poems of apparent "American sprawl"?

We can test the theory in reading "Chinese Journal," a series of apparently unrelated images marked off from each other by section breaks. The poem begins with reference to a Morandi still-life drawing:

> In 1935, the year I was born,
>                     Giorgio Morandi
> Penciled these bottles in by leaving them out, letting
> The presence of what surrounds them increase the presence
> Of what is missing,
>                     keeping its distance and measure.          (*World* 199)

Some thoughtful shaping of the line is apparent here. The dropped line both separates and unites the poet to the painter, and the repetition of "presence" balances the line in a paradox of absence. But we do not perceive the spider's web by examining its parts alone. To see the design, we must find the pattern repeated. Except for the fourth image (a two-line stanza where, briefly, "everything comes to rest" [*World* 199]), each stanza has four lines, two of which are dropped (making the stanza look like six). This is not a neat symmetry such as Williams tends to obey, since line lengths (and the location of dropped lines) vary. Nor is it simply a symmetry based on the page. Indeed, a pattern of paradox in the thought and imagery—presence/absence, stillness/motion, smallness/vastness—informs the subsequent stanzas in a similar rhythm. A still life by Morandi seems an odd way to start a poem called "Chinese Journal," and in fact there is nothing Chinese in the poem, unless it be the formal organization. The stanzas that follow form loose haiku, each presenting a brief image, though it doesn't obey a strict syllable count.

> The purple-and-white spike plants
> > stand upright and spine-laced,
> As though poised to fight by keeping still.
> Inside their bristly circle,
> The dwarf boxwood
> > flashes its tiny shields at the sun. (*World* 199)

By beginning the poem with Morandi, Wright has invited us to read subsequent images as still lifes, and to see how not only the images but also the lines themselves increase "the presence of what surrounds them." The vertical plants stand like Morandi's bottles, against the horizontal of the text and its "two-ply air." In the next stanza, the Pothos plant dangles down "heart-leaves in the nothingness," in countermotion to the defiant spikeplants. These stanzas mirror each other while remaining distinct. Each section begins and ends with a dropped line. Lines are mostly initiated by prepositions (*in, of, inside, into, as under, to*) probing the space, in contrast to the emphatic thrusts of "Morandi" and other poems in *China Trace*. End words are generally nouns: *measure, sun, nothingness, rest,* and *dust.* The penultimate stanza is more abstract and marks closure by its brevity, matching in pattern only to the first half of the other stanzas, opening into the white space. "To shine but not to dazzle. / Falling leaves, falling water, / everything comes to rest" (*World* 199). The poem that began with the poet's birth and the artist's drawing pauses on the word *rest,* which brings life (or death) and creativity together again. The poem appears "loose" indeed, but its deep structure abides in a formal design that only becomes apparent in the whole. The poem ends, however, on a relinquishment of any claim to have captured the ultimate pattern of things in the form of the poem. "What can anyone know of the sure machine that makes all things work?" (200). The spatial and aural gesture of the line yields to the emptiness of white space in the last line. No extension into a low-rider here; we are up against a limit: "An inch of music is an inch and a half of dust" (200).

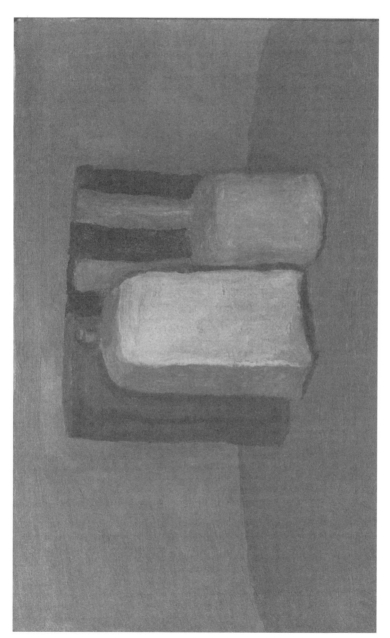

Giorgio Morandi, *Natura Morta*, c. 1957. The University of Iowa Museum of Art.
Gift of Owen and Leone Elliott (1986.36). Copyright The University of Iowa Museum of Art.

In the three volumes collected in *Negative Blue*, form has become subject matter more explicitly than ever before. The danger in such thematic foregrounding is the neglect of form at the non-semantic level, where it properly belongs. As form becomes an idea, does it lose its relation to form (reversing Cézanne's achievement)? Some readers have criticized Wright's recent discursive turn, suggesting that it converts his skeptical metaphysics into a kind of dogma. But a careful study of the poems reveals much creative struggle carried on at the level of the line even as gnomic utterance supplants image. In recent poems, he has worked toward a binary palette, a chiaroscuro effect, in which images largely recede, exposing the "black zodiac" (as he calls his 1997 volume) that is writing. The painterly world of the ten thousand things has been reduced, as in Morandi, to a few bare objects in a linguistic plane. He calls his poem after Morandi "Still Life with Stick and Word" as if to remind us that the artist's work inhabits the threshold of reference and medium (*Negative* 60). Again, Wright does not describe Morandi's painting. In this case, no painting appears at all in the poem, though it is identified in the notes (that *Natura Morta* is from the University of Iowa collection, 1958).

The spirit of Morandi's stripped-down painting informs Wright's poem: "better to concentrate on something close, something small. / This stick, for instance. This word." Wright's conflation of landscape and still life in the poem evokes Morandi's two sole genres, which become metaphors for the movement between outside and inside. As the poem continues, the outside itself becomes architectural, full of corridors and entrances into the emptiness. Wright returns repeatedly to his minimalist scene just as Morandi returns to his cluster of bottles, to discover the unreal in the real: "how unlike it is. How like." "Next week. Back in the same chair." But the same is never the same, is seen differently each time, its light/dark values reverse: "Out into absence. Night chair. [. . .] A slide of houselight escapes through the kitchen window" (*Negative* 60).

Morandi's visual surface emerges synesthetically at the end of the poem. "White. It covers my tongue like paint." Paint on the tongue silences speech. To utter "white" is to evoke the silence of the unmarked page. White, the "great eviscerator," is more negative than darkness as this poem pursues an inversion of values. Like words on the page, "Yips in the dog dark [. . .] mirror the overburn." The stick at the beginning has pointed the way to infinity; the white spots on its bark (the reverse of white page and black letters) become "star charts to ford the river of heaven" (*Negative* 60).

Morandi's is not an art of epiphany, however, and few lines in Wright's late work have the visionary thrust that erupts even in the "loose" lines of *The World of the Ten Thousand Things*. The line is still the governing unit of the composition, but the effects are slower and more accreted. A certain awe arises in the repetition of "word" (from the title) once it is disclosed to be "white," but the language never becomes rhapsodic: "I say it and light forms, / Bottles arise, emptiness opens its corridors" (*Negative*

60). The movements from object to text, from stick to word, from outside to inside and back out again, mark a sub-narrative. But the poem is deliberately weighted in a rhetoric of measured time. The lines are made up of diary notations. "April is over. May moon"; "Next week. Back in the same chair"; "Out into absence. Night chair." Such two-fragment lines punctuate each five-line stanza, leading off into a second, longer, line that drops and extends across the page. The broken line leads in turn to two full or enjambed lines, but returns to the two-fragment line to close. The lineation marks a rhythm of containment or occlusion and release, moving toward the final sense of the world as uncanny.

The voice in this poem couldn't be more casual. The intensity is rather in the design. While the conception of the poem may derive from Morandi's painting, its effects are primarily aural in "spore-pocked" and "rose constellations rise" and in the *o*'s and *w*'s ("inside now. The word is white") and *o*'s against *a*'s ("April is over. May moon") and the rhythmic play of short and long vowels ("white yips in the dog dark that mirror the overburn. / A slide of houselight escapes through the kitchen window" [*Negative* 60]). These are not just local effects but rather a sound-scheme that defines the shape and relation of the lines. As Charles O. Hartman has observed of successful free verse, each poem as a whole must establish some general prosodic scheme (92). And Wright has remained committed to a further principle, that each line must have some special weight, some definition of its own. The confidence of these sonorous lines is marked in their spatial patterning and rises to the example of Morandi's spatial definitions.

For both Morandi and Wright, the line, which evokes descriptive and discursive subject matter, also draws the beholder into its inscription, where it becomes a map of the invisible. As a poet rather than a painter, Wright approaches this metaphysics through a different physics, one vigorously acoustic. Yet in his way of organizing the line he keeps the visual reality of the page, which he shares with the Italian master, constantly in his mind. The optical space of the poems informs their ultimate mental space. It is not only through the manipulation of sounds against silence, but also of shaped, written words against the white page, that Wright creates the metaphysical dimension into which he perpetually directs his desire.

## WORKS CITED

Altieri, Charles. *Painterly Abstraction in Modernist American Poetry*. Cambridge, UK: Cambridge UP, 1989.

Bedient, Calvin. "Tracing Charles Wright." *The Point Where All Things Meet: Essays on Charles Wright*. Ed. Tom Andrews. Oberlin: Oberlin College P, 1995. 21–39.

———. Slide-Wheeling around the Curves." *The Point Where All Things Meet: Essays on Charles Wright*. Ed. Tom Andrews. Oberlin: Oberlin College P, 1995. 39–52.

Bond, Bruce. "Metaphysics of the Image in Charles Wright and Paul Cézanne." *The Point Where All Things Meet: Essays on Charles Wright*. Ed. Tom Andrews. Oberlin: Oberlin College P, 1995. 264-74.

Bourjea, Serge. "Eye, Dance, Trace: The Writing Process in Valery's Rough Drafts." *Yale French Studies: Boundaries: Writing and Drawing* 84 (1994): 136-54.

Braun, Emily. "Speaking Volumes: Giorgio Morandi's Still Lifes and the Cultural Politics of *Strapaese*." *Modernism/Modernity* 2.3 (1995): 89-116.

Bryson, Norman. *Looking at the Overlooked: Four Essays on Still Life Painting*. Cambridge, MA: Harvard UP, 1990.

Cushman, Stephen. "The Capabilities of Charles Wright." *The Point Where All Things Meet: Essays on Charles Wright*. Ed. Tom Andrews. Oberlin: Oberlin College P, 1995. 223-41.

Hartman, Charles O. *Free Verse*. Princeton: Princeton UP, 1980.

Hubert, Renée Riese. "The Postmodern Line and the Postmodern Page." *The Line in Postmodern Poetry*. Ed. Robert Frank and Henry Sayre. Champagne: U of Illinois P, 1988. 133-46.

Lawler, Justus. *Celestial Pantomime*. New Haven: Yale UP, 1974.

McGann, Jerome. *Black Riders: The Visible Language of Modernism*. Princeton: Princeton UP, 1993.

*Morandi*. Exhibition catalogue. New York: Rizzoli, 1988. [First published in Italian by Mazzotta Publishers, Milan.]

Perloff, Marjorie. *The Dance of the Intellect*. Cambridge, MA: Cambridge UP, 1985.

Reid, Martine. Editor's Preface. "Legible/Visible." *Yale French Studies: Boundaries: Writing and Drawing* 84 (1994): 1-12.

Wilkin, Karen. *Giorgio Morandi*. New York: Rizzoli, 1997.

Wright, Charles. *China Trace*. Middletown, CT: Wesleyan UP, 1977.

———. *Country Music*. Middletown, CT: Wesleyan UP, 1982.

———. *Halflife: Improvisations and Interviews, 1977-87*. Ann Arbor: U of Michigan P, 1988.

———. *Zone Journals*. New York: Farrar, Straus & Giroux, 1988.

———. *The World of the Ten Thousand Things*. New York: Farrar, Straus & Giroux, 1990.

———. *Quarter Notes: Improvisations and Interviews*. Ann Arbor: U of Michigan P, 1995.

———. *Appalachia*. New York: Farrar, Straus & Giroux, 1998.

———. *Negative Blue*. New York: Farrar, Straus & Giroux, 2000.

# Charles Wright's *Via Mystica* (2004)

" The modern sequence is the decisive form toward which all the developments of modern poetry have tended," M. L. Rosenthal and Sally Gall once claimed. "It . . . is a response to the lyrical possibilities of language opened up by those pressures in times of cultural and psychological crisis, when all past certainties have many times been thrown chaotically into question" (3). Although poets like T. S. Eliot and Ezra Pound, emulating "the mythical method" of James Joyce's *Ulysses*, modeled their long poems on classical works, their epics traced personal obsessions rather than journeys of heroes intent on returning home or building an imperial city or finding heavenly paradise. In short, modern epics tended to trace the mind's wanderings and wonderings rather than the picaresque quests of culture heroes. The sequence form, which has become a genre in its own right, is musical in the way it plays variations on diverse themes, recording emotional highs and lows in a non-narrative progression. "It usually includes narrative and dramatic elements, and ratiocinative ones as well," Rosenthal and Gall point out, "but its structure is finally lyrical" (9). One might add that the modern poet's lyre-like music, if it is epic in scope and unconstrained by a traditional plot, can go on—as in Pound's case—for as long as the poet lives.

Charles Wright, one of the most ambitious and distinguished of the contemporary epic lyricists, has devoted most of his career to a quasi-Dantesque "trilogy of trilogies." He remarked in an interview: "In the same way that *Country Music* was a trilogy that was a kind of small-time *inferno, purgatorio,* and *paradiso, Chickamauga, Black Zodiac,* and *Appalachia* are a small-time *inferno, purgatorio,* and *paradiso*" (*Southbound*, 56). After composing his third *paradiso* (*Appalachia*), Wright came to a logical conclusion, but his quest continued. Would Dante have considered exploring a new region of the soul in *The Divine Comedy* after reaching the Trinity in the Empyrean's Celestial Rose, or Homer allowed Odysseus to undertake further adventures after rejoining his family in Ithaka? Epic poets of the past tended to narrate one arc of a cycle—a journey down and up, or out, around, and back. As Aristotle argued in his *Poetics*, classical narratives were supposed to have definite beginnings, middles, and ends. Disagreeing with Aristotle's orderly world-view, Wright's Modernist precursors mapped ongoing cycles of mind, body, culture, and nature in their disjunctive epics. In his "trilogy of trilogies," Wright does the same.

If the ghost structure supporting Wright's grand trilogy is *The Divine Comedy* (a work he studied as a Fulbright scholar in Italy during the mid-1960s and several years later as a professor at the University of California,

Irvine), the way he fragments Dante's architectonic design, scattering shards of infernos, purgatories, and paradises throughout his sequence, owes its largest debt to Pound. The catalyst for his writing career, Wright has acknowledged in poems and interviews, was Pound's "Blandula, Tenulla, Vagula," a rather old-fashioned poem commemorating Catullus's idyllic villa on Lake Garda's peninsula of Sirmione (Wright visited the place in 1959). "What hast thou, O my soul, with paradise?" Pound asked at the beginning of his poem. In *The Cantos*, Pound, for the most part, abandoned his archaic style, but not his obsession with finding paradises among history's ruins. To embody his cyclical quest among history's cycles, he developed an incantatory, ritualistic style that made constant use of anaphora—the repetition of phrases for rhetorical effect. Wright inherited Pound's ritualistic imagination, anaphoric style, and moody lyricism, adapting them to similar preoccupations with the past and its transcendence.

In an interview with editor and translator David Young, Wright explained that his principal concerns fell into the pattern of a trilogy: "There are three things, basically, that I write about—language, landscape, and the idea of God" (*Quarter Notes*, 123). His entire *oeuvre* amounts to a journey toward God in or beyond language and landscape. The journey has no end because God, for Wright, is elusive—a mystery forever attracting and repelling, beckoning and vanishing. Speaking of the Buddhist as opposed to the Christian search for God, he admitted: "I cannot find that still, small center in my self or in the world that will make me at one with my world. But I look for it. In fact I look for that more than I would look for . . . a Christian resolution. I was brought up in a Christian atmosphere . . . so my reference points, my linguistic touchpoints, all tend to be Christian. . . . But I would think, as I get older, my steps would be in the service of something more along the line of a Buddhistic journey than a Dantesque journey" (*Quarter Notes*, 123-124). In fact, his journey has always been both Eastern and Western, worldly and otherworldly, marked by a rhythm of emotional rises and falls. His meditative critiques of words circle back to the Word; his invocations of landscapes invoke a Creator of landscapes that remains absent. What impels the melancholic ground note of his poetry is the recognition that orthodox Word, God, and Heaven are fictions of a previous age—enticing souvenirs that realistic intellects can no longer believe.

If there is "one story and one story only" playing itself out in Wright's poetry, it harks back to the Biblical myth of Eden, Adam's fall, and Christ's redemption. The paradise he continually elegizes is that imaginary place and time in which God, landscape, and language were one. In an essay on Gerard Manley Hopkins, he expresses nostalgia for the Jesuit poet's ability to see "God's fingerprint and face on everything." Bolstered by his Catholic faith, Hopkins could claim that the "inscape" of a landscape or natural object "is knowable and tactile through language"; he could affirm an Edenic harmony between God's "book of nature" (His word-world) and poetic words; he could believe "that the heart of the mystery, the pulse at the very unspeakable center of being, is apprehensible through writing about it" (*Quarter Notes*, 24). By transcribing God's "book" into his poems, Hopkins and, in turn, his readers could commune with the supreme Author. Echoing Hopkins's lush, alliterative music and poignant nature imagery, Wright repeatedly expresses an unrequited longing for the sort of faith that made Hopkins's linguistic idealism possible.

Wright's postlapsarian and postmodernist world, however, differs radically from the Christian world inhabited by Hopkins. Referring to language's ability to unify God and landscape into a poetic "book of nature," Wright remarks: "One no longer believes this is possible. One more often now knows the only answer to inscape is silence. How marvelous, however, to see how the world once seemed, how Adamic it all was before the word and world became separate. And the Word and the world became separate" (*Quarter Notes*, 24). In his numerous references to himself as a pilgrim, Wright identifies with the old Adam evicted from Eden who searches for a Christian redemption that inevitably proves fleeting or non-existent. He identifies with the new Adam—Jesus—because he feels crucified by personal, linguistic, and philosophical quandaries. Nevertheless, his communions invariably underscore his unlikeness and separateness from Jesus. His religious imagination (in the sense of *re-ligare*, of binding back) constantly tries to resurrect sacred places and significant events from the past by linguistically re-membering them, but Mnemosyne provides only fleeting consolation. His ritualistic invocations of ancestors, poetic precursors, landscapes, gods, paintings, and other artifacts culminate in wistful recognitions that the past is ineluctably past, that Edenic unities are dead and gone. Redemption, if it comes at all, is always momentary. It is engendered by a mystical attentiveness (both Buddhist and Christian) to events and objects in an everyday environment (to what Wright perceives from his study window or a deck chair in his backyard) and by the process of writing itself.

The rhythm of joy and sorrow that throbs through Wright's poetry originates, in part, from his ambivalence toward both his everyday life and his attempts to transcend it. If Wright were content to simply record in realistic fashion the goings-on outside his house, his long poems in *Zone Journals* and later books might more closely resemble the sequences of William Carlos Williams and Williams's Imagist and Objectivist heirs. Working against Wright's Buddhist acceptance of things-as-they-are is an unquenchable desire for a Dantesque paradise or mystical sublime beyond landscape, beyond language, beyond thought, and even beyond God. Because he knows his inveterate leaps for the sublime will end in painful falls to earth, he struggles all the more to embrace the principle of desireless enlightenment, even though his Christian and Buddhist feelings of transcendence usually end in disillusionment. As his poems commemorating his youthful training at North Carolina Bible camps and

Episcopal schools attest, his religious temperament, with its introspective and transcendentalist tendencies, constitutes a kind of Nessus shirt, an "intolerable shirt of flame / Which human power cannot remove," as Eliot put it in the *Four Quartets* (196).

In Wright's late poem "Reading Lao Tzu Again in the New Year," he complains that he can't wriggle free from this shirt woven out of conflicting religious desires. As one year passes into another, he remains bound by old afflictions: "I stand in the dark and answer to / My life, this shirt I want to take off, / which is on fire." In an attempt to extricate himself, he recalls the lessons of Taoist Buddhism. Lao Tzu, its founder, encouraged disciples to accept the *tao*, "the way," which was a *via negativa* through contemplative darkness toward an awareness of the mystery of being (what he called the "ten thousand things"—a phrase Wright appropriated for the title of his second "trilogy"). At the beginning of the *Tao Te Ching*, Lao Tsu wrote:

> The Tao that can be told is not the eternal Tao. . . .
> The nameless is the beginning of heaven and earth. . . .
> Ever desireless, one can see the mystery.
> Ever desiring, one sees the manifestations.
> These two spring from the same source but differ in name;
>     this appears as darkness.
> Darkness within darkness.
> The gate to all mystery. (3)

To apprehend the mysterious source of the cosmos, according to Lao Tsu, the mind first must empty itself of mundane desire, knowledge, and language. Wright aspires to this mystical state of equanimity and insight. In what might be a repudiation of the evangelical teachers of his youth, he declares: "I've heard that those who know will never tell us, / and heard / That those who tell us will never know . . . / Desire discriminates and language discriminates: / They form no part of the essence of all things." (Wright paraphrases the fifty-sixth section of the *Tao Te Ching*: "Those who know do not talk. / Those who talk do not know" [58].) Searching for a still point beyond the painful wheel of illusion and disillusionment set in motion by desire, and beyond his "shirt of flame," Wright acknowledges that the "secret is emptiness" and contemplative silence.

As a poet, professor, and citizen, however, Wright can no more shed concepts and language than he can shed his skin. The paradox, which is at the core of Eastern and Western mystical literature, is also at the core of Wright's trilogies. In his poems about language, landscape, and God, he bemoans the futility of poetry, the deceptions of language, the fleeting beauties of landscape, and the obsolescence of God. He knows that he will never be able to fly from his linguistic and conceptual labyrinth—at least not for long—without plunging back into it. Language and concepts are the ineradicable stuff of his poetic imagination. They constitute the tradition he depends on to be understood and to make a living. Like the Christian and Buddhist mystics who attract him, he uses liturgy, ritual, and sacred texts in order to get beyond their "language," but in the end he and his poetry remain ensnared in what it seeks to escape. "Like a grain of sand added to time, / Like an inch of air added to space, / or a half-inch, / We scribble our little sentences," he writes in a typical deflation of his art, "'When You're Lost In Juarez, in the Rain, and It's Eastertime Too.'" Then he counters: "There's been no alternative / Since language fell from the sky. / Though mystics have always said that communication is languageless. / And maybe they're right— / the soul speaks and the soul receives." Because the soul continues to receive "voices" and speak in "voices," because the body continues to desire what it can't have (e.g., an Easter resurrection and transcendence), Wright continues to write about a mystical zone beyond the confinements of space and time even while recognizing his attempts to reach it are doomed.

Like those scientists brooding on the origin of the universe in order to discover a "Theory of Everything," Wright persists in his search for words and concepts to describe "the heart of the mystery, the pulse at the very unspeakable center of being." Unlike the scientists, he readily admits that he can only offer myths and fictions for that "unspeakable center." In koan-like lines ("What God is the God behind the God who moves the chess pieces? . . . / What mask is the mask behind the mask / The language wears and the landscape wears?" ["'It's Turtles All the Way Down'"]) and in expressions of bewilderment and humility, Wright follows the path of mystics who for centuries have denied the efficacy of language and reason to represent God and Creation. His poetry is both "cataphatic" (positive) and "apophatic" (negative). It entertains the belief that words and concepts can represent the divine mystery and it contradicts that belief by suggesting that divinity and being are beyond words and concepts.

In *Negative Blue* and in poems collected in earlier books, Wright frequently espouses a central tenet of the apophatic or "negative theology" inherent in most mysticisms—that God can only be approached through a *via negativa*, a purging of the mind's cognitive and linguistic functions, and that God can only be hinted at through negative statements delineating what He is not. From the perspective of negative theology, God is an absence, a wholly "other" nonbeing; representations that affirm His presence, in fact, misrepresent Him. In his poem "Absence Inside an Absence," which was inspired in part by an unpublished essay, "The Apophatic Image: The Poetics of Effacement in Julian of Norwich" (*Negative Blue*, 203), Wright declares: "Our lives are language, our desires are apophatic, / The bush in flame is the bush in flame, / Imageless heart, imageless absence between the hearts." We live our lives by using language, but Wright's transcendental desires lead him beyond life and language toward an apophatic God who stymies communion and refuses to communicate. Unlike Jehovah speaking to Moses through the burning bush on Mt. Horeb, Wright's God is not present in nature and is not

representable in words. His poems repeatedly use tautologies to empha-
size that things-as-they-are are simply things-as-they-are. Bushes are
bushes, he argues, not divine oracles infused with God's presence, as
Moses or Hopkins envisioned.

"If we cry out, / if once we utter our natural sounds,"Wright says, echo-
ing Rilke's *Duino Elegies*, "Even the angels will hide their heads / Under
their blue wings, /. . . . / So better forget that, better forget the darkness
above the tongue, / Its shortings of words, its mad silence and lack of
breath." Drawn to the sort of communion with higher beings that faith al-
lows, Wright constantly finds his yearnings rebuffed by hard facts.
Mimicking a Scholastic theologian of the Middle Ages, he likes to tease
himself and his readers with braintwisters such as "the idea of absence in-
side an absence / Completing a presence." (Perhaps our brains, in their
struggle to conceive of even the most arcane possibilities, can turn "absence
inside an absence" into an image, a presence.) Wright pays homage to me-
dieval mystics like Julian of Norwich, whose most famous treatise was ti-
tled *Showings* ("the showings foretold / Unseeable through the earthly
eye" ["Absence Inside an Absence"]), only to reject the mystical assump-
tion that God's presence can be known and/or loved. In the end, Wright
can only acknowledge his distance from Julian's cataphatic visions of a
bleeding Christ and well-mannered, loving patriarchal God and her
apophatic visions of an "uncreated God" illuminating the "soul [that] . . .
has despised as nothing all which is created" (*Showings*, 132). Drawn to the
mystic's "unearthly" eye,Wright concludes "Absence Inside an Absence" by
affirming the matter-of-factness of our earthbound lives and discourse:
"The earth in our cracked hands, / the earth dark syllables in our mouths."

Wright's nostalgia for the traditional mystic's union with the divine is
perhaps most succinctly stated in his prayerful request "St. John of the
Cross, Julian of Norwich, lead me home," which appears in the poem
"Apologia Pro Vita Sua." (The Latin title means "explanation or justifi-
cation of my life" and was used by John Henry Newman for his account
of converting to Catholicism.) In his "Apologia," Wright says nothing
about a conversion to Catholicism. Instead, he touches on some of the
reasons Catholic mystics like St. John and Julian attract him, and why
their Catholicism remains inaccessible to him. In a discussion of his
propensity for migraines and the neurological phenomena that accom-
pany them ("strict auras and yellow blots, / green screen and tunnel vi-
sion, / Slow ripples of otherworldliness, / . . . / Feckless illuminations"),
Wright suggests that these "illuminations" or "showings" are the sort of
false "mystical" experiences that afflict him in his actual home.The home
for which he yearns is an archetypal place, like Eliot's "significant soil . . .
where prayer has been valid" in the *Four Quartets* (190, 192)—where the
mystic's traditional communions and unions with God have been ac-
cepted as genuine.

In his trilogies,Wright calls on a series of saints, monks, and contem-
plative writers (Plotinus, Pseudo-Dionysius, Dante, St. Augustine, St.

Francis of Assisi, St. Ignatius of Loyola, St. Xavier, Ruysbroeck, Richard of St. Victor, St. Teresa of Avila, Meister Eckhart, Simone Weil, and others) to act as representatives of and guides to this sacred "home." Following Dante, who in the *Paradiso* ascended toward a union with God after multiple communions with saints and mystics, Wright addresses the shades of past masters who can lead him to a "home" in the Empyrean. This heavenly home, however, proves to be as mercurial as his former homes in Tennessee, North Carolina, California, Italy, and elsewhere. (Referring to Dante's Christian faith, which made possible his journey beyond the fixed stars into the Empyrean, Wright told an interviewer: "I would love to be a believer. But I'm not. And that's why everything always ends . . . at the heaven of fixed stars" [*Southbound*, 56]). Like Elizabeth Bishop in "The End of March" and other poems, Wright tries to return to "proto" or "crypto" dream homes through rituals of remembrance, but he inevitably concludes that such homes are mainly figments of the imagination. Because the mystical "home" that St. John of the Cross and Julian of Norwich point to is a type of transcendent Eden, Wright—again like Bishop—sees himself as a "homeless" pilgrim, always looking over his shoulder longingly at an illusory paradise as he moves through the world.

Wright's longing for a churchlike "home" of contemplative silence harks back to the origins of Christian mysticism in the mystery cults of ancient Greece. The etymology of "mystical" and "mystery" reveals a legacy of obsession about abandoning language (keeping quiet, keeping secrets) while in the presence of rituals associated with the divine fecundity of the landscape. "Mystery" derives from Greek words such as *mustērion* (secret rites), *mustēs* (one initiated into secret rites), and *muein* (to close the eyes or mouth); "mystical" from *mustikos* and *mustēs* (an initiated person who was expected to remain silent). Both words share the root *mu*, which is related to "mute" and "mum." In the Eleusinian mystery cult that celebrated Demeter's rejuvenation of the landscape in spring, initiates took a vow of silence. A sacred and silent mist was supposed to enshroud the rituals. In Christian tradition, "mystical" originally referred to the secret, hidden, or difficult meanings of the Bible that only strenuous allegorical interpretation could reveal. Meditation, for early Christians, consisted of repeated close readings—often out loud—of the Scriptures to unlock their divine meanings, their mysteries. In "Mysticism: An Essay on the History of the Word," Louis Bouyer recalls: "For the Greek Fathers the word 'mystical' was used to describe first of all the divine reality which Christ brought to us, which the Gospel has revealed, and which gives its profound and definite meaning to all the Scriptures. Moreover, mystical is applied to all knowledge of divine things to which we accede through Christ" (47). Later on, "mystical" denoted the presence of Christ in the Eucharist's symbolic bread and wine. Many of the so-called mystics (the label gained currency in the seventeenth century), from Pseudo-Dionysius on, declared that communion or union with God was the goal of contemplation, which was seen as a higher form of meditation. During the climax of mystical experience, which was often brought about by ecstatic love for God, the soul enjoyed a revelation of God's magisterial otherness, His utter mystery. If closed eyes and closed mouths were necessary to apprehend God, cognitive blindness and linguistic silence were the results of union with Him.

Scholars of the *via mystica* tend to regard the contemplative approach to God in epic terms, as a heroic journey with difficult rites of passage and rituals of communion that proceed to a redemptive end. The hero departs from home, is initiated into an otherworld of supernatural wonders and trials, and after unifying with God returns home to dispense life-enhancing boons. At the beginning of her encyclopedic study *Mysticism*, which influenced numerous twentieth-century poets (from Eliot and Theodore Roethke to Seamus Heaney and Charles Simic), Evelyn Underhill said of Eastern and Western mystics: "Their one passion appears to be the prosecution of a certain spiritual and intangible quest: the finding of a 'way out' or a 'way back' to some desirable state in which alone they can satisfy their craving for absolute truth. This quest, for them, has constituted the whole meaning of life. . . . Mysticism, then, offers us the history, as old as civilization, of a race of adventurers who have carried to its term the process of a deliberate and active return to the divine fount of things" (3, 35). For Underhill, the *via mystica* was "an inward Odyssey" (91) with an archetypal plot that involved a journey away from habitual perception and conduct, a recognition of the central mystery of the universe, and a return to society. In an attempt to schematize this journey, she argued that the traditional three-stage itinerary proposed by theologians such as Origen and Pseudo-Dionysius (purification, illumination, and union) should be expanded to five: 1) the joyous "awakening" of the self to the divine; 2) the self's painful realization of its imperfections and consequent desire to purge them; 3) the detachment from sensory experience that brings about "the contemplative state par excellence . . . , a certain apprehension of the Absolute, a sense of the Divine Presence"; 4) the radical purification of the spirit referred to as "mystic death" or the "dark night of the soul"; and 5) the ecstatic union in which "the Absolute Life is not merely perceived and enjoyed by the Self, as in Illumination: but is one with it" (169-170). According to Underhill, who sometimes disparaged the goals of Eastern mysticism, the Western quest was cyclical rather than vertical; the mystic's journey ended with a return to redemptive work in the world rather than a static, blissful union in the void. "This systole-and-diastole motion of retreat as the preliminary to a return remains the true ideal of Christian Mysticism in its highest development" (173), she contended.

In "An Ordinary Afternoon in Charlottesville," Wright reveals his awareness of these mystical schemas and writes about them in an ecumenical way that Underhill sometimes repudiated. Meditating on his hometown landscape, he characteristically regards it as language—as a text or "book of nature"—that is both Eastern and Western, Buddhist and Dantesque. In his imagination, shadowy Chinese ideograms merge with Italian words for stages of the *via mystica*:

> Under the peach trees, the ideograms the leaves throw
> Over the sun-prepped grass read
> *Purgatio, illuminatio, contemplatio,*
> Words caught in a sweet light endurable,
> > > > unlike the one they lead to,
> Whose sight we're foundered and fallowed by.
>
> Meanwhile, the afternoon
> > > fidgets about its business,
> Unconcerned with such immolations,
> Sprinkle of holy grit from the sun's wheel. . . .

The tripartite structure—purgation, illumination, contemplation—recalls the mystical itinerary of Pseudo-Dionysius and his heirs, but also the language and tripartite structures of Dante, who twice paid homage to Pseudo-Dionysius in the *Paradiso*.

Having passed through hell and purgatory, Dante travels with Beatrice through a series of illuminations made possible by the "sweet lights" of heaven (the planets and sun appear to him as wheels of revolving lights). A master of contemplation, Saint Bernard of Clairvaux, leads Dante to his climactic vision of the Celestial Rose, Beatrice's assumption among the angels, and God's presence in the Trinity. In the final canto, like mystics before him, Dante reiterates that his beatific vision is incommensurate with his mind's conceptual and linguistic abilities. As he approaches God, he says: "From that moment my vision was greater than our speech, which fails at such a sight, and memory too fails at such excess" (481). In the last sentence of *The Divine Comedy*, Dante records the successful completion of his contemplative odyssey. His intellectual powers have been usurped; he is now at one with God and the whole universe that moves harmoniously according to a spirit of love: "Here power failed the high phantasy [Dante's divine vision], but now my desire and will, like a wheel that spins with even motion, were revolved by the Love that moves the sun and the other stars" (485).

Wright ends his contemplative poem about an "ordinary afternoon in Charlottesville" quite differently. The Empyrean's fires have been extinguished. In their absence, Wright feels "the cold / glacier into the blood stream." A sublime communion with a loving God that moves the universe seems impossible. His communion wafer is an "iron disk" on his tongue. He hears no choir of heavenly angels, only "the birds oblivious, / . . . [and] their wise chant, *hold still, hold still. . . .*" If the birds admonish him to remain in contemplative stillness, they also signal they are oblivious to his disillusionments with the *via mystica*. The traditional boon of union with God, he avers, is beyond him. The "iron disk" ritually recalls

the iron in his own blood and his mortality, not Christ's blood that prom-
ises redemption and eternal life. His unity at poem's end is with the ele-
ments (iron), nature (oblivious birds), and impending death (the glacier
in the bloodstream). Having envisioned the sort of divine light that
Dante eulogized in the *Paradiso*, Wright is not so much uplifted as dis-
combobulated and silenced ("foundered and fallowed"). The unen-
durable light that seems to emanate from an apophatic Creator empties
Wright momentarily (such purgatorial emptyings are typical of the "dark
nights" and "clouds of unknowing" that attend the mystic's *via negativa*).
But Wright's "fallow" moment does not prepare him for a fulfilling en-
counter with God's presence. Like his other poems, "An Ordinary
Afternoon in Charlottesville" traces a contemplative journey that ends
with the sort of aporias common in negative theology and postmodernist
criticism. It moves from an ordinary place and time (a stand of peach
trees in the afternoon) to a vision of something extraordinary beyond
place and time, and then cycles back to the hard facts of ordinary life.
Unlike Dante's comedic plot, Wright's plot ends in disenchantment. "The
pulse at the very unspeakable center of being," he implies, is not a heav-
enly rose; it is an unendurable light. Having witnessed this mystical light,
the ordinary light of his backyard is nearly unendurable as well. Wright
can endure it only by struggling to "hold still."

If Dante provided Wright with an epic model and ideal goal for the
*via mystica*, St. John of the Cross provided him with a detailed and astute
analysis of its purgatorial obstacles. Wright read St. John for the first time
during the late 1950s while serving as an intelligence officer in the army,
then more thoroughly during the late 1960s and 1970s at the University
of California. St. John's sixteenth-century treatise on contemplation, *The
Dark Night*, which is an elaborate interpretation of a poem he wrote, is
full of the sort of wise counsel that Wright evinces in his poems. St. John
implores the "distracted and inattentive spirit" (331) to persevere calmly
during its passage through the "dark night of the soul." To be "illumined,
clarified, and recollected by means of the hardships and conflicts of the
night" (331) is no easy matter, as his metaphors of wars, prisons, and
burnings attest. The soul's *via negativa*, he asserts, is "a method of true
mortification, which causes it to die to itself" (297) and to its "sensory
and spiritual parts," that is, to "all the faculties, passions, affections, and
appetites" (362). "This negation of self and of all things" (297), which
causes the contemplative to suspect God has disappeared, is essentially a
struggle to empty the mind and "hold still." "My house," which for St.
John is a metaphor for his mind, must be "all stilled" (296), he says, be-
fore the contemplative journey toward "a wondrous and delightful spiri-
tual communication [with God], at times ineffably sublime" (385), can
begin. The soul must survive crucifixion before it can ascend to union in
heaven.

The plot of St. John's *Dark Night*, which charts the journey of a lover
through the night toward an ecstatic tryst with a beloved, resembles

Dante's in *The Divine Comedy*, but on a much smaller scale. It has a happy, romantic end. St. John's exemplary contemplative recounts: "I abandoned and forgot myself, / Laying my face on my Beloved; / All things ceased; I went out from myself, / Leaving my cares / Forgotten among the lilies" (296). According to St. John's allegorical interpretation of his poem, the questing soul enjoys a rapturous tête-à-tête with God. Underhill in *Mysticism* added an aesthetic gloss to St. John's "dark night of the soul" by insisting that it signified "an extreme form of that withdrawal of attention from the external world and total dedication of the mind which also, in various degrees and ways, conditions the creative activity of musician, painter and poet"(299). In other words, St. John could be writing a primer for artists, who must also struggle in contemplative solitude and silence. It was St. John's relevance to the creative process as much as his religious message that originally attracted Wright.

St. John's account of the vagaries and ecstasies of the contemplative journey may have encouraged Wright to read other mystics of the "dark night," such as Pseudo-Dionysius and the anonymous author of *The Cloud of Unknowing*. In *The Dark Night*, St. John pointed to Pseudo-Dionysius's discussion of a "cloud of unknowing" in the *Mystical Theology* as one of his primary sources. St. John wrote:

> When the divine light of contemplation strikes a soul not yet entirely illumined, it causes spiritual darkness, for it not only surpasses the act of natural understanding but it also deprives the soul of this act and darkens it. This is why St. Dionysius and other mystical theologians call this infused contemplation a "ray of darkness"—that is, for the soul not yet illumined and purged. For this great supernatural light overwhelms the intellect and deprives it of its natural vigor. . . . Clouds and darkness are near God and surround Him, not because this is true in itself, but because it appears thus to our weak intellects, which in being unable to attain so bright a light are blinded and darkened. (335-36)

St. John referred to these dark clouds as symbols of "unknowing" (344), of the contemplative's annihilating "night" that "purges the intellect of its light and the will of its affections, but also the memory of its discursive knowledge" (344). In *The Ascent of Mount Carmel* he declared: "A man must advance to union with God's wisdom by unknowing rather than by knowing" (80). According to St. John, blind faith, grace, and love—rather than reason and will—were the prerequisites for the *via negativa*.

Wright read the fifth- or sixth-century Syrian writer Pseudo-Dionysius (scholars have been unable to discover his real name or biography) in the mid-1980s. Perhaps the most famous expounder of negative theology, Pseudo-Dionysius merged Neoplatonism with Christianity in his treatises on the divine "Cause of all existence" (50). "Divine names," he argued in a book with that title, were useful in steering one's attention toward the divine source of all being, but could never fully represent that source. Anyone who contemplates the First Cause, in Pseudo-Dionysius's view, resembles Moses approaching God on Mt. Sinai: "He plunges into the truly mysterious darkness of unknowing [sometimes translated as a 'cloud of unknowing']. Here, renouncing all that the mind may conceive, wrapped entirely in the intangible and the invisible, he belongs completely to him [God] who is beyond everything. Here, being neither oneself nor someone else, one is supremely united to the completely unknown by an inactivity of all knowledge, and knows beyond the mind by knowing nothing" (137). Realizing that the Creator is utterly transcendent, the Mosaic contemplative also realizes that He is immanent in Creation, that He can only be hinted at in statements saying what He is not, and that religious icons, rituals, and scriptures that pretend to make him present can only pretend through misrepresentations. In *The Divine Names*, which codifies many of the paradoxes in mystical literature, Pseudo-Dionysius wrote: "God is therefore known in all things and as distinct from all things. He is known through knowledge and through unknowing. Of him there is conception, reason, understanding, touch, perception, opinion, imagination, name, and many other things. On the other hand he cannot be understood, words cannot contain him, and no name can lay hold of him" (109). God is both cataphatic and apophatic. In short, He is an oxymoron, an enigma.

In his poem "Easter 1989," Wright uses one of the Christian calendar's central days to reflect on God and Christ through the bifocals of Pseudo-Dionysius. At first Wright suggests that the sacramental spring landscape (the crocuses "in their purple habits / wet cowls") is a scene of crucifixions and resurrections that are merely biological. There is no attempt, in Pseudo-Dionysius's words, "to strive upward . . . toward union with him who is beyond all being and knowledge" (135). Echoing Dylan Thomas's biological fatalism in "The Force That through the Green Fuse Drives the Flower," Wright declares: "Instinct will end us. / The force that measles the peach tree / will divest and undo us. / The power that kicks on / the cells in the lilac bush / Will tumble us down and down." These divestings and fallings, however, initiate a mystical turn from cataphatic representations of divinity toward apophatic ones. Although Wright's dismissal of orthodox beliefs in Christ's resurrection (he seems to be treating Easter, as Eliot did in *The Waste Land*, as a vegetation rite gone bad) might seem atheistical, in the end he sides with Pseudo-Dionysius's attempt to "pack away the workings of childish imagination regarding the sacred symbols" and "to cross over to the simple, marvelous, transcendent truth of the symbols" (283). The truth, for Wright as for Pseudo-Dionysius, is that the Creator is an unknowable nothingness that defies rational belief:

> Belief is a paltry thing
> and will betray us, soul's load scotched
> Against the invisible.
> We are what we've always thought we were—
> Peeling the membrane back,
> amazed, like the jonquil's yellow head

Butting the nothingness—
>
> in the wrong place, in the wrong body.

The definer of all things
>
> cannot be spoken of.

It is not knowledge or truth.

We get no closer than next-to-it.

Beyond wisdom, beyond denial,
>
> it asks us for nothing,

According to Pseudo-Dionysius, which sounds good to me.

"You must turn to all of creation" to find God, Pseudo-Dionysius said in *The Divine Names*, but what you ultimately find is the dark, dazzling "supra-essential being of God . . . , the truth which is above all truth . . . [and] at a total remove from every condition, movement, life, imagination, conjecture, name, discourse, thought, conception, being, rest, dwelling, unity, limit, infinity, [and] the totality of existence" (54). Contentions like these have provoked some scholars to question whether Pseudo-Dionysius was an atheist posing as a Christian. Although his encounters with divine nothingness instilled in him an "amazed" appreciation of the divine mystery behind and within all beings, his ideas always possessed a whiff of heresy. His mix of traditional and untraditional Christian views made him an appealing ally for Wright.

Wright alludes to *The Cloud of Unknowing*, which was directly inspired by Pseudo-Dionysius's *Mystical Theology* (a work the author of *The Cloud* translated) in his long sequence "A Journal of the Year of the Ox," written in the mid-1980s. His verse-journal, like many of his other poems at the time, reveals the ambivalence toward memory and reason apparent in *The Cloud*. The gist of *The Cloud* is that God can be loved, but never known or expressed. To enter a mystical state of contemplation in which "nothing occupies your mind or will but only God" (61), the fourteenth-century author stipulates, "you must . . . put a cloud of forgetting beneath you and all creation," obliterate all awareness of physical and spiritual realities, and enter a "cloud of unknowing" (66) because God "cannot be comprehended by our intellect" (61). "How am I to think of God himself, what is he?" the author imagines his reader asking. With the same combination of colloquial profundity and nonchalance that characterizes Wright's style, the *Cloud*'s author replies: "I cannot answer you except to say 'I do not know!' For with this question you have brought me into the same darkness, the same cloud of unknowing where I want you to be!" (67).

At the beginning of "A Journal of the Year of the Ox," Wright expresses sorrow for his alter ego, the contemplative pilgrim who struggles to transcend both present and past realities in order to pass from "the cloud of forgetting" into "the cloud of unknowing." "Pity the poor pilgrim, the setter-forth, he says, "pity his going up and his going down." He is pitiful partly because he is at war with himself. He seeks transcendence, but he also wants to remain attached, through memory, to the world that often fills him with guilt, remorse, and horror. Amnesia is both a boon and a bane to this perplexed soul:

> Each year I remember less.
> This past year it's been
>                         the Long Island of the Holston
> And all its keening wires
>                         in a west wind that seemed to blow constantly,
> Lisping the sins of the Cherokee.
>
> How shall we hold on, when everything bright falls away?
> How shall we know what calls us
>                         when what's past remains what's past
> And unredeemed, the crystal
> And wavering coefficient of what's ahead?

Later in the poem, Wright's memory of historical troubles improves; he recalls in abundant detail how "the Cherokee's mystic Nation," which was more sinned against than sinning, was decimated on the Holston River and how the Indians were evicted from Tennessee only to be further decimated on a "Trail of Tears." To "hold on" and "hold still" in the wake of such disasters remains the goal of Wright's *via mystica*.

Having wandered once again through history's inferno, Wright conjures up a Dantesque ghost who in some ways resembles the author of *The Cloud*. This ghost visits Wright "in the night garden" by his house and urges him to persevere in his contemplative pilgrimage. "*Concentrate, listen hard,*" he says. Rather than God's voice, however, Wright hears "A motor scooter whine up the hill road, toward the Madonna." Loving unions with a transcendent God seem a long way off. "*Attention is the natural prayer of the soul,*" the voice reminds him, paraphrasing *The Cloud*. Wright's attentive, prayerful consciousness eventually finds signs of hopeful change. Endings merge with beginnings, as in Eliot's *Four Quartets*, which draws on many of the same mystical sources as Wright's "trilogies." At the end of his "Journal," which records the end of 1985, Wright looks forward to the soul sloughing its temporal burdens and moving toward a redemptive "timeless moment" at the cycle's center. "Tomorrow the rain will come," he predicts, "And the soul will start to move again, / Retracing its passage, marking itself / back to the center of things." The future, unfortunately, is not so propitious. On Christmas day, a time when many remember "the center" or source of Christian salvation, Wright recalls the beginning of Christian "things" mainly to underscore his distance from them. His ritual return doesn't end with an affirmation of contemplative union with Christ or God, but with unresolved questions about the value of contemplation: "What is a life of contemplation worth in this world? / How far can you go if you concentrate?" Not very far, Wright implies. Spiritual transcendence, for which he still pines, seems blocked: "The afternoon shuts its doors. / The heart tightens its valves." If he works in a "cloud of unknowing," no access to divinity appears forthcoming. Wright finishes with aporias—with pore-like doors and arteries blocked rather than opened to God's presence.

Wright's Modernist sequences often amount to collages of quotations and paraphrases from books by or about mystics that attract him, but whose Christian idealism goes against the grain of his skeptical, down-to-earth intellect. Like monks of old, he meditates on theological texts with the hope of making a contemplative journey toward communion and union with the sacred "center of things," only to realize that the cyclical processes of nature and culture perpetually draw him away from this "center." Nietzsche once remarked: "When skepticism mates with longing, mysticism is born" (Buber, *Ecstatic Confessions*, xiv). The aphorism appears in Martin Buber's collection of Eastern and Western mystical writings, *Ecstatic Confessions*, shortly before the editor's discussion of the German author Fritz Mauthner, whose "'godless' mysticism" (xiv) and skepticism about language's ability to represent reality influenced Buber. Wright, whose skepticism and longing mate to form a similar atheistical mysticism, uses a quotation from this discussion as an epigraph to his poem "Ostinato and Drone": "The mystic's vision is beyond the world of individuation; it is beyond speech and thus incommunicable" (xv). Wright acknowledges the fourteenth-century German mystic Meister Eckhart in his note to the poem because Mauthner cited Eckhart as a kindred soul.

Wright found especially riveting Meister Eckhart's tract, which appeared at the end of *Ecstatic Confessions*, about a woman's confession of her mystical experiences. The woman, according to Eckhart, told her priest that she had envisioned the void before her bodily creation and even before God's Creation. Having entered a primordial cloud of unknowing, she said: "I am where I was before I was created; where there is only bare God in God. In that place there are no angels or saints or choirs or heaven. . . . You should know that all that is put into words and presented to people with images is nothing but a stimulus to God. Know that in God there is nothing but God. Know that no soul can enter into God unless it first becomes God just as it was before it was created" (156). The woman's experience confirmed Eckhart's concept of the "Breaking-Through to the Divine Ground" (Eckhart, 47) where the mystic realized the intractable otherness of God. The purpose of contemplation, Eckhart once claimed in a sermon, was to somehow return to "the hidden darkness of the eternal divinity" that defied understanding. This divinity, he explained, "is unknown, and it was never known, and it will never be known" (Eckhart, 196). Like the negative theologies of his precursors, Eckhart's mysticism had an atheistical inflection. "I pray to God that he may make me free of 'God,' for my real being is above God if we take 'God' to be the beginning of created things" (202), he said. "If I say: 'God is a being,' it is not true; he is a . . . transcending nothingness" (207). Such nihilistic views were not welcomed by the Church, which posthumously condemned them.

"Undoing the self is a hard road," Wright observes at the beginning of "Ostinato and Drone." The purgatorial process is a dénouement—literally an "unknotting"—that requires "tenderness that's infinite" and "loneliness that's infinite." As if alluding to Eckhart, Wright says, "There's nothing that bulks up in between" or at the end of these two infinities. Having glimpsed the void's paradoxical "Radiance," Wright's contemplative is left "Speechless. Incommunicable. At one with the one." His sense of aporia, of being blocked at the edge of the void, evokes a sardonic aside: "Some dead end—no one to tell it to, / nothing to say it with. / That being the case, I'd like to point out this quince bush, / Quiescent and incommunicado in winter shutdown." Wright compares the quiet, incommunicado mystic to a wintry bush, then to Moses' burning bush irradiated by God's presence. Who or what speaks through Wright's humble quince bush? "The voice continuing to come back in splendor," he writes, is the voice of ordinary reality. If it is radiant with a mysterious otherness, that's because it has no intrinsic meaning ("the word [is] still not forthcoming"), only the poetic or religious meaning imposed on it by language. "We're talking about the bush on fire," Wright comments, alluding to Moses' metaphoric bush. Then, to stress the fact that a mystic's godly bush is still just a bush, he says: "We're talking about this quince bush, its noonday brilliance of light." For many mystics, Moses conversing with God on various mountain summits was the archetypal contemplative. For Wright, Moses is an archetype of the imagination that feels compelled to talk with and about God, that transforms ordinary bushes and clouds into divine ones because it can't help deifying the world with words.

Wright's *via mystica*, with its "ostinato"—its musical repetitions—of birdlike flights between contemplative sublimities and mundane realities, may best be summed up by the twelfth-century Scottish mystic Richard of St. Victor. Wright was introduced to Richard by Dante, who saluted him (along with Pseudo-Dionysius and Augustine) in the tenth canto of the *Paradiso* (Dante wrote: "in contemplation [he] was more than man" [153]). Responsible for organizing into an orderly, Scholastic system the insights of Pseudo-Dionysius, Augustine, and other contemplative writers who preceded him, Richard argued that the soul in contemplation progressed toward the divine through six stages. It began in enlightened wondering about corporeal things and ended in ecstatic union—made possible by grace—with God. Wright typically shuns this sort of romanticized and programmatic view of the mystical journey. (Drawing on the "Song of Songs," Richard saw the "marriage" between the soul and God's "divine secrets" [274] as an occasion for spiritual inebriation, dancing, singing, and exultant "alienation of mind" [316].)

Despite his qualms, as his poem "Bicoastal Journal" reveals, Wright agrees with Richard's assessment of the quick, birdlike fluctuations of the contemplating mind through memory, imagination, and reason. His poem alludes specifically to Richard's *The Mystical Ark*, an allegorical interpretation of the Biblical ark of the covenant that Jehovah described to Moses from Mt. Sinai's "cloud of unknowing." Richard stressed the quixotic nature of the soul in a way Wright found particularly attractive:

> That penetrating ray of contemplation is always suspended near something because of greatness of wonder, yet it operates neither always nor uniformly in the same mode. For that vitality of understanding in the soul of a contemplative at one time goes out and comes back with marvelous quickness, at another time bends itself, as it were, into a circle, and yet at another time gathers itself together, as it were, in one place and fixes itself, as it were, motionless. Certainly if we consider this rightly, we see the form of this thing daily in the birds of the sky. Now you may see some raising themselves up on high; now others plunging themselves into lower regions and often repeating the same manner of their ascent and descent. You may see some turning to the side, now to the right, now to the left, and while coming down a little ahead now in this part, now in that, or advancing themselves almost not at all, repeating many times with great constancy the same changes of their movements. (158)

"The contemplative soul goes out and comes back with marvelous quickness— / Or bends itself, as it were / into a circle," Wright says in "Bicoastal Journal," co-opting Richard's language to trace geographical journeys between West and East Coasts (Wright's homes in California and Virginia) as well as contemplative journeys between different landscapes and different ideas of God. Moving from Richard's humble birds to the Scholastic abstractions they signify, Wright continues:

> There are six kinds of contemplation,
> 　　　　　　　　　　St. Victor adds:
> Imagination, and according to imagination only;
> Imagination, according to reason; reason
> According to imagination;
> 　　　　　　　reason according to reason;
> Above, but not beyond reason;
> 　　　　　　　above reason, beyond reason.

In a birdlike swoop, Wright quickly brings these highfalutin speculations down to earth by noting his current situation in wintry Charlottesville: "First month, third day, 32 degrees. / Overcast afternoon, / cloud cover moving from west to east / As slow as my imagination." Everything in Wright's landscape—clouds, white pines, wind, water, fire—undulates lethargically like his spirit, which, he confesses, would "rather be elsewhere."

Caught up in a contemplative "cloud cover" that he finds both inspiring and constricting, Wright acts like one of Richard's birds flitting between contraries. If wintry Virginia represents the *askesis* of focused concentration, he longs for the easygoing, hedonistic lifestyle and natural beauty of the California coast: "I'd rather be loose fire / Licking the edges of all things but the absolute / Whose murmur retoggles me. / I'd rather be memory, touching the undersides / Of all I ever touched once in the natural world." If he complains about being bound to "the absolute," he also admits that its "murmur" (a word sharing the etymological root, *mu*, with "mysticism" and "mystery") attaches him like a toggle bolt or toggle switch to something—either metaphysical or physical—that electrifies him. As for Richard of St. Victor, for Wright the *via mystica* is dialectical—a bicoastal flight that is both harrying and creative. "All things come about in accordance with strife" (114), Heraclitus wrote in a book Wright read around the time he composed "Bicoastal Journal." Strife between "the absolute" and "the natural world," East and West, God and Creation, motivates and determines the route of his contemplative journey throughout his "trilogies."

If the classic epic plot depended on faith in an empire (Greece or Rome) or an imperial religion (Christianity), the modern poetic sequence allows for a more equivocal stance. In Wright's case, it allows for an expression of ongoing ambivalence toward the boons of the mystical quest. Like Richard's soul-birds, "repeating the same manner of their ascent and descent," their retreat and advance, Wright repeatedly communes with textualized landscapes and landscaped texts in order to pursue his mystical idea of "the God behind the God"—the "transcending nothingness" from which all being originated. Despite the best efforts of scientists and theologians, Wright reminds us, the source of the Creation remains an unfathomable mystery. Cataphatic by vocation, apophatic by temperament, Wright continues to puzzle over enigmas that have made thinkers scratch their heads (and writing implements) for millennia. Can one know and describe the source of all being, or is that source unknowable and indescribable? Is there a Supreme Being accessible through love and faith, if not through reason and language? Can we commune with the Creator through the "book of nature" or the "book of religion," or are landscape and language dead ends? What do rituals, icons, and scriptures tell us about ourselves and our gods? Can words and concepts adequately represent reality, or are they essentially misrepresentations, fictions, lies? What is the proper attitude toward nature and culture, its long history of disasters and splendors?

Wright's ambiguous responses to these conundrums are partly responsible for his melancholic lyricism, but like Richard of St. Victor's birds, his music is cyclical; it follows a rhythm of dispiriting "downs" and inspirational "ups," cautious retreats and bold advances. In a conversation about his "trilogy of trilogies," he said: "As I look back on it, the whole thing does seem to be a kind of searching . . . , an emotionally organized movement, in an ascending path" (*Southbound* 44). He then compared it to the sort of wandering pilgrimage toward God Augustine recorded in his *Confessions*, which he called "the iconic book of my life" (44).

Although Augustine's Church-centered *via mystica* had a profound effect on most of the Christian mystics who followed him, Wright, characteristically, accepts the general drift and values of Augustine's journey without adhering to the orthodox faith he reached at the end of it. Love and praise for the mystery of creation, whether divine or human, are the goals Wright shares with Augustine and his successors. As he writes in "December Journal,"

> Every existing thing can be praised
> > when compared with nothingness. . . .
> Love what you don't understand yet, and bring it to you.
>
> From somewhere we never see comes everything that we do see.
> What is important devolves
> > from the immanence of infinitude.
> In whatever our hands touch—
> The world is here, just under our fingertips.

A reverence for the natural world, which Wright also finds enshrined in poetry from the T'ang Dynasty, the Romantic tradition, and the American Imagist tradition, is everywhere apparent in his work. Awe before the original "nothingness" and "the world of the ten thousand things" that arose from it is the catalyst for his reverence. Although St. Augustine once claimed "God should not be said to be ineffable [because] . . . the ineffable is what cannot be said, [and] . . . what is called ineffable cannot be ineffable" (Kessler, *Mystics*, x), Wright's *via mystica* constantly veers toward an ineffable and unknowable Creator whose Creation is intrinsically mysterious. His epic voyage, like a river full of eddies, keeps curving back on itself to question its direction, destination, origins, and contents. His questions impel his quest, and his masterly craft entices us to follow him as he charts one of the most ambitious courses in twentieth-century poetry.

## WORKS CITED

Anonymous. *The Cloud of Unknowing* (trans. Clifton Wolters). Harmondsworth: Penguin, 1961.

Bouyer, Louis. *Understanding Mysticism* (ed. Richard Woods). New York: Image Books, 1980.

Buber, Martin. *Ecstatic Confessions*. San Francisco: Harper & Row, 1985.

Dante. *The Divine Comedy: Paradiso* (trans. John D. Sinclair). New York: Oxford Univ. Press, 1939.

Eckhart, Meister. *The Essential Sermons, Commentaries, Treatises, and Defense*. New York: Paulist Press, 1981.

Eliot, T. S. *The Complete Poems and Plays*. London: Faber & Faber, 1969.

Heraclitus. In *Early Greek Philosophy* (ed. Jonathan Barnes). Harmondsworth: Penguin, 1987.

Julian of Norwich. *Showings* (trans. Edmund Colledge and James Walsh). New York: Paulist Press, 1978.

Pseudo-Dionysius. *The Complete Works* (trans. Colum Luibheid). New York: Paulist Press, 1987.

Richard of St. Victor. *The Mystical Ark* (trans. Grover A. Zinn). New York: Paulist Press, 1979.

Rosenthal, M. L. and Sally M. Gall, *The Modern Poetic Sequence*. New York: Oxford Univ. Press, 1983.

St. Augustine. In *Mystics* (eds. Michael Kessler and Christian Sheppard). Chicago: Univ. of Chicago Press, 2003.

St. John of the Cross. *The Collected Works of St. John of the Cross* (trans. Kieran Kavanaugh and Otilio Rodriguez). Washington, D.C.: ICS Publications, 1973.

Suarez, Ernest. *Southbound*. Columbia: Univ. of Missouri Press, 1999.

Tsu, Lao. *Tao Te Ching* (trans. Gia-Fu Feng and Jane English). New York: Vintage, 1989.

Underhill, Evelyn. *Mysticism*. Oxford: Oneworld, 2001.

Wright, Charles. *Quarter Notes*. Ann Arbor: Univ. of Michigan Press, 1995. Quotations from Wright's poems come from *Country Music* (Hanover: Wesleyan Univ. Press, 1982); *The World of the Ten Thousand Things* (New York: Farrar, Straus & Giroux, 1990); *Negative Blue* (Farrar, Straus & Giroux, 2000).

WILLARD SPIEGELMAN

# Charles Wright and "The Metaphysics of the Quotidian" (2005)

> . . . being unable to find peace within myself, I made use of the external sur-
> roundings to calm my spirit, and being unable to find delight within my heart,
> I borrowed a landscape to please it.
>
> —T'u Lung (T'u Ch'ihshui)

The creative impulse arises from an aching inner void, a longing for completion that only art can provide. Thus Wallace Stevens: "And not to have is the beginning of desire" ("Notes Toward a Supreme Fiction").[1] We speak of expression and fulfillment as equivalent terms even though they are linguistically opposed to each other, one an outpouring and the other an influx. But the first can produce the second and consequently stand in its place: we fulfill ourselves by self-expression. Likewise, the aesthetic and the erotic are at least in part overlapping, and sometimes virtually synonymous. From the story told by Aristophanes in Plato's *Symposium* down to Jacques Lacan's psychoanalytic theory, most Western mythographers have based their versions of Eros on some dream of finding, in a sensuous or aesthetic quest, one's better half, the "partner in your sorrow's mysteries" (Keats, "Ode on Melancholy"). In Shelley's neo-Platonic allegory "The Sensitive Plant," the titular figure "desires what it has not—the Beautiful." It is no wonder that this central "character" has often been taken as an allegorical representation of any aspiring artist, of, for example, Shelley himself.

The place of "landscape," the natural world, in such quests has usually been as a backdrop for, an external projection or a representation of the human drama played out upon or against its stage. In Charles Wright's work we find something peculiar if not unique in contemporary poetry: the use of landscape as a virtual replacement for sexuality. For all his sensuousness, he is not an erotic poet. His work is essentially neither allegorical nor symbolic, nor is it merely reportorial and empirical. It is a poetry of longing, but this longing is not directed at erotic fulfillment,

---

1. Wallace Stevens, *The Collected Poems of Wallace Stevens* (New York: Knopf, 1954), 382, hereafter *CP*.

social or familial coherence, or ecological sanity. The landscape, everything that comes into our view, is the only possible access to spiritual wholeness, but it offers no guarantee of anything. For Wright, the world is implicitly *not* everything that is the case, but it is all that we can be sure of. If there were a word for a style that takes the natural world as its subject without hankering after physical fulfillment, that combines lushness with austerity, visible bounty with spiritual doubt, and that proceeds by way of anecdotes that still manage to obscure important people, things, and events in the poet's present adult life, such as his wife and son, that word would be Wrighteous.

In the great title poem of her 1965 *Questions of Travel*, Elizabeth Bishop wonders: "*could Pascal have been not entirely right / about just sitting quietly in one's room?*" Like traveling, through which we expect to look closely and eagerly at foreign landscapes, just examining the more domestic details of nature in one's backyard can stem from a comparably inarticulable dread, failure, or void within one's heart. The excerpt from T'u Lung above, placed carefully at the end of *China Trace*, qualifies as a legitimate epigraph to all of Charles Wright's work. Borrowing a landscape means trying to please the spirit. Other people seek and find such pleasure in the consolations of religion. Wright, too much a skeptic to believe in the Episcopalian faith of his childhood, is held too much in its sway to let it go.[2] Just as his idiosyncratic style conceals his personality and many of the details of his lived life, so his lush cravings for the spirit indwelling within the physical never point toward a doctrinal God. All is aspiration; fulfillment comes only in partial glimmers. As he said in an interview: "Roethke wrote that all finite things reveal infinitude. What we have, and all we will have, is here in the earthly paradise. . . . I'd say that to love the visible things in the visible world is to love their apokatastatic outlines in the invisible next."[3]

"Apokatastatic" comes from a man who is not afraid of abstruse, technical terms (here, the Greek word for renovation or restoration), but whose diction by and large does without such theological words, and also without the scientific terminology used by such other ardent poetic observers as A. R. Ammons, Alice Fulton, and Richard Kenney. It swerves away from the overly scintillating linguistic gestures and baroque, sinuous syntax of Amy Clampitt and James Merrill. Wright's poems often filter the lushness of Hopkins through the incomplete utterances—phrases rather than clauses—of Pound (who was Wright's first and greatest inspiration). Where John Ashbery moves in one continuous, seamless maneuver, often losing his

---

2. See, inter alia, Wright's interview with Matthew Cooperman, in *Quarter Notes: Improvisations and Interviews* (Ann Arbor: University of Michigan Press, 1998), 167, or the interview with Sherod Santos, in *Halflife: Improvisations and Interviews, 1977-87* (Ann Arbor: University of Michigan Press, 1991), 109-110.

3. Interview with J. D. McClatchy, *Quarter Notes*, 120.

reader in the delicate modulations of tone, gesture, scene, or subject, Wright, like Jorie Graham, seems to sputter his way hesitatingly, building a poem by accretion but with plenty of detours along the path. He has announced, "Parts are always more than the sum of their wholes" and "Poems should be written line by line, not idea by idea."[4] The second of these remarks is a variation on Mallarmé's famous advice to Degas (a poem is made not with ideas but with words), but the first virtually warns a reader not to expect a luminous, organic wholeness in Wright's poems. His negotiations with nature are unusual precisely because his poems do not progress solely along the lines of the Romantic nature lyric (written to the formula: "Here I am and this is what I see"), or those of the Whitmanian travelogue (such as the prototypical "There was a child went forth"), both of which accumulate details in order to portray a thinking or monarchic self. Nor do they sound, except occasionally, like delicate Imagist or Symbolist miniatures in which the observed data necessarily stand for an unspecified or unspecific numinous presence. Somehow Wright's poems partake of all these genres separately, or all at once, especially within the capacious boundaries of his "journal" works.

The most interesting treatment of Wright would proceed synchronically rather than diachronically or historically. His stylistic and thematic development, though visible, is less important than the changes we might identify by examining the collected poetry as a single landscape (and attending to the landscapes *within* that landscape). Wright has developed and maintained a poetic persona while often remaining unforthcoming about the merely personal details of his life. We can define him much more through his use of context, place, situation, anecdote, and natural description than through any even momentarily overt confessions. Framing himself within a recollected or perceived landscape, he enacts a pilgrimage toward self-portraiture (which means self-understanding) by painting himself *into* the landscape. In *The Southern Cross*, five poems entitled "Self-Portrait," along with "Portrait of the Artist with Hart Crane" and "Portrait of the Artist with Li Po," impart a vision of Wright, the man and the poet, just at the moment before he transforms his style from the stanzaic poems of the earlier volumes to the jagged, long-lined meditations of the journals. We observe, in other words, the poet on the verge of breakup, *sparagmos*, and poetic reconstitution.

The assembled self-portraits tremble on the margins of evanescence and disappearance. Written in the poet's midforties, the lyrics waver between past, present, and future time. The poet collects memories, stations himself in moments of contemplation, and prepares for his future dispersal and possible restoration by natural or human forces. Of these five portraits, the first is by all standards the most conventional. Three five-line stanzas begin with

---

4. *Halflife*, 28, 34.

a realization of discovery (By whom? For what? It is not at all certain) and death ("Someday they'll find me out, and my lavish hands"). The poem continues with an accommodation in the present ("Till then, I'll hum to myself and settle the whereabouts") and ends with an invocation (rarely used by Wright) for unspecified spiritual salvation ("Hand that lifted me once, lift me again").[5]

In the three stanzas of the second self-portrait (*World*, 13), the poet in the present moment is the *hardest* thing to see. He seems to bracket himself in the blank space between stanza 1, in which he remembers Italian nights, or relives them in memory, or regards a picture of himself on his wall; and stanza 2, in which he anticipates his posthumous condition:

> Charles on the Trevisan, night bridge
> To the crystal, infinite alphabet of his past.
> Charles on the San Trovaso, earmarked,
> Holding the pages of a thrown-away book, dinghy the color of honey
> Under the pine boughs, the water east-flowing.
>
> The wind will edit him soon enough,
> And squander his broken chords
>                         in tiny striations above the air,
> No slatch in the undertow.
> The sunlight will bear him out,
> Giving him breathing room, and a place to lie.

As if to negotiate between a collectable past and a predictable future, the poem ends in the eternal present of description:

> And why not? The reindeer still file through the bronchial trees,
> Holding their heads high.
> The mosses still turn, the broomstraws flash on and off.
> Inside, in the crosslight, and St. Jerome
> And his creatures . . . St. Augustine, striking the words out.

Supposedly significant details are blurred rather than clear. What are these reindeer accompanied by saints? It took a letter to and a reply from the

---

5. Charles Wright, *The World of the Ten Thousand Things: Poems 1980-1990* (New York: Farrar, Straus and Giroux, 1990), 11, hereafter *World*. All references to Wright's poetry are from either this volume, which includes poems from *The Southern Cross*, *The Other Side of the River*, *Zone Journals*, and *Xionia*, or from *Country Music: Selected Early Poems* (Middletown, Conn.: Wesleyan University Press, 1982); the most recent volumes are *Chickamauga*, *Black Zodiac*, and *Appalachia* (all New York: Farrar, Straus and Giroux, 1995, 1997, 1998, respectively), subsequently gathered together in *Negative Blue: Selected Later Poems* (New York: Farrar, Straus and Giroux, 2002). The phrase from the title to this chapter ("the metaphysics of the quotidian") appears in the commonplace book whose name gives the title to *Halflife*, 22.

poet to certify that they are in the form of postcards that hang above his desk, one from Finland, two from Venice reproducing Carpaccio's pictures of the Church fathers. As a self-portrait, this poem is curiously frustrating, not only for its failures to explain, but also for its polite depiction of a third-person "Charles" in stanza 1, a more distant "him" in stanza 2, and a total removal of references to him in stanza 3. The poet is his book ("earmarked" and soon to be edited) or postcards, as Wallace Stevens, the Ariel in "The Planet on the Table," is the collected pages of his own world.

The desire to be delivered, whether by God, ancestors, progeny, readers, or unnamed spiritual forces that will shape his ends, is apparently the initial and transcendental motive for Wright's self-portraits. These brief lyrics reproduce the substance and much of the technique of all his volumes taken together. It is a sign of his reticence that the third self-portrait, a consideration of old photographs, does not even mention the poet until its third stanza, as if getting to him randomly in a list of other people. And significantly, too, the self-portrait disappears as the act of pointing moves on to other objects. What comes to portray the self is names. Or photos, postcards, and mementos. By the fourth portrait (*World*, 19) Wright settles on a technique that he uses almost exclusively in his later work and that marks his legacy from Pound, whom he read passionately while serving in the Army in Italy, near Verona:

> Marostica, Val di Ser. Bassano del Grappa.
> Madonna del Ortolo. San Giorgio, arc and stone.
> The foothills above the Piave.
>
> Places and things that caught my eye, Walt,
> In Italy. On foot, Great Cataloguer, some twenty-odd years ago.
>
> San Zeno and Caffè Dante. Catullus' seat.
> Lake Garda. The Adige at Ponte Pietra
> —I still walk there, a shimmer across the bridge on hot days.

Phrases instead of clauses, names instead of actions, places instead of people, moments instead of extended linear narratives: thus Wright begins to locate himself amid flashes, collected and set aside like candid snapshots in an album reopened by chance or choice years later, and by the very person whose life they constitute. He has condensed both the Whitmanian catalogue and the giant Whitmanian ego. In such a portrait the first-person self makes the briefest appearance, quite literally centered through a recollection of a repeated action:

> —I still walk there, a shimmer across the bridge on hot days,
> The dust, for a little while, lying lightly along my sleeve—
> Piazza Erbe, the twelve Apostles. . . .

And then it vanishes from the poem, which subsides into a one-sentence stanza containing a single last vignette, and then retreats into the randomness of naming:

> Over the grave of John Keats
> The winter night comes down, her black habit starless and edged with
>     ice,
> Pure breaths of those who are rising from the dead.
>
> Dino Campana, Arthur Rimbaud.
> Hart Crane and Emily Dickinson. The Black Château.

I take this self-portrait as emblematic of Wright's newer methods of painting a self into a poem by largely ignoring it, and by attending to everything that looks initially secondary, random, or of the background. For one thing, phrases lead up to sentences, and then succeed them, just as the lyric "I" embeds itself within a recollected landscape or a series of pen-and-ink sketches never fully colored in. And, more important, the stanza itself (a staple of Wright's poetry in *Country Music: Selected Early Poems*) has begun an inexorable breakdown and expansion. From *The Southern Cross* on, the line and the paragraph will replace the pretty stanzaic rooms that have started to crumble. Like the series of self-portraits by Francis Bacon on which this sequence is based, Wright's collection dramatizes the loss of the self as a means of building it up. Just as Bacon's images ooze and flow, so Wright locates his self through the things that surround him and the things he has read, bracketing the middle three portraits with the two more conventionally confessional, external "frames." And, like Bacon's self that vanishes from the canvas, Wright sees himself in the last picture "in a tight dissolve," imploring: "Angel of Mercy, strip me down."

Such self-locating gestures in these five lyrics, or in the other two, where Hart Crane and Li Po precede the Charles Wright who makes his appearance only in their wake and as a kind of afterthought, look like a product of routine Southern politeness and of an aesthetics that forswears both self-revelation and extended narrative ("I can't tell a story. Only Southerner I know who can't," Wright once confessed in an interview).[6] Other poets in this century, Pound most noticeably, have preached a doctrine of impersonality; it is Wright's distinctive achievement to have avoided the cryptic coldness of Pound at his worst (or of his followers, like the Welshman David Jones), and to have reshaped the characteristic self-centeredness of lyric by extending it: extending its lines and stanzas quite literally and extending the scope of its traditional concerns in order to move beyond the demands of the ego without advancing into the

---

6. *Quarter Notes*, 107.

larger epic forms that have tempted most American male poets from Walt Whitman through James Merrill. (As Howard Nemerov wittily puts it in an epigrammatic truth: most American poets "start out Emily and wind up Walt."[7]) In Wright, the lyric, not the ego, has expanded, and it has done so, paradoxically, by concentrating even more closely on landscape and the poet's place within those landscapes he recalls, inhabits, or symbolically recreates in the formal frames of his poetry.

In "Roma II" (*World*, 97), Wright proposes a hypothesis with the forceful clarity he always summons up when delivering a pointed truth. He waxes for the moment didactic and wise: "The poem is a self-portrait / always, no matter what mask / You take off and put back on." Aphoristic plainness is matched by a personal modesty, as the poem began with a recollection of looking at his "mother's miniature" while living in Rome. And it continues briefly in the pluperfect, referring to the earlier time when his mother was alive. Then, after the epigram, it continues with a present-tense description of Irish poets who are making a group sketch of people at a city bar: "they draw till we're all in, even our hands." Drawing draws everyone in; the painters' hands make a metaphoric connection with the hands of their subjects. (And they should recall for us, as well, the poet's own "lavish hands," which I discuss above.) The self-portrait, like the lyric "I," makes only momentary appearances. By the last stanza, all specificity has been left behind for a mythic generality and an acknowledgment of the emptiness from which all creative work springs:

> Surely, as has been said, emptiness is the beginning of all things.
> Thus wind over water,
> > thus tide-pull and sand-sheen
> When the sea turns its lips back . . .
> Still, we stand by the tree whose limbs branch out like bones,
> Or steps in the bronchial sediment.
> And the masters stand in their azure gowns,
> Sticks in their hands, palm leaves like birds above their heads.

We can take this conclusion as Wright's version of Stevens's famous austere pronouncement:

> From this the poem springs: that we live in a place
> That is not our own and, much more, not ourselves
> And hard it is in spite of blazoned days.
> > ("Notes Toward a Supreme Fiction," *CP*, 383)

---

7. Howard Nemerov, "Strange Metamorphosis of Poets," in *The Collected Poems of Howard Nemerov* (Chicago: University of Chicago Press, 1977), 451.

But it is also something more. The epiphany allows him to inhabit a land-scape sadly but not alone. He has transformed his Irish poet-sketchers into a combination of Yeats's Byzantine mosaic sages and his scarecrows (in "Sailing to Byzantium" and "Among School Children"), shadowed by Stevensian palm trees. The bronchial sediment recalls the reticulations of the "bronchial" trees in the second "Self-Portrait"; Wright cannot desist from simultaneously separating from and inserting himself in a landscape that contains human and superhuman figures. As a reparative elegist in the tradition of Stevens, Wright has no contemporary equal.

Such elegy takes many forms in Wright's extended work. At its sim-plest, it involves an exemplary vignette, as of an adolescent Charles Wright on a whiskey run with pals, fleeing from the cops and generally hooting it up with the boys. He revels in past glory and recognizes its in-sipidity:

> Jesus, it's so ridiculous, and full of self-love,
> The way we remember ourselves,
> > and the dust we leave . . .

> Remember me as you will, but remember me once
> Slide-wheeling around the curves,
> > letting it out on the other side of the line.
> > ("Gate City Breakdown," *World*, 40)

Momentary gestures like this make Wright sound like the Wordsworth of the "Intimations" ode, lamenting "the splendor in the grass" and the "glory in the flower" that nothing can ever bring back. He also sounds like a character out of Dante, delivering what amounts to a sentimental self-epitaph and asking to be recalled by his survivors or readers in a defining moment of passionate self-abandonment.

However moving this episode may be, it is among Wright's least inter-esting (because most conventional) elegiac maneuvers. At his best he is a memorialist of the common destiny. Here, for example, is the pluralized and therefore anonymous small lament entitled "Snow" (*Country Music*, 112):

> If we, as we are, are dust, and dust, as it will, rises,
> Then we will rise, and recongregate
> In the wind, in the cloud, and be their issue,
>
> Things in a fall in a world of fall, and slip
> Through the spiked branches and snapped joints of the evergreens,
> White ants, white ants and the little ribs.

This poem contains the jaggedness we associate with the later Wright in the apparent evenness of an ongoing, single-sentence lyric. Its fluid hy-potactic subordination keeps the poem braced along lines of tension, with a high Romantic rhetoric masking a simple statement. But the use of repetition interrupts as well as extends the rhythm of the argument. Everything ends as something else: we as dust, dust as snow, snow as white ants, trees as ribs of skeletons, rising as falling. The beauty of such considerations forswears the personal in favor of the communal, and mingles a diction of biblical cadence ("Dust we are") and romantic resignation. The lines move simultaneously in jumps, starts, hesitant afterthoughts, *and* as a nonstopped flow. Such a technique again calls our notice to Wright's effort to conjoin the spatial and the temporal (an effort I discuss in more detail below). The poem might easily be taken as a description of a little dime-store glass sphere containing a landscape, which, when turned upside down, lets loose a mini-snowfall over its world. Contemplation leads here to visual description. The world ends in an image.

Whether focused on himself or on our common humanity, Wright's elegiac temper, with its associated sadness, humility, and delicacy of perception, turns a famous Coleridgean obiter dictum on its head, or at least puts a new spin on it: "Elegy is the form of poetry natural to the reflective mind. It *may* treat of any subject, but it must treat of no subject *for itself*; but always and exclusively with reference to the poet himself."[8] By one way of looking at his work we can take Wright as always the subject, even if implicit. By another, we can see that he has heeded the religious truth expressed in the adage from *The Cloud of Unknowing* that he quotes in his longest poem, "A Journal of the Year of the Ox": *Attention is the natural prayer of the soul.* By fiercely and patiently watching an external scene, even if not by the strict procedures set down by Ignatius Loyola or other saintly contemplatives, Wright manages to treat many subjects both for themselves and for their ability to absorb him within their boundaries. Depending on his mood he may express a longing for something otherworldly, a haunting by something missing and aspired to, or he may simply turn his attention with no ulterior motives to the external world, as though painting were an end in itself. "I have no interest in anything / but the color of leaves" ("A Journal of the Year of the Ox," *World*, 186). In this alternation between things for their own sake (which we can label Wright's aestheticism) and things as talismans or symbols of spiritual valences (his residual religiosity), the poems document Wright's inheritance, and movement away, from all Romantic forebears.

Like the past, the future haunts and inspires in equal measure. It provokes anxiety and strength, just as the future and the invisible paralyze but augment the poet's deepest feelings. As usual, we can compare an earlier poem with subsequent ones to chart the road Wright has traveled along (although he may often seem to have remained in the same place).

---

8. Samuel Taylor Coleridge, *Table Talk*, in *Collected Works*, ed. Carl Woodring (Princeton Bollingen Series), 14, no. 1 (1990): 444–45.

"Reunion" (*Country Music*, 141) shows how the future has it in for us. It always wants to become the past. Time traps us coming and going; there is no escape:

> Already one day has detached itself from all the rest up ahead.
> It has my photograph in its soft pocket.
> It wants to carry my breath into the past in its bag of wind.
>
> I write poems to untie myself, to do penance and disappear
> Through the upper right-hand corner of things, to say grace.

Writing poems may untie and release, but such poems also reunite, join together, and commemorate. Wright sounds nostalgic for the future even though it beckons to him with a gentle menace, like the figure of Death in the medieval morality play who comes to take Everyman when he has it least in mind. This condensed lyric offers two takes, really, on death, giving the upper hand to neither. The first stanza implies the inevitable "ceas[ing] upon the midnight with no pain" that Keats contemplates in the "Ode to a Nightingale," while the second, with paradoxical counter-force, defends the poet from dissolution by getting the better of Death, making a creative assault not to immortalize the poet in the classic Horatian fashion ("Exegi monumentum aere perennius") but to dissolve him in the very act of self-commemoration.

Just a few years later, Wright reexamines his reasons for writing in the simply titled "Ars Poetica" (*World*, 38), a poem that is a partial holdover from his anaphoric and repetition-haunted earlier lyrics, but that is already moving toward the looser forms of his "journals." Once again, there is no exit, even though the rich Keatsian lushness of landscape offers its peculiar combination of temptation and frustration, fulfillment and desolation. Here the poet contrasts his present southern California setting ("I like it back here," he begins, and then repeats his proposition in a hallucinated way) with the interior space of a room (whether in California or in the South is unclear) filled with family ghosts and mementos. And the proposition proceeds almost logically. Instead of pitting one brief stanza against another, as he did in "Reunion," Wright works from thesis through antithesis to a synthesizing last section, beginning with a single, set-off line: "The spirits are everywhere." Escape is an impossibility. Once he calls those spirits down, he asks, "What will it satisfy?" He will still have

> The voices rising out of the ground,
> The fallen star my blood feeds,
>                    this business I waste my heart on.
>
> And nothing stops that.

Even by the Pacific, in other words, whether by choice or destiny, the past arises, satisfaction seems unlikely, and nothing is within the poet's control.

Wright's continual quest for a poetic technique that can bear dense emotional freight involves nothing less than a refiguring of the lyric so that it can encompass the concentrated delicacy of observation that he associates with those Asian poets with whom he would like to identify; the autobiographical and historical aspects of his own life as an individual and a Southerner; and the capaciousness of meditation. In these different kinds of poetry, it is always landscape that occupies the central position, because landscape alone allows the poet to move from present to past, from here to there, and from, the visible to the invisible. In "The Southern Cross" (*World*, 42), for example, a poem in the newer medley form that encourages the cross-stitching necessary to combine Wright's excursions among several genres, it is natural observation that frames and inspires his movement between the particular and the general. He wants the poem to be (like all of his "journal" poems) a combination of the three modes, so he starts with a single, ominous generalization, proceeds to four lines of individuated details, and symmetrically closes the opening section with another single-line dictum, in this case, a resignation:

> Things that divine us we never touch:
>
> The black sounds of the night music,
> The Southern Cross, like a kite at the end of its string,
>
> And now this sunrise, and empty sleeve of a day,
> The rain just starting to fall, and then not fall,
>
> No trace of a story line.

But a story line is exactly what Wright cannot avoid, even if he lacks the stereotypical Southern gift of gab and even if the line of story and poem is strung obliquely like the stars of the invisible Southern Cross. He segues immediately to recollections from early childhood, all of which lead him to the ambivalent conclusion that his "days were marked for a doom" but with the realization of "How sweet the past is, no matter how wrong, or how sad. / How sweet is yesterday's noise" (43). What intercedes between the first and the second of these realizations is, once more, the natural details whose perception allows him to move from his first tentative emotional response to the next one:

> The morning is dark with spring.
> The early blooms on the honeysuckle shine like maggots after the rain.
> The purple mouths of the passion blossoms
> open their white gums to the wind.
> (43)

I have picked this opening virtually at random. Other selections would make the same point: that although Wright's new kind of poetry has the appearance of casualness, it also forces us to understand his contemplative temperament as directly and intricately bound up with his descriptions of nature, into which he releases and redeems himself, and from which he then pulls himself together into new, although momentary states of thought and feeling. If at times a sense of personal failure predominates, at others visionary triumph breaks through the mundane details of the natural world. As he announces later in the poem, "the landscape was always the best part" (49).

So it may be in all of Wright's poetry. But the landscape is not the only part. Of the various strands interwoven throughout his work, we can unravel several (as I have already begun to do) to see how the whole fits together. One could collect simple aphoristic statements of failure: "Everyone's life is the same life / if you live long enough" ("The Southern Cross," 48); "The edges around what really happened / we'll never remember / No matter how hard we stare back at the past" (49); "Time is the villain in most tales, / and here, too" (51); "I can't remember enough" (52). But Wright plays off these sad admissions (in "The Southern Cross" and the other long poems) against virtually antiphonal statements of successes small and large, hopes entertained and not entirely defeated, compromises that constitute victory, sometimes with a muted Old Testament confidence or a Christian expectation of grace:

> Thinking of Dante is thinking about the other side,
> And the other side of the other side.
> It's thinking about the noon noise and the daily light. (45)

> The Big Dipper has followed me all the days of my life.
> Under its tin stars my past has come and gone.
> . . . . . . . . . . . . . . . . . . . . . . . . . . . . . . . . .
> It blesses me once again
> With its black water, and sends me on. (45)

> Everything has its work,
>                          everything written down
> In a secondhand grace of solitude and tall trees. (53)

> It's what we forget defines us, and stays in the same place,
> And waits to be rediscovered. (54)

With an almost metronomic sway between despair and hope, Wright moves equally evenly among gnomic generalization, precise observation, and recollected anecdotes. What Keats called "a life of sensations" everywhere balances that of "thought," although Wright's poetry makes a synthesis rather than a conflict of these potentially unharmonious constituents. Both "Lost Bodies" and the adjacent "Lost Souls" (*The Other Side of the River*) bear witness to disappearances, but the best comment on all the recollections in this volume is the toneless acknowledgment that "There is no stopping the comings and goings in this world, / No stopping them, to and fro" ("Italian Days," *World*, 89). And in two adjacent sections of any long poem one can find quicksilver changes of mood: "Despair, with its three mouths full, / Dangles our good occasions, such as they are, in its grey hands," followed by

> Nothing's so beautiful as the memory of it
> Gathering light as glass does,
> As glass does when the sundown is on it
> > and darkness is still a thousand miles away.
> > ("A Journal of the Year of the Ox," 166)

Such metaphoric visionary moments derive from and compensate for the losses, hauntings, and lassitude that often precede them. Wright makes reparations and keeps on going. "I keep coming back to the visible" ("December Journal," *World*, 209), he admits (just as Stevens keeps "coming back/ To the real," in "An Ordinary Evening in New Haven" [*CP*, 471]), and in the visible he encounters things themselves and as promises, portents, even symbols of something like salvation in an undoctrinal but thoroughly spiritual realm.

"We invent what we need," concludes a largely anecdotal family reminiscence ("Arkansas Traveller," *World*, 107). What Wright generally needs and invents—in the Renaissance sense of coming upon—is his landscapes. These contain the "ten thousand things" of his title, each of which, according to the Chinese sages, is "crying out to us / Precisely nothing, / A silence whose tunes we've come to understand" ("Night Journal," *World*, 147). The ambiguous, Stevensian "nothing" that things sing to us inspires us to an equivalent eloquence, which mingles the seen and the heard in our minds and recreates a landscape that comes to look more like a tapestry:

> —Even a chip of beauty
> > is beauty intractable in the mind,
> Words the color of wind
> Moving across the fields there
> > wind-addled and wind-sprung,
> Abstracted as water glints,
> The fields lion-colored and rope-colored,
> As in a picture of Paradise,
> > the bodies languishing over the sky
> Trailing their dark identities
> That drift off and sieve away to the nothingness
> Behind them
> > moving across the fields there
> As words move, slowly, trailing their dark identities.                (148)

A passage like this illustrates the shifting depths in Wright's poetry. Just as the things of this world are transient, our words equally ephemeral, and the next world unknowable, the very pattern of a single sentence—one perception, image, or metaphor melting into or being replaced by the next—proceeds along a double path of dissolution and accumulation. The minutest piece of beauty is first seen as intractable, but then as evanescent. The wind has no color of its own, but its visible effect on the fields produces mottled colors there. A whole sequence of tropings—a metamorphosis of metaphor—moves the poem onward: a mental chip of beauty is like words, which are the metaphorical "color" of "wind-addled" landscape, which is itself variegated like water. The natural scene then becomes a notional, depicted one ("as in a picture of Paradise"). What another poet might accomplish through a sequence of clauses Wright accomplishes through a series of self-transforming images, each turning into the next. Although he attaches himself to the things of this world, at the same time he announces (concluding this poem) that he would "never love anything hard enough / That would stamp me / and sink me suddenly into bliss" (149). No poet has ever so clearly resisted his own enthusiasms: to stamp means both to mark neutrally and to eradicate, to stamp out. He approaches ecstasy and then turns away from it because he cannot bear too much beauty, however mesmerizing he finds it.

Wright wants to see and to use the landscape the way one might look at a painting: first from a distance, to capture the totality of representation, the mimetic field of action, and then up close, to see the technique, the patina, the impasto, the planes of colors. First the forest, then the trees, then the branches and their leaves. For this as for other reasons, Cézanne is his great original. Although medieval and Renaissance religious art, the still lifes of Giorgio Morandi, the abstractions of Mondrian, and numerous miscellaneous photographs and sculptures frequently turn up in Wright's poems, it is Cézanne who presides as the tutelary spirit over the oeuvre. The "Homage to Cézanne" opens *The Southern Cross* and takes pride of place in Wright's poetry of the eighties. Significantly, the more recent volume, *Chickamauga*, which contains only short poems, has for a cover a sequence of photos, eleven close-ups of someone's mouth, presumably the poet's. Each poem has become the equivalent of a single, more traditional lyric utterance. The reasons for Cézanne's status as Wright's presider in the longer works from the eighties are not hard to discover. Cézanne's revision of spatial form, paving the way for the Cubists, who were his most grateful beneficiaries, has as its correspondence Wright's decision, starting tentatively with *The Southern Cross*, to break away from his earlier, smaller stanzaic units and to find suppler ways of effecting transitions in longer poems. The hemistich (the broken half-line) makes an image, phrase, or sentence *look* disjointed even when it is not syntactically so. It has the additional effect of filling in an entire printed page, which now seems to melt into its white boundaries instead of being tightly confined by them. Just as words and things (in "Night Journal") have ambiguously tangible and ephemeral realities, so the quasi-stanzaic units in the journal poems look compact and diffuse at the same time. The poems have a horizontal and a vertical thrust, as if the poet were deliberately drawing our eye along and down the page in one protracted sweep. A horizontal line has been broken up only to make us aware of it simultaneously as a vertical one.

Sometimes the cause or effect of the line break in the "journal" poems is to imitate an action described:

> The weeping cherries
> > lower their languorous necks and nibble the grass.
> > > (136)

The enjambment conveys the sense of downward movement: trees are progressively, metaphorically transformed into pasturing animals. We witness a complex pattern of figuration as the personified cherries, given their correct name ("weeping"), become, in the second line, perhaps human, and then, something other than human. Or:

> Last night, in the second yard, salmon-smoke in the west
> Back-vaulting the bats
> > who plunged and swooped like wrong angels
> Hooking their slipped souls in the twilight. (166)

Here grammatical transposition ("Back-vaulting the bats") and an enjambed subordination ("the bats / who plunged") produce both visual dazzle and referential obscurity. The gymnastic bats become fallen angels, but we can never be sure whose souls—bats' or angels'—are "hooked" in the twilight.

Sometimes the break is used in the service of a stilled description rather than an active one:

> The trees dissolve in their plenitude
> > into a dark forest
> And streetlights come on to stare like praying mantises down on us.
> > (154)

Here the doubled prepositional phrases ("in . . . into") call attention to the fact as well as the location of dissolution. Severed from the first part of the sentence, the second phrase amplifies and concentrates the description. The effect is like that of a zeugma (the yoking of two items by a single verb or preposition), but in addition to linking two objects ("plenitude" and "forest"), Wright also multiplies them: as the trees disappear, they are transformed *into* a dark forest. Especially in relation to the second half of the sentence (which details a coming into view rather than a disappearance), the divided first half serves a mimetic function. Or, here is a different example of descriptive stillness, this time without the force of an enjambment:

> Like the stone inside a rock,
>> the stillness of form is the center of everything,
> Inalterable, always at ease. (155)

In this case, the two phrases surround the main discursive epigram, like foils for a jewel. An independent clause, concerning the centrality of form, is itself located—easily, unalterably—within two kinds of qualifying descriptions.

Sometimes the break makes visible a hypothetical point, but without doing violence to syntax and without any unusual enjambment:

> —Structure is binary, intent on a resolution,
> Its parts tight but the whole loose
>> and endlessly repetitious.
>
> (136)

Or:

> The new line will be like the first line,
>> spacial and self-contained.
>
> (142)

The conflict between tightness and looseness, self-containment and repetition, works itself out on the page. In other words, by breaking the lines, Wright has devised a visually mimetic way of underlining his assertions. Form and fact coincide. Most of his experiments with lineation can be understood this way, with reference to localized rhetorical effects and descriptive accuracy.[9]

There may be a metaphysical reason for all of this. Like Jorie Graham, Wright longs for some ineffable presence, but whereas her recent work starts and stops and sputters before our eyes, all parenthetical asides, with less and less coherence in syntax or narrative, Wright's lines only look broken. They jolt us into a recognition of separateness but they roll fluently by. The small, the separate, the partial, and the individual all fit within the ongoing rush of the large, the whole, and the collective. Just as days strung together make a life, and as vignettes can cluster together into a biography, so the glittering pieces of Wright's crystalline observations yield a poetry of statement, observation, recollection, and aspiration.

---

9. Wright has described his breaking of the line as different from similar efforts by Pound, Williams, O'Hara, and Olson: he wants "to keep the line from breaking under its own weight. . . . It is always one line, not two, and broken in a particular place to keep the integrity of the single line musically" (*Quarter Notes*, 79-80). Although he maintains that his primary goal is the conversational musicality of his line, Wright would not be unsympathetic, I suspect, to the more individual "readings" of specific effects I have proposed here.

The artistic, rather than the metaphysical, analogy for such a style, if not its direct cause, is clearly depicted on the dust jacket of *The World of the Ten Thousand Things*. Cézanne's characteristic late planes, chunks and daubs of color, are distinct *and* blurred. Even the colors themselves haphazardly melt into the unpainted areas of the canvas in a way that seems random (when seen up close) and prescribed (when seen as part of the depicted landscape). In a brief commentary inspired by the anniversary of Cézanne's death, Wright matter-of-factly summarizes his legacy: "He made us see differently, where the hooks fit, and the eyes go . . . / Nothing is ever finished" ("A Journal of English Days," *World*, 127). It all comes down, in poetry as well as painting, to the making of connections, all of which are temporary, informal, casual, even random. Like a post-Impressionist painting, Wright's long poems give the paradoxical, simultaneous pleasures of partiality and incompletion ("there is more to notice here . . . these slapdash details are random," we might say to ourselves) and aesthetic totality (we say "the whole world has been successfully epitomized"). The poem is a diary, travelogue, or record of perceptions in time; it is also a composition, a rendering of the natural world, in space. "Nothing is ever finished" is one motto; its opposite (the last line of "March Journal," *World*, 137) is "Form is finite, an undestroyable hush over all things." Through acts of description the poet stakes out his claim to a territory where finite boundaries are ever on the move:

> The landscape was always the best part.
>
> ———
>
> Places swim up and sink back, and days do,
> The edges around what really happened
> > we'll never remember
> No matter how hard we stare back at the past.
> > ("The Southern Cross," 49)

Like Wordsworth in the opening paragraph of "Tintern Abbey," measuring his hedgerows and then blurring them ("hardly hedgerows"), seeing the "one green hue" that unifies and blurs the plotted landscape, or like Elizabeth Bishop in "At the Fishhouses," where a silver sheen covers multiple facets of a maritime scene, Wright searches for the visible form of the landscape (which he then translates for our benefit into the visible form of the printed page) as well as for the blurs, leaks, and blanknesses that appear, Cézanne-like, within it. He depicts space and time as a single synaesthetic continuum, with places on the move and even past time capable of being stared at. Parts, as he has said repeatedly, are greater than their sums.

He calls himself "*A Traveler between life and death*" and proceeds to ask himself one of those typical, unrhetorical questions that his poetry can never answer:

> Where is that line between sleep and sleep,
> That line like a wind over water
> Rippling toward shore,
> > appearing and disappearing
> In wind-rise and wind-falter—
> That line between rain and sleet,
> > between leaf-bronze and leaf-drop—
> That line where the river stops and the lake begins,
> Where the black blackens
> > and light comes out of the light.
> > ("A Journal of English Days," 129-30)

With such an interest in looking hard enough at the visible world to elicit a map of its "line after line after latched, untraceable line" (130) it is no wonder that Wright should achieve momentary frustrations, temporary triumphs, with nothing keeping put for long. He would doubtless approve Ammons's equivalently synaesthetic realization, in his most popular poem, "Corsons Inlet," that space and time are merely two facets of a single perceptual phenomenon, that a sand dune is as much an event in time as an organization of space, that "tomorrow a new walk is a new walk" because even more than we, nature itself is always changing.[10] It never stands still, neither in our observing nor in our remembering it. As typically happens in Wright's work, sentences that begin as meditations on place turn into ones on time. And, like Ammons's, Wright's poetry asks us to consider the line as that which binds, which leads into, and which dissolves.

"Homage to Paul Cézanne" stands vibrantly on the border between Wright's early and later technique. In its appearance and method it is all politeness: at only three places in eight pages does the poet cut a line in half, preferring to stay inside fixed stanzas, but—here's the novelty—the stanzas have differing lengths: groups of six, four, eight, two, and three lines toward the start and, at the end, a more random sequence. It is as if the poet decided on some aleatory principle of composition, an equivalent of Marianne Moore's syllabic stanzas. The poem's rhythmic forcefulness, its repetitions and anaphoric rhetoric recall Wright's earlier ways of depicting a sense of haunting. He fills the poem with images and metaphors of the dead, who occupy its space the way colors do that of a post-Impressionist landscape by Cézanne. By the middle of the poem the images actually become parts of a natural or imagined landscape:

---

10. Ammons is only one of several poets who make us compare the shape of poetry on the page to its effect on the mind and in the ear. Ezra Pound, Marianne Moore, Allen Ginsberg, and e. e. cummings make comparable demands, and the triads of William Carlos Williams, which even a conservative poet like Charles Tomlinson has adopted, make for a synaesthetic experience. In Wright's case, lineation becomes a visually mimetic homage to observed and depicted landscapes.

> The dead are a cadmium blue.
> We spread them with palette knives in broad blocks and planes.
>
> We layer them stroke by stroke
> In steps and ascending mass, in verticals raised from the earth.
>
> We choose, and layer them in,
> Blue and a blue and a breath,
>
> Circle and smudge, cross-beak and buttonhook,
> We layer them in. We squint hard and terrace them line by line.
>
> (6)

Such a mingling of the poem's human characters and their metaphoric equivalents in a painting leads to the poem's resigned conclusion, which locates human life somewhere at the junction of death, in a landscape at once real and painted:

> What we are given in dreams we write as blue paint,
> Or messages to the clouds.
> At evening we wait for the rain to fall and the sky to clear.
> Our words are words for the clay, uttered in undertones,
> Our gestures salve for the wind.
>
> We sit out on the earth and stretch our limbs,
> Hoarding the little mounds of sorrow laid up in our hearts.
>
> (10)

Again, where Stevens sadly announced that "not to have is the beginning of desire," Wright hoards the trials of his senses as though they were necessary preparatory stages in a creative program.

Wright's aphorisms and other abstract statements often pepper his longer poems. But such statements typically work in relation to metaphor and the poet's changing perceptions of an external scene. For this reason, we must turn to a closer examination of Wright's landscapes as objects of aesthetic focus, intimations of unseen spiritual presences, and foils for the self-portraiture that he always, if obliquely, wishes to create. At times, he makes an easy equation between the ten thousand things of this world and their correspondences with the next or the other. Like Stevens, who keeps "coming back to the real,"

> I keep coming back to the visible.
>                    I keep coming back
> To what it leads me into,
> The hymn in the hymnal,
> The object, sequence and consequence.
> By being exactly what it is,
> It is that other, inviolate self we yearn for,

> Itself and more than itself,
> >               the word inside the word.
> It is the tree and what the tree stands in for, the blank,
> The far side of the last equation.
>
>               ("December Journal," *World*, 209)

This equation comes from the poetic equivalent of an elementary algebra textbook. Statements of being are statements of self-as-other. The visible is "more than itself"; it is the tree and also a compensation for the tree. What Wright calls in the same poem "the immanence of infinitude" (211), the relation of the "lust of the eye" (210) to what its searches lead to in the next world, brings him to the comforting assurance that "The other world is here, just under our fingertips" (211). Such is the Augustinian side of Wright's temperament.

But this is always balanced by an Eastern, Confucian, or postmodern side. There are many other moments in Wright's poetry where the two halves of any tentative formula do not correspond, where blurs and inequalities rather than one-for-one correspondence prevail. Earlier in the same volume, "Chinese Journal" (*World*, 199) begins its series of five quasi-Oriental lyrics with a look at a Morandi sketch of bottles done in the year of the author's birth. The artist

> Pencilled these bottles in by leaving them out, letting
> The presence of what surrounds them increase the presence
> Of what is missing,
> >               keeping its distance and measure.

Subtraction rather than addition becomes the measure of wisdom, as a master announces in the previous poem: "for knowledge, add something every day, / To be wise, subtract" ("A Journal of One Significant Landscape," 198). And as Wright himself summarizes in an earlier poem: "Exclusion's the secret" ("Yard Journal," *World*, 122). One must put things together by taking them apart. Wright the anatomist is twin brother to Wright the synthesist. The impulse to expand, through noticing and accumulating one's responses to the external and internal worlds, must be met by an equivalent and opposing one to reduce and let go. Thus Wright's pull (like Ammons's) between poems large and small, or his composition of large poems made up of separate, smaller units. Thus, also, his interest in the poetic equivalent of painterly techniques of inclusion and exclusion, as a way of both allowing the visible to stand for the invisible and of reminding us of the unbridgeable gap between them. Remembering a discussion of painting with his army buddies, he asserts "that what's outside / The picture is more important than what's in." What he forgets exceeds what he recalls, and this polarity parallels the relation between form and formlessness in art: "nothing is ever ended" ("A Journal of the Year of the Ox," 152).

For Wright (as for Cézanne) a focus on borders rather than on mirroring or one-for-one correspondences may provide the truest calculation of the currents in which we circulate. Sometimes the borders are crisp, sharply etched; sometimes they are extended, run-over (or run-on), and blurred. Even in spring, earthly plenitude comes with its own frustrations: "it all twists into the dark, / The not [*sic*] no image can cut / Or color replenish. / Not red, not yellow, not blue" ("A Journal of the Year of the Ox," 158). A zero-degree January day, detailed several pages earlier in the same journal, provides opposite but equivalent frustrations: "How does one deal with what is always falling away, / Returning diminished with each turn? / The grass knows, stunned in its lockjaw bed, / but it won't tell" (154).

Wright looks to the natural world to answer such questions. At times he is requited, at other times frustrated. As I have suggested, his questions are never rhetorical, but even when answered, answered only for a brief time. There is no American poet who combines so neatly the rival tendencies to summarize, epitomize, or conclude (as Wright does in his gnomic pronouncements) and to speculate, wonder, and question. Flux provokes the poet's eye and mind, but even when excluding things from his view he makes no permanent or final commitments. Like Morandi with his bottles, Wright is capable of revising the composition of his world and of his poem on a daily basis.

Description, in other words, is a constantly changing adventure, even though Wright's themes and tropes are remarkably persistent, indeed repetitive (to the dismay of impatient readers). Other poets—Ammons and Nemerov come to mind—use perception as the starting point for discursive conclusions. With Wright one has the feeling that such speculation is never an end in itself but a temporary stopping point, as if the poet is gathering his breath and self-control before returning to the natural world, at once his home and his tempter. No other poet makes the world so vividly exciting merely to read about. Exciting and at the same time inevitable, the result of waiting and patiently looking, as he offhandedly remarks in "The Other Side of the River" (*World*, 80):

> I want to sit by the bank of the river,
> > in the shade of the evergreen tree,
> And look in the face of whatever,
> > the whatever that's waiting for me.

This little couplet-as-folk-song comes in the middle of one of Wright's typical maneuvers. He begins by locating himself, at Easter in southern California, and then segues to "For weeks I've thought about the Savannah River, / For no reason" (78). He reaches for some links, connections that appear only to vanish: "Something infinite behind everything appears, / and then disappears" (79). But to say that the poem merely follows Wright's standard method of stationing himself, recalling the past, contemplating the present, anxiously waiting for the future, combining anecdote with description and philosophical proposition, is to ignore the interrelationship among these various timbres and among their respective styles. In all of the registers, it is the landscape that does the work. Wright seems constantly aware that whatever he looks at is watching, and even waiting for, him in return.

His constancy of theme leads to or from a constancy of mood; in spite of glimmers of hope and confidence, Wright is our contemporary Tennyson, an anatomist of melancholy in its manifold moods, a glum examiner of his own life and its contexts. Like Tennyson he extends the Virgilian line of poets who conveniently associate melancholy with landscape details. (And like Virgil and Tennyson, as well, he is a poet of evening and of shadows.) But he is also a contemporary Rilke, one of those bees of the invisible turning the pollen of actuality into the honey of the spirit, at least at those rare moments when the numinous makes itself accessible. It should come as no surprise, then, that in terms of his dealings with the landscape he is also the premier American poet of what Ruskin scornfully dismissed as the pathetic fallacy. His landscapes are artfully viewed but also metaphorically or rhetorically humanized. Things momentarily stand in for other things, or at least come to resemble them.

Wright employs such "fallacies" ("figurations" would be a more exact term) as the basis for an entire short poem or as one device among many in constructing a longer, looser one. The chilly "California Spring" (*World*, 30) consists of five three-line stanzas. Each line is a single end-stopped sentence. In the sameness of iteration (variations on a simple subject-predicate construction), Wright builds a description from simple observation through menacing, humanized details. So, for example, the first stanza:

> At dawn the dove croons.
> A hawk hangs over the field.
> The liquidambar rinses its hundred hands.

After two lines of deliberate simplicity, the third sentence opens us onto a personified natural world that incorporates the human. At the end of the third stanza, a parallel image reverses the situation: "There is a spider that swings back and forth on his thin strings in the heart." So not only is nature humanized (a tree with hands), but now an arachnid image metonymically represents a human being from within. Later, as the sun rises higher, it is "caught like a kite in the drooped limbs of the tree." The common cliché ("limbs") disguises its origin as a catachresis, but by this point, if we have been properly following Wright's method, we realize the strange, not to say ominous, connections that obtain between the human and the nonhuman worlds, and between the perception of a scene and the encoding within it of suggestively animating details. The end is both shocking and appropriate:

One angel dangles his wing.
The grass edges creak and the tide pools begin to shine.
Nothing forgives.

The poem has hinted at religious possibilities from its first line, but now we realize we have been teased out of thought. The accumulated individual details have withheld more than we may have wanted them to deliver. Is the angel a bird? An imagined spirit hovering over the scene? A Paraclete in the landscape, or a figment of the poet's imagination? Light comes up as day proceeds, and the poem ends unforgivingly with a unique two-word line of nonfigurative, abstract language in the richly figured tapestry of description. Does the line undo everything that preceded it, or does it come as an inevitable conclusion? The shock of the line reminds us of moments in Rilke and James Wright; the mysteries of the pathetic fallacy prohibit any final knowledge of our place in the observed world rather than welcome us within it.

As an example of the same rhetoric at work on a large scale, one might take the opening nine-line section of "The Other Side of the River" (78):

Easter again, and a small rain falls
On the mockingbird and the housefly,
                                        on the Chevrolet
In its purple joy
And the TV antennas huddled across the hillside—

Easter again, and the palm trees hunch
Deeper beneath their burden,
                              the dark puddles take in
Whatever is given them,
And nothing rises more than halfway out of itself—

Easter with all its little mouths open into the rain.

Opening (as is his recent procedure) with a phrase rather than a clause, Wright gives us two takes on his ritualized scene ("Easter again, and . . . Easter again, and . . ."), as if acknowledging that Easter will always look like this. The observed details are both random and willful: the unmodified mockingbird and housefly ease us into a world where, it transpires, even the mechanical is animated (the automobile "in its purple joy" and the antennas "huddled"), and where the natural is humanized (the palm trees "hunch," the puddles "take in" the rain). The season of sacrifice, forgiveness, and reawakening is summarized in a quasi-allegorical phrase, as though Wright needed to end by epitomizing it: "Easter with all its little mouths open into the rain" looks like some primitive deity, sculpted or painted. Resurrection and rebirth never seemed so banal and unpromising.

As Wright moves through a recollection of quail hunting with his brother when they were teenagers, he keeps protesting his inability to analogize: "There is no metaphor for any of this" (79), while at the same time loading all of his description with, for the most part, momentary rather than extended metaphorical gestures. He insistently returns to catachresis, the rhetorical trope of misnaming or of transferring a word to a phenomenon with no proper word of its own (speaking of the "face" of a mountain, for example, or the "limbs," rather than the branches, of a tree, as above). Thus, he mentions "the plum trees preen[ing] in the wind," "the vine-lipped face of the pine woods," and "the vinca blossoms like deep bruises among the green." And, from the other side, he undoes and de-animates living things: "quail . . . bursting like shrapnel points" and "the trees balloon and subside." Moving up and down some imaginary scale of animation (another parallel to the vertical movement on his pages), Wright takes time out in the middle of the poem to announce his main obsession, one already indicated by his figurative language:

> It's linkage I'm talking about,
>                          and harmonies and structures
> And all the various things that tie our wrists to the past.
>
> Something infinite behind everything appears,
>                          and then disappears.
>
> It's all a matter of how
>                  you narrow the surfaces.
> It's all a matter of how you fit in the sky.                    (79)

That last sentence ambiguously announces two of Wright's long-standing concerns, as well as the connections between the artistic and the spiritual. "How you fit in the sky" means both how you manage to depict the heavens in your version of a landscape painting, and how or where you belong in the cosmic scheme of things. Like a jigsaw puzzle, like a painting in process, like a Charles Wright poem, one's arrangements with the divine partake equally of figuring things out and putting things in. Even when he stoically concludes his poem with the sad, sentence-long realization, "So to have come to this . . . / Is a short life of trouble," he is able to embed within the sentence's subject and predicate examples of the world's multiple beauties. As usual, he humanizes the natural world (n.b. the participles "whimpering," "cruising," and "thrusting" below), implicitly participating in it, and thereby mitigating his troubles and enabling his readers (if not himself) to escape from them:

> So to have come to this,
>                  remembering what I did do, and what I didn't do,
> The gulls whimpering over the boathouse,
>                          the monarch butterflies
> Cruising the flower beds,
> And all the soft hairs of spring thrusting up through the wind,

And the sun, as it always does,
> dropping into its slot without a click,
Is a short life of trouble.                                              (81)

Short, maybe; but suspended within that life as within the poem's epi-
grammatic conclusion are the beauties of the world, literally (as here)
sprawled out across the landscape of Wright's pages. The numinous ap-
pears, amassing itself even as the poet confesses that "there comes a point
when everything starts to dust away / More quickly than it appears" (80).
To record the evanescence renders it permanent; the details of the ob-
served world fill in the page just as Cézanne's squares and wriggles of
color become a landscape.

Wright complicates the entire question of looking at a landscape by
his mixing of genres. There are poems (like "Homage to Paul Cézanne")
that skirt the edge of painterliness and that tend toward the ekphrastic
while remaining faithful to the observed data in the natural, as opposed
to the represented, world. Occasionally he sounds reductive and Platonic
at once, as in a recent short lyric, "Morandi II" (*Chickamauga*, 67), which
renders the essence of the Bolognese painter without referring to a spe-
cific painting. Instead, Wright merely names shapes ("rectangle, circle,
square"), geometrical figures ("angle and plane"), painterly marks
("Scratches like an abyss") as representative "examples," before a con-
cluding couplet that summarizes the bare contents of Morandi's oeuvre:

> Corners of buildings, bottles, hillsides, shade trees and fields,
> Color and form, light and space,
> > the losses we get strange gain from.

Poems about abstract paintings are rare, but this lyric, although it con-
cerns a representational painter, approaches the limits of abstraction. Even
Wright's lists (and his general preference for nominal structures) allow
him to specify items, without description or ornament, before conclud-
ing with his paradoxical summary of lessons learned.

He puts description, and painting itself, to a somewhat different use
in "Homage to Claude Lorrain" (*World*, 82). A casual reminiscence
about army life (Verona, 1959) recalls a Claude picture that hung on the
bedroom wall: "a rigged ship in a huge sea, / Storm waves like flames
above my bed." Now, however, long lost, the picture is "Trapped in the
past's foliage, as so much else is / In spite of our constancy, or how / We
rattle the branches and keep our lights on the right place." Time and
space have merged. The past is a dense forest, and no matter how hard we
try to illuminate it, the darkness seems always to prevail. The poem
continues with a description of the poet's rooms before ending with a
second memory of Claude's picture, which now assumes iconic and psy-
chological power, as the poet occupies a symbolic middle space between
one body of water and another, with a depicted external fire and an

internalized one, and coming gradually to occupy an enclosed space as, once again, time and space come together:

> Between the sea fires of Claude Lorrain
> > and the curled sheets of the river,
> I burned on my swivel stool
> Night after night,
> > looking into the future, its charred edges
> Holding my life like a frame
> I'd hope to fit into one day, unsigned and rigged for the deeps.

Looking *at* Claude's work, Wright comes to occupy it, or some version of it, as he becomes both an anonymous picture ("unsigned") and a burning vessel ("rigged for the deep"). Figuration multiplies, in other words, as ekphrasis itself expands beyond mere description. Looking leads to absorption in space and through time. Specific detail leads to generalized significance. Often, one cannot determine which is more important to the poet: visual accuracy or abstract conclusion. Claude's picture becomes part of a gestalt, a scene, an inspiring memory.

"What matters is abstract," he remarks in a poem ("Yard Journal," 121) where the image precedes, rather than follows, the abstraction to which it is connected:

> —Deep dusk and lightning bugs
> > alphabetize on the east wall,
> The carapace of the sky blue-ribbed and buzzing
> Somehow outside it all,
> Trees dissolving against the night's job,
> > houses melting in air:
> Somewhere out there an image is biding its time,
> Burning like Abraham in the cold, swept
> > expanses of heaven,
> Waiting to take me in and complete my equation:
> What matters is abstract, and is what love is,
> Candescent inside the memory,
> > continuous
> And unexpungable, as love is.

This entire poem, cast in Wright's newer mode, allows us to see the intersections and overlappings not only between the abstract and the individual but also between the observed and the artistic. "Exclusion's the secret," as he has announced; what is visible is also what is missing. He grapples with whatever heaves into view or recedes from it, and whatever stands even momentarily still. Such struggle is another way of explaining Wright's hemistiches, his efforts to render the world continuous and stationary at once. Like lightning bugs, however, the images, details, and alphabets of the world flash on and off. Now you see them, now you don't.

Wright's poetry oddly combines particularity of observation, discreteness of detail and diction, with the haze on disjunctions caused by lineation, transitions, and other gestures that mimic the mind's transactions with external reality. As I have tried to show, many of his metaphors both clarify and mystify, calling attention to both sameness and difference in the two halves of their comparisons. The combination of simile and phrases, rather than clauses, has made many of Wright's newer, shorter poems seem like experiments in seeing and recording. Parts rather than wholes begin to overwhelm the page. Take, for example, these lines from "Meditation on Song and Structure" (*Black Zodiac*, 59):

> Swallows over the battlements
> and thigh-moulded red tile roofs,
> Square crenelations, Guelph town.
> Swallows against the enfrescoed backdrop of tilled hills
> Like tiny sharks in the tinted air
> That buoys them like a tide,
> arrested, water-colored surge.
> Swallows darting like fish through the alabaster air,
> Cleansing the cleanliness, feeding on seen and the unseen.

The thrice-mentioned swallows grow throughout the stanza, first merely located, then relocated and figured in terms of "sharks," and at last refigured as "fish" in the process of action ("cleansing"). As a sentence, the stanza is officially incomplete; as an experiment in amplified troping it embraces ever larger realms of vision and descriptive possibility.

Perhaps Wright's transactions—with vision, description, and similitude—are all epitomized in a series of plangent questions in "California Dreaming" (*World*, 116): "What if the soul is indeed outside the body . . . / What if inside the body another shape is waiting to come out . . . / What other anagoge in this life but the self?" The search for the soul and for the truth that lies outside it dissolves into a gray area where outside/inside, body/spirit, self/world, all the distinctions on which our poetic tropings as well as our philosophies and our self-interest depend, entirely dissolve.

Later in the same poem, Wright announces what might be called the truth of all poets, namely, the gradual half-life of metaphor, the failure to abridge disparate facts, the inadequacy of language. This sad truth lies at the center of all the other failures, the mysterious hauntings and losses, in the poet's heart, precisely because it is a poetic failure. He makes his announcement significantly in a poem about his own alienation from his nonnative landscape. California was never for Wright—perhaps unique among American poets in this regard—the Golden State. Instead, it was the desert of his seventeen-year exile before his return to Virginia. Not that the South is an unmitigated paradise, but at least the poet can feel there the ties that have bound him to family, landscape, and a recognizable contour for human emotions. "Out there where the landscape ends," however, he comes to a delicate self-knowledge:

> What I know best is a little thing.
> It sits on the far side of the simile,
>
> > the like that's like the like.
>
> > > (116)

No wonder that lines break where syntax bends; or that flora momentarily become fauna-like; or that one memory inspires another one, however disconnected; or, finally, that the poet seems terminally melancholic. Whereas a more linear poet like Bishop uses paratactic arrangements for acts of description ("Everything only connected by 'and' and 'and,'" as her famous line puts it in "Over 2000 Illustrations and a Complete Concordance"), Charles Wright prefers hypotactic, transformative syntax, as if to say "Everything only connected by 'like' and 'like.'" And nothing stays put or unchanged for very long. Everything falls away into the depths of forgetfulness, and even what we can recollect we must give up as partial.

We can measure Wright's distinctiveness by comparing his paths with those not taken. With his multiple images, his phrasal writing, his insistent anecdotes that appear only to vanish, and even his interest in non-representational painting, he might have become another Frank O'Hara. But the shape of a long Wright poem differs from the "I do this, I do that" casualness of O'Hara's diary jottings. Where O'Hara is light, Wright is by turns lush and austere; where O'Hara, like so many poets in the tradition of first-person observation, gives the sense of merely following a random path of actual scenes, thoughts, and events, Wright makes everything seem both irrational and inevitable. Probably no more succinct synopsis of Wright's metaphysical stance and of his poetic method exists than the birthday entry in his year-long "Journal of the Year of the Ox" (179), a summary of his place well after the *mezzo del cammin*:

> In my fiftieth year, with a bad back and a worried mind,
> Going down the Lee Highway,
>
> > the farms and villages
>
> Rising like fog behind me,
> Between the dream and the disappearance the abiding earth
> Affords us each for an instant.
>
> > However we choose to use it
>
> We use it and then it's gone:
> Like the glint of the Shenandoah
>
> > at Castleman's Ferry,
>
> Like license plates on cars we follow and then pass by,
> Like what we hold and let go,

Like this country we've all come down,
                                        and where it's led us,
    Like what we forgot to say, each time we forget it.

With its combination of country ballad and Old Testament diction
(Ecclesiastes: "the earth abideth forever"), this heartbreaking stanza reit-
erates Wright's central truth. Repetition—automobile-travel down an old
country highway or a string of similes—leads in one direction only: to-
ward our disappearance. The details of the road have been ravishing; the
landscape takes us in and welcomes us; then we go.

# Bibliography

## Part One: Primary Works

POETRY

*The Voyage*. Iowa City: Patrician Press, 1963.
*Six Poems*. London: Royal College of Art, 1965.
*The Dream Animal*. Toronto: Anansi, 1968.
*Private Madrigals*. Madison, WI: Abraxas Press, 1969.
*The Grave of the Right Hand*. Middletown, CT: Wesleyan University Press, 1970.
*The Venice Notebook*. Boston: Barn Dream Press, 1971.
*Backwater*. Santa Ana, CA: Golem Press, 1973.
*Hard Freight*. Middletown, CT: Wesleyan University Press, 1973.
*Bloodlines*. Middletown, CT: Wesleyan University Press, 1975.
*Colophons*. Iowa City: Windhover Press, 1977.
*China Trace*. Middletown, CT: Wesleyan University Press, 1977.
*Wright: A Profile*. Iowa City: Grilled Flowers Press, 1979.
*Dead Color*. Salem, OR: Charles Seluzicki, 1980.
*The Southern Cross*. New York: Random House, 1981.
*Country Music: Selected Early Poems*. Middletown, CT: Wesleyan University Press, 1982.
*Four Poems of Departure*. Portland, OR: Trace Editions, 1983.
*The Other Side of the River*. New York: Random House, 1984.
*Yard Journal*. Richmond, VA: Laurel Press, 1985.
*Five Journals*. New York: Red Ozier Press, 1986.
*A Journal of the Year of the Ox: A Poem*. Iowa City: Windhover Press, 1988.
*Zone Journals*. New York: Farrar, Straus & Giroux, 1988.
*Xionia: Poems*. Iowa City: Windhover Press, 1990.
*The World of the Ten Thousand Things: Poems 1980-1990*. New York: Farrar, Straus & Giroux, 1990.
*Chickamauga*. New York: Farrar, Straus & Giroux, 1995.
*Black Zodiac*. New York: Farrar, Straus & Giroux, 1997.
*Appalachia*. New York: Farrar, Straus & Giroux, 1998.
*North American Bear*. Winona, MN: Sutton Hoo Press, 1999.
*Negative Blue: Selected Later Poems*. New York: Farrar, Straus & Giroux, 2000.
*Night Music*. Exeter, UK: Stride, 2001.
*A Short History of the Shadow*. New York: Farrar, Straus & Giroux, 2002.
*Buffalo Yoga*. New York: Farrar, Straus & Giroux, 2004.
*Snake Eyes*. Exeter, UK: Stride, 2004.
*The Wrong End of the Rainbow*. Louisville, KY: Sarabande, 2005.

PROSE

*Halflife: Improvisations and Interviews 1977-87*. Ann Arbor: University of Michigan Press, 1988.
*Quarter Notes: Improvisations and Interviews*. Ann Arbor: University of Michigan Press, 1995.
*Uncollected Prose: Six Guys and a Supplement*. Roanoke, VA: Roanoke College, 2000.

## TRANSLATIONS

Campana, Dino. *Orphic Songs.* Oberlin, OH: Oberlin College Press, 1984.
Montale, Eugenio. *The Storm and Other Poems.* Oberlin, OH: Oberlin College Press, 1978.
————. *Motets.* Iowa City: Windhover, 1981.
————. *Selected Poems.* Translated by Jonathan Galassi, Charles Wright, and David Young. Oberlin, OH: Oberlin College Press, 2004.

## Part Two: Secondary Works

*Note: A star indicates that the work is included in this volume. A double star denotes a work that appeared in* The Point Where All Things Meet *but is not included here.*

Agena, Kathleen. "The Mad Sense of Language." *Partisan Review* 43, no. 4 (1976): 625-30.
Albright, Daniel. "Noble Savagery and Its Opposite: American Art Right Now." In *America Today: Highways and Labyrinths: Proceedings of the XV Biennial Conference, Siracusa, November 4-7, 1999,* edited by Gigliola Nocera, 51-65. Syracuse, Italy: Grafià, 2003.
Altieri, Charles. "The Dominant Poetic Mode of the Late Seventies." In *Self and Sensibility in Contemporary American Poetry*, 32-51. Cambridge: Cambridge University Press, 1984.
Andrews, Tom. "The Point Where All Things Meet: Improvisations on Charles Wright's *The World of the Ten Thousand Things.*" Review of *The World of the Ten Thousand Things. Iron Mountain Review* 8 (1992): 9-13.★
————. "Via Negativa: A Symposium." Review of *Chickamauga. Ohio Review* 56 (1997): 123-37.
————. ed. *The Point Where All Things Meet: Essays on Charles Wright.* Oberlin, OH: Oberlin College Press, 1995.
Axelrod, Steven Gould. Review of *The Southern Cross. World Literature Today* 57, no. 1 (1983): 111.
Bagby, George F. "Wright Sets Autumn of Life to Verse." Review of *Chickamauga. Richmond Times-Dispatch*, 23 July 1995, city edition, sec. F, 4.
————. "Spiritual Theme Marks Wright's New Verse." Review of *Appalachia. Richmond Times-Dispatch*, 27 June 1999, city edition, sec. F, 4.
Baker, David. "On Restraint." Review of *Chickamauga. Poetry* 168, no. 1 (1996): 33-47. Reprinted in *Heresy and the Ideal: On Contemporary Poetry* (Fayetteville, AR: University of Arkansas Press, 2000).★
Beasley, Bruce. Review of *Appalachia. Bellingham Review* 22, no. 1 (1999): 115-8.
Bedient, Calvin. "Tracing Charles Wright." *Parnassus* 10, no. 1 (1982): 55-74.★
————. "Slide-Wheeling around the Curves." *Southern Review* 27, no. 1 (1991): 221-34.★★
————. "Poetry and Silence at the End of the Century." Review of *Chickamauga. Salmagundi* 111 (1996): 195-207.
————. "Wanted: More Complexity." Review of *Chickamauga. Southern Review* 33, no. 1 (1997): 136-49.
Beer, John. Review of *Night Music. Chicago Review* 47/48, no. 4/1 (2001): 263-70.
Blasing, Mutlu Konuk. "The American Sublime, c. 1992: What Clothes Does One Wear?" Review of *The World of the Ten Thousand Things. Michigan Quarterly Review* 31, no. 3 (1992): 425-41.★★

Bond, Bruce. "Metaphysics of the Image in Charles Wright and Paul Cézanne." *Southern Review* 30, no. 1 (1994): 116-25.★

Boyle, Peter. "Tradition and Wisdom in Charles Wright's *Black Zodiac* and *Chickamauga.*" *Verse* 15/16, no. 3/1 (1998): 102-8.

Branam, Harold. Review of *Appalachia.* In *Magill's Literary Annual 1999,* edited by John D. Wilson. Pasadena, CA: Salem Press, 1999, 61-63.

Brier, Peter. Review of *A Short History of the Shadow.* In *Magill's Literary Annual 2003,* edited by John D. Wilson and Steven G. Kellman. Pasadena, CA: Salem Press, 2003, 741-45.

Bromwich, David. "I Showed Her My Darkness, She Gave Me a Stone." Review of *China Trace. Poetry* 133, no. 3 (1978): 169-76.

Brown, Ashley. Review of *Negative Blue. World Literature Today* 74, no. 4 (2000): 821-22.

Buckley, Christopher. "From Here to There." Review of *The Southern Cross. Telescope* 4, no. 1 (1985): 81-94.

———. "A Light in Our Eyes." Review of *The Other Side of the River. Bluefish* 2, no. 3/4 (1984/85): 147-57.

———. "Charles Wright's Hymn." Review of *Xionia. Poet Lore* 86, no. 3 (1991): 59-65.★

Butterick, George F. "Charles Wright." In *Dictionary of Literary Biography Yearbook: 1982,* edited by Richard Ziegfeld. Detroit: Gale Research Company, 1993, 389-400.

Byrne, Mairéad. Review of *Black Zodiac. Sycamore Review* 9, no. 2 (1997): 146-50.

Carpenter, John R. "The Big Machine." Review of *Hard Freight. Poetry* 125, no. 3 (1974): 166-73.

Chaser, Mike. Review of *Appalachia. Texas Review* 20, no. 1/2 (1999): 116-18.

Chitwood, Michael. "Gospel Music: Charles Wright and the High Lonesome." *Iron Mountain Review* 8 (1992): 23-25.★

Clark, Kevin. "Stature." Review of *Zone Journals. Café Solo* 5, no. 3/4 (1989): 63-68.★★

Cohea, David. Review of *Appalachia. Florida Review* 24, no. 2 (1999): 106-16.

Collins, Floyd. "Metamorphosis within the Poetry of Charles Wright." Review of *The World of the Ten Thousand Things. Gettysburg Review* 4, no. 3 (1991): 464-79.

———. "A Fine Excess." Review of *Chickamauga. Gettysburg Review* 9, no. 2 (1996): 331-52.

———. "A Poetry of Transcendence." Review of *Black Zodiac. Gettysburg Review* 10, no. 4 (1997): 683-701.

Conarroe, Joel. Review of *The Southern Cross. Washington Post Book World,* 27 June 1982, 10.

Costello, Bonnie. "The Soil and Man's Intelligence: Three Contemporary Landscape Poets." *Contemporary Literature* 30, no. 3 (1989): 412-33.★★

———. "Charles Wright's *Via Negativa*: Language, Landscape, and the Idea of God." *Contemporary Literature* 42, no. 2 (2001): 325-46.

———. "Charles Wright, Giorgio Morandi, and the Metaphysics of the Line." *Mosaic* 35, no. 1 (2002): 149-71.★

Cushman, Stephen. "The Capabilities of Charles Wright." *Iron Mountain Review* 8 (1992): 14-22.★

Daniels, Kate. "Porch-Sitting and Southern Poetry." In *The Future of Southern Letters,* edited by Jefferson Humphries and John Lowe, 61-71. New York: Oxford University Press, 1996.

———. "Old Masters." Review of *Appalachia. Southern Review* 35, no. 3 (1999): 621-34.

Davis, William V. "Making the World with Words: A Reading of Charles Wright's 'Appalachian Book of the Dead.'" In *Latitude 63° North: Proceedings of the 8th International Region and Nation Literature Conference, Östersund, Sweden 2-6 August 2000,* edited by David Bell, 255-70. Östersund, Sweden: Mid-Sweden University College, 2002.

Eshleman, Clayton. "Life as a Poetic Puzzlement." Review of *The Other Side of the River*. *Los Angeles Times Book Review*, 19 August 1984, 7.

Francini, Antonella. "A Poet's Workshop: Charles Wright Translating Eugenio Montale." *Anello Che Non Tiene* 4, no. 1/2 (1992): 44-71.

———. "'The Pale Hems of the Masters' Gowns': Mediterranean Voices and Shadows in the Poetry of Charles Wright." In *America and the Mediterranean: AISNA, Associazione Italiana di Studi Nord-Americani, Proceedings of the Sixteenth Biennial International Conference, Genova, November 8-11, 2001*, edited by Massimo Bacigalupo and Pierangelo Castagneto, 85-92. Turin: Otto, 2003.

Frank, Elizabeth. "The Middle of the Journey." Review of *The Other Side of the River*. *Nation*, 7 April 1984, 421-24.

Gall, Sally M. "Seven from Wesleyan." Review of *Hard Freight*. *Shenandoah* 21, no. 1 (1974): 54-70.

Gardner, Thomas. "Restructured and Restrung: Charles Wright's *Zone Journals* and Emily Dickinson." *Kenyon Review* 26, no. 2 (2004): 149-74.

Garrett, George. "New Poems by Four Appalachian Masters." Review of *Buffalo Yoga*. *Appalachian Heritage* 32, no. 3 (2004): 74-82.

Garrison, David. "'An Old Song Handles My Heart': Charles Wright and the Sweet Failure of Music." *Kentucky Philological Review* 6 (1991): 9-14.

———. "From Feeling to Form: Image as Translation in the Poetry of Charles Wright." *Midwest Quarterly* 41, no. 1 (1999): 33-47.

Gitzen, Julian. "Charles Wright and the Presences in Absence." *Mid-American Review* 14, no. 2 (1994): 110-21.★

Gregerson, Linda. "Short Reviews." Review of *Zone Journals*. *Poetry* 155, no. 3 (1989): 229-39.

Gussow, Mel. "A Good Ear for the Music of His Own Life." *New York Times*, 16 April 1998, late edition, sec. E, 1.

Hahn, Robert. "Versions of the Mediterranean in American Poetry." In *America and the Mediterranean: AISNA, Associazione Italiana di Studi Nord-Americani, Proceedings of the Sixteenth Biennial International Conference, Genova, November 8-11, 2001*, edited by Massimo Bacigalupo and Pierangelo Castagneto, 57-63. Turin: Otto, 2003. A revised version appears in *Poetry International* 6 (2002).

Hart, Henry. Review of *Chickamauga*. *Verse* 14, no. 1 (1997): 114-18.

———. "Charles Wright." In *American Writers: A Collection of Literary Biographies*. Supplement 5, edited by Jay Parini, 331-46. New York: Scribner, 2000.

———. "Charles Wright's *Via Mystica*." *Georgia Review* 58, no. 2 (2004): 409-32.★

Hart, Kevin. "'La poesia è scala a Dio': On Reading Charles Wright." *Heat* (Artarmon, N.S.W.) 1, no. 6 (1998): 92-109.

Henry, Brian. "Charles Wright Puts Past to Good Use." Review of *Black Zodiac*. *Richmond Times-Dispatch*, 21 September 1997, city edition, sec. K, 4.

———. "Southern Cross: The Inheritance of Charles Wright." *Quarterly West* 46 (1998): 196-202.

———. "New Scaffolding for New Arrangements: Charles Wright's Low Riders." *Virginia Quarterly Review* 80, no. 2 (2004): 98-112.

Hirsch, Edward. "The Visionary Poetics of Philip Levine and Charles Wright." In *The Columbia History of American Poetry*, edited by Jay Parini, 777-806. New York: Columbia University Press, 1993.★★

Hix, L. H. "Charles Wright and a Case of Foreshortened Influence." *Notes on Contemporary Literature* 18, no. 1 (1988): 4-6.

Hosmer, Robert Ellis, Jr. "Poetry Roundup." Review of *Black Zodiac*. *America*, 20 December 1997, 23-28.

Hurley, Tom. "A Universe in the Back Yard: Collection Reflects Eighteen Dark and Light Months of Poet Charles Wright's Soul." Review of *Appalachia. San Francisco Chronicle Book Review*, 24 January 1999, 2.

Ingalls, Zoë. "Charles Wright, Poet of Landscape, Melds Tradition and Innovation." *Chronicle of Higher Education*, 18 September 1998, sec B, 10–11.

Jackson, Richard. "Worlds Created, Worlds Perceived." Review of *China Trace. Michigan Quarterly Review* 17, no. 4 (1978): 543–62.

Jarman, Mark. "The Trace of a Story Line." Review of *The Other Side of the River. Ohio Review* 37 (1986): 129–47.★

———. "The Pragmatic Imagination and the Secret of Poetry." Review of *Zone Journals. Gettysburg Review* 1, no. 4 (1988): 647–60.★

Kalstone, David. "Lives in a Rearview Mirror." Review of *The Other Side of the River. New York Times Book Review*, 1 July 1984, 14.★

Kennedy, X. J. "Lovers of Greece, Women, and Tennessee." Review of *Hard Freight. New York Times Book Review*, 17 February 1974, 6.

———. "A Tenth and Four Fifths." Review of *The Southern Cross. Poetry* 141, no. 6 (1983): 349–58.

Kessler, Edward. "The Shortest Distance between Two Poets." Review of *Hard Freight. Washington Post Book World*, 5 May 1974, 3.

Kinzie, Mary. "Haunting." Review of *The Southern Cross. American Poetry Review* 11, no. 5 (1982): 37–46.

Kirsch, Adam. "Between Heaven and Earth." Review of *Appalachia. New York Times Book Review*, 28 February 1999, 21.★

Kitchen, Judith. "What Persists." Review of *Chickamauga. Georgia Review* 51, no. 2 (1997): 332–55.

LaFemina, Gerry. Review of *Chickamauga. Colorado Review* 22, no. 2 (1996): 214–23.

Lake, Paul. "Return to Metaphor: From Deep Imagist to New Formalist." *Southwest Review* 74, no. 4 (1989): 515–29. Reprinted in *New Expansive Poetry: Theory, Criticism, History*, edited by R. S. Gwynn (Ashland, OR: Story Line, 1999).

Langdon, Hammer. "Ways of Seeing." Review of *A Short History of the Shadow. Los Angeles Times Book Review*, 18 August 2002, 6.

Levine, Philip. "Citation: Philip Levine." *American Poet*, Winter 1996/97, 25.

Lewis, Leon. Review of *Buffalo Yoga*. In *Magill's Literary Annual 2005*, edited by John D. Wilson and Steven G. Kellman, 98–103. Pasadena, CA: Salem Press, 2005.

Logan, William. "Season to Season, Day to Day." Review of *Zone Journals. New York Times Book Review*, 4 September 1988, 9.

———. "Hardscrabble Country." Review of *Black Zodiac. New Criterion* 15, no. 10 (1997): 69–76.

———. Review of *Appalachia. Washington Post Book World*, 10 January 1999, 11.

———. "Falls the Shadow." Review of *A Short History of the Shadow. New Criterion* 20, no. 10 (2002): 75–82.

Longenbach, James. "Poetry in Review." Review of *Chickamauga. Yale Review* 83, no. 4 (1995): 144–57.★

———. "Between Soil and Stars." Review of *Black Zodiac. Nation*, 14 April 1997, 27–30.

———. Review of *Appalachia. Boston Review* 23, no. 6 (1998/99): 54–55.★

———. "Under the Sign of the Sun." *Los Angeles Times Book Review*, 27 June 1999, 4.

———. "Disjunction in Poetry." *Raritan* 20, no. 4 (2001): 20–36.

Lucas, Dave. Review of *Buffalo Yoga. Meridian* 13 (2004): 150–53.

Marcus, Jacqueline. "The Imperishable Quiet at the Heart of Form: Charles Wright's *Black Zodiac*." Review of *Black Zodiac. Literary Review* 41, no. 4 (1998): 562–66.

Mason, David. "Poetry Chronicle." Review of *Chickamauga*. *Hudson Review* 49, no. 1 (1996): 166-72. Reprinted in *The Poetry of Life and the Life of Poetry: Essays and Reviews* (Ashland, OR: Story Line, 2000).

McClatchy, J. D. "Recent Poetry: New Designs on Life." Review of *Bloodlines*. *Yale Review* 65, no. 1 (1975): 95-105.

———. "Reading." In *White Paper on Contemporary American Poetry*. New York: Columbia University Press, 1989, 21-75.★

———. "Amid the Groves, under the Shadowy Hill, the Generations Are Prepared." Review of *The World of the Ten Thousand Things*. *Poetry* 158, no. 5 (1991): 280-95.

———. "Ars Longa." Review of *Appalachia*. *Poetry* 175, no. 1 (1999): 78-89.★

McCorkle, James. *The Still Performance: Writing, Self, and Interconnection in Five Postmodern American Poets*, 171-211. Charlottesville, VA: University of Virginia Press, 1989.★

———. "Charles Wright." In *Dictionary of Literary Biography*. Vol. 165, *American Poets since World War II, Fourth Series*, edited by Joseph Conte, 267-82. Detroit: Gale Research Company, 1996.

McGuiness, Daniel. "The Long Line in Contemporary American Poetry." *Antioch Review* 47, no. 3 (1989): 269-86.

Meinke, Peter. Review of *Hard Freight*. *New Republic*, 24 November 1973, 25-27.

Miller, Christopher R. "Poetic Standard Time: The Zones of Charles Wright." *Southern Review* 34, no. 3 (1998): 566-86.★

Mobilio, Albert. "The Word's Worth." Review of *Black Zodiac*. *Village Voice,* 29 April 1997, 55.

Morris, John N. "Making More Sense Than Omaha." Review of *Hard Freight*. *Hudson Review* 27, no. 1 (1974): 106-18.

———. "The Songs Protect Us, in a Way." Review of *Bloodlines*. *Hudson Review* 28, no. 3 (1975): 446-58.

Muske-Dukes, Carol. "Ourselves as History." Review of *Bloodlines*. *Parnassus* 4, no. 2 (1976): 111-121.

———. "Guided by Dark Stars." Review of *Black Zodiac*. *New York Times Book Review*, 31 August 1997, 11-12.★

Oser, Lee. Review of *Black Zodiac*. *World Literature Today* 71, no. 4 (1997): 794-95.

———. Review of *Appalachia*. *World Literature Today* 73, no. 3 (1999): 535-36.

———. Review of *A Short History of the Shadow*. *World Literature Today* 77, no. 1 (2003): 105-6.

Pankey, Eric. "The Form of Concentration." Review of *Zone Journals*. *Iowa Review* 19, no. 2 (1989): 175-87.★★

———. "'Perilous Interface': Recent Poetry." Review of *Black Zodiac*. *Partisan Review* 66, no. 2 (1999): 344-49.

———. "What Hast Thou, O My Soul, with Paradise: Charles Wright's *Appalachia*." Review of *Appalachia*. *Verse* 16, no. 2 (1999): 165-70.

Parini, Jay. "From Scene to Fiery Scene." Review of *Country Music*. *Times Literary Supplement*, 1 March 1985, 239.

———. "Charles Wright: The Remembered Earth." In *Some Necessary Angels: Essays on Writing and Politics*, 181-200. New York: Columbia University Press, 1997.

———. "A 'Thirst for the Divine.'" Review of *A Short History of the Shadow*. *Nation*, 20 May 2002, 30.

Pettingell, Phoebe. "Through Memory and Miniatures." Review of *The Other Side of the River*. *New Leader*, 20 August 1984, 17-18.

Pinsky, Robert. "Description and the Virtuous Use of Words." Review of *Hard Freight*. *Parnassus* 3, no. 2 (1975): 134-46. A revised version appears in *The Situation of Poetry: Contemporary Poetry and Its Traditions* (Princeton, NJ: Princeton University Press, 1976).

Prado, Holly. "Respecting Poetry's Possibilities." Review of *The Southern Cross*. *Los Angeles Times Book Review*, 7 February 1982, 3.

Pratt, William. Review of *Chickamauga*. *World Literature Today* 70, no. 4 (1996): 967.

Pugh, Christina. Review of *Negative Blue*. *Harvard Review* 21 (2001): 177-78.

Rand, Richard. Review of *Buffalo Yoga*. *Harvard Review* 27 (2004): 203-5.

Rauschenbusch, Stephanie. "Serving a Darker Music." Review of *Appalachia*. *American Book Review* 21, no. 1 (1999): 27.

Rector, Liam. Review of *Appalachia*. *Harvard Review* 16 (1999): 116-18.

St. John, David. "Raised Voices in the Choir: A Review of 1981 Poetry Selections." Review of *The Southern Cross*. *Antioch Review* 40, no. 2 (1982): 225-34. Reprinted in *Where the Angels Come Toward Us: Selected Essays, Reviews, and Interviews* (Fredonia, NY: White Pine Press, 1995).

————. Review of *The Other Side of the River*. *Washington Post Book World*, 20 May 1984, 6.

————. "Charles Wright's *Country Music*." Foreword to *Country Music: Selected Early Poems*, 2nd ed., xiii-xxi. Middletown, CT: Wesleyan University Press, 1991. Reprinted in *Where the Angels Come toward Us: Selected Essays, Reviews, and Interviews* (Fredonia, NY: White Pine Press, 1995).★

Sampson, Dennis. "Poetry Chronicle." Review of *The World of the Ten Thousand Things*. *Hudson Review* 44, no. 2 (1991): 333-42.

Santos, Sherod. Review of *Zone Journals*. *New Virginia Review* 8 (1991): 369-72.★

Schuldt, M. D. "Search Light: Charles Wright Scans the Landscape of Language." Review of *Negative Blue*. *Tucson Weekly*, 16 November 2000, 34-35.

Simic, Charles. "You Can't Keep a Good Sonnet Down." Review of *A Short History of the Shadow*. *New York Review of Books*, 26 September 2002, 40-42.

Smith, Ron. "Charles Wright Excels Once More in New Collection of Verse." Review of *Negative Blue*. *Richmond Times-Dispatch*, 12 November 2000, city edition, sec. F, 4.★

————. "Wright Continues Lyrical Trips in Nature" Review of *A Short History of the Shadow*. *Richmond Times-Dispatch*, 29 September 2002, city edition, sec. F, 4.

Spiegelman, Willard. "Poetry in Review." Review of *Black Zodiac*. *Yale Review* 85, no. 4 (1997): 166-75.

————. "Landscape and Identity: Charles Wright's Backyard Metaphysics." *Southern Review* 40, no. 1 (2004): 172-96. A revised version appears in *How Poets See the World: The Art of Description in Contemporary Poetry* (New York: Oxford University Press, 2005).★

Stewart, Pamela. "In All Places at Once." Review of *The Southern Cross*. *Ironwood* 19 (1982): 162-66.

Stitt, Peter. "The Inward Journey." Review of *Bloodlines*. *Ohio Review* 17 (1976): 91-92.★★

————. Review of *China Trace*. *Georgia Review* 32, no. 2 (1978): 474-80.★★

————. "Problems of Youth . . . and Age." Review of *The Southern Cross*. *Georgia Review* 36, no. 1 (1982): 183-93.★★

————. "The Circle of the Meditative Moment." Review of *The Other Side of the River*. *Georgia Review* 38, no. 2 (1984): 402-14.★★

————. "To Enlighten, to Embody." Review of *Zone Journals*. *Georgia Review* 41, no. 4 (1987): 800-13.★★

————. *Uncertainty and Plenitude: Five Contemporary Poets*. Iowa City: University of Iowa Press, 1997.★

Suarez, Ernest. "The Year in Poetry." Review of *Negative Blue*. In *Dictionary of Literary Biography Yearbook: 2000*, edited by Matthew J. Bruccoli, 90-101. Detroit: Gale Group, 2001.

Sullivan, James. Review of *Chickamauga*. In *Magill's Literary Annual 1996*, edited by Frank N. Magill, 103-6. Pasadena, CA: Salem Press, 1996.

———. Review of *Black Zodiac*. In *Magill's Literary Annual 1998*, edited by John D. Wilson, 117-20. Pasadena, CA: Salem Press, 1998.

Taylor, Henry. "Land of the Poets: Charles Wright and Eavan Boland Tell of the Landscapes of Fact and of Poetry." Review of *Appalachia*. *Boston Globe*, 13 December 1998, city edition, sec. M, 1.

Tillinghast, Richard. "From Michigan and Tennessee." Review of *Country Music*. *New York Times Book Review*, 12 December 1982, 14.

———. "An Elegist's New England, a Buddhist's Dante." Review of *The World of the Ten Thousand Things*. *New York Times Book Review*, 24 February 1991, 18-19.★

Unsino, Stephen. Review of *The World of the Ten Thousand Things*. *America*, 25 April 1992, 361-62.

Upton, Lee. *The Muse of Abandonment: Origin, Identity, Mastery in Five American Poets*. Lewisburg, PA: Bucknell University Press; London: Associated University Presses, 1998.★

Van Winckel, Nance. "Charles Wright and the Landscape of the Lyric." Review of *Zone Journals*. *New England Review and Bread Loaf Quarterly* 12, no. 3 (1990): 308-12.★★

Vendler, Helen. "False Poets and Real Poets." Review of *Bloodlines*. *New York Times Book Review*, 7 September 1975, 6-18.

———. "The Transcendent 'I.'" *New Yorker*, 29 October 1979, 160-74. Reprinted in *Part of Nature, Part of Us: Modern American Poets* (Cambridge: Harvard University Press, 1980).★

———. "Travels in Time." Review of *Zone Journals*. *New Republic*, 18 January 1988, 34-36. A revised version appears in *The Music of What Happens: Poems, Poets, Critics* (Cambridge: Harvard University Press, 1988).★

———. "The Nothing That Is." Review of *Chickamauga*. *New Republic*, 7 August 1995, 42-45.★

Walker, David. Review of *The Southern Cross*. *FIELD* 26 (1982): 87-97.★

Walton, Anthony. "The Journey Within." *Oxford American* 37 (2001): 67-73.

Ward, David C. "The Mask of Battle." Review of *Chickamauga*. *PN Review* 22, no. 6 (1996): 67-69.

Wojahn, David. "Survivalist Selves." Review of *Black Zodiac*. *Kenyon Review* 20, no. 3/4 (1998): 180-90.

Wright, Stuart. "Charles Wright: A Bibliographic Chronicle, 1963-1985." *Bulletin of Bibliography* 43, no. 1 (1986): 3-12.

Young, David. "Language: The Poet as Master and Servant." *FIELD* 14 (1976): 68-90. Reprinted in *A FIELD Guide to Contemporary Poetry and Poetics*, revised ed., edited by Stuart Friebert, David Walker, and David Young (Oberlin, OH: Oberlin College Press, 1997).

———. "The Blood Bees of Paradise." Review of *The World of the Ten Thousand Things*. *FIELD* 44 (1991): 77-90.★

———. "Looking for Landscapes." Review of *Black Zodiac*. *FIELD* 58 (1998): 74-90.★

Zawacki, Andrew. "Reading Wright in the Wrong Country." *Thumbscrew* 8 (1997): 74-78.

# Contributors

The poetry of **TOM ANDREWS** (1961–2001) has been collected in *Random Symmetries* (Oberlin College Press, 2002). He also wrote a memoir, *Codeine Diary* (Little Brown, 1998), and edited collections of criticism on two contemporary poets: *On William Stafford: The Worth of Local Things* (University of Michigan Press, 1995) and this book's precursor, *The Point Where All Things Meet: Essays on Charles Wright* (Oberlin, 1995).

**DAVID BAKER'S** most recent books include *Midwest Eclogue: Poems* (W. W. Norton, 2005) and *Heresy and the Ideal: On Contemporary Poetry* (University of Arkansas Press, 2000). His edited volume *Radiant Lyre: Essays on Lyric Poetry* is forthcoming from Graywolf Press. He is Poetry Editor of the *Kenyon Review*.

**CALVIN BEDIENT**, Professor of English at UCLA, is the author of four books of criticism, including *He Do the Police in Different Voices: The Waste Land and Its Protagonist* (University of Chicago Press, 1986), and two collections of poetry: *Candy Necklace* (Wesleyan University Press, 1997) and *The Violence of the Morning* (University of Georgia Press, 2002).

**BRUCE BOND** is the author of five books of poetry, most recently *Cinder* (Etruscan Press, 2003) and *The Throats of Narcissus* (University of Arkansas Press, 2001). His poems have appeared in *The Best American Poetry* anthology series, *Paris Review*, *Georgia Review*, and elsewhere, and he has received fellowships from the NEA, Bread Loaf, the TCA, and other organizations. He is Professor of English at the University of North Texas and Poetry Editor for the *American Literary Review*.

**CHRISTOPHER BUCKLEY** teaches in the Creative Writing Department at the University of California, Riverside. His recent books of poetry include *Sky* (Sheep Meadow Press, 2004) and a forthcoming volume entitled *And the Sea*. His second book of creative nonfiction, *Sleep Walk*, is due in 2006 from Eastern Washington University Press, who also published *A Condition of the Spirit: The Life and Work of Larry Levis*, which he co-edited with Alexander Long.

**MICHAEL CHITWOOD** has published four collections of poetry, most recently *Gospel Road Going* (Tryon Publishing, 2002), and a book of essays, *Hitting Below the Bible Belt* (Down Home Press, 1998). He has a book of essays and stories and two books of poetry in press. He teaches in the Creative Writing Program at the University of North Carolina at Chapel Hill.

BONNIE COSTELLO is Professor of English at Boston University, and the author of *Marianne Moore: Imaginary Possessions* (Harvard University Press, 1981), *Elizabeth Bishop: Questions of Mastery* (Harvard, 1991), and *Shifting Ground: Reinventing Landscape in Modern American Poetry* (Harvard, 2003). She is the general editor of *The Selected Letters of Marianne Moore* (Knopf, 1997). Her current book project is *Planets on Tables: Poetry, Still Life, and the Turning World*.

STEPHEN CUSHMAN is the author of two volumes of poetry, two books of literary criticism, and a nonfiction reflection on the Civil War. His next book, a collection of poems entitled *Heart Island*, is due out in 2006 from David Robert Books. He is Robert C. Taylor Professor of English at the University of Virginia.

JULIAN GITZEN'S critical articles appeared in a number of Australian, English, and American journals, including *Modern Poetry Studies, Critical Quarterly, Critique*, and *Essays in Arts and Sciences*. He taught at Victoria College at Toorak, Deakin University, and Aichi Bunkyo University.

HENRY HART has published critical studies of Robert Lowell, Seamus Heaney, and Geoffrey Hill, as well as two books of poetry. His biography *James Dickey: The World as a Lie* (Picador, 2000) was runner-up for a Southern Book Critics Circle Award. He teaches English at the College of William and Mary.

MARK JARMAN'S latest collection of poetry is *To the Green Man* (Sarabande Books, 2004). His collection *Questions for Ecclesiastes* (Story Line Press, 1997) won the Lenore Marshall Poetry Prize for 1998. He has published two books of essays on poetry: *The Secret of Poetry* (Story Line, 2001) and *Body and Soul* (University of Michigan Press, 2002). He teaches at Vanderbilt University.

DAVID KALSTONE is the author of a study of Elizabeth Bishop, *Becoming a Poet* (Farrar, Straus and Giroux, 1989); a collection of essays on contemporary American poets, *Five Temperaments* (Oxford University Press, 1977); and *Sidney's Poetry* (Harvard University Press, 1965). He was Professor of English at Rutgers University from 1967 until his death in 1986.

ADAM KIRSCH is the book critic for the *New York Sun*. He is the author of *The Thousand Wells: Poems* (Ivan R. Dee, 2002) and *The Wounded Surgeon: Confession and Transformation in Six American Poets* (W. W. Norton, 2005).

JAMES LONGENBACH is the author of three books of poems, *Threshold* (University of Chicago Press, 1998), *Fleet River* (Chicago, 2003), and a forthcoming volume, *Draft of a Letter*, as well as five books of criticism, most recently *The Resistance to Poetry* (Chicago, 2005) and the forthcoming *Art of the Poetic Line*. He teaches in the Warren Wilson MFA Program and at the University of Rochester, where he is the Joseph H. Gilmore Professor of English.

**J. D. MCCLATCHY** is the author of five collections of poetry, most recently *Hazmat* (Knopf, 2002). His literary essays are collected in *White Paper* (Columbia University Press, 1989) and *Twenty Questions* (Columbia, 1998). He has edited several books, including *The Vintage Book of Contemporary World Poetry* (Vintage, 1996). He teaches at Yale University and since 1991 has been Editor of the *Yale Review*.

**JAMES MCCORKLE** is the author of *Evidences* (Copper Canyon Press, 2003), which received the APR/Honickman First Book Prize in Poetry. He is an associate editor for the *Greenwood Encyclopedia of American Poets and Poetry* (Greenwood, 2005), the editor of *Conversant Essays* (Wayne State University Press, 1990), and the author of a critical study of postmodern poetry, *The Still Performance* (University of Virginia Press, 1989). He teaches at Hobart and William Smith Colleges.

**CHRISTOPHER R. MILLER** is an Associate Professor of English at Yale University. He is author of the forthcoming book *The Invention of Evening: Perception and Time in Romantic Poetry* (Cambridge University Press, 2006) and articles on a variety of topics in lyric poetry.

**CAROL MUSKE-DUKES** is the author of seven books of poems, most recently *Sparrow* (Random House, 2003), three novels, and two collections of essays: *Women and Poetry: Truth, Autobiography, and the Shape of the Self* (University of Michigan Press, 1997) and *Married to the Icepick Killer: A Poet in Hollywood* (Random House, 2002). She is Professor of English and Creative Writing at the University of Southern California.

**DAVID ST. JOHN** is the author of nine collections of poetry, most recently *The Face: A Novella in Verse* (HarperCollins, 2004). He is Director of the Ph.D. Program in Literature and Creative Writing at the University of Southern California.

Poet and essayist **SHEROD SANTOS** is the author of five books of poetry, most recently *The Perishing* (W. W. Norton, 2004). He is also the author of a book of literary essays, *A Poetry of Two Minds* (University of Georgia Press, 2000), and a new collection of translations, *Greek Lyric Poetry: A New Translation* (Norton, 2005). He teaches at the University of Missouri–Columbia.

In 2005 **RON SMITH** was awarded the Inaugural $10,000 Carole Weinstein Prize in Poetry; he is now one of the curators of this annual prize. His poetry and prose have appeared in reference works and in the *Nation, Georgia Review, Kenyon Review, Southern Review, New England Review, Virginia Quarterly Review,* and several anthologies. His book *Moon Road* is forthcoming from LSU Press. Like Charles Wright, he travels often in Italy.

**WILLARD SPIEGELMAN** is the Hughes Professor of English at Southern Methodist University and the Editor-in-Chief of the *Southwest Review*. His most recent books are *How Poets See the World: The Art of Description in Contemporary Poetry* (Oxford University Press, 2005) and *Love, Amy: The Selected Letters of Amy Clampitt* (Columbia University Press, 2005). He writes frequently for the Leisure and Arts page of the *Wall Street Journal*.

**PETER STITT** is the author of two books on twentieth-century American poetry: *The World's Hieroglyphic Beauty* (University of Georgia Press, 1986) and *Uncertainty and Plenitude* (University of Iowa Press, 1997). From 1976 to 1987 he was the regular reviewer of poetry for the *Georgia Review*, with pieces in forty-four consecutive issues. He is the founding and current Editor of the *Gettysburg Review*.

**RICHARD TILLINGHAST** has published seven books of poetry as well as a critical memoir of Robert Lowell called *Damaged Grandeur* (University of Michigan Press, 1995). His most recent book is a collection of essays, *Poetry and What Is Real* (Michigan, 2004). Professor Emeritus at the University of Michigan, he is currently living in the country near Kilkenny in Ireland.

**LEE UPTON'S** poetry, fiction, and criticism appear widely. She is the author of four books of poetry and four of criticism, most recently a study of how poets claim their own distinctiveness, *Defensive Measures* (Bucknell University Press, 2005). She is a Professor of English and the Writer-in-Residence at Lafayette College.

**HELEN VENDLER**, the Porter University Professor at Harvard University, has written books on Yeats, Stevens, Herbert, Shakespeare, and Heaney. Her most recent book is *Invisible Listeners: Lyric Intimacy in Herbert, Whitman, and Ashbery* (Princeton University Press, 2005).

**DAVID WALKER** teaches English and creative writing at Oberlin College. He is the editor of *American Alphabets: 25 Contemporary Poets* (Oberlin College Press, 2006) and *Poets Reading: The FIELD Symposia* (Oberlin, 1999).

**DAVID YOUNG** has edited *FIELD*, a journal that often features work by Charles Wright, since 1969. His own books include *Black Lab* (Knopf, 2006), *Six Modernist Moments in Poetry* (University of Iowa Press, 2006), *The Poetry of Petrarch* (Farrar, Straus and Giroux, 2004), and, with Jonathan Galassi and Charles Wright, *Montale: Selected Poems* (Oberlin College Press, 2004).

# Acknowledgments

*Every effort has been made to obtain permission to reprint the selections in this collection.*

Tom Andrews. "Improvisations on Charles Wright's *The World of the Ten Thousand Things*" first appeared as "The Point Where All Things Meet: Improvisations on Charles Wright's *The World of the Ten Thousand Things*" in the *Iron Mountain Review* 8 (1992).

David Baker. "On Restraint" first appeared in *Poetry* 168, no. 1 (1996). Used by permission of the author.

Calvin Bedient. "Tracing Charles Wright" first appeared in *Parnassus* 10, no. 1 (1982). Used by permission of the author.

Bruce Bond. "Metaphysics of the Image in Charles Wright and Paul Cézanne" first appeared in the *Southern Review* 30, no. 1 (1994). Used by permission of the author.

Christopher Buckley. "Charles Wright's Hymn" first appeared in *Poet Lore* 86, no. 3 (1991). Used by permission of the author.

Michael Chitwood. "Gospel Music: Charles Wright and the High Lonesome" first appeared in the *Iron Mountain Review* 8 (1992). Used by permission of the author.

Bonnie Costello. "Charles Wright, Giorgio Morandi, and the Metaphysics of the Line" first appeared in *Mosaic: A Journal for the Interdisciplinary Study of Literature* 35, no. 1 (March 2002). Used by permission of *Mosaic* and the author.

Stephen Cushman. "The Capabilities of Charles Wright" first appeared in the *Iron Mountain Review* 8 (1992). Used by permission of the author.

Julian Gitzen. "Charles Wright and Presences in Absence" first appeared in the *Mid-American Review* 14, no. 2 (1994).

Henry Hart. "Charles Wright's *Via Mystica*" first appeared in the *Georgia Review* 58, no. 2 (2004). Used by permission of the author.

Mark Jarman. "The Trace of a Story Line" first appeared in the *Ohio Review* 37 (1986). "The Pragmatic Imagination and the Secret of Poetry" first appeared in the *Gettysburg Review* 1, no. 4 (1988). Both selections used by permission of the author.

David Kalstone. "Lives in a Rearview Mirror" first appeared in the *New York Times Book Review*, 1 July 1984.

Adam Kirsch. "Between Heaven and Earth" first appeared in the *New York Times Book Review*, 28 February 1999. Used by permission of the author.

James Longenbach. "Earned Weight" first appeared as "Poetry in Review" in the *Yale Review* 83, no. 4 (1995). "*Appalachia*" first appeared in the *Boston Review* 23, no. 6 (1998/99). Both selections used by permission of the author.

J. D. McClatchy. "Under the Sign of the Cross" appeared as part of the essay "Reading" in the author's book *White Paper on Contemporary American Poetry* (New York: Columbia University Press, 1989). "Ars Longa" first appeared in *Poetry* 175, no. 1 (1999). Both selections used by permission of the author.

James McCorkle. "'Things That Lock Our Wrists to the Past': Self-Portraiture and Autobiography in Charles Wright's Poetry" first appeared in the author's book *The Still Performance: Writing, Self, and Interconnection in Five Postmodern American Poets* (Charlottesville, VA: University of Virginia Press, 1989). Used by permission of the author.

Christopher R. Miller. "Poetic Standard Time: The Zones of Charles Wright" first appeared in the *Southern Review* 34, no. 3 (1998). Used by permission of the author.

Carol Muske-Dukes. "Guided by Dark Stars" first appeared in the *New York Times Book Review*, 31 August 1997. Used by permission of the author.

David St. John. "Charles Wright's *Country Music*" appeared as the foreword to the second edition of Charles Wright's book *Country Music: Selected Early Poems* (Middletown, CT: Wesleyan University Press, 1991). Used by permission of the author.

Sherod Santos. "*Zone Journals*" first appeared in the *New Virginia Review* 8 (1991). Used by permission of the author.

Ron Smith. "An Enchanted, Diminished World" first appeared as "Wright Continues Lyrical Trips in Nature" in the *Richmond Times-Dispatch*, 29 September 2002. Used by permission of the author.

Willard Spiegelman. "Charles Wright and 'The Metaphysics of the Quotidian'" appeared in the author's book *How Poets See the World: The Art of Description in Contemporary Poetry*, copyright 2005 by Oxford University Press, Inc. Used by permission of Oxford University Press, Inc.

Peter Stitt. "Resurrecting the Baroque" appeared in the author's book *Uncertainty and Plenitude: Five Contemporary Poets* (Iowa City: University of Iowa Press, 1997). Used by permission of the author.

Richard Tillinghast. "An Elegist's New England, a Buddhist's Dante" first appeared in the *New York Times Book Review*, 24 February 1991. Used by permission of the author.

Lee Upton. "The Doubting Penitent: Charles Wright's Epiphanies of Abandonment" first appeared in the author's book *The Muse of Abandonment: Origin, Identity, Mastery in Five American Poets* (Lewisburg, PA: Bucknell University Press; London: Associated University Presses, 1998). Used by permission of the author.

Helen Vendler. "The Transcendent 'I'" appeared in the author's book *Part of Nature, Part of Us: Modern American Poets* (Cambridge: Harvard University Press, 1980). "Travels in Time" appeared as "Charles Wright" in the author's book *The Music of What Happens: Poems, Poets, Critics* (Cambridge: Harvard University Press, 1988). "The Nothing That Is" first appeared in the *New Republic*, 7 August 1995. All selections used by permission of the author.

David Walker. "*One for the Rose* and *The Southern Cross*" first appeared in *FIELD* 26 (1982). Used by permission of the author.

David Young. "The Blood Bees of Paradise" first appeared in *FIELD* 44 (1991). "Looking for Landscapes" first appeared in *FIELD* 58 (1998). Both selections used by permission of the author.